Imperial Culture and the Sudan

Imperial Culture and the Sudan

Authorship, Identity and the British Empire

Lia Paradis

I.B.TAURIS
LONDON • NEW YORK • OXFORD • NEW DELHI • SYDNEY

I.B. TAURIS
Bloomsbury Publishing Plc
50 Bedford Square, London, WC1B 3DP, UK
1385 Broadway, New York, NY 10018, USA
29 Earlsfort Terrace, Dublin 2, Ireland

First published in Great Britain 2020
This paperback edition published in 2021

Series design by Adriana Brioso
Cover image: First post office established in Dilling, Kordofan
Province from the Sudan Archive at Durham University.

A catalogue record for this book is available from the British Library.

A catalogue record for this book is available from the Library of Congress.

ISBN: HB: 978-1-7883-1899-0
PB: 978-0-7556-3753-9
ePDF: 978-1-7883-1901-0
eBook: 978-1-7883-1900-3

Typeset by Integra Software Services Pvt. Ltd.

To find out more about our authors and books visit www.bloomsbury.com
and sign up for our newsletters.

For Edmund

Contents

Acknowledgements

This book took a very long time to finish. Its first iteration was as my dissertation at Rutgers University. The history faculty I worked with there showed me what good colleagues, good teachers and good scholars look like. My advisor, John Gillis, has always been exactly what I needed – critical, enthusiastic and patient, in equal measure. I was lucky that he saw something in my original proposal and then let me take the time to discover something much better. He's been a very good friend and an excellent role model as both a professor and a mentor. Similarly, I'm grateful to my dissertation committee – Matt Matsuda, Joan Scott and Al Howard – who all gave not only guidance and criticism but also the space to follow my own path. Dorothy Helly, my mentor since undergraduate years at Hunter College, continues to demand my best effort and I thank her for it.

The conversations and debates with fellow students shaped me as a historian, as have the friendships with other members of the Rutgers alumni I've been lucky enough to remain close to today. I would never have finished this book without the intellectual engagement I've had, then and now, with Brady Brower, Lindsay Braun, Brian Crim, Gary Darden, Justin Hart, Sarah Gordon, Patrick McDevitt, Tammy Proctor, Jennifer Tammi and Chuck Upchurch. Their respect and support have been a great gift.

I worked on this project intermittently for many years. During that time, core members of the Midwest Conference on British Studies kept me inspired and excited through their work and offered me a community where I could continue to engage with fellow British Studies scholars even when I wasn't able to publish. There were many others whose contributions to MWCBS conferences informed my work, but I'd like to thank in particular Jennifer McNabb, Jason Kelly, Eric Tenbus, Bob Bucholz, Christine Haskill, Warren Johnston, Carol Engelhardt and Jennifer Hart.

Alice Ritscherle and Susie Steinbach read portions of the manuscript. I want to thank them for their incredibly useful critique, as well as the feedback from anonymous readers and my editor, Tomasz Hoskins, at I.B. Tauris/Bloomsbury. I would also like to thank Anna Davin for her generosity and encouragement. Two other British historians are completely unaware of how much they are responsible for this book being published. James Vernon and Susan Kent were encouraging at a moment when I was ready to abandon it altogether. My colleagues at Slippery Rock University are a pleasure to work with and I thank them for their support. I'm very lucky to be among peers who see traditional scholarship as part of a larger package of intellectual engagement.

My research took me to many archives and libraries where I had the good fortune to be helped by literally dozens of excellent archivists, librarians and technicians. I want to mention two of them. Jay Barksdale, the long-time librarian in charge of the Wertheim Study at the New York Public Library, always found room for me there during the narrow windows when I was able to work. And Jane Hogan, the head archivist of the

Sudan Archive at Durham University, was (and still is) incredibly knowledgeable and a pleasure to work with. Her contribution cannot be overstated.

I want to thank Sylvie Bertrand, Brian Gallagher and Kara Stanley for decades of love and support. Finally, my parents, Barbara and Jerome, raised their daughter to be intellectually curious, up for adventure and stubborn. Their unflagging confidence in me was probably their greatest gift. I wish my father were still here so that he could read the final product. My husband, Edmund, who has lived with this project almost as long as I have, is a blessing to me every day. Thank you.

Introduction

In 1989, Martin Daly and Francis Deng published a collection of interviews with British and Sudanese government officials during the period of British rule in Sudan from 1898 to 1956, when the country was officially the Anglo-Egyptian Condominium of the Sudan. Most of the British contributors to *Bonds of Silk* make the wonderfully contradictory assertions that knew nothing about the Sudan or its people before they began their careers there, but they remembered being enthusiastic about joining the administration because of what they had heard about the place.[1] How can both statements be true? Britons who went to the Sudan made a particularly momentous decision when they chose colonial careers that would separate them from their families, friends and communities because they were not, for the most part, from multigeneration imperial families. It seems counterintuitive that they would choose to go to a country and rule over a people they knew nothing about; the second statement – that they were motivated by their knowledge of the place – seemingly makes more sense. They did their homework; they familiarized themselves with the history of the country, its people, religions and geography and then decided on careers that would take them there. But this simply wasn't the case. The British interview subjects don't hesitate to admit their ignorance before they landed. And yet the country and its people brought them there.

This book aims to reconcile those two statements. These men, and later their wives and other women who joined the Sudan government, thought they knew the Sudan before they got there. They also thought they knew what being colonial administrators was all about. This 'knowledge' motivated them to pick the Sudan as the location and colonial administration as a career. Only once they got there did they realize just how deeply ignorant they were about the country and its people and about the work they had chosen.[2] They spent the rest of their careers slowly moving away from this starting point of absolute confidence and total ignorance. But as they charted their own journey they increasingly diverged from the metropolitan 'knowledge' of the Sudan and colonial administration. They struggled to be who their friends, families and government thought they were, while coming to grips with just how little – in their view – the British public and its decision-making bodies understood imperial territories in general, the Sudan in particular and the many peoples under their control.

One reason for the administrators' paradoxical responses to Deng and Daly's interview question was that the Sudan figured large in the imperial adventure stories, poems, songs and movies they had encountered as children and adolescents. And the Sudan's entrance into the British public's consciousness coincided with the beginning of mass marketing of the Empire – the advent of High Imperialism – in the 1880s and 1890s. A shared vocabulary of the Sudan stretched across multiple media platforms with a vividness and coherence that earlier and later colonial narratives lacked. The tragedy of General Charles Gordon and the siege of Khartoum in 1884, and General Herbert Kitchener's triumph and the reconquest of the Sudan in 1898, were events collectively experienced by the British public – produced and responded to in new media and a new context of representational mass politics.

From the moment probationary officers were accepted into the Sudan government, they were confronted by different texts about the Sudan and about colonial careers than those their metropolitan peers had consumed. In the early days of the Anglo-Egyptian Condominium, many of these journals, memoirs and treatises reinforced established images of Gordon and Kitchener rather than debunked them. After the Great War, however, the demand from the British government and officials in the Sudan government for improved and modernized training resulted in a substantial, standardized period of inculcation prior to their departure. These interwar recruits were exposed to a curriculum that undermined the knowledge that mass-produced literature about the Sudan had led them to believe they possessed.

Imagining the Sudan

Part One, 'Metropolitan Britain Writes the Sudan', is located at the intersection of scholarship on New Journalism, New Imperialism, the study of readership in the new mass society and the growing interest in colonial careers and training (both official and cultural).[3] As Andrew Griffiths argues, the newspaper campaign to get Gladstone's government to send Gordon to Khartoum, and then to send a party to rescue him months later, marks the convergence of these late-nineteenth-century developments.[4] The simultaneous rise of New Imperialism and New Journalism exploited the potency of the newfound personal relationship readers could have with imperial actors even though the 'emotions of the moment were constructed and experienced not on the streets but in and through newspapers and journals'.[5] In the British imagination, the Sudan as a territory, the Sudanese as a subject people and British administrators in the Sudan as an imperial 'type' were all born from this moment when popular press, politics and culture were fixated on the same imperial story.[6]

The prologue sets out the first act of creation in this process: W. T. Stead's campaign to send Gordon to evacuate Khartoum and then, once Gordon was under siege, the campaign to rescue him. The prologue identifies ingredients central to Griffiths's argument that the Gordon campaign should be considered the quintessential intersection of New Journalism and New Imperialism. This event introduced the British reading public to the Sudan and established the ideal of the colonial hero in the metropolitan imagination. Public engagement with personalities rather than policies, and with moral questions rather than strategic ones, seemed to directly bring about geopolitical consequences in a distant territory.

Chapter 1 examines the literary legacy of the Gordon saga and the subsequent (re)conquest of the Sudan by Kitchener in 1898. In an earlier era, novels by, say, Sir Walter Scott could pit internal enemies against each other. By the second half of the nineteenth century, great sweeping stories of risk, patriotism or sacrifice, taking place within Great Britain, were no longer a safe source for plotlines in an era of competitive nationalism.[7] Fictional Scots and English, rich and poor, needed to cooperate to ensure that Britain didn't look bad compared with France or Germany. And Britons were united in the cause of Empire. In this environment, the formulae of national literature – the novels, poems and tracts that explain a nation's people to themselves – were successfully repurposed and moved into the Empire.[8] Formulas work precisely because they fit new plots, characters and locations into an established vocabulary. The nation-building romance of earlier eras became the imperial romance and centred on the British hero or subaltern villain.[9]

The effect on metropolitan imperial imaginary varied depending on the reader's class and age.[10] Scholarship since Edward Said's *Orientalism* has explored the discursive construction of a knowable and colonizable Other in the literature consumed by European metropolitan elites.[11] The Western, Orientalist scholar emerged from the nineteenth-century European imperial impulse precisely because he gave ongoing legitimacy to the policies and narratives of European institutions of power, both governmental and cultural. The Gordon myth, however, was perpetuated not through scholarly texts but through the newly democratized knowledge of colonial life disseminated in popular publications to the Edwardian reading public. This bypassed the traditional sources of imperial expertise.

Patrick Brantlinger and others have explored how popular culture in Britain created an African Other with far-reaching usefulness in the metropolitan national narrative of progress and civilization. Scholars have illustrated the importance of middle- and lowbrow literature in the cultural creation of any imperial Other for a society's ever-evolving process of self-definition.[12] As Kelly Boyd notes, the stories in inexpensive boys' magazines during this period 'formed the central core of young male reading'.[13] But the stories that fired working- and lower-middle-class boys' imaginations during the fin de siècle were never really so 'adventurous' as they seemed, despite hand-wringing about their lack of wholesomeness. Reading them more closely, Boyd argues, they weren't intended to show those boys how to change their world, but rather how to fit into it.[14] Fears of a less-educated electorate and the growing strength of the Labour Party at the start of the twentieth century prompted editors to feature stories that advocated community over class loyalties and a paternalistic view of social-reform efforts.[15]

By contrast, the middle- and upper-middle-class boys destined to be the social and political leaders of Britain and its Empire consumed slightly more expensive adventure novels and middlebrow popular fiction for adults by authors such as G. A. Henty, who also edited a boys' journal at the end of the nineteenth century.[16] In these, recent political and military events were backdrops for stories of personal development and the responsibilities of noblesse oblige.[17] These books assumed that prep-school textbooks provided the requisite knowledge about geography and Britain's imperial history and reinforced the expectation that these boys would act upon a global, imperial stage, either indirectly as voters or directly as policymakers, administrators, businessmen or educators.[18]

Fiction and non-fiction alike, aimed at adolescents and adults, fixed the Sudan in the minds of two generations of readers. The popular fiction of G. E. Henty and A. H. Mason was leavened with supposedly more cerebral non-fiction by such authors as Count Carl von Slatin, who went from being Gordon's underling to a long-term prisoner of the Mahdists; Winston Churchill, who soldiered in and reported on Kitchener's Nile campaign; and Rudyard Kipling. Stitching all of these contributions together was the imperial catechism found in schoolbooks, Boy Scout songs and the popular press. The territory, the climate, the indigenous population and the role of the imperial hero in the Sudan story were refined and codified in hundreds of texts in various registers.

Chapter 2 returns to Gordon, this time looking at his *Journals* and his ideas about the roles and responsibilities of colonial administrators. It then considers what others wrote about him. This was what a young man would read when considering a colonial career and what was on the reading list for Sudan Political Service (SPS) probationers. Just as Gordon would forever stand, still, at the top of the staircase in the ubiquitously reproduced image of him, George William Joy's *Death of Gordon*, a web of mutually referencing literature dating from before the Great War, similarly focused the Sudan narrative on imperial heroism.[19] But Gordon's simultaneous sainthood and much-recorded subordination were tricky to navigate for young men looking for role models.

Berny Sèbe's recent analysis of Gordon as the Ur-hero of High Imperialism is the starting point for this chapter, as it examines the implications of Gordon for the specific individuals who became administrators in the country founded on his heroic legacy. Additionally, the two heroic types identified by Geoffrey Cubitt – the Great Man and the exemplar – inform the analysis. The Great Man shapes history not only by determining the course of a nation or civilization but also by being of it. The source of the exemplar's heroism comes from sitting outside society's norms, expectations and ambitions.[20] As Sèbe rightly asserts, Gordon fit squarely in the second category until his persona dominated the imperial heroic imaginary that it became an imperative. Along these lines, Robert MacDonald frames Gordon as the personification of a 'pattern-book of heroism'.[21] For MacDonald, Gordon's 'appeal to feelings that overrode reason, such as love of country or pride of race', meant that certain moral questions could be ignored or highlighted as needed.[22] In what MacDonald calls 'Deeds of Glory' narratives, evangelical imagery could also be deployed to legitimize militarism because in this context Christianity was civilizational as much as religious.[23]

John Tosh argues that even for adult men, imperial literature was a potent medium for the prescriptions of normative masculinity.[24] This was reinforced when other men in imperial leadership hailed Gordon as an imperial martyr without agreeing on whether he died a Great Man – representative of the British nation – or an exemplar. Even as the administrative culture of the 1920s Sudan government shifted away from prewar literary representations of imperial heroism, they were regularly referenced in British-Sudani letters, indicating confidence that most Britons back home still possessed this shared memory cum fantasy of the Sudan.[25]

Strictly speaking, the Anglo-Egyptian Condominium of the Sudan was never a colony. It was never governed from Britain through the Colonial Office; it was officially a sovereign state. The Sudan's interactions with Britain came under the umbrella of the Foreign Office because, technically, Britain was always dealing with a foreign government.[26] The officials of the Anglo-Egyptian Sudan could thus imagine themselves independent contractors in a universal project of uplift, rather than representatives of a specific national version of that project. What was the *symbolic* ideal for other colonial administrators – to be selfless stewards of uplift for benighted peoples – was, in the Anglo-Egyptian Sudan, the *explicitly* constituted relationship. Yet their worthiness to be the governors and servants of the Sudanese depended precisely on the claim that they embodied Great Britain's values and culture. Christopher Prior quotes Orwell's 'Shooting an Elephant' to ask the extent to which administrators were consciously aware of and comfortable with the performative embodiment of imperial Britishness. His conclusion that while 'civilian officials never completely abandoned the notion that performance had a part to play ... over time, a greater proportion of officials ... increasingly considered the use of prestige a means to an end'.[27]

In the 1910s, university-educated officials in the new Sudan government began asserting a more systematic regimen of bureaucratic civilian authority.[28] Led by these university men, the Sudan government expanded in numbers and scope between the wars, staffing projects in economic development, public works, sanitation and education. They embraced indirect rule and consulted anthropologists, linguists and other colonial theorists. Basic introductory courses in law and Arabic, accompanied by a suggested reading list, became a systematized training year by the late twenties.[29]

Chapters 3 and 4 follow these developments. Recruits to the colonial territories and the SPS received formal training in theories of colonial administration, cultural anthropology and infrastructure planning and development before they left Britain. This endowed the SPS probationers with expertise beyond that of the general public, in harmony with the imperial policy experts in Whitehall and in the proconsul palaces of colonial capitals. These chapters consider the impact this new training regimen had on SPS officials' understanding and execution of their jobs. Historians and later officials have since explored the substantial negative impact of indirect rule (or native administration) on African societies, but the administrators trained in the 1920s and 1930s saw themselves as modernizers, implementing development priorities such as educational institutions and expanded commercial infrastructure. Paternalism still underlay the assumptions of colonial administrative policy, but the means by which the 'uplift' myth was achieved had changed.

Belonging to Britain

Part Two, 'Authoring the "British-Sudani" Identity', explores the tensions created as the British administrators in the Sudan came to recognize the distance between expectation and lived experience. These people weren't so stupid as to think that a Kipling poem, or a Korda Technicolor extravaganza, was the same as living day in and day out in the Sudan. But the *remembered* Sudan of their childhood reading and viewing was the metropole's only Sudan. Colonial administrators and their wives accumulated experiences that separated them from metropolitan counterparts. Many British-Sudanis worried in their writing that different life paths meant they were developing a different sense of what it was to be British. Letters and diary entries suggest they consciously worked to create strong relationships with family and friends while living in the Sudan to ensure they would fit in again once they returned. There was never a smooth intersection of the British imperial 'story' and that of Britain's imperial agents; little in the public sphere acknowledged those rough edges.

Ann Laura Stoler and Frederick Cooper warn that 'it does us no service to reify a colonial moment of binary oppositions so that we can enjoy the postcolonial confidence that our world today is infinitely more complicated, more fragmented and more blurred'.[30] Rather, 'hybridities of richly varied sorts existed' for colonized and colonizer.[31] The British-Sudani articulated – through repetition, reiteration, sarcasm, irony or silence – their own anxieties about hybrid identities. Their adult identity was as the purveyors and implementers of British expertise to the Sudanese and as experts on the Sudan, Arab culture, Middle East politics and a host of other topics when communicating with the metropole.[32] This dual status was simultaneously embraced as the life they had chosen and downplayed out of fear that the accumulation of Sudan experience and expertise might dilute their British identity.

Chapters 5 and 6 examine the correspondence circuit of British-Sudanis and their families and friends back in Britain; they employed epistolary strategies to establish a virtual 'third space', to borrow a term from Homi Bhabha, in which slightly different, more compatible versions of the Sudan and Britain were cultivated.[33] The British-Sudanis created a continuous narrative of their lives in what James How calls 'common spaces', overriding the geographic separation they experienced for decades. Carolyn Steedman examines a related phenomenon of letter-writing where intentions jockey for position in the epistolary equivalent of Jürgen Habermas's public space of personal articulation. Dena Goodman conceptualizes letter-writing as a 'reciprocal exchange' forming an epistolary bridge between public and private actors. These are all useful approaches when analysing British-Sudani correspondence because colonial administrators' identities are so tied up with the country they represent that 'public' and 'private' have different meanings for them than for private citizens.[34]

Chapter 7 examines one moment when this textual 'third space' was challenged by events in the Sudan: the Egyptian Army Mutiny in the Sudan after the assassination of the Sudan's governor general, Sir Lee Stack. In Britain, the 1924 Mutiny was about Egyptian claims of sovereignty. But for individual administrators in the Sudan, it threatened their self-identification as experts on and caretakers of the Sudan. The recent interest in the idea of modern European empires as 'networks' of contingent interplay (cultural, economic or other) encourages us to analyse both the agency of and the impact on the individual colonial actor.[35] As David Lambert and Alan Lester point out, 'The agendas of colonial interest, their representations of colonized places and peoples, and their practices in relation to them, were not only differentiated, but also often constructed in opposition to one another.'[36] In the metropolitan press and policy circulars in Whitehall, pundits and politicians focused on the implications for British foreign policy with Egypt, in stark contrast with the personal way the Mutiny was addressed in letters written by British-Sudanis to people living in Britain.[37]

They thought their role as experts would be reinforced in this rare moment when the modern Anglo-Egyptian Sudan entered the British public's consciousness. British-Sudanis worried about how outsiders would assess British-Sudanese relations in the context of the Mutiny. The post–First World War civilian-ization of the SPS was already destabilizing the corporate identity of the Sudan government, and British-Sudani correspondents used the Mutiny to argue for and against the older and newer models of imperial administration.[38] Despite their assertions of expertise, however, they were unable to control the meaning of the Mutiny in the metropole.

Remembering the Sudan

By the end of the interwar period, administrators could no longer comfortably assert a single model of civilization and expect it to be valorized across the European imperial landscape. After the Second World War, the Cold War demanded fresh allies. Imperial powers were forced to double down on the benefits of global capitalism and hope the indigenous populations of colonies saw it their way.[39] The independence movement in the Sudan was complicated and accelerated by Egypt's ongoing claims to control over the Sudan. Forced into a politically untenable position between Sudanese political groups arguing for full Sudanese independence and those backed by Egypt calling for the 'unity of the Nile Valley', British officials had to choose. 'Sudanization', the process by which Sudanese took over from British administrators, sped up. British governors became the reluctant stewards – even champions – of Sudanese independence, defending against the possible replacement of British with Egyptian (nationalist and even socialist) influence.[40] An original plan for a twenty-year transition was pared down to ten and then six. Sudan became independent on New Year's Day, 1956.

In this process, the British government and the Sudan government grew more distant from each other. Echoes of Gordon could be heard in British-Sudani critiques of Whitehall and Westminster. Colonial Service memoirs are rife with examples of frustration between those who set policy from a distance and those who implemented it on the ground. As a colonial memoirist succinctly put it, 'in his sheltered life in the Colonial Office', officials did not want to hear 'the forthright speech of a man accustomed to deal with men rather than with papers'.[41] This was a prevalent attitude among British-Sudanis during Sudanization and independence, as well.

While this disconnect between colony and metropole had geopolitical implications, it also raised existential ones. To what communities do the British-Sudani belong? Could these men and women be wholly British again? On whose terms would their post-Sudan identities be fashioned? Part Three, 'Remembering the Sudan', concerns reintegration and redefinition. During the period of decolonization, huge numbers of European nationals, some of whom had never set foot in Europe before, descended on the 'motherland' or 'fatherland'. Thousands of men (and some women) retired at the end of colonial careers. Every soldier, clerk, railway man, missionary, teacher and administrator who returned at the end of a colonial career faced the challenges of reinserting themselves into a community.[42]

A life in the imperial arena changes a person. In E. M. Forster's *A Passage to India*, Adela Quested is reunited with her fiancé, Ronny, only to find that living in the Anglo-Indian cantonment in Chandrapore has changed him. And Virginia Woolf's Mrs. Dalloway thinks her old flame, Peter Walsh, feels distanced from British society and the moral code that goes with it because he sees it from the outside now, having spent years in India. Literary moments like these quietly articulate doubt and nervousness about the boundaries of Britain and just how long and how far one could go careering in the Empire before it was too late to come back.[43] Similar doubts, anxieties and questions prevail in the writings of the administrators and in the complaints of their impatient bosses in Whitehall.

There was no organized programme for the reintegration of ex-colonial staff into Britain or educational programmes established for the children of Colonial Service employees.[44] The potential for trouble from exposure to a different climate and culture was seemingly best left unacknowledged. On behalf of Britain, the colonizer embodied the colonizing power: walking, talking, eating and simply being Britain. Nevertheless, Forster and Woolf articulated an uneasy suspicion that it was impossible in the imperial setting to maintain one's Britishness, no matter how superior and resilient that identity. A person didn't need to 'go native' to provoke certain questions: Just how well could Britons, and therefore Britain, endure the constant exposure to otherness? What community does a colonial administrator belong to at the beginning of a career and at the end?[45]

The most useful framework for thinking about these subjects involves cultural and social theory; much of the analysis is interpretive. Georg Simmel's social forms, the most famous of which is the Stranger, established the centrality of social networks for identity. Simmel's Stranger has come into one society from another, not as an enemy or a refugee but freely, as a trader, who must interact with the community, know its desires and cater to it, but never belong.[46] The colonial administrator similarly traded – this time in the wares of Western society and the promises attached to their acquisition. Simmel ascribes to the trader this quality of strangeness only while 'out in foreign lands' and in relation to the society *out there*.[47] The fate of the Stranger once back 'home' is left unexamined. Movement, a key element of modernity, is both psychologically and physically disruptive. Durkheim, who, like Simmel, theorized in an era of accelerated imperial movement, observes that the conditions of modernity encourage anomie because our sense of self and our well-being are attached to our social networks.[48] Julia Kristeva observes that in the modern world 'foreignness is within us'.[49] In the context of European imperialism, or globalization, she asks, 'If one is oneself uprooted, what is the point of talking to those who think that they have their own feet on their own soil?'[50] Thinking that subjects' locations are unproblematic because they are 'on their own soil' can influence psychological geography as much as spatial.

Britain's postwar commitment to abandon imperialism, however reluctantly, imposed a caesura between a national-identity narrative that was necessarily post-imperial and the personal identity narrative of the Empire's most active participants.

Colonial administrators were characterized as 'of the past' – best denied and forgotten. Metropolitan society sought to culturally quarantine itself in case the now retrograde occupation of former colonizers might stunt the growth of a new, modern Britain. As Frederick Cooper argues, returning colonizers' 'assertions of particularity and claims to recognition' were at odds with the prevailing anticolonial sentiment because their 'identity politics … resonated badly with its time and social context'.[51] For the metropolitan society, the ex-administrators' desire to be acknowledged as good civil servants and faithful citizens was extremely problematic. '[These] were not recognition claims like any other', Cooper observes. 'They were assertions of a past that risked getting in the way of a future.'[52] The newly trained colonial technician – the development man – derided Whitehall for being old-fashioned. 'Care must be taken', writes one in his memoirs, 'to bring the [metropolitan] official's knowledge up-to-date from time to time – to avoid the menace of the "expert" who is thinking in terms of long past days'.[53] But metropolitan certainty about colonial belatedness silenced similar voices.

Migrants' internal perceptions of their locations are at odds with the external social meaning attached to their movements.[54] Recent scholarship on travel and home reveals how travel can produce two responses. A person can create a fantasy of the seamless wholeness of the departure point.[55] The 'home' culture becomes a talisman protecting the traveller from alien influences.[56] Or the distance can provide perspective, the traveller becoming aware of the contingent nature of the 'home' culture and, therefore, identity.[57] When the dominant contemporary articulations of identity are firmly located in spatially defined nationalist narratives, both of these responses are challenges to the traveller's community membership.[58]

Chapter 8 examines the ongoing process of returning home over the decades both before and after Sudanization was implemented. British-Sudanis were anxious to maintain their connection to the metropolitan life and so any discrepancy or disagreement with the national narrative was acutely felt the closer they came to the moment of return. Initially, British-Sudani celebrations and commemorations before departure suggested their enthusiasm for marking the passage from the Sudan to Britain. Upon their return, however, the lack of fanfare, or even support structure, suggested an awareness of their marginal place. Said calls the people caught in this twentieth-century moment 'colonial hybrids': 'Insofar as these people exist between the old and the new, between the old empire and the new state, their condition articulates the tension, irresolution, and contradiction in the overlapping territories shown on the cultural map of imperialism.'[59] Said is talking about colonized subjects as hybrids, but for colonial returnees, 'what is truth in one context of the individual's social career becomes wrong in the next', creating an ironic distance between British-Sudanis and the community to which they returned.[60]

After the British decision-making and opinion-forming institutions embraced, or at least became resigned to, the divestiture of Empire in the 1960s and the 1970s, colonial administrators needed to be different so British society could become postcolonial, post-imperial, post-racial – post-everything – as quickly and smoothly as possible. The previous fantasy that the administrator and the nation were indissoluble was rearticulated with gusto but to a different purpose. The totalizing figure of the colonizer now became the embodiment of an ex-colonizing power.[61] By fixing the persona of the administrator in an earlier version that was a product of the metropolitan fantasy of the type, British society could be 'post-' all the sooner.[62] This imperial typecasting allowed the metropole to be fluid and dynamic. Britain could radically change its identity and yet remain British by insisting that these administrators had truthfully embodied an authentic Britain. It was merely one that had passed.

Chapter 9 considers British-Sudani efforts to establish a relationship to the British public sphere.[63] Associational participation, Habermas tells us, bridges the gap between public and private space, made particularly problematic when the private citizen has embodied a public institution.[64] The Sudan Government British Pensioners' Association (SGBPA) was formed to act as the representative organ of the entire British-Sudani population, specifically in its attempts to gain pension parity and security. They were forced to reimagine themselves, abandoning their corporate identity as officials of an independent country and embracing an unfamiliar role as the supplicants of Her Majesty's Government. Associational culture is regulatory, but it also provides a framework for resistance.[65] In the psychic space of oscillating identity and the ambivalence of cultural difference, we must explore whether the concurrent British-Sudani discourses of master and servant in their struggle for pension rights manifested their continuing hybrid condition.[66]

The process of reimagining their identity as Britons was also one of retrieving and preserving their British-Sudani identity. In Chapter 10, particular associational configurations become sites for the articulation of both general and specific British-Sudani experiences and their meanings. The Anglo-Sudanese Association rewrote the last years of the Condominium as a story of partnership between the British and the Sudanese. Susannah Radstone suggests that memory work is a primary location for the negotiated truce between fragmentary subject positions.[67] In the context of a nascent multiracial and postcolonial Britain, these retrospective efforts at presenting a cogent narrative of the Anglo-Egyptian Sudan were as much about who the British-Sudanis were presumed to be as about who they had been in the Sudan.[68] The formation of the Sudan Archive at the University of Durham was another commemorative effort, but the lack of a regulatory framework allowed a 'fictive kinship' to develop within the archive.[69] Individual contributions expanded the definition of the imagined community of the Anglo-Egyptian Condominium; as a collection of individual actions and articulations of memory, the archive does not support a monolithic narrative of the Condominium. Rather, its mandate is to preserve the records of any individual who was connected to the Sudan at any time during British rule. The archive privileges personal experience and individual memory over national memory and identity, whether that identity is British, Sudanese or the hybrid identity of a postcolonial subject.[70]

Conclusion

British-Sudani knowledge of the Sudan begins with an imagined territory and the expectations of a life there that were constructed long before the physical journey began.

A wide swathe of the British public visited this Sudan virtually and then imagined they had experienced it firsthand. They clearly knew this wasn't so, but British metropolitan society was engaged in its most overt articulation of imperial cultural investment during the Edwardian period; the sheer volume of texts and their variety, as well as the remarkable consistency of the Sudan narrative they articulated, became 'knowledge' of the Sudan.[71] Literature, newspapers, memoirs, journals and poetry created layers of imagery and opinion that populated the narrative space until the textual Sudan became almost as messy and multifarious as the experience of real life.

The British-Sudani formed a unique identity within, and in response to, the framework already established before they set foot in the country. This biography of an administrative cohort tracks the strategies they employed to counter others' expectations of their lives, push back against the limitations of metropolitan imaginations and forge a new legacy in the face of public disinterest and disapproval. They clearly articulated a desire to shape British knowledge of the Sudan and colonial careering, during and after the Empire.

Prologue: The story begins

In November 1883, a large Egyptian Army force, led by Hicks Pasha, was annihilated while trying to suppress the expanding reach of the Mahdi, the Sudanese religio-military leader of an uprising against Egyptian occupation of the Sudan. The British-Egyptian relationship had first caught the British public's attention in 1879. The Egyptian Khedive Ismail had dreams of empire and stretched Egypt's finances so far that Britain forced his resignation when he wouldn't allow it to step in and manage the situation. Under the new, more pliant khedive, Tewfik, Sir Evelyn Baring took up the post of consul-general and began to restructure the nation's finances to benefit European investors. This prompted a nationalist uprising in 1882; when Tewfik was unable to quell it, the British Navy bombarded the port of Alexandria and then took greater control of the Egyptian Army, putting down the insurrection. By 1883, the British government was caught between two contradictory positions. Officially, Tewfik ruled Egypt and led its military. But British officials controlled the nation's finances and British officers led its forces. Prime Minister William Gladstone and Lord Granville, his foreign secretary, did not want Britain to rule Egypt directly, but they wanted to control the Suez Canal. They didn't want France to have more influence. And they wanted to fill the ever-increasing vacuum left by a declining Ottoman Empire. Restructuring Egypt's finances, government and military, including abandoning the expensive occupation of the Sudan, was difficult without taking over completely. But that was not an option. Egypt was still nominally under Ottoman rule, and Gladstone and his supporters were strongly opposed to expansion of British imperial responsibilities. Similarly, although the British public was beginning its late-Victorian jingoist phase, people wanted imperialist adventures; they just didn't want to pay for them. The question was how to get Egypt to financial health and out of the Sudan without Britain launching a major military expedition against the Mahdi.

W. T. Stead assumed the editorial reins at the *Pall Mall Gazette* (*PMG*) shortly before the Hicks campaign's defeat. His approach to the next few months' events included journalistic choices that hastened the process by which a broader newspaper-reading public became a policy-making body – or at least imagined it should be. Stead's editorial techniques were honed during the 'Gordon for the Sudan' campaign, resulting in a potent textual relationship between the British and Gordon, creating a unique bond between this particular imperial hero, the quasi-imperial territory and the British public.

The recent expansion of the franchise and the establishment of near-universal literacy gave that campaign its force. The government for the first time had to consider public opinion when making imperial policy. As Andrew Griffiths notes, 'Stead and Gordon were, respectively, the foremost representatives of the New Journalism and the New Imperialism and ... their meeting inaugurated an unprecedented period of symbiosis between empire and press.'[1] The perceived threat of public ire if Gordon had not been sent, or if a relief expedition to rescue him had not been approved, may have been greater than its actual impact.[2] Nevertheless, Stead asserted a right to weigh in on the decision-making process that he had, in fact, authored.[3]

By 1880, newspapers were beginning to organize their content differently. Columns of reprinted parliamentary debates (most notably in the *Times*) were replaced as editors created connections for readers, linking speeches to letters to the editor to dispatches, and so on.[4] This new style was compelling for readers, and Stead embraced it earlier and more enthusiastically than most.[5] Recent scholarship by Rachel Matthews and Tony Nicholson points out that regional papers were at the forefront of New Journalism. Political radicalism, industrialization and non-conformity went hand in hand with expanded literacy in the north in particular. It is reasonable to suspect that Stead's experiences meant he had strong ideas about how to engage the provincial readership and whatever risks were attached to pursuing a new style would be worth it.

Matthews shows the provincial press is where many of the characteristics of New Journalism were first developed.[6] Early iterations of his morality campaigns appeared while he was still editing the *Northern Echo*, increasing circulation numbers and bringing him notoriety on the national stage. He experimented with establishing a personal relationship with the reader by asserting a recognizable 'voice' in the pages of his paper.[7] The newspaper campaign was a logical extension of this development; the editor's moral outrage and hunger for information drove the campaign, and he modelled informed civic engagement for his readership. Nicholson argues that Stead's successful adoption of this new model was what led to his move to the *PMG*, and his methods ultimately produced the 'Maiden Tribute' campaign.[8] But the 'Gordon for the Sudan' campaign was his first foray into campaigning at a paper with national readership.[9]

In addition to the unique intersection of social and cultural developments that led to his successful experiments at the *Northern Echo*, the Gordon campaign also exploited a unique transitional, or hybrid, period in Liberal attitudes towards imperial undertakings. Furthermore, his techniques helped to drive that transition. In the Conservative press of the day, British identity and power were synonymous. The right to control Egyptian finances and political decisions was assumed if doing so were in Britain's self-interest. In the establishment of Liberal press, the rationale for imperial action was slightly different. Britain exceeded the capabilities of all non-European and most European societies – that was a given. But there was still faith that the Empire was a tool of progress for benighted peoples, which sentiment justified imperial exploits. Stead launched his campaign in the context of this Liberal assumption: that British power included the power to bring real improvements to the lives of Egyptians, Sudanese and others.[10] By the end of the campaign, however, Stead had successfully challenged traditional periodicals' claim to authoritative debate about what those improvements would be and how they would be achieved.[11] Expansive empire-building for moral reasons underlay *PMG*'s editorial stance. This served the hawkish faction in Gladstone's government and the popular mood.[12]

At the *PMG*, Stead made the fact-gathering process appear transparent, encouraging readers to see themselves as investigators.[13] As he had at the *Northern Echo*, Stead positioned himself and his paper as the facilitator rather than the author of public opinion.[14] Traditionally, reviews and essays in periodicals were where informed debate took place; their contributors were seen as responsible for 'forming national opinion'.[15] In this new age, however, events were moving fast. The time to ruminate on policy was contracting. The *PMG*, a cheaper, daily paper, whose audience was not typically the gentlemen of the clubs, was part of the modern information revolution. By 1883, Stead was already living by the credo he articulated in 'Government by Journalism' in 1887:

> The enormous advantage of being up to date … is undoubtedly the chief source of the inferiority of the influence of Parliament to that of newspapers. But the Press has many other advantages. It has freer access to experts. Let any question … come up, and within a week an energetic editor can have sucked the brains of every living authority in England or in Europe, and printed their opinions in his columns. Parliament can listen to no expert unless he is a British subject … [a member of Parliament, and] the subject must be brought on in some debate in which he can catch the Speaker's eye. Failing any one of these essentials, the expert's voice is dumb so far as Parliament is concerned, and of course, … for five months of the year, … Parliament itself is not sitting. … The parliament of the Press has no such arbitrary limitations. It … is ever open in a public forum in which everyone who is qualified to speak is freely heard.[16]

A new middle-class reader/expert was being created. And by empowering readers to articulate strong opinions, Stead's campaign vastly expanded the notion of the 'expert' and changed the definition.[17]

On 22 November, news arrived in London of the complete annihilation of Colonel Hicks and his forces in the western part of the Sudan. Initially, the press debated whether to respond to the Mahdi in the west, where Hicks and his men had died, or whether Egypt, with Britain's help, should simply try to hold onto the Sudan east of the Nile and north of Khartoum. But Hicks's defeat was an opportunity for Gladstone, supported and encouraged by Baring in Cairo, to extract all the Egyptian Army troops from the Sudan. This financial and strategic necessity was turned by Stead into a moral debate. Could the British leave the Sudan honourably? Between 22 November 1883 and 9 January 1884, Stead, and other newspapers that followed, had created the fantasy of a well-considered verdict being reached after an exhaustive, objective investigation by the British public.

Stead's support for Gordon's appointment may have rested on his strong belief that Egypt (and Britain) shouldn't abandon the Sudan.[18] But he was, first and foremost, a newspaperman. He altered his own declared stance along the way, likely trying to see which position would gain traction, not only with his readers but with regional and the other metropolitan papers. But he made these shifting positions part of the performance of fact gathering and responsible weighing of evidence.

His first expert was Sir Samuel Baker, who had served in the Sudan with Gordon in the 1870s. Baker had written letters to the editors of the *Times* between the Hicks debacle in November 1883 and the next, on 4 February 1884, when a large force under the command of Samuel's brother, Valentine, was defeated by the Mahdi's military leader, Osman Digna, at El Teb. Within a week of Hicks's death, Stead published an article drawing on Baker's expertise. Stead summarizes Baker's position and identifies him as an 'experienced Anglo-Egyptian' whose 'interesting and instructive' assessment is that 'the prevailing panic is, as usual, unreasonable'.[19] Stead's instinct was to support the position of Gladstone's government and the consul-general in Cairo, Sir Evelyn Baring, that Egypt needed to reduce its territorial reach in the Sudan. But Stead also saw room for outrage and debate in the aftermath of what the *PMG* dubbed 'the Soudan Catastrophe'.[20]

Was it untenable to maintain effective control of the Sudan, given Egypt's dire financial problems and the increasingly popular uprising of a religio-military leader, the Mahdi? Stead's *PMG* apparently took as a given the need to reduce Egypt's territorial reach, but to what point and who should be sent to implement it? Rumour had it that Zubayr Pasha, the leader of the slave kingdom of Darfur, was the preferred choice.[21] Stead pointed out to his readers in late November that 'Sir Samuel Baker writes a very interesting letter to the *Times*, lamenting that English officers were sent without a representative of the Prophet'.[22] And he goes on to agree that '[Baker's] proposal to employ the chief of the slave-traders to crush the Mahdi and to reestablish the kingdom of Kordofan would have been better than the dispatch of Colonel Hicks, and it may be that this suggestion will even now be put into execution'.[23] On 4 December, the *Times* built on this expectation by printing a telegraph message, obtained from a Reuters correspondent in Cairo, stating that Zubayr Pasha would command the 'new Soudan expedition', calling him a 'native of the province of Darfour, whose name is held in much awe throughout the Sudan'.[24]

By the time Stead was invoking Baker's expertise to support a change in editorial position, however, the British government realized the British public would never approve of appointing a known slave trader to, in essence, represent British interests. And Stead must have come to that realization as well. On the same day the *Times* printed the Reuters telegraph, Charles Allen, president of the British and Foreign Anti-Slavery Society, wrote to the *PMG* explaining that Zubayr's role in expanding nominal Egyptian sovereignty in Darfur included establishing his own slavery-funded fiefdom there, something that should not be rewarded or repeated. Allen supported his argument by quoting Gordon, whose anti-slavery credentials were unimpeachable, as saying, 'Darfur ought to be abandoned and the Khedive's forces concentrated on the Nile'.[25] Allen tied General Gordon's expertise to a moral imperative about the nature of British engagement in Egypt. From then on, the anti-slavery aspect of Gordon's earlier work and the unacceptability of Zubayr as a representative of British and Egyptian interests were linked in *PMG* coverage. In less than a month, Stead provided a variety of insider information, often conflicting, incomplete and soon repudiated. But his editorial efforts gave his reading public the sense that they were participating in a real-time discussion of foreign affairs.[26]

Then a more intensive educational process began. Beginning with the 4 December issue, readers were presented with briefs: 'The War in the Sudan' covers an entire page and includes a map. Factual details are interspersed with subjective analysis. The Mahdi's movement is described as slow, his future actions easily predicted. 'There will be plenty of time', the writer asserts, 'to throw any reinforcements that may seem necessary [into Khartoum] ... provided that route remain[s] open'.[27] A few days later, a letter to the editor appeared: 'The Soudan from an Abyssinian Point of View'. A former aide to King Johannes indicts the expansionist policies of the Khedive and accuses nominally independent British actors, such as Samuel Baker, of making promises of military control that couldn't be sustained, helping drain Egypt's resources. His solution reinforced what soon became the *PMG*'s declared position. The letter-writer, Habib Habeshi, asserts that the only way to pacify the region and thwart the slave trade – the two objectives that concerned the British public – was to save Khartoum and then create telegraph stations and military outposts along the entire Nile, into Abyssinian territory.[28] The potential commercial, military and political benefits to Abyssinia of such a plan go unmentioned.

Another recent expert on Egypt was drafted to support the fantasy of dispassionate public debate. Henry Villiers-Stuart, MP for County Waterford, had been sent to Egypt after the bombardment of Alexandria in 1882 to report on conditions in the country. Stead reproduces a letter that Villiers-Stuart had sent to the *Times*, suggesting that strategically placed forts could defend Egypt from the Mahdi. Again, Stead provides a map and some geographical context, observing that the territory south of the Assuan [Aswan] Dam was virtually impassable anyway, implying that a retreat to the boundaries of Egypt proper might be strategically preferable to continued military efforts in Sudan territory.

The invocation of experts and the 'education' of readers by the *PMG* were key to the new relationships between the reader/voter, the government and the imperial actor. Stead's efforts supported the illusion that the public was acquiring knowledge that extended beyond the immediate question of the Mahdi and was, therefore, comprehensive. Stead modelled the process for his readers by ostentatiously replacing his initial stance, reluctantly supporting Baring and the government, with the one held by General Charles Gordon.

By early January, Gordon's expertise had been asserted by both Charles Allen (a moral expert) and Samuel Baker (a military expert). On 8 January, Stead approached the man himself. Interviewing Gordon was revolutionary, an innovation from America that many in the British press found distasteful and unhelpful. Stead travelled to Gordon's home and described his participation as reluctant and unvarnished and the reading public equated candour with wisdom. 'With characteristic modesty', Stead assures us, 'General Gordon begged to be excused'. But Stead insisted that because 'he of all men now in the country was best acquainted with the Soudan', Gordon should speak. Further establishing Gordon as a cool-headed expert, Stead assured his readers that Gordon spoke 'with the utmost clearness and emphasis upon all the phases of the question of the hour'.[29] The public was riveted.

On 9 January 1884, on the front page of the *PMG*, Stead offered his argument for sending Gordon to the Sudan. Stead doesn't challenge Evelyn Baring's assertion, which was also Gladstone and Granville's inclination, that the full evacuation of the Sudan was necessary to save money. Stead simply states that he sees 'no option but reluctantly to acquiesce to his [Baring's] decision'.[30] The respect he pays to Baring's expertise is necessary to give weight to his own experts, pointing out that 'every authority' who looks at the issue from the perspective of Egypt's welfare rather than Britain's disagrees with Baring completely.[31] This carries an air of objectivity; it implies that disregarding British interests in favour of Egypt's must, by definition, be more objective than the self-interested considerations of those who are, like Baring, thinking of Britain. In the previous few weeks Stead had provided a series of conflicting opinions precisely so they might slowly be honed into the *PMG*'s official position.

The *Extra* that was published to launch the full campaign, set in motion after the 'Gordon for the Soudan' editorial, illustrates how the *PMG* distilled various currents into a single question. By 10 January, Stead could confidently ask the British public, 'Who Is to Have the Sudan? Gordon or the Slave Traders?' But this was after the slow accretion of 'knowledge' from 22 November through 9 January. In the *Extra*, Stead claims to support evacuation, just as Gordon claims he will facilitate an evacuation once he arrives in Khartoum. And yet the headline states the opposite. But Gordon has assured the British public that he can save Khartoum and, consequently, control of the Sudan, which, by this point, is the only moral alternative offered. To abandon the Sudan is fiscally responsible and militarily prudent, but it isn't British.

On 16 January, two days before Granville and Gladstone capitulate and order Gordon to Cairo, Baker returned to the pages of the *PMG*. His 'opinion' supported what, by this point, appeared to be the unanimous position of an informed British reading public. This apparent unanimity resulted partly from Stead's editorial innovation, ensuring that his efforts were amplified far beyond his paper's direct circulation. Papers customarily carried summaries of other papers' coverage under subheadings such as 'The Epitome of Opinion'. Stead modified this to create an 'expert' public that saw itself as part of a larger body politic. Later, in his *Review of Reviews*, Stead would do this in journal format, reprinting longer pieces he felt were worth disseminating. There was a serious difference, however, between reproducing wire-service stories and explicitly compiling independently written editorial content from national and major regional papers on a single topic. The latter fosters an awareness in each reader of other readers, other newspapers, other publics in other cities, who collectively agree with or at least entertain a particular editorial position. Through the feedback loop of 'The Epitome', the public became aware that it was obsessed with the successful execution of one goal: getting Gladstone to appoint Gordon.[32]

In 'Government by Journalism', Stead calls this a useful strategy for provincial papers to employ to influence Westminster and Whitehall, speaking from experience. He notes:

> The odd thing is that while members are frequently swayed from side to side by the utterances of the provincial Press, it is a rare exception for any of them to study that Press intelligently. They are dependent for the most part upon the more or less fragmentary excerpts from the rural oracles which the London papers dignify with the title of 'Epitome of Opinion.' The swing of the Ministerial pendulum has

> been frequently decided by those extracts, which in times of crisis are much more influential with both parties, but especially with the Liberals, than any London editorials.[33]

Stead took the methods first adopted by provincial papers to sway politicians by creating the sensation of a national debate. And he understood that because that debate was taking place in the pages of the paper rather than in Parliament, it seemed more immediate to the readership and more dangerous to the politicians. It couldn't be ignored.

The shifting position of the *PMG* did not damage Stead's credibility; by making information-gathering a seemingly transparent process, Stead made his readers 'experts'. Gentlemen who read the long essays in the fortnightly and monthly reviews presumed the authors possessed a high level of expertise gathered over years and conveyed to the reader fully formed. Stead performed the process in full view of his readership: political, military and economic data were collected, experts were consulted, maps were perused and consensus was reached. The voices of individuals on the ground, such as Baring and Wood, no longer seemed to be voices of expertise.

'Who Is to Have the Sudan? Gordon or the Slave Traders?' By this point, Stead had framed the question and answered it; the rest of the press amplified it. The *Manchester Times* summarized the issue on 12 January:

> The immediate question … [is] the manner in which the Soudan rebellion is to be dealt with. If we are to believe the statement current, Sir Evelyn Baring has advised the total withdrawal of the Egyptian forces … thus involving the abandonment of Khartoum. Whatever Sir Evelyn says is necessarily of the utmost importance, but on the other hand we have the opinion of General Gordon, who tells us plainly that the Egyptian troops cannot be withdrawn from Khartoum and other places outside the proposed frontier, simply because there are no means of transport. General Gordon in short says that it is impossible to abandon the Soudan if we would, unless we are prepared to leave to their fate the garrisons now threatened by the Mahdi. In the midst of the conflict of opinion amongst men who are all eminently qualified to judge the Government has no easy task to find the safest path.[34]

Once the government sent Gordon, it had acknowledged that the public's view was right. Stead didn't let the story go; he kept it in the public imagination for months. This was aided by carefully leaked information from secure communication between Baring and various ministers, some of whom constituted a hawkish and rebellious faction within Gladstone's government.[35] And when, months later, the government seemed reluctant to send an expedition to rescue Gordon, Stead's 'expert' public weighed in again – or at least Stead and the hawks suggested it was likely they would at the ballot box.[36]

The Sudan was a mythic place where the active, Christian heroes of the Empire would champion civilization against its enemies: the military-religious leader the Mahdi and the ruthless slave trader Zubayr Pasha. Its servants were reluctant. And relative to Great Britain, it was distant and independent. The British government was reluctant to claim responsibility for the Sudan in 1884. By 1898, Kitchener's Nile campaign was explained as retribution for Gordon's death – but also as atonement for abandoning the Sudanese. The logic of imperial heroism had entwined that narrative within the broader identity of the British public. Young boys had shared prickly adolescent thrills when they witnessed Gordon's doom courtesy of an Edwardian adventure story or pored over Winston Churchill's first-hand account as one of Kitchener's men. The utility of heroic myths came from the disassociation between the cultural fascination with these myths and their political, economic and social utility.

Part One

Metropolitan Britain writes the Sudan

1

A child's journey to the Sudan

Many of the junior officers who (re)conquered the Sudan with Kitchener in 1898 were teenagers or younger when, in 1884, they had followed the newspaper accounts of Gordon's doomed journey to Khartoum and the relief expedition sent to save him. By the end of the Great War, many of those members of the Nile Expedition had become senior members of the fully fledged Sudan government. That was the last generation of officials who had personal memories of the Gordon affair.[1] A narrow range of years containing all the formative events in British-Sudan history – from Gordon through Kitchener – coincides precisely with a period when various technological sea changes and the radicalization of politics combined to rock the existing social and cultural structures of imperial Britain.[2] These events generated a long-lasting and prolific industry in Gordon- and Kitchener-related literature that coincided with the growth of New Journalism and continued unabated for decades, entertaining and influencing boys who became men and colonial administrators.[3] The Education Act of 1870 brought near-universal literacy and standardized curricula. The extension of male suffrage into the working classes in 1889 encouraged both public and private interests to reach out to this new reading public. Newspaper editors like Stead understood that the increased power of the popular press and growth of the publishing industry were caused by the resultant explosion in readers and potential subscribers.[4] He was also at the forefront of editors and publishers who began to couch geopolitical complexities in the narrative structures of fiction and sensational exposés.[5] The traditional collaborations between governments and newspapers like the *Times* – shaping official opinion and disseminating it to the reading public – no longer controlled the conversation.[6] Politicians and editors increasingly had to contend with an actively engaged, larger and less-educated readership.[7]

In Britain between 1884 and 1918, at least sixty-one non-fiction works were published with Gordon's name in the title. His own journal, written during the siege, became an instant best-seller in multiple formats. And by the end of the First World War, at least twenty-one novels had been written about Gordon, the siege of Khartoum or Kitchener's reconquest.[8] The analysis here builds on Berny Sèbe's assertion that heroes like Gordon were directly deployed to 'further imperial aggrandizement', but 'they were also of interest to indirect hero makers: politicians, lobbyists, and the leaders of professional or charitable organizations could find in them an attractive way of furthering their causes'.[9] Advertising, sports, music, art, political campaigns and mass literature were new opportunities to increase sales, boost circulation or win votes. Stories from the Empire could reliably recast narratives previously employed for domestic socialization and regulation, such as children's adventure stories.[10] The reinforcing efficacy of interlocking modes of representation – consumption, leisure, politics, education – aided the overarching purpose: to elaborate on the story of the nation and include every voting, consuming and reading subject in it.

Literary sources had a cumulative effect on the British public's specific imaginary of the Sudan.[11] Reductive metropolitan knowledge of British colonial possessions was not unusual. But the new conditions of mass society influenced both the tenor and the content of the late-century imperial agenda (particularly in Africa), as Stead, novelist and publisher G. A. Henty and poet, novelist and textbook author Rudyard Kipling well knew.[12] Legitimated by textbooks, made more accessible by boys' adventure novels and given gravitas by non-fiction tomes bestowed as prizes in the upper forms or pulled from a father's bookcase at home during half-term break, the narratives of Empire grew more influential with every contribution.[13] The vast constellation of mass consumed, imperial literature consistently appealed to multiple generations of readers. Rider Haggard's Alan Quartermain series – begun in the late 1880s, within the emotionally heightened moment immediately following Gordon's death – helped establish an easy relationship for readers between heroism, adventure and Africa in popular fiction.[14] And Edgar Wallace's Sanders series – begun just before the Great War and first printed as a series of short stories in *The Tale-Teller* – articulated explicitly racist imperial narrative tropes aimed at the down-market end of the readership spectrum.[15] They, along with Henty, Kipling and many more, constituted a vast complex of imperial literature consumed by a voracious reading public in a variety of formats.

The popular fiction and non-fiction examined here, however, are texts which specifically outlined the Sudan's history in the service of developing 'character' in young British readers. Published between 1892 and 1907, these poems, novels and textbooks would have been read by British-Sudanis who entered the Sudan government between the wars. Boys who would eventually become members of that government enveloped themselves in detailed descriptions of the Sudan and experienced the smells, noises and sights that vivid literature can conjure. But these literary forms were not functioning in isolation from each other. The reiteration of themes, facts and arguments in different registers and across genres created an imaginary of the Sudan that was far more mutually reinforcing than texts in a single format – children's fiction, or school-sanctioned textbooks, or middlebrow adult non-fiction – ever could, no matter how expertly drawn.[16]

Schooling on the Sudan

In 1901, *A School History of England*, produced by 'teachers of experience', aimed to give a 'concise, correct and elementary view of English history'.[17] It was intended as a preliminary survey for younger students at the preparatory 'feeder' schools from which middle- and upper-middle-class students went on to public schools. Substantial scholarship details the relationship between the Victorian preparatory and public-school systems and the staffing of the Empire. J. A. Mangan and others have established these institutions' centrality in creating and promoting the imperial service ethos.[18] Some public schools were promoted as providing 'practical' value for money, reassuring up-and-coming upper-middle-class families that the fees were worth it because there was a direct conduit between the school halls and the halls of government, domestic or imperial – and that athleticism was key to success in all things.[19]

The *School History* begins before the Norman Conquest, and most monarchs get a chapter each unless their reign was particularly short, dull or both. Subsections within each reign chart domestic political history interspersed with issues and events at home and in the Empire, such as 'Religious Liberty', 'The Irish Potato Famine' and the creation of 'the Dominion of Canada'. The final, full chapter covers the reign of Victoria – a very long chapter. But at the very end of the book there is an odd, disconnected demi-chapter, 'Recent Events, 1881–1901', focusing on the later Gladstone and Salisbury ministries and Victoria's death. But four international events are deemed important enough to get their own entries. The granting of Australian statehood on New Year's Day, 1901, was so recent it was more of a current event. And two other unresolved topics were included: the war in South Africa and the fallout from the Boxer Rebellion. The one other issue deemed worthy of mention: 'Egypt and the Sudan'. In little more than a page, the authors set out the circumstances by which the 'reckless and spendthrift Ismail Pasha' forced the British to take control of Egypt. They then explain that the 'greater … danger from the Sudan' of the 'fanatical revolt' of the Mahdi brought about the defeat of Egyptian Army forces in the Sudan, under the leadership of an English general, Hicks. The few garrisons left were trapped. Without discussing whether the garrisons could be saved, by force or diplomacy, they simply state that 'a man of heroic mould, General Gordon' was sent to ensure their withdrawal. The importance of these imperial events to a metropolitan schoolroom audience is assumed. The students took in this classroom lesson about the character of Gordon and the inadequacies of the Egyptian Pasha. Even those who would never actively participate needed a strong understanding of imperial history to ensure their ongoing support of colonial policies. After all, without domestic support, men of character (Britons) might not be able to step in where men of dubious abilities (Egyptians) could not.[20]

Still, even in this oversimplified treatment of Gordon and the eventual reconquest of the Sudan, anxieties about British imperial action seep through. The debates of previous decades were not revisited, but the tone suggests nothing had been resolved. 'When he reached Khartum [*sic*]', the authors explain, 'he saw that strong and prompt measures alone could save the Sudan. But the English cabinet was deaf'.[21] According to them, Gordon was decisive. This sounds right. The cabinet must have been 'deaf' not to hear the rightness of the argument made by their man in the field; certainly that's what a boy reading this would think. How could they not listen to this brave man, there on the scene? Wasn't the empire built on the fearless and astute assessments of soldiers and adventurers who saw what was needed and provided it?

This 'elementary' version of English history elides the issues and arguments of the original debate; it sounds unproblematically legitimate. The authors, likely men who remembered the *PMG*'s 'Gordon for the Soudan' campaign, reproduced the contested premise that underlay the arguments fifteen years earlier. The *School History* explains,

'At last, when Gordon's position was known to be hopeless, the Government, powerless against popular indignation, sent ... an expedition up the Nile to relieve him and his garrison. Help came just too late. ... Khartum was betrayed and Gordon slaughtered.'[22] Here the implied sin was inaction, not incorrect action. In the context of the events in China and South Africa, the textbook reflects that basic imperial principle. 'It seemed', the authors say, 'as if Mr. Gladstone's cabinet would have been stung into action' by the shame of criticism.[23] But no. Gordon died; Khartoum was not only lost, it was 'betrayed', and the Sudan suffered under indigenous but incompetent rule for another thirteen years.

This critique of British policy and policymakers might have been harsh, but there was no need to worry. The authors make it quite clear that among the blessings the students enjoy as subjects of the UK is that governments change and policymakers learn their lessons. 'Ten years later Lord Salisbury's Government understood that to make Egypt safe we must reconquer the Sudan. ... By this time, Lord Cromer's law, order, and economy had given Egypt prosperity, and the patient efforts of Sir Herbert Kitchener ... had built up a native army which could inspire confidence.'[24] This same Kitchener, in the year of the textbook's publication, had the fate of British soldiers in the South African war in his hands. His patience and skills, which had created an effective Egyptian force (substantially supported by British troops), could reassure the sons and daughters of the men fighting under his command in South Africa; those attributes, so valued by a wise British public in 1884, even in the face of governmental resistance, still pertained. By the 1910s, Kitchener had become the heroic senior general who glared out from the hoardings to exhort these enlistment-aged youth of the nation to join the armed forces. And he died an uncommon death, in 1916, ensuring that he would stay safe from criticism in the pages of textbooks for a long time to come.[25]

A School History of England was rather dry. Nevertheless, it was still in circulation when a completely different but identically named preparatory school textbook was published in 1911. Co-written in a chatty style by Rudyard Kipling, it tried to describe British involvement in Africa for a young readership destined to be the colonial administrators of an empire now at its apex but soon to be at war; in this text historical facts are augmented by more explicit moral arguments. The rationale for British colonial acquisition during the Scramble for Africa, for instance, is explained retroactively through its benefits and differentiated from, let's say, German ones: 'The natives everywhere welcome the mercy and justice of our rule, and they are no longer liable, as they were before we came, to be carried off as slaves by Arab slave dealers.'[26] Kipling et al.'s *School History* barely mentions Gordon or the Sudan, merely asserting that the fierceness of the Sudanese wasn't fully appreciated and, as a result, the world lost a 'gallant general'. But boys reading either of these textbooks would have had numerous other ways to connect the contemporary empire to the events of 1884–85, including the novels and poetry of Henty and Kipling.

Two of the greatest heroes of the fin de siècle, General (later Earl) Kitchener and Lieutenant-General (later Lord) Baden-Powell, had direct connections to Gordon and the siege of Khartoum that kept Gordon central to the imperial narrative. As the war began in 1914, Kitchener had to be persuaded to leave his position as consul-general of Egypt to become secretary of war. Although he quickly moved on from the Sudan to the war in South Africa, Egypt and the Sudan were where he spent most of his career. Kitchener's sudden death in 1916, as his ship was sunk by German mines, only added to his renown. As the nation mourned, many an adolescent likely traced Kitchener's career back until it intersected with the Ur-martyr of the Empire, Gordon.[27] A hunger for all things Kitchener inevitably leads back to the siege of Khartoum.

Robert Baden-Powell, accessible to schoolboys through his *Scouting for Boys: A Handbook for Instruction in Good Citizenship*, was a great hero of the Boer War. 'Fresh from the glories of Mafeking', as a local paper billed him, he visited his alma mater, Cottesmore School in Brighton, in 1902 and connected his actions with the lessons being taught.

> While we are doing hard work [in South Africa] week after week, losing lives, and having very few pleasures, we do it because it is very pleasing and encouraging to us to go on when we know our efforts are being appreciated by those at home – and more especially when we know that the boys of England are watching and learning from us so that when their turn comes to do their duty for their country they will know how to do it.[28]

These boys were watching and learning through mass-produced textbooks and illustrated news reports. During the Boer War, journalists travelled along with soldiers. The Siege of Mafeking, which made Baden-Powell a household name, trapped newsmen along with civilians and soldiers.[29] The intimate coverage of imperial military exploits by 'embedded' journalists encouraged elaborate memoirs and inspired poems and songs, adventure tales and learned treatises.

When, just six years later, he published his *Handbook*, Baden-Powell uses General Gordon as the example of a man who puts his 'duty before all'.[30] He connected scouting to Gordon effectively when he appropriated Sir Henry Newbolt's poem *Vitaï Lampada*, which he renamed 'Play the Game', and incorporated it into scouting material:

> There's a breathless hush in the Close to-night –
> Ten to make and the match to win –
> A bumping pitch and a blinding light,
> An hour to play and the last man in.
> And it's not for the sake of a ribboned coat,
> Or the selfish hope of a season's fame,
> But his Captain's hand on his shoulder smote
> 'Play up! play up! and play the game!'
>
> The sand of the desert is sodden red, –
> Red with the wreck of a square that broke; –
> The Gatling's jammed and the colonel dead,
> And the regiment blind with dust and smoke.
> The river of death has brimmed his banks,
> And England's far, and Honour a name,

But the voice of schoolboy rallies the ranks,
'Play up! play up! and play the game!'

This is the word that year by year
While in her place the School is set
Every one of her sons must hear,
And none that hears it dare forget.
This they all with a joyful mind
Bear through life like a torch in flame,
And falling fling to the host behind –
'Play up! play up! and play the game!'

In three stanzas, Newbolt moves from the cricket pitch to the battlefield of Abu Teb, where forces sent to rescue Gordon were beaten by the Mahdi army, and then to the conflicts these boys will experience as men.[31] Gordon's sacrifice and legacy were deployed for new audiences by biographers, editors, textbook writers, youth leaders and novelists; his philosophy of colonial service became the romance of High Imperialism.

Kipling's exotic familiar

In the interview collection *Bonds of Silk*, many British-Sudanis identify their first experience of the Sudan as Kipling's poem 'Fuzzy Wuzzy'. Despite the derogatory name, Kipling's description of the Sudanese as worthy adversaries left a strong, positive impression in young boys' memory. The *Barrack Room Ballads* collection that contained 'Fuzzy Wuzzy' saw seven editions in India in two years; the year it was published in Britain, 1892, four editions were printed.[32] Kipling immortalizes the bravery and skill of the warriors in the Mahdist army who managed to 'break the square'. Years later, one SPS officer noted that this recounting of the Sudanese feat of piercing supposedly impregnable British defences 'eclipsed' all other knowledge that the British who went there had of the Sudan and the Sudanese.[33]

Kipling's ballad mixed violent images and humour in a perfect combination for boyhood imaginations. In the poem, war is an adventure; the losses experienced on both sides are sanitized by the jokey and domestic language of Kipling's Cockney soldier narrator. A young probationary officer recalled decades later including a shotgun and a medicine chest in the list of supplies he needed to purchase before his first tour and being encouraged to go and watch dissections at the Radcliffe Infirmary to get used to the sight of death. He was thrilled but not surprised. Kipling's narrator had already warned him as a child what was in store for him. The violent 'Fuzzy Wuzzy' must not be underestimated: 'before we know, 'e's 'ackin' at our 'ead; 'E's all 'ot sand an' ginger when alive, An' 'e's generally shammin' when 'e's dead'?[34]

For adult men, imperial literature was a potent medium for conveying normative masculinity; for boys it offered another world in which their alter egos could flourish.[35]

Part of Kipling's genius was his ability to make the imperial arena familiar and unthreatening, even if exotic. As Boyd puts it, these boys 'roamed the globe carrying British ideas and arrogance in their baggage'.[36] The ever-cheery narrator of the *Barrack Room Ballads* conveys the naturally simple view of the world held by 'Tommy' in the Empire through sentimental language describing honour, battle, love, drunkenness and sorrow. He does his duty, understands some things but is bored by the complexity of others, is undervalued by the civilian population back home and yet sees the world through a British cultural lens. To Tommy, Fuzzy Wuzzy is 'a daisy, 'e's a ducky, 'e's a lamb!' And the Englishman finds himself toasting not only his adversary but also 'the missis and the kid. . . . '

Kipling's poem exemplifies the classic imperial tension between the illusion of familiarity and the titillation of the exotic. The domestication of Empire suggests that all is knowable and controllable, yet the irreconcilable differences justify policies of conquest and control. Kipling's *Plain Tales*, his novels and his poetry shared the top of the sales lists in the 1890s with Lord Roberts's memoir of life in India and, briefly, with a work destined to be forever connected to the Sudan: Slatin Pasha's account of captivity under the Mahdi.[37] This range of imperial literature is co-existing and mutually reinforcing despite their obvious differences. And Kipling's Nobel Prize for Literature in 1907 brought additional gravitas to the popular favourite right when boys who would become administrators after the Great War were first of an age to read his work.

In the *Barrack Room Ballads*, the middle and upper classes could enjoy an inside look at the attitudes and experiences of Britain's soldiers, the working classes could see themselves represented, finally, in the literature of Empire, and little boys could enjoy reading subject matter beyond their tender years. 'Danny Deever' describes a soldier's death for the crime of desertion; another poem bemoans the bad reputation soldiers have (unfairly) acquired; another is an utterly unapologetic paean to drunk and disorderly behaviour. The collection has something for everyone. But 'no single ballad . . . had such a furore of success' as 'Fuzzy-Wuzzy'.[38]

The Fuzzy Wuzzies were the Hadendoa, a subgroup of the Beja people. Their nickname arose from their elaborate hairstyles, in which their hair was worn long and impregnated with butter to help it stand up and out. According to Kipling's Cockney admirer, the greatly respected and fierce-looking Hadendoa fighter 'cut our sentries up at Sua'kim'. Suakin was once the key port on the Red Sea, and for a time, Egyptian and British soldiers' last redoubt in Sudan territory at the height of the Mahdi's reach. Every probationary administrator arriving in Port Sudan would likely have recalled Kipling's admiring description of the warriors:

'E 'asn't got no papers of 'is own,
'E 'asn't got no medals nor rewards,
So we must certify the skill 'e's shown
In usin' of 'is long two-'anded swords:
When 'e's 'oppin' in an' out among the bush
With 'is coffin-'eaded shield an' shovel-spear . . .

In 1926, Nancy Robertson arrived in Suakin with her husband James, who would eventually head the SPS as civil secretary. She recalled, 'Having read Kipling, as everyone had in those days, I was expecting to see them standing with their long spears, romantically silhouetted against the sky.'[39] Whatever youthful administrators consciously expected of the Sudan, we can imagine Kipling's stanzas running in their heads like a familiar song that can't be dislodged.[40]

Henty's Egypt/Sudan trilogy

For the young public-school reader, the metropolitan fantasy of the Sudan was difficult to differentiate from knowledge of the Sudan. His Egypt/Sudan trilogy provided a vivid narrative embellishment for the terse descriptions of the same events found in the young boys' textbooks. They cover all the key moments, from the bombardment of Alexandria to Gordon's expedition to Khartoum and the failed rescue attempt to Kitchener's conquest of the territory. The first in the trilogy, *A Chapter of Adventures; or, Through the Bombardment of Alexandria*, published in 1891, offered a version of the events that led to Britain becoming embroiled in Egyptian affairs nine years earlier.[41] Henty usually waited before crafting tales about recent events. Five or six years pass between the Zulu and Ashanti Wars, or the Battle of Kandahar, and Henty's fictional treatments of them. Similarly, it took him almost a decade to commit the bombardment to paper. But he followed *A Chapter of Adventures* with *Dash for Khartoum* only a year later. The second novel concerned the peripheral battles waged by the British-led Egyptian Army against the Mahdi before Gordon's attempt to evacuate the city and then the Gordon relief expedition. Henty likely saw the two novels as a continuing, connected saga. And in *Dash for Khartoum*, as in Kipling's poem of the same year, the author assumes his readers have more than a passing familiarity with the Sudan saga of 1884–85.

Henty's third novel about the Sudan, *With Kitchener in the Soudan*, published in 1903, reaches back to the events resulting in the 'loss' of the Sudan two decades earlier and connects them to Kitchener's conquest in 1898. Kitchener had gone straight from the Nile Campaign to the Boer War, his exploits eagerly covered by the copy-hungry press. He had acquired a reputation for efficiency – and ruthlessness. At the Battle of Omdurman, the lives of 11,000 Sudanese troops were taken at the cost of roughly 300 Britons. And in South Africa, Kitchener incarcerated women and children in concentration camps to prevent civilian aid reaching the Afrikaner guerilla fighters. The war was won, but approximately 27,000 (white) women and children died in the camps.[42] Most British readers continued to hail him as the greatest imperial hero since Gordon. But in the war's aftermath, these ugly statistics became fodder for critics of the Empire, notably members of the new Labour Party. In *With Kitchener*, for the first time Henty puts the reader in the same narrative frame as the imperial hero. Readers are also instructed in the preface to adopt a favourable interpretation of Kitchener's actions and their historical relevance. By 1903, the Boer War, the Boxer Rebellion and the debate over America's future as an imperial power had changed the stakes for narratives of imperial derring-do.

A Chapter of Adventures

A Chapter of Adventures ostensibly describes events surrounding the British bombardment of Alexandria in 1882. In it, three junior midshipmen (boys, really) who are in the merchant navy take shore leave just before civil unrest erupts in the city. They accidentally find themselves in the midst of the action, as plucky lads often do in Henty's novels. They are caught up in the initial rioting and seek shelter with an Italian shopkeeper; later they are held prisoner by Egyptians. Eventually, Jack, Jim and Arthur escape and climb a hill outside the city, just in time to watch the British naval bombardment from a safe distance. At last, they find their way back to the British authorities, much to everyone's relief.

For the young men, the causes of the bombardment are distilled to what individuals tell them on the ship and on the streets, which Henty offers as facts. The initial riot 'began in a quarrel between some Maltese and natives', Henty explains through one of the senior officers. 'But this quarrel seemed to be accepted by the latter as a signal for a general attack and they rushed from their houses armed with heavy sticks and knives and attacked the Europeans.'[43] The boys are taken prisoner by an Egyptian man who sees them fleeing angry 'natives', recognizes their potential worth as hostages and has them carried away, shrouded so that they'll be mistaken for Egyptians who died at the hands of the European shopkeepers.

In Henty's version of history, the original uprisings that result in the bombardment were caused by individuals rather than institutions. Henty creates a fictional 'wealthy bey' who was 'the brother of one of the leaders of the insurrection at Cairo'.[44] Henty explains that 'his agents had assisted to bring about the riot ... by exciting the greed of the lowest classes of the town by pointing out how great was the wealth they could obtain by looting' the Europeans' shops and warehouses.[45] The deaths of dozens of Europeans (including women, Henty points out) and hapless, gullible Egyptians are the tragic outcome of an event completely denuded of wider political and economic implications.

The ramifications of the extremely controversial 'capitulations' – Europeans' exemptions from taxes and other laws that Egyptians were subject to – were elided. The British public's understanding of Egyptian financial and political failure was based on a racial and religious teleology that allowed the reader to abdicate all responsibility for understanding the wider context. Rather than characterize Egypt as unstable *because* of Britain's (and Europe's) intervention, in Henty's narrative Egypt's a priori instability necessitates Britain's intervention. Fiction's demands for streamlined narratives and clear plot arcs helped shape the narrative of history. What is lacking in these early novels finds its way into some of the adult non-fiction treatments of the same subject, years later. Lord Cromer, for example, devotes quite a bit of time to complaining about the continued detrimental impact of the capitulations even in the 1910s, in his introduction to Sidney Low's review of Egypt and the Sudan, *Egypt in Transition*.[46]

From the perspective of the young midshipmen of *A Chapter of Adventures*, however, economic and political forces that had long contributed to the weakening authority of the khedive were reduced, in Henty's telling, to the Egyptian military wanting more 'privileges' and 'natives' wanting Europeans removed from government. Henty also says that it's likely 'the French are at the bottom of it' because they 'have always been jealous of [British] influence in Egypt'.[47] The book's central character, Jack, who had been taken aboard a merchant ship because his widowed mother couldn't support him at home, is told this about Egypt as he is about to go ashore in Alexandria with his pals.

The ship has stopped there to deliver iron railway sections – so the reason Jack was in Egypt was Britain's support of Egypt's commercial and economic growth. According to Henty, the reason for the unrest was the Egyptians' being easily led by the French to demand the removal of British governors who had their best interests at heart. Little differs between this fictional distillation of the standard narrative of reluctant and altruistic British intervention, written in the 1890s, and John Buchan's non-fiction account of the history of the Sudan, written in 1934. Buchan explains that 'in 1883 the government of the Soudan was a jerry-built monstrosity which would have fallen from its own weight even if there had been no alien force to batter it. Ismail was the typical Oriental despot whose imagination, especially in money matters, far outran the prosaic fact'.[48] In a classically ambivalent comment, Buchan goes on to admit, admiringly, that there was still 'an element of greatness in [Ismail's] folly. When he was asked concerning the gauge of his proposed railway, he replied, "Make it the same as South Africa; it will save trouble in the end"'.[49] The difference between ambition and overreach was never quite settled when it came to Egypt – either for Britain's Egyptian 'partners' or for British policymakers themselves.

For the three central characters in the novel, the unrest is sudden and unexpected. 'Rumours had for some time been current among [the rebellious Egyptians] that the Christians intended to conquer Egypt and put down the Mahomedan religion and in their excited state a spark caused an explosion.'[50] But the officers on the merchant ship thought it safe to send the lads on shore leave; it is carefully explained that the riot took hold only in the poor quarter of the city. So the immediate cause of violence was the unreasoning fear of simple-minded Muslims that Christian Europeans were planning to outlaw their faith. The boys' senior officers couldn't have been expected to predict this kind of irrational behaviour, Henty suggests.

Henty describes how ineffectual governance endangers the peaceful inhabitants of the city because the riot isn't put down. The unpredictable and violent 'natives had entirely their own way [in the streets] from three o'clock in the afternoon until seven in the evening'. The lads almost die as Egyptian looters set fire to the shop of Italians who tried to rescue them. Their fate was sealed because 'the [Egyptian] police made no attempt whatever to put down the riot'. 'Some seventy Europeans, including ten or twelve women were killed', Henty reports, but the European business centre was not affected because the entrepreneurial class armed itself and, at heart, the 'Egyptians are timid people'.[51] The Egyptians are portrayed simultaneously as destructive and timid – much like children. Thus, imprisoned by Egyptians, Jack, Arthur and Jim are among equals. This explains how, over time, the boys are able to manipulate the native adults and determine the best outcome for themselves. They come into the situation as equals, British children among childlike natives, but they will ultimately be rational British adult men of Empire, which gives them a leg up.

In *A Chapter of Adventures*, Henty tries to explain why the British should continue to be involved with Egypt and the Egyptians. When the book was published in 1891, the British were even more directly in control of Egypt's finances, the Canal and government decision-making. According to Henty, the appropriate interpretation of these events was that the 'outbreak was... the result of the hatred existing among the lower class against the riffraff of the various nationalities gathered in Alexandria, whose conduct frequently gave good grounds indeed for the feeling entertained against them'.[52] *Greater* British involvement was the answer. Henty was expressing the increasingly interventionist trend in metropolitan imperial sentiment in the early 1890s. The prime minister and foreign minister during much of this period, Lord Salisbury, ostensibly pursued a policy of 'splendid isolation', but in practice increasingly favoured imperial action.[53] Jack, Arthur and Jim, in Alexandria in 1882, would have been unaware of Salisbury's predecessors and his colleagues debating these issues. Gladstone, Granville and other ministers are absent from Henty's stage. Nevertheless, this novel of 1891 helped subsequent generations of young readers understand Britain's relationship with Egypt and the Sudan in a certain way.

The denouement of the novel is the actual bombardment of Alexandria in July 1882. When, weeks after they're taken captive, the British gunboats mass in the harbour and begin their bombardment, their (by then) admiring captors take Jack, Jim and Arthur to safety on the bluffs outside the city. The boys are awestruck, watching the evidence of Britain's power, but out of harm's way. They witness Britain's military might and benefit from it; they are rescued once the city is pacified. Henty limits the boys' exposure to larger events. They interact with individual Egyptians in acts of violence and generosity. Their interpersonal negotiations are the hallmark of the British imperial project. The incredible destructive and coercive power of the British guns, on the other hand, is described from a distance and never experienced by them.[54] The successful negotiation of interracial imperial relations by individuals on the ground is bolstered by the threat and ultimate power of the British military machine. The message is that the character of the men engaged in the imperial project ensures its success, through individual virtue and the judicious use of violence.

For British policymakers, this definition of colonial administration is highly problematic, but for the common reader, it makes complex power dynamics threaded through three continents and countless governments both real and manageable. In literature, the individual's character is given far greater weight than the administrative structure and broader geopolitical considerations of policymakers back in Westminster.[55] 'Britain' exists as ships on the horizon and as part of an anonymous community of industrious Europeans. The successful individuals (Jack, Jim and Arthur) are separated from Britain, from the structures of government, and succeed by choosing action over consultation and one-on-one relationships over established hierarchies and institutions. Along the way, the controversies swirling around the bombardment – debated in London, across Europe and in Egypt – are distilled by Henty into manageable issues, easily addressed and resolved. The young male readers of Henty might not have characterized their reading experiences as briefings, but they were being trained to think about the Empire in a particular way and to consider their literary experience of colonial events as a legitimate source of knowledge.

Novels as news

The bombardment of Alexandria set in motion events that, less than two years later, resulted in Gordon's arrival in Khartoum, at the behest of the Egyptian and British governments, to evacuate British and Egyptian troops before the total domination of the Sudan by the Mahdi and his followers. The metropolitan understanding of these events is illuminated by the second in Henty's trilogy, *The Dash for Khartoum: A Tale of the Nile Expedition*, published in 1891.[56] The story begins in an enclave of British India with the switching of babies at birth and ends years later with each man proving his worth, thanks to the opportunities for heroism presented by the Mahdi's aggression and Gordon's need of rescue. This was published in the same year as *A Chapter of Adventures*; Henty invited his young readers into a Sudan governed by the same epistemology. No revelations had changed the vocabulary, nor had any political or cultural shift in British metropolitan society recast the events discussed in the first novel. Whether a young reader decided to read Henty's novels in the order they were written or according to the subject matter, *The Dash for Khartoum* would have followed *A Chapter of Adventures*.

Youthful readers would also, however, be introduced to these texts as news – their first information about historical events in Egypt and the Sudan. They encountered these texts not as fictional counterpoints to memories of newspaper coverage of actual events but as *the* source. Henty assumed while writing that the locations, events and characters would already be familiar to the audience; a reader today would find the book virtually incomprehensible.[57] This easy appropriation of events, and the second novel's compression of complex political and military strategies into the fictional tale of two men's journey into selfhood, further illustrates that the sources of 'knowledge' that later administrators drew from were not clearly separated in their memories. To read *Dash for Khartoum* was to revisit Kipling's 'Fuzzy Wuzzy'; Henty's Khartoum under siege recalled the basic imperial catechism of textbooks.

Edgar, our hero, arrives in Suakin with his battalion in advance of the famed battle of Tokai, one of the two battles Kipling referred to where the square was broken. We (and he) are witness to a debate about the relative merits of trained British soldiers and passionate, but undisciplined, natives. 'What chance have they got against regular troops?' asks one of the soldiers. 'I don't know, Johnson', the more battle-tried sergeant replies. 'The Zulus were savages, and they made a pretty tough fight against us.' The novice soldier is reminded that the Sudanese had already 'cut Hicks Pasha's army into mincemeat'. But the young reader who had read his Kipling would also have the delicious knowledge that Edgar and his mates didn't – the breaking of the square was soon to come. 'If you think this is going to be no harder work than a field-day in Aldershot, I think you are likely to find you are mistaken.'[58] But the reader knows better.

Knowing what will happen turns the reader's attention to the pending test of these men's valour and our protagonist's manhood. This depends on the quality of the enemy. 'You don't suppose … that these naked beggars are going to stand for a moment against a charge of eight hundred cavalry?' the soldier asks incredulously. The sergeant replies, 'It does not seem possible these Arabs can stand for a moment against our charge; but, you see, we do not understand these fellows … When you have got to reckon with men who don't care the snap of a finger whether they are killed or not, you never can count upon an easy victory however badly they may be armed, and however, undisciplined they may be.'[59] The Hadendoa may not be equals of the British soldiers, Henty asserts, but they are fearless. And this is reinforced and amplified by Kipling's 'Fuzzy Wuzzy'. The Sudanese were fearless but undisciplined, poorly led but faithful, treacherous but not dishonourable, whether one was reading Henty or Kipling.

So events whose meanings were highly unstable in contemporary public discourse and the subject of heated debate in the world of adults – such as Gordon's assignment in the Sudan and whether an expedition should have been sent to rescue him – existed as unproblematic 'knowledge' for these adventure novels' original adolescent readers. Later generations of readers also assumed that the novels' narratives were framed with unassailable facts. Even today, Henty novels are used widely as reliable histories for homeschooling.[60] In the decades of their greatest popularity, the imperial arena was portrayed as fixed in time not only in terms of development, race relations and conceptualizations of administrative policy but also with regard to social mores, class identities and gender dynamics.

In *Dash for Khartoum*, impossibly complex geopolitical considerations that brought down a British government and crippled the Egyptian economy are reduced to casual campfire conversations. Henty has a character articulate the prointervention side of the argument that Stead championed Stead in the *PMG*, split the cabinet, was opposed by Baring and Wood in Cairo and resulted in dispatching Gordon:

> 'It seems to me,' [the soldier] said, talking it over with several of his chums, 'that sooner or later we must have some fighting in Egypt. I cannot understand how it is that some of the regiments there have not long ago been sent down to Suakim. We have smashed up the Egyptian army, and it seems to me that as we are really masters of the place we are bound to protect the natives from these savage tribes who are attacking them down on the Red Sea and up in the Soudan. The Egyptians always managed them well enough until we disbanded their army. If Hicks Pasha had had, as he asked for, an English regiment or two with him, he would never have been smashed up by the Mahdi's people; and it seems to me awful that the garrisons of Sinkat and Tokar should be deserted when we have a lot of troops lying idle at Cairo, while Baker is trying in vain to get up a native force to march to their relief'.

No one voices the counterargument; the position is presented as so obvious that an untrained, casual participant is able to see clearly its rightness. Memoirs abounded with similar narrative devices, reinforcing the illusion that clear pathways were available to righteous imperial decision-making.

Adventures in the Sudan

Two books that were likely to sit near each other in family bookcases were Henty's *Dash for Khartoum* and Count Rudolph von Slatin Pasha's *Fire and Sword in the Sudan*. Slatin's book was recommended reading for young probationary administrators heading out to the Sudan, even in the interwar period, whereas the Sudan government would likely have been insulted at the suggestion that Henty's novel might provide similar information. Nevertheless, central to the plot of both books is that our 'hero' finds himself a captive of the Mahdi. For later generations, the stories would resonate, adding weight to *Dash for Khartoum* and the allure of boys' adventure tales to Slatin's memoir.

Slatin was the Egyptian khedive's governor in Darfur when first cut off from his superiors by the advancing Mahdi forces in 1883. Like Edgar, Henty's hero, Slatin Pasha was captured at the time of Gordon's defeat at the end of 1884 and held as a (privileged) prisoner/slave for the next decade. Finally escaping in 1895, he wrote his memoirs, and the English translation of his *Fire and Sword in the Sudan* appeared in 1896.[61] But Edgar's adventures were not a fictional version of Slatin's ordeal; Slatin's account, published five years after *Dash*, is so rich with Henty's literary tropes that it's hard to remember that it was intended as adult non-fiction, not a derivative knockoff. And yet its 'expertise' on the Sudanese was valued well into the interwar period. The portrait it draws of the Sudan was consistent with earlier newspaper reports and fiction and reconfirmed by later versions of the same: an entire constellation of imagery that gained legitimacy from, rather than being undermined by, slight inconsistencies across the various sources.

Another book also offered a 'captured by the Mahdi and made a slave of the Dervishes' plot, published only a year after *Dash*. Father Joseph Ohrwalder's *Ten Years Captivity in the Mahdi's Camp: 1882–92* recounted how he was taken prisoner by one of the Mahdi's generals and held for a decade. His story is the least swashbuckling of the three, but the shared narrative gained impact from their contemporaneous publication. Ohrwalder's persona is burnished by his heroic – albeit fictional – counterpart in Henty; Henty's young hero becomes all the more 'real' for the readers in 1892 and after.[62] These tales of captives recall Linda Colley's book of the same name. Part of Colley's argument is that the narrative of captivity helps distract from the narrative of conquest, or at least invasion, by British forces.[63] Rather than think why Christian missionaries or Austrian mercenaries were in a position to be captured, these accounts, reinforced by Henty's story of Edgar, emphasize the positive aspects of the individual's character, tested by adversity.

The interdependency of various literary genres seems to increase over the decades when it comes to the Sudan 'story'. The final installment in Henty's trilogy, *With Kitchener in the Soudan: A Story of Atbara and Omdurman*, took young readers back to the Sudan once again, in time for the Nile Campaign of 1898 to (re)conquer the country from the Mahdi's successor. Henty did his part to burnish Kitchener's persona in the wake of the horrific revelations of incompetence and brutality in the South African campaign. Published in 1903, Colonel Kitchener's journey up the Nile and the eventual Battle of Omdurman are not presented with any of the even grudging admissions of barbarism and unnecessary brutality that Churchill and Bennett each attest to in their eyewitness accounts – *The River War* and *Downfall of the Dervishes* – despite their overall positive assessment of the actions of the officers and commanders alike. Churchill's and Bennett's books remained on the reading list for young recruits to the SPS well into the 1940s, likely because their occasional criticism of British military and diplomatic policy, as well as their lengthy assessments of the Sudanese, qualified them as intellectual non-fiction rather than popular reading. Kitchener's campaign up the Nile had barely concluded when Henty wove a narrative around it, and it leans heavily on the recent reportage of both special correspondents. Churchill, whose work includes a bibliography, makes use of romanticized first-person accounts to clarify or establish points of historical narrative. The result is a collage of Sudan non-fiction enriched by myths and ripping yarns legitimized by eyewitness accounts.

The imperial romance is a self-referential cultural production. *The River War* saw its origins in serialized newspaper dispatches to the *Morning Post*.[64] Lord Cromer cites it enthusiastically in his much-quoted *Modern Egypt*, published in 1906; Slatin and Father Ohrwalder are the only experts other than Gordon himself that Churchill cites during his lengthy recounting of the events that culminated in the Nile Expedition in 1898 and Kitchener's conquest.[65] Slatin and Churchill went on to political careers, and so their earlier literary efforts retroactively acquired the legitimacy of 'governmental', 'policy' documents. And Cromer was synonymous with governance and authority in Egypt and the Sudan for decades. But the voice with which Slatin and Ohrwalder spoke to British readers, including Churchill, who depended on them so heavily for his background material, was the voice of Kitchener's successor, Reginald Wingate. Before arriving in the Sudan, most of the recruits to the SPS may have been introduced to Wingate's Sudan long before they experienced its legacy in person during the interwar years.

In 1902 came the publication of Henty's final Sudan journey, *With Kitchener in the Soudan*, Churchill's one-volume, best-selling version of *The River War*, and yet another classic of Sudan popular literature, A. E. Mason's *The Four Feathers*. Earlier events haunt the characters or narrators of these texts. The Sudan was something personally experienced, but what brought men there was a series of events known by all. In the preface to *With Kitchener in Soudan*, Henty 'reminds' the reader about the history covered in his previous two Egypt/Sudan novels, offering a particular characterization of political debates and policies connected to Gordon and the Sudan as the accepted truth. He describes Kitchener as 'the moving spirit of the enterprise [to reconquer the Sudan]'. Although Kitchener was in 1898 the military leader 'whose marvelous power of organization had secured its success', by 1902 he was at the centre of criticisms regarding decisions made during the Boer War. But Henty redirects his reader back to the Sudan. He explains that the work of Kitchener and Wingate took 'a land that had been turned into a desert by the terrible tyranny of the Mahdi and… restored [it] to civilization'. In the process, Henty assured his trusting readers, 'the stain upon British honour caused by the desertion of Gordon by the British ministry of the day was wiped out'.[66] Kitchener redeemed the honour of the British government; actions on behalf of the British government in South Africa should, perhaps, be left unexamined.

Henty then returns to the central events of his first book set in Egypt. Ten years passed between his two versions of the bombardment, but for many young readers in the first half of the twentieth century, the gap could have been a matter of weeks, as they read one Egypt/Sudan-themed Henty book after another. The brief retrospective, woven into the novel, of the 'real' history would have encouraged any boy who happened to read *With Kitchener* first to seek out Henty's previous two Egypt/Sudan novels.

An officer recruited to the SPS in the 1920s might have read the Kitchener novel in the 1900s or early 1910s, after having had Kitchener mania dominate the media landscape his entire life. The difference between fiction and non-fiction, and adult and juvenile literature, would hardly register, contemporaneously or in memory.[67]

The hero of Henty's novel this time is Gregory Hilliard, the son of a devoted father who brought his tubercular wife to Egypt just before the bombardment of Alexandria and who then disappeared while fighting the Mahdi under the ill-fated Hicks Pasha. Sixteen years later, the son is hand-picked by Lord Cromer to act as an interpreter in Kitchener's expeditionary force. Through pluck and happenstance, Hilliard manages to be present at every major event of the following years, from Atbara to Fashoda. Henty rewarded readers familiar with the details of the Gordon story – certainly the fathers of the boys who were raptly reading *With Kitchener* – with an homage to Gordon, in the form of a diary. Written by Hilliard père and discovered by Hilliard *fils*, it informs the son that the father had been in the direct service of Gordon and had left Khartoum, under Gordon's orders, with Stewart and Mr. Power, who, every adult reader knew, ran aground and were killed in September 1884 trying to reach help.

This literature cast British imperial projects as the narratives of individuals and focused on dilemmas and anxieties universally understood within the metropole across class boundaries.[68] It employed a vocabulary of character, personal challenge and self-realization. The Sudan became both an exotic locale and an internal, psychic space.[69] Mason's classic Sudan novel, *The Four Feathers*, is as much interior narrative as action story. It is about bravery (and the fear of cowardice). Mason used the familiar events in the Sudan to frame the most fundamental question of young manhood: Would I, faced with the prospect of my own death, be a coward? Its enduring popularity suggests that *The Four Feathers* tapped into the psyche of successive generations of young men. The book follows Harry Feversham out to the Sudan as he tries to disprove the accusations of cowardice levelled against him by helping shape the course of history:

> The sun rose toward the centre of a colourless, cloudless sky, the shadows of the camels shortened up on the sand, and the sand itself glistened white as a beach of the Scilly Islands. There was no draught of air that morning to whisper amongst the rich foliage, and the shadows of the branches lay so distinct and motionless upon the ground that they might themselves have been branches strewn there on some past day by a storm. The only sounds that were audible were the sharp clank of weapons, the soft ceaseless padding of the camels' feet, and at times the whirr of a flight of pigeons disturbed by the approaching cavalcade. Yet there was life on the plateau, though of a noiseless kind. For as the leaders rode along the curves of sand, trim and smooth between the shrubs like carriage drives, they would see from time to time, far ahead of them a herd of gazelle start up from the ground and race silently, a flash of dappled brown and white, to the enclosing hills. It seemed that here was a country during this last hour created.[70]

The Sudan was a desolate place, its silence the result of its emptiness, the people of the Sudan barely registering except as members of the marauding Mahdi army – more a uniquely Sudanese force of nature than a population.

Fuzzy Wuzzy hadn't disappeared. But Mason's novel abandoned a key element of the Henty-style adventure novel: the surprise plot twist that rewards the selfless hero with a title, a fortune or both. The heroes of *The Four Feathers* are enriched by the Sudan because their experiences in its bleakness help them find peace within themselves. They prove themselves worthy through their appreciation of the Sudanese people, an appreciation so great that they are successfully able to impersonate them as well as master them. Mason's representation of the Sudan as a space for personal growth and testing is an interesting companion to the boys' adventure novel and the war reporter's first-hand account. Mason might not have written 'literature', but as at least one critic pointed out, he was 'a remarkable raconteur'.[71] It was reissued year after year, in the United States as well as Britain, and, tellingly, was a perennial favourite of Tauchnitz, the publisher of lightweight paperback editions of the most-popular current titles, sold to English-speaking travellers in bookstores around the world.[72] It was also brought to the screen no less than four times before the outbreak of the Second World War. One can assume that the *bildungsroman The Four Feathers* would have cohabitated with Gordon in the imaginations of administrators and the metropolitan public throughout these decades.

Events experienced by one generation of colonial actor, in the 1880s and 1890s, became the fodder for literary escapism for the next generation – a strange reversal of the usual characterization of the colony as always one step behind the metropole.[73] The young reader/future administrator was introduced to the Sudan, and other British controlled territories, through popular literature and then through works such as Churchill's book, which lays claim to authority and non-fiction detachment but was really literary sensationalism for the middlebrow. The literature read by young men and women destined for the Sudan placed them within the social context of the imperial governor rather than governed.

Henty's fictional account of the 1898 campaign was located within a narrow range of possible narratives of the Empire. Churchill and Bennett continued the established narrative of the Sudan into the twentieth century for further generations of colonial observers and actors; their non-fiction accounts held on to certain tropes of the Sudan and, like Henty and Mason, reduced the vast geopolitical influences of the British imperial fin de siècle to their own personal experiences.[74] The images of multiple literary journeys to the Sudan found a permanent place in readers' imaginations.[75]

Furthermore, imperial ideology was formed by these images as much as it predicted the form they would take.[76] The sense of authenticity in these imperial representations in popular literature, in advertising and in art was reinforced by coverage of the Empire in supposedly objective media and through the policies and actions of the government. The middle-class reader may have thought himself mature and subtle in his understanding of colonial events in the colonies, but he didn't necessarily reject diversions such as Henty's. One reviewer in the *Public School Journal* in 1916 'admitted that [he] was for some years addicted to the Henty book habit'.[77] He read them but felt guilty about it; he also felt superior because he read the higher-brow newspapers, which provided extensive, and at times didactic, coverage of overseas events. So even ripping yarns like Henty's served to emphasize that 'realism' could reliably be recognized by the British middle-class reader, precisely because Henty's books didn't represent it. The tension between the unknowing-but-policy-driving metropole and the knowing-but-bound-to-implement-policy empire is repeatedly seen in these narratives. Popular support for government policies was bolstered by the public's perception that it understood the reasons for imperial engagement and expansion.

The SPS was considered 'elite'; this was supported by popular representations of the Sudanese as superior to other populations whom the British governed. Organizational language and practical training were instituted by the 1920s to help prepare these young men for where they were going and whom they were governing.[78] But most of these young recruits would have begun their reading about Egypt and the Sudan years earlier. Literature of all kinds would have formed an indelible image in their minds of what it was to be a British servant of the Empire in the Sudan as they travelled along with Mason's hero, or Henty's, or with Gordon himself. Henty's understanding of the Empire came from his experience as a journalist in far-flung locales, but he and others were focused on the moments of conflict and the stories of adventure and sacrifice rather than the day-to-day slog of colonial administration. The heroes of Henty's stories are also boys whose talents and intelligence become apparent from their quick responses to extraordinary situations, rather than their academic prowess or respect for authority. In reality, however, the colonial services were increasingly about training, expert analysis, technical and engineering ability and an orderly administrative structure that discouraged mavericks and opportunists.

2

General Gordon's legacy

Freewheeling colonial actors had a privileged place in the late-Victorian metropolitan imagination and Gordon was the quintessential and original specimen.[1] Berny Sèbe identifies the 'logistics of imperial heroism' unique to this moment. Heroes of High Imperialism 'gave rise to a series of cultural constructions that helped shape, but were also influenced by, the dominant beliefs and worldviews of the societies that engendered them. Their exemplarity was a potent justification for imperial development, further embodied their country's supposed genius, and set powerful precedents for self-sacrifice'.[2] The advent of a mass reading public shaped imperial policy, which in turn shaped popular narratives. As the competition among European powers grew at the fin de siècle, European free agents in the employ of African rulers became rarer. Imperial rivalries were increasingly high risk. Previously, imperial aggression carried out by proxies in territories not officially under European rule enabled those powers to denigrate and sideline the agenda of African rulers while gaining the metropolitan benefits of imperial bluster.[3] But Little Englanders were replaced by jingoists as Germany entered the imperial arena, France expanded its influence in Africa, and the economic ramifications of control over the Suez and the Cape were clearly established for politicians, newspaper editors and the British public.[4] Global competition, rapid communication and modernizing militarism changed the stakes.

Egypt and the Sudan were at the nexus of these developments. Egypt had long been an unofficial colony, and economic concerns – whether over the Suez Canal, the Nile or the Sudan – had prompted military action again and again. When the Sudan was reconquered in 1898 and the Anglo-Egyptian Condominium established, the debate about the relative merits of military or civilian expertise, and the ongoing entanglements of pseudo-imperialism, entered a new chapter. In the previous decades, whether in music halls or Salisbury's cabinet, action (and, therefore, the military acumen to lead it) was touted.[5] Now, in the popular press and best-selling memoirs, a more-nuanced argument was emerging. The 1885 Berlin Conference mandated the expansion of administration in colonies. But after the atrocities in King Leopold's Congo were exposed in 1900, structures of responsible and effective colonial administration, as defined by both Westminster and Whitehall, got greater attention.

By odd coincidence, the careers of decision-makers and opinion-shapers from the first two decades of the twentieth century – with lengthy resumes from across a vast empire – intersected with Egypt or the Sudan. To readers a generation or two after Gordon's death, it looked as if imperial prestige and a connection to Gordon were de rigueur. Lord Cromer, Viscount Milner, Kitchener, Wingate and Churchill were all involved in some way. And subsequent chapters in their imperial stories – in the Boer War, the Great War or Egyptian independence – meant another opportunity to revisit Gordon. His ubiquity was both a beacon and a bait-and-switch for men attracted to and then working in the civilian Sudan government, well into the twentieth century.[6]

Popular imperial heroes in the late Victorian and Edwardian eras were soldiers, like Gordon and Kitchener, or missionaries like David Livingstone, not mid-level bureaucrats simply trying to implement policies.[7] Rhetoric about the responsibilities of colonial administration might hint at a religious mission but were more often focused on imperial soldiers or explorers.[8] But expeditions, wars and annexations tended to end before the governing began.[9] Military success and diplomatic prowess are seldom found in the same leader. Gordon had been a childhood hero for men in the Sudan government, but he was hardly a useful role model.

Berny Sèbe describes the shift from

> 'the early years of imperial heroism, when celebrated figures tended to appear as mavericks who stood on the margins of society and seemed to overstretch the boundaries of the national project'.

For Sèbe, if Gordon was one of these figures, then Kitchener epitomized

> 'the proconsul turned hero [who] embodied the shift from conquest to administration'.

As the (re)conqueror of the Sudan he was hailed a hero, but Kitchener's contribution to Pax Britannica was as the founder of the Anglo-Egyptian Sudan.

He complicated the ideal for young men thinking about careers in the service of the Empire, particularly the Sudan, because he overshadowed any other version of colonial actor in the British imagination. Many young men saw the Sudan government as a good career path with a generous pension, and the careers of men in the SPS, or the Indian Civil Service (ICS) for that matter, seldom played out as imperial romances or cautionary tales. Their peers didn't carry expectations drawn from boyhood narratives of bravery and character-building into their careers as accountants or stockbrokers. John Kenrick, who rose through the ranks of the SPS but also served as an officer in the Sudan Defense Force during the Second World War, had a fair understanding of his job before he arrived. He was 'playing a part in ... the administration of justice and the development of education, agriculture and economic affairs'.[10] But probationers commonly approached the job as H. A. Nicholson, who retired at the rank of provincial governor, described it. 'We were all excited and keen to arrive and get involved in our work [with only] a very vague idea of what this would be.'[11] His contemporary Thomas Owen similarly admitted that 'the secret of the Sudan's fascination' was that 'experience' was the only way he could find out what his job entailed.

Many British-Sudanis make reference to Gordon's *Journals*, which were written by Gordon while under siege and published soon after his death. They weren't assigned as reading but were an obvious addition for young men preparing to interview with the selection committee. They also read the accompanying commentary of the *Journals*' editor, A. Egmont Hake. Hake was instrumental in framing the Gordon narrative in 1885, building on the persona established by Stead in the original campaign and then amplified by the popular press in the breathless coverage of the siege and the relief expedition. Originally published in 1885, the book was reprinted with huge press runs. Gordon's vivid and compelling *Journals*, and Hake's packaging of them, described a militaristic, adventurous and highly romanticized version of the colonial administrator.

These young men read the *Journals* out of order, in a sense – after the novels and poems discussed above rather than as original influences for those works. They confirmed the characterizations by Henty, Kipling and others, providing a non-fiction foundation for those adventure narratives. As these recruits evolved into senior officials, the distance between Gordon's version of colonial administration and the reality of the job was increasingly apparent, and critiques of Gordon were not uncommon. While fantasies of Empire might spur young men's enlistment in the SPS, their subsequent training necessitated that they read more-detached and analytical authors such as Lord Cromer and Viscount Milner. In each of their texts, these authors explicitly discuss political decisions and the implementation of government policy, administrative competency, technical skills and professionalization. In some cases, they explicitly respond to Gordon and Hake. Naturally, the *Journals* come down squarely on the side of soldier hero. By contrast, the longer reading list assigned by the SPS to probationers never quite decides which side it wants to emphasize – the soldier hero or the competent administrator. This ambivalence towards Gordon's legacy reflects the ambivalence of the associational culture of the Condominium, particularly until after the Great War, when a first wave of change takes place because of the total demilitarization of the service, followed by the ad hoc process of preparation being replaced by an increasingly elaborate training regimen in the 1920s.

A hero's impact

Young recruits to Colonial Service in the interwar period could easily misunderstand what lay in store for them. Gordon represented to these young men a peculiar notion of what colonial careering would be like. As Robert MacDonald describes the attraction of Gordon's brand of imperial heroism, the 'appeal to feelings that overrode reason, such as love of country or pride of race', meant that certain moral questions could be ignored or highlighted as needed. Evangelical imagery could also be deployed to legitimize militarism; in this context Christianity was civilizational as much as religious.[12] This was further reinforced when other men in imperial leadership continued to hold up Gordon as the epitome of imperial martyrdom without an agreement about whether he died a representative of the British nation, an anomalous exemplar of universal heroism or an irrational romantic.[13]

Gordon left a conflicting legacy for administrators serving in the Sudan. By the turn of the century, he was associated with a geographically bounded, extremely specific set of events, concentrated in a short period. His earlier nom de guerre, 'Chinese' Gordon, was earned putting down the Taiping Rebellion against China's

Qing Dynasty in the 1860s.[14] But 'Chinese' Gordon was wholly eclipsed by the 1884 events in Khartoum. 'Gordon of Khartoum' was the vivid, obsessively revisited and therefore familiar persona.[15] Even as the administrative culture of the Sudan government in the 1920s shifted away from prewar literary representations of colonial actors, the narratives of imperial heroism at the centre of the Sudan romance were regularly referenced by British-Sudanis in their letters. John Tosh observes that these potent narratives first encountered by a child weren't easily abandoned because they helped shape the man he became. They might be ironically referenced, critiqued and consciously set aside, but they were part of the framework of imperial masculinity.[16] His imperial story was finite. The tragedy was clear. And yet the meaning of the story remained unresolved.

The journals Gordon wrote during the siege – smuggled out of Khartoum just days before his death – were made public almost immediately. They became his voice from the grave. In 1885, readers could choose from two versions of his *Journals* to read the doomed hero's account of the last few months of his life. The more expensive edition was a facsimile of the sixth and final notebook smuggled out of Khartoum just days before its fall. The run was only five hundred copies and the lucky few able to obtain one could pore over his handwritten entries.[17] His scribblings, including crossed-out comments, writing that turned up the sides of pages, and little sketches, were all faithfully reproduced. The newspaper articles that he had clipped and pasted on the back of his own journal pages – including his handwritten, ranting marginalia – were also reproduced on the backs of pages in this limited edition. This all created an intense experience unmediated by an editor.

There was also a popular, inexpensive version, edited and with a foreword written by A. Egmont Hake, who had already written a biography of Gordon in his China days.[18] Members of the SPS and the Sudan Civil Service who acknowledge having read the *Journals* before they began their careers in the Sudan probably read this version. Hake tells his readers about the newspaper clippings attached to the original that Gordon references throughout and paraphrases them when necessary. But they aren't reproduced. The maps, sketches and caricatures are all reproduced, but they aren't where they were in relation to the original text, where the doodles are part of the barrage of thoughts. Nevertheless, in any form, the *Journals* are haphazard, a stream of consciousness representing an impulsive tendency Gordon was already known for.

In his cover letter for the last of the journals, he writes that he has included '*private* opinions upon certain facts'. He addresses an unspecified 'you', giving the reader the sense that Gordon is talking to him or her directly. These facts, he confides, 'perhaps it is just as well you should know confidentially. You can of course make extracts of all official matter, and will naturally leave my private opinions out in the case of publication'. And on the cover of the journal he writes, 'To be pruned down if published'.[19] Gordon has been characterized as an extremely private man, but that doesn't mean he shied away from myth-building and renown. It's clear that despite his solitude, as a lone Englishman leading non-English, as an expert being asked his opinion by a newspaper editor, or as a hero among hero-worshippers, he was conscious of going through life with an audience, made up either of his contemporaries or of posterity.[20] He expected an edited version of his writing to be shared with the public.

And within the departments of government involved in the events in the Sudan, he is completely unbothered by his writings' reception.

This matters when thinking about how the *Journals* would have been consumed decades later by prospective or probationary members of the administration. Young men at the turn of the century, and certainly after the Great War, would have been less likely to read the *Journals* in their youth. Stories about Gordon and about Kitchener's avenging had adventure-story appeal. The *story* of Gordon would have likely been familiar to most readers, as opposed to the *voice* of Gordon. Recent analyses of the Gordon myth are concerned with the diffused idea of him and the purposes to which his myth was put.[21] The impact of Gordon on the broader British reading public was oblique. But men anticipating a career in the Sudan, through the *Journals*, have a direct relationship with Gordon, the colonial servant and soldier. Suddenly, it was personal. His use of the second-person voice gives the *Journals* an immediacy. And the raw haphazardness of the content encourages the reader to assume that Gordon is, indeed, providing a peak behind the curtain of official imperial narratives.

Other voices in the *Journals* try to mediate that relationship. In the facsimile version, we find just Gordon's main text, clippings from a 7 September English-language Cairo newspaper that told him a force has been sent to rescue him, and his scribbled comments directed at the authors of the newspaper articles and the public figures mentioned in them. But in the mass-produced version, Hake's introduction and essays by Gordon's brother, Sir Henry W. Gordon, act as interpretive guides before the reader finally arrives at the General's own words, which often contradict those interpretations. Gordon's unedited personal observations are, perhaps, the first (certainly the most vivid) exposure that young men who planned to join the Colonial Service would have had to an administrator writing about what he is doing and the policies he is expected to carry out. It is not a tidy image.

Before the reader begins to read Gordon, Hake sets the sentimental scene:

> We cannot bring him back to life. Yet from his death we may learn at least how fit he was to teach us while he lived, how fit to hold his country's honour in his hand, how fit to judge of what was right and what was wrong. His journals are his last words to the world as much as they are instruction and information to his Government, and Englishmen who value England's honour may well read them with a heavy heart – with eyes dimmed by tears.[22]

Hake intended this passage to be instructional, offering himself as the public's guide for an 'appropriate' emotional response to the tragedy. 'We can do much he would have done for us had he been allowed to live.... His journals tell us how we can best repair mischief already done, and they tell us what is best for the Soudan. In the interest of this unhappy land he devoted much of his life; in its interest he died.'[23] Encountering this more than thirty years later, the probationer would know that something *had been* done, even though it took more than ten years. The vanquishing of the Mahdiyya, decades of relative peace and the criminalization of slavery would allow the reader a moment of satisfaction, despite the intervening decades. The ubiquity of the earlier struggles foreshortened those years in the popular imagination.[24]

The *Journals* bring the reader back to the Gordon era; he finds himself immersed immediately in a world of warring opinions. His suggestion that Gordon's words could instruct future governments is coupled with more veiled implications: 'It would seem the fate of those who devote their lives to the cause of humanity to be foiled instead of aided in their aim … In all his efforts for the blood of these blacks Gordon met with every form of interference whence he might at least expect support.' But the trope of the ungrateful native also figures prominently. 'The Khedive himself was not always mindful of the many difficulties to be encountered. But Gordon said, to blame the Khedive for his actions you must blame his people, and blame their Creator; they act after their kind, and in the fashion they were made.'[25]

The British government was morally bound to support Gordon, and in Hake's formulation, 'as a gentleman' Gordon was morally bound to remain in the Sudan until every British and Egyptian person under his authority was safely removed. Furthermore, Gordon's failure was the result of being 'constantly thwarted and never supported' by HMG.[26] In this scenario, Gordon best served civilization by being a bad servant of his own state.

Central to the Gordon myth was that the eradication of the slave trade was his primary goal, and that during the years of his absence from the Sudan, between 1879 and 1884, the authorities in Cairo erased any progress he had made in that area. 'The new rulers', as Hake described it, 'were in favour of slavery, in favour of oppression, in favour of backsheesh'.[27] The predatory loans made by European governments to multiple generations of Egyptian rulers, the usurious interest and the unforgiving repayment schedules, were not included as explanations for the Egyptian eagerness for 'backsheesh' – nor the Canal profits not being directed towards the general well-being of the Egyptian population, nor that the capitulations had exempted Europeans from taxation. Hake's characterization of Egyptian malfeasance in the events leading up to Gordon's death is a distillation of the prevailing sentiment in the popular press at the time, reinforced in fictional characterization of the rapacious and opportunistic Egyptian. But if Gordon could explain the supposed failings of the Egyptians and the Sudanese as divine will, Hake could also characterize Gordon's arrival that way. If he had died so that others might live, in a Christ-like sacrifice, then the question became: who were those 'others' – the men who found themselves administering this territory because of Gordon's sacrifice – going to be?

Michael Coray, in his exploration of the Gordon cult, focuses on the language of Christian martyrdom surrounding Gordon. Churchill, in *The River War*, has Evelyn Baring stating that 'as the movement in the Soudan was partly religious they [meaning him as the spokesperson for Egyptian government opinion] were "very much averse" to the appointment of a Christian in high command'.[28] Here, calling Gordon a Christian meant zealotry rather than devotion. But Coray correctly notes that it is difficult to appreciate how unselfconsciously the Victorian and Edwardian public admired Gordon's Christian fervour. Religious faith could help articulate constellations of attributes that, when gathered together, made up character and duty. The Empire was a Christian project, if not for the purposes of religious conversion, certainly for cultural conversion. Gordon's self-sacrifice and his self-discipline were culturally admirable characteristics in the 1880s and 1890s. But his Christian mysticism became less appealing (or appropriate) to administrative culture over the decades. By the 1930s, the Sudan government was not interested in hiring men who came to it because of the Christian fervour of its most famous administrator. But this doesn't mean those young men in the Sudan weren't still subconsciously measuring themselves against Gordon's level of selflessness from the moment they arrived.

He was hard to escape. His statue stood outside the palace in Khartoum, the anniversary of his death was a national holiday (in the Sudan) and there seemed always to be an appropriate occasion to eulogize him. The 'Gordon symbol', as Coray calls it, needed to be treated delicately. What made Gordon excessive also made him the patron saint of the Anglo-Egyptian Condominium. Unlike other romantic inventions of late-Victorian and Edwardian sentimental literature, Gordon couldn't be cast aside when priorities shifted. His passions had to be explained.

Edwardian popular Christianity in the Sudan was long represented by Bishop Llewelyn Henry Gwynne, who first arrived in 1905 and led the diocese of the Sudan until 1946. Gwynn wrote biographies of central figures in Sudan history, including Gordon. If Gwynn's biographical sketches were used in some form in sermons in the later years of his career, his characterizations would have made many in his congregation of senior government officials uncomfortable. Gwynn describes Gordon's death as 'the one and only happening that could begin the redemption, the civilizing and educating, the progress of the people of the Sudan'.[29] For him, Gordon was a necessary sacrifice, much as Christ had been. His death stirred 'the people of his own race to redeem and lift up and develop the people bought by his sacrifice'.[30] For Gwynn, development is next to godliness and because of the 'administration' brought by Gordon's sacrifice, 'never in … history has a people so benefited from another race as the people in the Sudan have from the British'.[31] In the interwar years, Gwynne's fervent hagiography and description of colonial development in religious terms would have a diminishing audience in the British-Sudani community.

The change in administrative cultural attitudes is evident in a lecture Douglas Newbold, the civil secretary, gave on the occasion of the sixtieth anniversary of Gordon's death in January 1945. Newbold asserted that 'there is no need to canonize Gordon – he would have hated it'. That perhaps is going too far; Gordon seems to be working towards his own canonization in his journal writing during the siege. But Newbold adds, 'We need not be ashamed – least of all in a world war – to commemorate his courage and his service to the Sudan', even while rejecting the religious framing.

Indeed, Newbold's critique of Gordon could probably have been articulated only in the Sudan, rather than in Britain, and by a government official surrounded by Gordon's administrative descendants. Gordon received a cooler assessment by officers who had contributed decades of decidedly unromantic governance to the Sudan after youthful consumption of the Gordon popular-culture myth in the metropole. They would have been far more comfortable with Newbold's clear-eyed description of Gordon's relationship with the Sudan and the Sudanese. 'He *did* have his faults and he did make mistakes', Newbold declares, 'but on that day 60 years ago he paid for them in full'.[32] For Newbold and his peers, Gordon's 'sacrifice' was substantial, but so were his faults. The events in Khartoum in 1884 were, it seems, a just punishment for, or at least an expected and reasonable outcome of, the flaws in his character.

Gordon as governor

Hake saw himself as a partisan player in the drama in 1885. In his introduction, Hake talks about Gordon being 'better able to form a judgment than anybody' and quotes government ministers saying the same. Hake references details of the original manuscript that are not included in the mass-produced, typeset version, as evidence of his uncompromised authority. For example, he tells readers that on a certain page in the notebook there are twelve lines that Gordon crossed out, but that underneath he wrote, 'Abuse of Baring and Co.'[33] The infuriating claim by officials at home that they too know the ins and outs of events in the colonial arena might, one imagines, resonate with readers in the aftermath of the Great War. But Hake argues that references to 'General Gordon's peculiar views' and 'his disobedience of orders' arose only when the British government realized they were powerless both to control Gordon and to get information without him.[34] This might be tricky for a young man inspired by Gordon but about to enter a career in service of the postwar version of Baring and Co.

Gordon repeatedly declares his independence. 'If the Expedition comes here before the place falls (which is doubtful)', he writes on November 22, 'and if the instructions are to evacuate the place at once, and leave Kassala and Sennar, etc., I will resign, and have nothing more to do with the Government of the place, or of the Soudan; and this I have a perfect right to do, and no one, not even the Soudan troops or people, could say one word'. Hake offers an editorial footnote here, quoting a letter from Baring to Gordon earlier in the year reminding him to 'bear in mind the main end to be pursued is the evacuation of the Soudan'. Hake stresses that Gordon had not been ordered to merely evacuate Khartoum and abandon the rest.[35]

One of the most horrifying events in the final volume of the *Journals* is not a battle or an outbreak of disease. It's the seemingly accidental arrival of an English-language newspaper from Cairo. A dispatch from Kitchener managed to make its way to the palace in Khartoum. Kitchener's material was, according to Gordon, of little importance but it was wrapped in a newspaper whose contents Gordon, certainly lacking much in the way of diversion, obsessed about for days. The horror lay in its juxtaposition of the outside world – stories of officials and policy and appointments – and Gordon's isolation. It established for the reader the limited reach of civilization and of British power and, as a result, heightened the perception of Gordon's bravery. Gordon's *Journals* force the incredulous reading public to see the limitations of communication, transportation and infrastructure in the (ostensibly) 'modern age'.

'A curious thing has happened', Gordon writes on 5 November:

> My friend Kitchener sent up the post; he wrapped the letters in some old newspapers (he gave me no news in his letter), the old newspapers were thrown out in the garden: there a clerk who knew some English found them blowing about … The doctor saw the date *15th September*, and secured them for me; they are like gold, as you may imagine, since we have had no news since 24th February, 1884![36]

For the reader, the time lapse between the date the paper was published and the date on which Gordon first mentions getting it reinforces the distances between Britain,

Cairo, and Khartoum, between civilization and the absence of it, defined by the reliability and timeliness of information.[37]

Contradicting the voice of metropolitan knowledge represented in the columns of the single newspaper in his possession was evidently one of the few forms of entertainment Gordon had. A brief mention of an Egyptian cabinet shuffle drew a derisive comment. 'By these papers, miraculously secured, I see we have made Minister of Interior Abdel Kader Pasha; according to all accounts up here, he is Abdel Kader and the Forty Thieves *in one*.'[38] In the later stages of the siege, Gordon repeatedly says he does not understand the cause for delay and argues with the newspaper cuttings, in lieu of available government representatives. One cutting states that 'owing to the unprecedented lowness of the Nile no confidence is felt in the practicability of hauling boats over the cataracts til the end of September'. And Gordon replies in the margin: 'It was not a low Nile – it was an average Nile, only you were *too late*.'[39]

The newspaper recounts the departure of General Wolsley, whom it was finally decided should lead an effort to rescue Gordon from Khartoum after he had been unable to get himself out. Gordon was livid that the terms of the effort represented the ongoing conservative approach of Gladstone's government to potential imperial entanglements. 'Lord Wolsley seen off at Victoria Station, for the *Gordon relief expedition!!*' Gordon scribbles in the margins. '*NO! for the relief of Soudan garrisons*.'[40] He adds, 'I expect that the naming of the expedition the Gordon Relief Expedition is because the fiction *"that Her Majesty's Government has no responsibility towards the Soudan and its garrisons"* is going to be held to, and that the object of the expedition thus named, will be considered as accomplished, if Khartoum is reached.'[41] That was, indeed, Gordon's original remit; he was to negotiate the evacuation of Egyptian Army troops trapped in Khartoum – not to defend all the outposts that the overextended army had been unable to maintain. This concerned him little once he was there and, thanks to Stead, Hake and many other admiring biographers, is little remembered. But Gordon's outbursts and scribbled marginalia obfuscate the actual mission and establish the popular narrative on which his myth is built.

Gordon apparently imagines numerous changing audiences for the *Journals*. Returning to his obsession with the arrival of the newspaper, for example, Gordon writes, 'These papers gave us far more information than any of your letters. Did K. send them by accident or on purpose?' Whom is he speaking to? The first sentence seems to suggest it's Kitchener, spoken to in the second person. He was the one whose letters were expected. But the next sentence has Kitchener in the third person, and the audience is ... whom? This reinforces the reader's sense of Gordon's isolation but also establishes that Gordon thinks of himself as being in conversation with the metropolitan authority – and its agents – that he is supposedly representing.

It becomes apparent that Gordon's mental state altered – one might say eroded – over time. But to someone heading out to work in the Sudan, this ideal colonial administrator would have seemed wonderfully blunt and honest. What the reader wouldn't have appreciated was that the doomed Gordon knew he wouldn't have to deal with the fallout from his lack of circumspection. Gordon appeared free of the self-regulation that a middle-class civil servant in the metropole would have to practise because Gordon was beyond the reach of British officialdom. But in truth, it was the inevitability of his death that freed him. Nevertheless, this fantasy of autonomy continued to influence the popular conception of colonial actors.

Gordon as muse

The exegesis of Gordon's words and of the many words written about him or because of him were supported by an old guard in the Sudan, many of whom had first arrived in the country as part of the force to avenge Gordon's death. Officials in the interwar Sudan government liked to collect stories of the 'bog barons', eccentric men seconded from the Egyptian Army in the early days of the Condominium to govern the southernmost reaches of Sudan territory. Mostly unmarried, they seldom went on leave. And unlike their university-educated and pension-scheduled civil-servant counterparts in the Northern Provinces, they weren't rotated out of their posts to make their way up the career ladder. Their eccentricities were attributed to their isolation. Some of the earliest of these were bloodthirsty despots, inclined to the kinds of excesses that Joseph Conrad ascribes to Colonel Kurtz.[42] But many stories were told about the more-benign ones, usually highlighting the delicious freedom of living beyond the surveillance of British society. One officer, for example, was known for having his cook bring him a bowl of porridge before bedtime. As he explained to a bemused guest from the north, 'It saves time in the morning.'[43]

The highly romanticized memoirs of early colonial officials in the territory, and their longevity as authoritative texts by influential authors, suggest how the governing institutions of the Sudan and the literary characterizations of the country were interdependent. One compelling case: the Austrian count and soldier for hire, Carl von Slatin. Once Gordon's second-in-command, Slatin, wrote a first-hand insider account of historic events in the Sudan of the 1880s and 1890s because of his own years as a captive of the Mahdi and his successors. Published in 1896, *Fire and Sword in the Sudan* refreshed the outrage of the reading public and bolstered support for Salisbury's decision to approve Kitchener's plan for (re)conquest and to commit British men and arms to the campaign. For many readers Slatin's memoir was a reminder why the 1896–98 campaign was not only necessary but righteous.[44] An ostensibly dispassionate eyewitness account, it offered readers the titillation of moral outrage under the guise of education.

In his account of the battles surrounding Hick's defeat in western Sudan the year before the battle of Tokai, Slatin's language is almost identical to Henty's. The Mahdi had 'worked up his fanatical followers to a pitch of the wildest enthusiasm'. In both fiction and non-fiction the Sudanese are consistently portrayed as worthy in equal measure because of their authentic passion and bravery and because of their skill and focus.[45] This and other echoes of imperial romance – including the requirement for the soldier to have a worthy adversary and for the colonial administrator to have a grateful native to uplift – seem to find voice in novel and a memoir. Slatin's work held its place on young officers' reading lists with all the status and weight attached to carefully selected non-fiction texts.

The lines between an imaginary Sudan and a real colonial territory subject to the bureaucratic control of a colonial civil service were blurred. *Fire and Sword* was translated into English by Reginald Wingate, then a lieutenant colonel and director of military intelligence of the Egyptian Army. Wingate helped negotiate Slatin's release, had already written what was considered the authoritative account of the rise of the Mahdi, published in 1891, and was eventually responsible for the death of the Mahdi's successor in 1899. Wingate became the first governor general of the new Anglo-Egyptian Condominium after the victory of the Nile Army. He ruled the Sudan for its first seventeen years, with Slatin as his second-in-command until the beginning of the war in 1914.

The book on the Mahdi, the translation of Slatin's memoir, and then Wingate's construction of the early government in the Sudan were all forms of non-fiction 'authorship' of the Sudan narrative, with the British (and occasional Austrian) as the protagonists. As Robert Collins describes it, Wingate's 'adroit orchestration' primed 'the British public ... to demand vengeance for [Gordon's] death by a host of popular books about tyrannous conditions in the Sudan.'[46] The idea of authorship isn't metaphorical here. Wingate literally wrote the book on the Mahdi and then killed the Mahdi's successor and made sure his Mahdi book and his translation of Slatin's memoir were included on the required reading list.

Not only following the Nile expedition, but also in preparation of it, there was another sharp increase in Sudan-related non-fiction and fiction focused on Kitchener's exploits. Gordon begat Kitchener, but they were not of a type. Sèbe observes, 'In stark contrast with the early years of imperial heroism, when celebrated figures tended to appear as mavericks who stood on the margins of society and seemed to overstretch the boundaries of the national project, the proconsul turned hero embodied the shift from conquest to administration.'[47] But this still occurred within the construction of heroism that was deployed for political purposes. 'Kitchener epitomized this type [... becoming] a national hero as the architect of the "reconquest" of the Sudan and the founder of modern Anglo-Egyptian Sudan.'[48] Kitchener belonged to the society he championed – definitely one of Cubbitt's 'Great Men'. Perhaps this is why the carnage witnessed by war correspondents at the battle of Omdurman and the consequences of the concentration camps he established in the Transvaal three years later were so disturbing to those who made it their business to know about them and so easy for the vast majority of the British public to ignore. He was the quintessential British imperial soldier. As Robert MacDonald has argued, there is little consistency between the behaviour of imperial heroes and the moral framework that they are supposed to represent.[49]

The first challenge to the established narrative was also the text that firmly cemented the events of Kitchener's Nile campaign as a redemption narrative. In 1900, Churchill published his account of Kitchener's campaign up the Nile to reconquer the Sudan and avenge Gordon's death. *The River War* drew from Churchill's dispatches to the *Morning Post*.[50] Churchill was not alone in writing about the campaign. Rival newspaper correspondents G. W. Steevens and Ernest Bennett did also. First publishing an article in the *Contemporary Review*, Bennett expanded his serialized coverage into a book immediately following the conquest.[51] And sales of Steevens's account benefited from his name recognition as a popular reporter for the *PMG* and then the *Daily Mail.* But Steevens tragically died from typhoid in the Boer War while reporting from inside the siege of Ladysmith in 1902. And Bennett's work fell into obscurity in part due to his interwar membership in the Anglo-German alliance. These events, as well as Churchill's rise to fame and power, meant that Churchill's two-volume work came to serve as an authoritative coda to the Gordon affair; it is perhaps the most-read treatment of Kitchener's campaign even today. These accounts all ensured that the Sudan had produced yet another larger-than-life character in Kitchener. But he was also profoundly unhelpful as a representative of colonial administrative temperament, priorities and attitude towards metropolitan authority.[52] He had the contemporary popular-culture status of a rock star, but Kitchener couldn't be portrayed as a martyr, a saint or a lone figure travelling through a non-Christian wilderness. He was, instead, an unapologetically belligerent figure whose popular legitimacy started from Wingate's success at framing the (re)conquest as vengeance for Gordon's death.

The River War's importance lies in Churchill's insistence on taking the reader back to Gordon; he doesn't just recount – he relitigates the Gordon saga. Churchill, having reviewed the available records, emphasizes the rightness of the official mind of the era, which was decidedly not in favour of Gordon. With the hindsight of almost twenty years, he informs his readers that Cromer was right to be adamantly opposed to Gordon's appointment. Churchill had no illusions that Cromer (who at the time of these events was Sir Evelyn Baring) could have resisted metropolitan authorities or popular sentiment. The historical record was clear: 'The pressure was too strong for [Baring] to withstand. Nubar Pasha, the Foreign Office, the British public, everyone clamoured for the appointment [of Gordon]. Had Baring refused to give way, it's probable that he would have been overruled.'[53] Egypt, Whitehall and every newspaper reader in Britain were in agreement – and, in Churchill's estimation, all wrong.

Churchill complicated the adversarial relationship, set up by Hake, Henty and others, between the soldier-hero Gordon and the administrator-bureaucrat Lord Cromer. Churchill, like Henty and Hake, is sympathetic to the man on the ground. But there's a twist – it's a different man whose expertise was calculated differently. Churchill had faith in the assessment of the man who was also the trained and capable governmental authority: Cromer. Not Gladstone nor Granville in London. But also not the man of action whose credentials consisted primarily of military victories. Churchill identifies Cromer as the man who seems singularly aware of the dangers of Gordon and who 'feared the feverish complications to Egyptian politics of the man who had always been identified with unrest, improvisation, and disturbance'.[54]

Churchill continued this characterization of Gordon in a 1933 profile in the *Overseas Daily Mail* in which he separated Gordon's actions and attributes: 'His place in our history is assured. But above all, [he] will be remembered [for] that sense of honour which united him to a helpless Native community whose safety and welfare had been committed to his charge.'[55] More than thirty years after his own participation in Kitchener's campaign to conquer the Sudan in Gordon's name, Churchill relegates the events surrounding Gordon's death, which were to a great extent the result of the excesses in his own nature, to 'a place in our history'. But memoirists continue to rehash the basic Gordon hagiography decades later, even if the rest of their texts hardly warranted it.

H. C. Jackson joined the SPS as one of a class of eight university men recruited in 1907. When writing in 1954, he still felt bound to begin his memoir with an account of the Gordon saga.[56] Then, recounting his own early experiences in the Sudan, he still finds Gordon around every corner. Despite saying that he and his fellow recruits 'were thrilled to be starting new life in a country of which we knew but little', upon arrival in Khartoum, he describes his 'memories' of a city he'd never before visited.[57] 'Cities have the power to evoke memories… Khartoum commemorates the devoted life and sacrificial death of General Gordon, a Christian victim of Islam.'[58]

For the metropolitan reading consumer, as well chronicled in a number of recent studies, Gordon was a powerful tool in the service of New Imperialism. His myth was further used to shape ideals of masculinity, argue for a virtuous form of Christian soldier, and sell mass-produced literature and newspapers.[59] For the men who entered the SPS, however, he and the many texts that orbited his central *Journals* informed and complicated their understanding of what a colonial administrator was supposed to be. The constant slippage between imperial melodrama and historic or religious treatise made the works of Gordon, Slatin and Churchill both compelling and unsettling. In the early decades of the Condominium, with few other sources of either training or information about the Sudan, there was little competition for the attention of young men hungry for guidance and clear job descriptions. Young officers knew that the Sudanese 'broke a British square at the battle of Tamai', or that they were 'first-class fighting men', or that there would be substantial 'adventure and wild life' – but this was not helpful. The public-school notion of the White Man's Burden – the 'feeling that the British have something worth giving for the development and progress of the world, economically and politically' – was a commonly expressed sentiment but still only a vague description of a colonial administrator's remit. These little bits of information were items that Gordon, Hake, Slatin and Churchill reinforced.[60] But all of it was equally available simply by reading Kipling. And Lytton Strachey's caustic observation about 'Chinese Gordon's' earlier exploits would have rung true to seasoned SPS officials: 'It is significant that Gordon found it easier to win battles and to crush mutineers than to keep on good terms with the Chinese.'[61]

'Responsible authorities on the spot'

Despite what Churchill wrote about the events surrounding Gordon's appointment, *The River War* wasn't written primarily for that purpose, and the argument was overshadowed by Churchill's account of the Nile campaign itself. So the relationship the wider British public had with the myth of Gordon went unchanged. Recruits in the 1910s, however, found themselves confronted for the first time with contemporaries of Gordon, Viscount Milner and Lord Cromer, who turned a critical eye on the Gordon affair, introducing these young men to the realpolitik of Britain's policy in Egypt. By 1905, training was deemed wise for recruits to the SPS. Some recruits enjoyed additional terms at university; by the 1910s all received a list of recommended readings.[62]

Alfred Milner, later Viscount Milner, was seen as hugely influential in the Anglo-Boer War at the turn of the twentieth century and then in the execution of British strategy in the First World War. He helped to set the course of Britain's last half century of Empire in Africa and continued to influence British-Egyptian relations. Before that, though, he was the undersecretary for finance in Egypt from 1889 to 1892, under Cromer's leadership and, like Gladstone and others, on the receiving end of Gordon's ridicule. Milner was central to the recuperation of Egypt's finances in the late nineteenth century and, therefore, the stability of British interests in the Middle East and the Canal Zone.

Serendipitously, Milner, who began his career as a journalist, once served as assistant editor to Stead, the editor of the *PMG*, who arguably started the entire Gordon cult. Perhaps he had not completely shed his persona as an investigative 'New Journalist' when he wrote bluntly and critically of the diplomatic legerdemain employed by multiple British governments in his 1893 volume, *England in Egypt*. Milner does not, however, ground his critique in the emotive language used by Stead or Hake. He argues that it was foolhardy for Britain to attempt to reform Egypt's financial situation – and that no other Egyptian affairs were any responsibility of the British government.

> The theory of our limited liability for the management of the affairs of Egypt is one that has played a great part in the history of the last ten years. Its genesis is not difficult to explain. As has been already shown, we plunged into the business of setting Egypt on her legs without any conception of the extent or the difficulty of the task. As the magnitude of our undertaking began to reveal itself to us, we strove by every means in our power to limit our obligations, and to narrow the field of our interference. We felt that we were bound to see Egypt out of trouble in vital issues, but that in all other things she had better look after herself.[63]

At this point Milner is clear in his condemnation of British policy towards the Sudan, but for Britain's sake, not the Sudan's.

> We averted our eyes from what was going on in the Sudan and hugged ourselves with the fiction that we were not responsible for the action of the Egyptian Government in that region. ... We met with a tremendous punishment. ... Millions of pounds had to be spent, thousands of lives to be sacrificed before we could extricate ourselves from the consequences of our original neglect.[64]

Agreeing on little else and writing in a quite different tone, Milner and Gordon agree on this point. In his *Journals*, Gordon makes the same point and even uses some of the same language: 'the FICTION that it is the Egyptian Government which governs Egypt ... it is a *silly* story, for everyone sees through it'.[65]

Despite his time working with Stead, Milner was as dismissive of public opinion as Cromer, Gladstone and the other professionals: 'The idea of abandoning [the Sudan] was intensely unpopular, and they could not make up their minds to accept the bitter necessity, which yet was palpable to every clear-sighted observer.' The public, clamouring for military action to save Gordon *and* pacify the Sudan, was obviously not part of this clear-sighted cohort.[66] Milner, not yet a professional 'race patriot', as he would call his form of imperial boosterism years later, fully agrees with Cromer's decision to abandon the Sudan. He might have been Stead's assistant editor a decade earlier, while Stead was campaigning for Gordon to find another solution, but by 1893, he was a pragmatist.

> [Baring's] view was that Egypt could by no possibility retain the Sudan, and that, this being so, her only wise course was to cut it adrift at once and altogether, and keep every man and every shilling that remained to her for the defense of her own frontier. And the British Government unhesitatingly adopted the advice of its representative. Throwing to the winds its previous attitude of indifference, it instructed Sir Evelyn to inform the Egyptian Cabinet that the Sudan must be abandoned with all possible promptitude.... Thus did we ourselves give the lie direct to our long-cherished theory that the policy of Egypt with regard to the Sudan was no business of ours.[67]

Milner was quite clear that the British Empire shouldn't continue the crypto-imperialism that shaped the careers of Gordon and other British officer-administrators in places like China and Egypt. But neither should British officials formulate policies without considering the practicalities on the ground. Britain and particularly its colonial officials could not be held captive by romantic metropolitan notions of the glories of imperial conquest and the inferiority of resistant indigenous forces.[68]

Milner, Churchill and Cromer all agree with Gordon on this key point, and it would have been readily apparent to all the probationers who dutifully worked their way through the reading list given to them. The officials in London were woefully ill-equipped to question the opinion of 'authorities on the spot'. While still Sir Evelyn Baring, he condemned the growing influence of British public opinion on policy decisions. Gordon suggested that a notorious slave trader, Zubayr Pasha, be sent to negotiate the withdrawal from Khartoum because he was possibly the only Sudanese in 1884 who could command as much respect as the Mahdi. In support of this, Cromer wrote, 'Whatever may be said to the contrary, [Britain is] responsible for any arrangements that are now desired for the Sudan.... Any attempt to settle Egyptian questions by the light of English popular opinion is surely productive of harm, and in this, as in other cases, it would be better to follow the advice of responsible authorities on the spot.'[69] Also implicated was the metropolitan luxury, not experienced by Cromer or Gordon, of adhering to fictions that events on the ground gave lie to. The British public rejected the possibility of a slave trader governing in the Sudan, but it wasn't interested in full British commitment in terms of blood and treasure, and it was invested in continuing a narrative of conquest and protection in the region.

'Not the mediocre by-products of the race'

Fifteen years later, Lord Cromer was quite specific in his description of the ideal Sudan administrator, and it wasn't Kitchener's model military aggressor of previous decades.[70] More influential than his entire memoir was Cromer's brief passage about the preferred characteristics of colonial administrators in his introduction to Sir Sidney Low's survey of Egypt and the Sudan as of 1913, *Egypt in Transition*.[71] Apparently, Cromer struck a chord; short sections of his description were compulsively reproduced in virtually every monograph, memoir and administrative manual about the Sudan for years to come.[72]

He begins by pointing out that all the work in the new Anglo-Egyptian Condominium of the Sudan, both administrative and military, was initially done by military men. But because the Anglo-Boer War demanded the reallocation of officers, the Sudan government suddenly found itself losing seconded military officials.[73] Cromer explains that when men know they can be transferred at any time, they are less likely to develop an emotional attachment to the territory they are governing. He warns, 'To any one sitting in a London office the removal of half a dozen young officers and the substitution of others in their place may not seem a matter of vital importance.'[74] But Cromer says it is impossible 'to fill at once the vacuum caused by the abrupt departure of even a very few trained men'. So it was 'manifestly desirable to do all that was possible to obviate any such risks in the future'.[75] This seemed to tilt the scales in the direction of university men, not soldiers. It wasn't a matter of indifference after all.

Cromer says that hand-picked civilian recruits reduced the chance for 'indiscretion or want of judgment' that could lead to 'venial errors'.[76] To be blunt, the 'best safeguard against the committal of any such errors is to discard absolutely the practice of selecting for employment abroad any who for whatsoever reason have been whole or partial failures in other capacities at home'.[77] Not one but three figures who loomed largest in the history of the Sudan prior to its loss in 1885 were exactly that type of man, and Baring had dealt with all of them: Gordon and the two Baker brothers, Samuel and Valentine. Gordon's excesses were not necessarily venial, although his erratic behaviour might be the result of alcohol. Lytton Strachey declared Gordon's alcoholism as fact in *Eminent Victorians* (although facts were not really Strachey's strong point as a biographer).[78] But Gordon's personality, including his obsession with Christian mysticism and his utter disregard for social and political protocols, made Gordon unsuited for more direct service to the British nation – even if he was sober. His best work was done as a proxy, in China and in Africa, far from the observant eyes of the press and the institutional hierarchies in the metropole.

The Baker brothers, on the other hand, were exactly the type Cromer meant when he wrote about metropolitan misfits. Samuel Baker was Gordon's predecessor in the Sudan in the 1860s and 1870s.[79] Although he had retired to the life of a country gentleman in Devon by the time of the Gordon affair, he could never be fully embraced by the British establishment; he may have bought his wife, Florence, from an Armenian slave-trader when she was as young as twelve or thirteen, and travelled with her for years before marrying her in 1865. The press said he was the only man to rival Gordon in expertise on the Sudan. He was a regular letter writer to the *Times* about Sudan policy and was the first person to suggest in print Gordon as the man to send.[80] But in Cromer's opinion, Baker's expensive adventuring years earlier had encouraged the khedive to mistakenly equate brief military conquest for the successful imposition of colonial authority. The overextension of Egypt's reach – and its finances – was due in part to the illusion that flamboyant characters like Samuel Baker (or Gordon, for that matter) could stand in for sober governors. Cromer was dealing with Samuel Baker's legacy on the ground in Egypt during the entire Gordon affair, while also having to refute Baker's interfering letters to the editor of the *Times*, promising, once again, things that Baring had no faith in anyone being able to deliver.[81]

Samuel's brother, Valentine, was even more problematic. He had been forced to pursue a foreign-service career after being convicted for sexually assaulting a young woman on a train in England in 1874. He led a hastily formed and ill-trained force against the Mahdi's general, Osman Digna, in 1882, which resulted in an abject defeat and required the intervention of British forces. It seems unclear what level of ineptitude and negligence was necessary to get fired from an imperial sinecure. He never returned to Britain.[82]

Colonial government in the twentieth century was for the professionals. Striking a blow against this Victorian-Edwardian colonial '"type"', a truncated version of Cromer's description of the new ideal became the unofficial motto of the SPS. The sections that get quoted are often presented as a single passage but came from two sections, one from his discussion of the military period of the administration, and the other from the civilian era. We can see how the approach to governing was changing in the colonial territory, even if that shift wasn't necessarily recognized yet at home. He assures his reader that he can't 'generalise on the subject of [the] respective merits' of military and civilian men. 'In the present case my feeling was that *a certain number of active young men endowed with good health, high character, and fair abilities were required* to assist in governing the country, and that it was a matter of complete indifference whether they had received their early training at Sandhurst, or at Oxford or Cambridge.'[83] Colonial government in the twentieth century was for the professionals now. And so Cromer describes the men who were beginning to populate the Sudan government as '*not the mediocre by-products of the race, but the flower of those turned out from our schools and colleges*.'[84] For Cromer, university men were desired because they wouldn't be sent elsewhere; training wouldn't be wasted on them; their dedication to the people they served would grow and mature over time because administration rather than soldiering would be their primary identity. Put together, these passages became a value-laden justification for the later civilian service: a certain number of active young men endowed with good health, high character and fair abilities were required, not the mediocre by-products of the race, but the flower of those turned out from our schools and colleges.

Conclusion

In 1879, Gordon wrote an essay in which he offered a philosophy of colonial administration much more measured and in line with the evolving, modern idea of what constituted an officer's responsibilities articulated by Cromer. Under the title 'Foreigners in the Service of an Oriental State', Gordon asserted:

> As to his facon d'agir, I maintain the foreigner should, for the time, entirely abandon his relations with his native land; he should resist his own Government, and those of others powers, and keep intact the sovereignty of the Oriental state

> whose bread he eats; he should put himself into the place of a native when he has to advise the Sultan, Ameer, or khedive, or any questions which his own, native, or any foreign Government, may wish settled, and his advice should be sealed by – first, what is universally right through the world; and, secondly by what is best for the Oriental state he serves. I do not mean best for the ruler of the Oriental state, but best for the people. Thus, acting as a native of the country, he will take care that the peculiar habit and customs are considered.[85]

This was included with the contract of employment, lists of kit to purchase, and the detailed pension and leave terms sent to new probationers.[86] What was a recruit to make of that? Was the Anglo-Sudanese Condominium of the Sudan advocating that officials should resist His Majesty's government as servants of the Sudanese? Coupled with Cromer's paean to the civilian SPS, was the message that the officials in Whitehall and Westminster could be ignored or defied, in good conscience, as long as the right kind of men were doing it?

When Hake writes in the introduction to Gordon's *Journals* that 'volumes have been already written on this subject, and there are probably volumes yet to come',[87] his later readers have, in fact, consumed what Hake predicts. Within Britain, this textual echo chamber froze Gordon and the ideals of imperial heroism in time. It also tended to stop the narrative at the moment when soldiers' work was done and administrators' work was beginning. Acceptance into the Sudan government, though, served as an initiation into a more nuanced, evolving discussion. This much smaller cohort of men would first encounter descriptions and discussions of complex geopolitical tensions because of the texts they were directed to read. They were prompted to question what constituted effective colonial administration and evaluate the bureaucratic mechanisms evolving in the British-governed Sudan in the early decades of the twentieth century. The earliest version of this process of self-conscious questioning was haphazard and contradictory – following an inconsistent path through Gordon and Hake to Churchill, Cromer and Milner. Gordon was never absent from the corporate identity of the SPS, but eventually his position in it shifted. It was the subsequent development of more-elaborate training programs for both the Sudan government recruits and those in the broader Colonial Service that would clarify the nature of colonial administration and the responsibilities of its officers. This would widen the divide between them and the metropolitan civilian understanding of imperial careering in the twentieth century, even before these men embarked from British shores.

3

The colonial administration course

In 1922, Charles Edward Fouracres, a veteran of the Great War, arrived for his interview with the SPS selection board. By his account, he 'was twenty-four and a half and for the past six years … had knocked about and had had experiences far beyond' his years.[1] As a result, he was fairly confident about his chances for acceptance, his preparation not going far beyond reading 'a few books'.[2] His confidence grew when he saw the dozen or so Oxbridge graduates sitting in the waiting room. He 'could not help thinking this group, with a few exceptions, looked like a lot of pink-faced schoolboys'.[3] The seven men chosen that year were from that group of Oxbridge 'schoolboys'. Fouracres's rough and ready 'university of life' education wasn't valued as much as he thought it would. Instead, he was offered the chance to transfer his officer's commission to the Egyptian Army and given a secondment to the Sudan government's Audit Department.

In that context, he recalls being told by another 'bimbashi' (a ranking officer) that he shouldn't refer to the civilian administrators – no matter how senior – as 'Sir' because he was an officer and they were not.[4] This recollection was very much in line with the sentiment of the period. In the 1920s, the military members of the Sudan government were still very resistant to the argument that the Sudan was now, after twenty-five years of British governance, better served by a civilian rather than military administration. Fouracres's story illustrates that young recruits in the 1920s and 1930s were sometimes confused about how they should be thinking about the Sudan and colonial administration, and that members of the Sudan government were struggling to adapt.

This chapter explores two fairly basic observations: first, ideas about what administrators needed to know evolved during the interwar period and so the training evolved too. The overwhelming majority of colonial administrators had been the products of public schools since before Gordon's time. Certain schools were created precisely to produce young men suited to being civil servants or colonial administrators and assumed a broad range of humanities disciplines were what young colonial administrator needed. Then university dons served as imperial talent spotters without acknowledging that any particular professional preparation might also be necessary. As far as the institutions were concerned, their 'mission was education, not training'.[5] After the Great War, however, attitudes slowly changed. The Mandate system, the creation of the League of Nations and the expansion of civilian administration throughout the Empire created a demand for more effective and 'forward thinking' officers. Under the aegis of the Colonial Office, as a result of pressure from both career civil servants and scholars, young recruits received longer and more detailed training.[6]

The second observation is that the postwar demand for civilian administrators to replace military officers lost during the conflict became a corporate ethos within the Sudan government (and others). By the 1930s, administrative success was defined economically, through infrastructure development, urban planning, the expansion of sanitation and medical programs, and the establishment of educational institutions. Projects that crisscrossed the Sudan with telegraph lines, railways, roads and irrigation systems were the death knell for these romanticized colonial figures.[7] University men saw colonial relationships through the lens of an education that now included a greater emphasis on the social sciences and economics.

There were new geopolitical priorities in a post-Paris Conference world that demanded attention. Then, a decade later, the metropolitan exigencies of Depression budgeting put additional pressures on administrators to be first-class managers.[8] All of this, plus a conscious policy decision to engage in what Cain and Hopkins call 'moral rearmament', prompted the interwar emergence of the development man.[9] Steeped in training and confident in the power of education and economic initiatives, he was determined to leave his own imperial legacy, but this time in hygiene initiatives and town planning.

Simultaneously, Indirect Rule, the new colonial administrative method first implemented by Lord Lugard in Northern Nigeria, was embraced. It devolved local governance to native administrators drawn from indigenous leadership. Between the wars, Indirect Rule was the cutting edge of imperial administrative theory. It appeared to embrace cultural relativism and value the thoughtful social scientist over the military man in the field. By the 1930s, however, even its greatest proponent, Margery Perham, would begin to critique the unthinking application of it as a recipe for stultification.[10] The argument against it wasn't that colonial governments needed to return to the earlier model. Rather, it was that development and education projects on the one hand, and native administration on the other, created contradictory and frustrating cul-de-sacs of limited opportunity for colonized populations.[11]

In 1924 a committee was created to explore the interwar staffing needs of the Empire and recommend a course of action to meet it. Led by Lord Milner until his death and then by Lord Lovat (who headed the Forestry Service – the first of the colonial services to create a formalized training regimen for new recruits), the committee finally produced a report penned by Ralph Furse, his private secretary. By the time the report was published in 1927, it served more as retroactive justification.[12]

Furse had deemed the short course provided by the Imperial Institute in South Kensington 'not a very satisfactory piece of cramming' and enjoined imperial historians at Oxford and Cambridge to create something more vigorous. Margery Perham, the preeminent scholar on African colonial administration in that era, was instrumental in developing the Oxford version but also consulted more broadly.[13] The Tropical African Service course was thus established in 1926.[14] In 1933, this became the Colonial Administrative Service course, wherein recruits spent a year steeped in practical and analytical disciplines that Furse, Perham and others felt were important to the recruits' specific career field and territory.[15]

The report confirmed what was already understood: the colonial administrator was someone who needed to be trained, rather than merely cultivated, and there was a specific collection of tools they needed to be taught.[16] The evolution of colonial training from the early version of SPS training established by the end of the Great War, through to the more deliberate and elaborate Colonial Service training course in place by the early 1930s, was motivated by widely acknowledged political and economic conditions. Nevertheless, men who entered the Sudan government during this period found the shift towards practical fields of knowledge disorienting, and some expressed resentment. These were interdependent developments: practical needs motivated a more deliberate authorship of training regimens and influenced their content. These curricula, in turn, shaped colonial administrators' expectations of colonial careering. This chapter traces the changes during the interwar period. The next chapter traces their impact.[17]

The journey to a colonial career

Bill Henderson, who served in the SPS from 1927 until 1953, and retired as the governor of Kordofan Province, was a prolific writer on the subject of the Condominium. He asserted that 'a large number of the Sudan Government officials were the sons... of doctors and clergymen. I imagine there were more clergymen's sons in the Sudan than any other profession'.[18] The historian Robert Collins contradicts Henderson, describing the SPS as comprised largely of English Squireocracy and its lesser, landed brethren.[19] There's little evidence to support either position although it's interesting to note they fit with existing perceptions. J. A. Mangan and Anthony Kirke-Greene provide more data-driven analyses. Solidly middle class, the product of public school and university educations, members of the Sudan government were usually born and raised in Britain, most from outside the Home Counties and only very occasionally coming from gentry families of local fame and influence. They were often Scottish, Welsh and Irish, sometimes lower-middle class, occasionally scholarship boys from the upper working class, and were seldom from colonial or commercial dynasties.[20]

After the First World War, often on the advice of family friends who worked in India, potential colonial recruits looked elsewhere because Indian independence seemed increasingly imminent. Bill Henderson had 'read an awful lot about India as a boy' and dreamed of a career there.[21] But he also had a clear memory of what he thought of the Sudan: 'It seemed to me that in 1895 practically all of Africa was in a comparatively peaceful condition except the Sudan which was... groaning under the rule of the Khalifa al-Mahdi.' In the 1920s, when Henderson entered the service, the pre-(re)conquest conditions of 1895 still lived on, and joining the Sudan government was the next best thing to India.[22]

Ralph Furse describes his own journey to a Colonial Office career as a process of seduction that included the Sudan in a central role. He remembered that as a child 'the queer romantic episode of Fashoda' caught his imagination. Furse wasn't interested in Kitchener who, 'his laurels fresh on his brow, leaving his army behind... and steaming up-Nile with his gunboats to sit down in that outlandish spot', was a 'rather overbearing figure'. For Furse, it was another lone figure in the desert, a la Gordon: Major Marchand. 'The slight French major … had struggled so far from the west, across Africa', in his attempt to thwart Britain's Cape to Cairo dream. Furse's 'sympathies were with the French major and his forlorn little hope', and he was 'glad when he was allowed to march out … with the honors of war'.[23]

But Furse, perhaps indicative of his subsequent role as the preeminent champion of professionalization for colonial administrators, then charts a straight line from the romance of Fashoda as a boy to a fascination with governors as a youth. His father's library was open to him. He started with Seeley's *Expansion of England*, a highly influential text that was the intellectual foundation of late-nineteenth-century imperial policy. But he quickly moved on to 'Cromer, and *England in Egypt*'. Although he read about India, Furse remembers that 'Clive and the Lawrences have never meant so much to me as Milner and Cromer; and, later, Lyautey'.[24] As Furse matured, the administrators won out over the soldiers, privateers and Christian martyrs of the Empire. And,

> by such little pulls and pushes, too slight to be noticed at the time, and, often years beforehand, are we conditioned … to make the right choice when the moment of decision arrives … [so that] one morning in December 1910 I sat down for the first time at my desk in the Colonial Office, as Assistant Private Secretary (Appointments). [25]

In Furse's telling, the impulse to modernize and, perhaps, extend the life of the British Empire and what he saw as its positive legacy began with a childish fascination with heroes that then matured into an admiration for administrators.

John Phillips, a member of the SPS who would later become Ambassador to Sudan in the 1970s, describes his own imperial background at the beginning of a memoir. 'Distinctly military and Indian: my earliest memories are dominated by the aura, not to say aroma, of tiger-skins, ivory elephants, sandal and other aromatic wood, silver and brass … and ponies.'[26] His father, while 'an officer in an Indian Light Cavalry regiment … had broken many bones and lost an eye in an aeroplane crash'. Phillips could 'not remember him other than with a black patch over his right eye which made him look like a pirate'. Sounding like a character from a Frances Hodgson Burnett novel, he provides a sterling imperial pedigree. 'He had, until his accident, owned and successfully ridden steeplechasers in India … He had played much polo and was … a keen rider to hounds … Master of his regimental pack.'[27] Phillips's mother was 'the daughter of the Resident of Hyderabad', where he spent the first seven years of his childhood. Phillips's credentials to tell the story of his imperial life, he seems to be saying in these opening sentences, are not to be challenged.

Nor does he stop there. His invocation of Indian imperial types establishes his credibility, but he also claims a personal connection to the romance of the Sudan. His 'paternal grandmother was … cousin to Sir Herbert Stewart who died of wounds … during the unsuccessful attempt to rescue General Charles Gordon at Khartoum in 1884–5'.[28] And, by 'remarkable coincidence, Charles Gordon's brother, Sir Henry Gordon, was [his] mother's maternal grandfather'.[29] And yet after having conveyed all of these layers and details of imperial tropes to a reader who has been lulled by the familiarity – the rightness – of his autobiography, Phillips asserts 'he had no recollection of his family history influencing his decision to join the Sudan Political Service in any way'.[30]

It seems impossible to take this claim seriously. But it can be seen as proof of two things: the utter ubiquity of Gordon and the intimate relationship everyone felt they had with him, and Phillips's strong desire years later to distance himself from the characterization of colonial administration still being tied to colonial adventuring. Both could be true simultaneously. By the time he was writing, Phillips was a senior member of the Foreign Office, charting a post-imperial path for British international relations. Even to him, his own family history must have certainly seemed distant, exotic and not of his world.

Phillips was not alone in having an Egypt/Sudan family connection, although it was unusual. Edward Haseldon had a grandfather and father in Egypt in the cotton trade. Educated at Cheltenham and Cambridge, Haseldon joined the SPS and finished his career as the Sudan Agent.[31] And men who worked in the technical branches often also had an Egyptian legacy. Reuben Cairo Garrett bears evidence of it in his name. His father was long in the service of the Khedive before joining the Audit Department, and Reuben served briefly in the Sudan Service himself after the Second World War.[32]

As the 1920s become the 1930s, however, the origin stories of administrators read more as realistic decisions made by middle-class men based on personality, family circumstances and opportunity, in economically perilous times. Numerous members of the SPS and the rest of the Sudan government offer up some account of their decision-making process and it is strikingly similar to what Colonial Service recruits report as well. This class of young men became ever more proactive in their pursuit of desirable careers. Particularly as a result of the unemployment problems of the early 1920s and then the slump in the early 1930s, they could no longer rest their career ambitions on their public school pedigree, and their university years were crucial.

Many of them began playing their strategic cards early and building their resumes. Paul Daniell joined the SPS in 1937. While still weighing his career options, he writes in his diary, 'The Master tells me that … I am not likely to get a 2nd but [thinks] I have "played my cards well" it being far more important in my line to become Secretary of the OUAC [Oxford University Athletic Club] and the Master thinks I am a dead [cert] for the Colonial.'[33] Daniell wound up with a Third level honours degree in Jurisprudence but his calculated choice to pursue associational leadership paid off – he was offered positions in both the Colonial Service and the SPS. E. G. Rowe, who was interviewed years after he had served in Tanganyika between the wars, found his way there through a similar process of practical reasoning. He went to Oxford on a Board of Education scholarship. Because he took time off when his father fell ill and then died, he fell behind and would have had to wait an entire year to take the teacher's exam. He was given permission to switch into the Colonial Course instead and requested East Africa because a university friend with connections there had peeked his interest. He readily admitted that 'if they had said there were no vacancies in the [Colonial] Administration … I might well have considered an Education Department' posting.[34]

Some young men were recruited by unofficial talent spotters, but others purposefully sought to gain entry into any branch of Colonial Service.

Rowe participated in one of the earliest iterations of the colonial services course at Oxford. The imperial romance was beginning to have less of an impact moving further into the 1930s. This is not to say that there weren't still men like Allan Arthur, a member of the SPS who joined after the Second World War and declared that watching *Sanders of the River* in 1935 was all it took for him to dream of a colonial career.[35] But alongside Arthur, a man like Daniell, after being accepted into the SPS, 'read bits of *a Life of Gordon*' and observed 'an awkward fellow to be first Governor-General of my Sudan'.[36]

First impressions of an imperial career

Substantial scholarship details the relationship between the Victorian preparatory and public school systems, and the staffing of the Empire. J. A. Mangan and others have established their centrality in creating and promoting the imperial service ethos. A number of public schools were founded and promoted on the basis of providing a sound 'practical' value for money – reassuring the families of the new upper middle class that the fees provided a direct conduit between the school halls and the halls of government, domestic or imperial.[37] Additionally, a wide range of technical schools also explicitly articulated an imperial purpose.[38] This holds true for the Sudan government as much as any other.

Nevertheless, the post-university training demanded of Sudan government recruits, and not others, was one of the ways that the elite status of the SPS was established in the early years.[39] Ralph Furse specifically acknowledges that he was inspired by what the Sudan government was already doing and understood that in the general lore of Oxbridge underclassmen, the SPS was considered 'elite' because it demanded additional training for its recruits.[40] When he was an undergrad, Furse recalls, 'The Colonial Service did not mean much ... but the Sudan Service did.'[41] He heard a much-admired classmate was staying at Oxford for an additional year because 'he was taking a probationary course for the Sudan Service'.[42] When the time came for Furse to argue to the Colonial Office that they needed to pursue new methods of recruitment to increase both the number and quality of their officers, he asserted a year-long training course would have a similar effect on the prestige of the colonial services. 'Twenty or thirty good men a year in each university who were likely to be prominent in college life, their presence for an extra year, scattered among the Oxford and Cambridge colleges, would attract the notice and rouse the curiosity of like-minded friends.'[43] Interestingly, despite Furse's perception and admiration, there was no codified training regimen for the SPS prior to the 1920s.

Collins and MacMichael have claimed that all probationers remained an extra year at university studying Arabic, then passed an exam and then set out for the Sudan. However, MacMichael's own description that he was able to 'arrange' for an additional year 'through the kindness of the College authorities' indicates that he is thinking of a later recruitment period than his own when he describes this universal course.[44] Other

SPS officials from the earlier era describe how they learned on the job. H. C. Jackson, mentioned earlier as a 1907 recruit, explains that he and the other probationers arrived in Khartoum without any extensive preparation. They were stationed in the capital for three months 'in order to acquire some insight into the machinery of government and methods of administration'.[45] This entailed trips to 'experimental farms, and to civil and criminal courts where we were instructed in legal procedure and learnt how the business of these courts was conducted'.[46] He makes no mention of any education he received before he arrived in Khartoum other than what he had learned from conversations with British Egyptian Army officers he met on the journey.[47] After those three months, the other seven were considered sufficiently trained and sent off to various provinces while Jackson spent an additional year in Khartoum.

At the time, he chafed at his ongoing stint in the capital but later understood the benefits of seeing 'how an office should be run and of learning about conditions in the Sudan through reading the monthly diaries sent in from all the provinces'.[48] Jackson experienced first-hand the casual approach to training and the prewar assumptions across the Empire that, as gentlemen and Britons, SPS officers possessed an innate ability to govern. For a brief period in 1908, Jackson was left in charge of five different governmental departments simultaneously because all of the senior officials were on leaves that overlapped. In 1954, he remarked that 'the mere fact that it was thought possible to leave so young and inexperienced an official in a position of such authority illustrates more clearly than words how times have changed'.[49] So it is likely that in the period when Furse was impressed that the Sudan Service required another year of training for its probationers, it wasn't yet standardized.

Students thinking of a colonial career often pursued tutorials with particular fellows who served as talent spotters for the various services. Or they gravitated to clubs and organizations with an imperial theme.[50] Professor E. G. Brown at Cambridge recruited a number of men beginning in the 1900s, including Harold MacMichael in 1905, who went on to be the civil secretary from 1926 to 1934, during which time he transformed that position into the de facto head of the Sudan government. Professor Margoliouth, an 'orientalist' scholar, professor of Arabic, and author of *Mohammed and the Rise of Islam*, was asked by Lord Cromer to fulfil that same role at Oxford.[51] These various talent spotters and mentors, however, were often two or three times the young man's age. And these fellows of the colleges had their students read texts, like Seeley's *Expansion of England*, that described an eighteenth- and nineteenth-century British Empire – one in the process of being understood, mapped, pacified and secured. There was less attention given to current scholarship on colonial administration.[52] Furthermore, undergraduates interested in a colonial career were often also drawn to organizations and clubs with a similarly older and less bureaucratically minded leadership, such as the Empire Club, the Corona Club and the Imperial Roundtable. These organizations often had the patronage of eminent men of letters and politics. These various influences gave students greater exposure to an older approach to imperial government throughout the interwar period.

After the Great War, however, the Sudan government selection committee ceased to be dominated by British senior officers in the Egyptian Army. This reflected a shift in the military to civilian ratio in the Sudan government in general. Increasingly, in the late 1910s and 1920s, senior civilian officials like MacMichael and Jackson were deciding the fate of applicants.[53] Additionally, a broader range of training options emerged. Most probationers received short introductory courses in law and Arabic at accommodating universities, not only Oxford and Cambridge but also at the School of Oriental and African Studies in London, as well as lectures in a relatively new field, anthropology. And by the end of the 1920s, training had expanded to become organized curricula over an entire additional year, studying eight subjects.[54] Once the combined Colonial Service was created in 1931, its sheer numbers relative to the Sudan government meant substantial demand and an economy of scale argued for the Sudan government probationers to attend the course Furse had standardized. While still trained as generalists, that general set of administrative skills and knowledge was being codified across the Empire.

New priorities in the Sudan

The Sudan government, in particular, underwent a striking shift in corporate culture that began during and immediately after the Great War. In 1916, Reginald Wingate left to become the High Commissioner in Egypt, and Kitchener died. In that one year, they ceased to provide the British public or the British in the Sudan with any connection to the era of the Mahdi and Gordon. Kitchener was killed in June, and in September Wingate took only a few hours to accept Sir Edward Grey's invitation to go to Cairo.[55] Wingate had created a fairly weak administrative structure in the Sudan with very little authority vested in any officials outside his personal coterie. And even once Wingate took up his new position in Cairo he insisted that his replacement, Lee Stack, have only 'Acting' status. Stack, who had been the civil secretary under Wingate, put up with this situation until Wingate's fall from grace as a result of the revolution in Egypt in 1919 that presaged full independence from British control less than three years later. Wingate may have wanted to stay involved in the Sudan from Cairo or thought of the Sudan as his safety net in case his time in Egypt wasn't successful. But it was also quite likely that Wingate saw himself as permanently connected to the Sudan, much like titled aristocracy – Wingate of the Sudan.[56] As acting governor general it might have been difficult for Stack to assert his authority, but he was also inclined to delegate, consult and bow to others' expertise by nature.[57] As a result, the culture of military hierarchy and authority that had been in place since Kitchener was no longer encouraged.

The war itself was equally important to the changing corporate identity in the Sudan. By the beginning of 1916, more than one hundred of the British officers and officials who were working in the Sudan, either in the Egyptian Army or seconded to the government, had left for war duty.[58] Many of these had arrived with Kitchener in 1898. But between 1919 and 1924, eighty-three new recruits entered the SPS, virtually all of them university graduates. Veterans like Fouracres were, eventually, able to transfer out of a civil service branch into the SPS. But they were exceptions.[59] By the time of Stack's death in 1924, thirteen of the fifteen provinces were headed by men with civilian rather than military backgrounds and the other two officers were the last remaining 'Bog Barons'.[60]

Britain's growing economic dependency on the Dominions and the colonies was a major factor influencing the bureaucratization of the various colonial services in the interwar period. Germany and the United States had outstripped British production levels when the war began and, particularly after the British Empire Conference in 1932 in Ottawa, the tariff agreements within the Empire that were intended to offer the Empire some sort of collective protection against the worst effects of the Great Depression also created an imperative for economic success.[61] In the immediate postwar period, domestic unemployment drove the demand for development policies for dependent colonies. Then, self-sufficiency (or, preferably, profitability) of colonial territories became increasingly important, particularly during the 1929–33 slump.[62]

The prevailing political wisdom was that unemployment in Britain could be alleviated by creating demand for industrial materials in the colonies.[63] Development investment in a number of African colonies after the First World War was also encouraged because the British government sought increased white settlement. It was thought that if governments in Uganda and Kenya guaranteed a certain level of transportation, communication and agricultural infrastructure, white farmers and entrepreneurs could be lured to the territories.[64]

Interest in imperial economics began to emerge in the 1920s as a specific field of study. Lillian Knowles, a professor at the London School of Economics, broke into the field with her survey, *The Economic Development of the British Overseas Empire*, in 1924, and two years later, Alan McPhee wrote what has been called the 'starting point' of African economic history: *The Economic Revolution in British West Africa*.[65] Nevertheless, as Margery Perham notes, there were few other extensive studies done on the business of colonial development during this era; part of the introduction she provides for a reading list is entitled 'The Paucity of Secondary Works on Colonial Administration'. Reports, studies and articles, such as appeared in *Sudan Notes and Records, African Affairs* and other journals, were what Perham, other lecturers and the student administrators depended on during the pre–Second World War period of the Colonial Administration course.[66]

In the Sudan, the economic relationships were slightly different than in other official colonies, but there were still substantial forces pushing for the creation of a civil service better equipped to promote and steward economic development in the interwar period. In addition to Khartoum, Cairo and London, there was one other locale that exerted great pressure: Lancashire. The British textile industry wanted Sudan's promise as a substantial cotton producer to be realized as quickly as possible. This meant the successful completion of a number of interconnected projects. The Gezira Scheme required the creation of a vast irrigation network in the rich soil between the two Niles supplied by waters made available upon the completion of the Sennar Dam. The project was first conceived of in 1914, and with pressure from Lancashire a loan was issued by the Treasury before the war necessitated the project be put on hold. Resumed in 1919, it became emblematic of the clash between older styles of colonial oversight and the demands of international economic rivalries. By 1920, the costs had skyrocketed and the pace of construction slowed, and an engineer was sent by the Treasury to determine where their money was being spent.

The financial secretary, E. E. Bernard, was responsible for the oversight of the dam project but, by the assessment of his peers, found its complexity utterly overwhelming. Over fifty, and therefore past the retirement age set out by Cromer, he had been in the administration since Kitchener's time.[67] 'He is frightened to death about the Irrigation Dept. and the Gezira Scheme works, and with much more cause than I think he realizes,' wrote his senior financial inspector, A. J. Forster.[68] As the Treasury's engineer, Forster wrote a scathing report in which he detailed the gross misuse of manpower – the eschewing of modern equipment for mass human labour – and the incomprehensible and inadequate bookkeeping practices. But crucially, he still praised the project itself and the eventual goal of mass agricultural production. On the strength of this report, Bernard was finally forced to retire. The professional engineer banished the military man.

The last of the civil secretaries who came to the Sudan with Kitchener and Wingate, C. E. Lyall was not the sort of man who could be counted on to oversee large and complex projects, either. He had long been the governor of Kassala Province, in the eastern Sudan, close to the Abyssinian border, and had become civil secretary purely due to seniority. Even once he was relocated to the seat of government in Khartoum he couldn't really understand 'anyone being busy in the morning'.[69] Under Stack, the governor general's council became a powerful body, and the Civil Secretaryship became the true day-to-day administrative head. Junior officers in all three divisions that were now collectively called the Political Service – Financial, Legal and Civil – were biding their time during these years. Forster and, Lyall's deputy, Harold MacMichael were of the handful of early university appointments from the first decade of the Condominium who were all but running the country – imposing new standards even while, or because, less capable men held the most senior posts above them.

The longest lasting of the Wingate era offices and personalities was the Intelligence Department and its head, C. A Willis. He took over from Slatin Pasha when Slatin was forced to resign during the war because of his Austrian citizenship. Slatin had built up an elaborate network of informants and 'secret agents' and had created a cult of personality around himself so that his position was more than that of security chief. He was, in many ways, the chief influence broker within the government and in relation to the elites within the Sudanese population. C. A. Willis, loath to give up the immense power that this position possessed, tried to perpetuate Slatin's style and methodology for as long as he could but was finally forced out in 1926. As Martin Daly bluntly puts it, 'By 1919 someone of the background and qualifications of Slatin Pasha already seemed a figure of antiquity.'[70] But back in Britain, this created the need for an educational infrastructure to produce this new creature – the colonial administrative professional.

The 'books of interest' reading list

At some point soon before or during the First World War, the 'List of Books of Interest – Recommended for Reading by Candidates Appointed to the Sudan Political Service' was compiled by more senior members of the SPS and sent out to incoming recruits. MacMichael's growing influence, the dominance of university graduates and the resultant shift in corporate culture suggested that recruits could reasonably be expected to read at least a fair number of them. Publication dates indicate that it was last updated in the 1920s even though it was still being given to candidates after the Second World War.[71] Its importance decreased when Furse created the Tropical African Services Course. Nevertheless, the Sudan Agent in London or the Civil Secretary's Office in Khartoum continued to hand it out, perhaps as a way to highlight the separate and unique nature of the Sudan. Even post-1945, grappling with the titles on this list was a rite of passage. Brian Carlisle, a member of the SPS in the 1950s, dutifully ticked off each book as he finished it, but also dryly noted in the list's margins comments such as 'dreadfully dull'.[72]

The first and longest section of the list is entitled 'Islam'. In it, religion is conflated with the broader culture, literature, history and law of its adherents. Classics, *Litterae Humaniores*, and Modern History graduates dominated the ranks of the SPS. It's unsurprising, therefore, that decision-makers like Harold MacMichael assumed recruits needed a crash course in Arabic and Islamic 'liberal arts'. This illustrates how Said's assertion that imperial power was consolidated through the imposition of an elite 'knowledge' about a European construction of the Orient was a cultural companion to Cain and Hopkins' thesis: city men were classmates of the colonial administrators, and gentlemanly capitalism and gentlemanly imperialism were grounded in the same education.[73]

In this context, the list is both telling and unsurprising. Professor Margoliouth, Cromer's Oxford recruiter to the SPS, heads up the 'Islam' section of the list with his 1905 text, *Mohammedanism, Mohammed and the Rise of Islam* and 1913 follow-up, *The Early Development of Mohammedanism*. It's likely that MacMichael, who was recruited in 1905, became personally familiar with both this text and its author. Margoliouth's scholarship drew, in turn, from earlier readings. Thus, it's understandable how Muir's 1861 *The Life of Mahomet*, and Ameer Ali's 1899 *Short History of the Saracens*, found their way onto the list despite being unlikely to provide recruits with practical knowledge about the twentieth-century Sudan. Even the recommended translation of the Koran, by Sale, was originally published in 1734.[74]

In the early twentieth century, there was a flurry of new translations of the Koran, most coming out of India, in reaction to the Christian characterizations and commentary accompanying earlier translations, including Sale's. The continued use of older texts suggests a Western reification of the country and its people, *a la* Said's thesis.[75] The rest of the suggested texts in the 'Islam' category reinforce this. As well as Bosworth Smith's 1889 *Mohammed and Mohammedanism* and T. W. Arnold's two texts from 1896 *The Preaching of Islam* and *A History of the Propagation of the Muslim Faith*; of three works listed by D. B. MacDonald, *Development of Muslim Theology, Jurisprudence, and Constitutional Theory*, *Aspects of Islam*, and *The Religious Attitude of Life in Islam*, none were published after 1911. I. Goldziher's *Lectures on Islam* was deemed 'a work of great importance' but was only available in German and French. The compilers of the list did indicate an English translation of P. H. Lammens's *L'Islam, croyances et institutions* was imminent. But as it arrived in 1929, and no other titles were added in the Islam section later than 1927, it's clear the list was seldom added too or culled after the Colonial Office courses took over as the main source of education for probationers.[76]

There were three other categories on the list: 'Administration, etc.', 'Sudan' and 'Anthropology'. Under the category of 'Administration, etc.' was Viscount Milner's 1893 *England in Egypt* and Lord Cromer's 1908 memoir of his own career, *Modern Egypt*. The list contained no other administrative advice to probationers from the 1900s and 1910s, and only two additions were made in the 1920s. The first was Volume I of the 1925 *Survey of International Affairs*. Edited by Arnold Toynbee, its subheading was *The Islamic World since the Peace Settlement*. It was noted as being 'of the utmost importance', containing multiple articles pertaining to Egypt, the Sudan and the Nile, and was the only item providing current political context for administrative decisions. Sir Frederick Lugard's 1922 *The Dual Mandate* was the other monograph from the decade. The administrative policy of Indirect Rule, developed by Lugard in Nigeria, had an oversized influence on administrative philosophy in the interwar period, although its prevalence, application and level of support from administrators on the ground are increasingly being re-examined.[77]

All titles listed under the 'Sudan' section have been discussed: Wingate's 1891 *Mahdism in the Egyptian Sudan*, Slatin's 1896 *Fire and Sword in the Sudan* and Churchill's *The River War*. It's possible that senior officials in the SPS may have thought the legacies of Mahdism extended into the first decades of British rule; the utility of Slatin's memoir is harder to imagine. The unclear delineation between authors and actors in the Sudan story is also apparent. The previously mentioned memoirist, H. C. Jackson, also wrote a 1924 biography of Osman Digna that is included. Osman Digna was the Hadendoa follower of the Mahdi who led the forces that managed to 'break the square', and inspired Rudyard Kipling to write 'Fuzzy Wuzzy'.[78] But there's little pedagogical argument to be made for the inclusion of his biography on a reading list for probationary officers.

The list lacks any works concerned particularly with administration in the Sudan until well into the 1930s. Civil secretary from 1926 to 1934, H. A. MacMichael's treatise *The Anglo-Egyptian Sudan* (which was the book that Carlisle considered dreadfully dull) and an edited volume of essays by SPS officials, *The Anglo-Egyptian Sudan from Within*, are published in the middle of the decade. These and the journal *Sudan Notes and Records*, which is also listed subsequent to its creation in 1918, are examples of ways in which the administration could reproduce itself through influence and inculcation.[79] Unusual due to their late addition to the list, they suggest an attempt to provide particular Sudan content to augment the generalized colonial administration course in the 1930s. Nevertheless, all other texts in this 'Sudan' section focused on the broader, Islamic world. R. A. Nicholson's *Literary History of the Arabs*, G. Huart's *History of Arabic Literature* and Rev. E. Sell's *Essays on Islam* were at least written since the formation of the Condominium. But it is difficult to find a rationale for including Richard Burton's 1855 *Personal Narrative of a Pilgrimage to Mecca and Medina* and J. Brown's 1868 *The Dervishes or Oriental Spiritualism*.[80] (As an aside, it is also telling that although the Wellcome Tropical Research Laboratories was founded in the Sudan in 1903, there is no evidence on the reading list of the Condominium's central place in scientific research and tropical medicine.)[81] Until the formal training course was established, it appears knowledge was defined by an impressionistic process and a focus on personal experiences, which reiterated the impression gained through reading the adventures of boys and young men years earlier; it was largely focused through the cultural analytical lens favoured by nineteenth-century Orientalist scholars, compounding recruits' misapprehensions about what constituted useful information.

Developing a modern colonial administration curriculum

When SPS began attending the colonial administration courses established by Sir Ralph Furse, it marked a shift in thinking for the SPS. SPS corporate identity was very much invested in its uniqueness, but the new course emphasized norms across all territories. H. E. Wraith, who developed the curriculum for the post–Second World War mid-career summer course for colonial administrators that came to be known as the Devonshire Course, derided the interwar iteration for its generalist approach.

> They taught a bit of history, a bit of anthropology, some I think fairly simple field engineering. They used to get possibly a local vicar who had been a missionary somewhere, to come and teach the language, and so on... They served their purpose well in the context of that time, but I do not think anyone would have accused them of intellectual rigour.[82]

This ungenerous assessment was coloured by hindsight.

In truth, the interwar Tropical African Services course and then Colonial Administrative Services course gradually developed elaborate curricula over two or three terms at either Oxford or Cambridge, with a territorially specific language course sometimes taken instead at the School of Oriental and African Studies or the London School of Economics. By the men involved, it was described at the time as quite demanding and remembered later as quite detailed. E. G. Rowe, mentioned earlier as a member of the Tanganyika Service, recalled specialized language courses and eight common subjects in the Tropical African Service course in 1928: 'Government, Local Government, history... criminal law and procedure and law of evidence, economics, tropical agriculture and forestry, [and] social anthropology.'[83] Observing that Indirect Rule was the established and pursued policy during the interwar period, Rowe recognized that his training began to teach him how to work with 'the true indigenous leaders'.[84] The growing post-45 sensitivity to, and fear of, political self-awareness in the Sudan and the colonies prompted retroactive critiques. Wraith points out, for example, 'There was nothing in this syllabus connected with what nowadays we would call political science... the study of the politics of developing countries.'[85] But, at the time, criticism of the curriculum was often that it was too detailed rather than that it didn't offer enough.

The largest intake groups for the SPS coincided with the first few years that the Tropical African Service was in place, from 1925 until the effects of the Crash resulted in a contraction of recruit numbers starting in 1931, including fifteen in 1926 and 1930, and fourteen in 1928. The cohort from these years were, incidentally, the

British administrators who oversaw the transition from Indirect Rule to 'Sudanization' and, finally, independence, years later. It is possible that exposure to a standard curriculum that included economics, native government and anthropology influenced that process. Many of these men went on to serve as decolonization specialists in other dependencies. Their theoretical training may have helped them to adapt their specific Sudan experience to other contexts later.[86]

Just as imperial economic analysis emerged in the 1920s, British social anthropology was also, arguably, in its most dynamic and innovative phase between the wars. Theoretical developments paralleled the developing critique of Native Administration theory. In this era, comparative research replaced an approach that leaned heavily on historical reconstruction. The first anthropologist of the Sudan territory was Charles Seligman, who posited the Hamitic theory of racial classification in which he asserts four descendent lines of Africa, one of which, the Hamites, constituted much of the northern Sudan population. In his 1913 work, 'Some Aspects of the Hamitic Problem in the Anglo-Egyptian Sudan', he argued that although 'a Negro admixture has taken place', throughout the Sudan, 'culturally if not always physically', the northern Sudanese Hamites were on a different trajectory than their southern counterparts.[87] Seligman's historical or ethnographic approach to anthropology presumed all societies to be on a trajectory towards modernity, just at different points along its path.

A. R. Radcliffe-Brown rejected this model in his 1922 work, *The Andaman Islanders*, where he began developing what he came to call 'coadaptation'. His social and cultural focus (that rejected Seligman and others' structural functionalist approach) leant itself particularly well to the professed goals of Indirect Rule. Radcliffe-Brown posited that it was through the creation of complimentary social practices and institutions that stable societies were maintained. Stability was promoted because groups seldom allowed contradictory or conflicting practices to flourish.

E. Evans-Pritchard, who did extensive fieldwork in the Southern Sudan in the late 1920s, was greatly influenced by this approach. By the late 1920s, recruits to the SPS were exposed to both scholars through the various bibliographies distributed during the course. Research that would become Evans-Pritchard's *Witchcraft, Oracles and Magic among the Azande*, and later three studies of the Nuer – *The Nuer, Nuer Religion*, and *Kinship and Marriage among the Nuer* – was presented in lectures to students in the Colonial Administration Service course when, by the mid-1930s, first Evans-Pritchard and then Radcliffe-Brown were lecturing at Oxford. Men like Paul Daniell, whose strategic pursuit of an SPS career was described above, not only read their works but interacted with them as student and teacher.[88] There is evidence in Margery Perham's writings that social anthropology was increasingly influencing her ideas about colonial administration, as well.[89] While Lugard himself was still lauded, by the 1930s, scholarship no longer assumed that his approach was universally applicable; it had become one methodology, not *the* methodology. The comparative approach in anthropology was influencing political theory.

Perham wrote numerous, regular articles and commentaries for the *Times*, *Spectator*, and other publications and was the primary lecturer at Oxford on Native Administration for the Tropical African and Colonial Administration Services course from their inception. Nevertheless, it wasn't until 1935 that the Rhodes Trustees, who had funded a number of Perham's research projects and trips, created a Research Lectureship in Colonial Administration for her. Perham wrote Lord Lugard's biography and was a strong proponent of Indirect Rule in the 1920s and 1930s. But the method of its application and the suitability of the location became issues of concern, as was the encouragement of new social practices and institutions. She did not necessarily see Indirect Rule as behind the times, end of story.[90] However, she did argue that 'there is a constant tendency of Indirect Rule to deteriorate into a policy of mere preservation. It is not only that development should be allowed: it should be stimulated and guided'.[91] Comparisons of local particularities and ways that Indirect Rule needed to adapt to them dominated Perham's teaching as the 1930s wore on. Earlier governmental models, Margery Perham argued, were inevitably based upon 'illusory views of the old Africa and of the impression it was bound to make upon men who had to deal with it as it was without the sociological skills or knowledge of recent years'.[92] The old Africa, she implied, was the product of an 'old' British administrative model that new training could correct. Drawing on the co-adaptive theory put forth by her anthropologist colleagues, she saw developmental connections in the colonial relationship were inevitable. Perham included a long list of anthropological studies in her many extensive bibliographies compiled as preliminary research for the various books, articles and speeches and disseminated to her students and to Colonial Office and Colonial Service officials.[93]

By the time her detailed analysis of Lugard's *Native Administration in Nigeria* was published in 1937, she clearly articulates her unease with the limitations and dangers of the methods as she applies the newly mainstream social sciences to a clear-eyed reassessment of Indirect Rule.[94] She states that more anthropological study of all of Africa's nations is necessary in order to appreciate Indirect Rule's level of disruption and bemoans the fact that 'as long as the obvious results of mishandling the human factor are not immediately apparent, it is to be feared that sociological investigation will remain the last of the many inquiries which [British colonial] African Governments finance'.[95] She cautions that 'at best this method is politically sterile'.[96]

Thomas Spear aptly points out that Indirect Rule 'offered a contradiction in terms. If colonial administrators were to capitalize on the illusion of traditional authority, their rule was limited by the need of those authorities to maintain their legitimacy'.[97] The only administrators in a position to know through whom and by what means 'native authority' could be deployed in the name of the colonizer were the men on the ground. And with the ostensibly independent Sudan government even further removed from the oversight of Whitehall, British-Sudanis were able to interpret, apply, reject and modify the various instruments of Indirect Rule as they saw fit, in the south and the north. Training gave SPS administrators the intellectual self-assurance to do so. Foreign Office officials often interpreted the Sudan government's resistance to their interference – and other colonial administrations' pushback against the Colonial Office – as some sort of colonial administrator-itis. Inevitably, the extensive training programme instilled confidence in administrators, and the nuanced knowledge acquired and applied by the man on the ground under Indirect Rule built on that. It was the price the Colonial and Foreign Offices paid for professionalizing colonial administration while also reducing their own direct responsibility for funding and staffing territories.

In this context, Perham resisted attempts to proscribe policy from a distance, but she was also prone to a certain blindness when it came to the limitations and foibles of administrators. Lessons are learned in the field, she argued, but officials aren't rewarded for their new insight. 'When, as so often occurs, by our misunderstanding of this factor, we find ourselves in very practical and expensive difficulties, we [the administrative authority in the colony] extricate ourselves by means of a common sense which prompts us to use the minimum of coercion and to combine it with investigation. We [authorities in Britain] do not,' she is sorry to say, 'seem to acquire the foresight which is the obvious lesson of these events'.

There is a gap between administrators' need to find ways to govern efficiently and with as little tension as possible, and policy makers' need to produce a report or a study that can quantify progress. 'To penetrate to the masses and discover their needs and the effects upon their lives of our measures is an exacting task which produces few results for presentation in annual reports.'[98] When Furse, Perham and others argued for, and succeeded in getting, colonial administration recognized as a profession in need of training, they were inadvertently supporting, and even institutionalizing, the British-Sudani corporate culture of elite independence. What was this new, modern training for, if men weren't then allowed to exercise their expertise?

It took time, however, for recruits to embrace the training as part of their corporate identity rather than a detriment to it. When Paul Daniell was on the course in 1937, he was both dismissive of the benefits of studying anthropology and, specifically, its theoretical or comparative nature. When Perham lectured to his cohort on 'Cultural Contact and Native Administration in North America', Daniell impatiently observed in his diary that 'we shall probably have to study use of the small tooth comb among the Esquimaux next'.[99] Throughout his first term, Daniell has nasty things to say about Perham, including referring to her as 'Pussy' Perham.[100] Interpreting his criticism, it's easy to suspect that he found her analytical and scholarly approach to colonial administration as a career and a field of study both strange and unsettling.

Lacking the congratulatory or romantic tone of past imperial literature, Daniell accuses Perham of sounding 'Smug and Superior [*sic*] in the consciousness of her inferiority'.[101] In her notes for introductory remarks to students during the Colonial Administration Summer Course, she exhorts students to freely discuss readings' implications for contemporary affairs.[102] This approach was probably what Daniell interpreted as 'her studied impromptu manner' which drove him 'nearly mad'.[103] Her students no doubt found it unsettling to be asked to offer an informed answer to questions that they hadn't even considered as questions before. Responding to an examination question, such as 'How far has the development of self-government in British dependencies been due to accident and how far to design', required them to think about the Empire differently.[104] With hindsight, Daniell comments that 'the development of my later hero-worship for Dame Margery Perham is interesting, from scorn to respect in one term'.[105]

Daniell's approach to his chosen profession could also be compatible with a romantic image of imperial careering. His anger at having the romance of empire turned into lectures on town planning, etc., is palpable in his diary entries; he resented Perham's role in the death of his fantasy. But his subsequent career path ironically illustrates the long-lasting impact of his training. Far from being disaffected, early in his SPS career he transferred to Gordon Memorial College in Khartoum. Over the years he became, in essence, 'Pussy' Perham to Sudanese students as the dean of the School of Administration, and then Dean of Law when it became a full-fledged university in 1951.

It is difficult to prove a negative, but organized and lengthy training in Britain before taking up a colonial post appears to have had a lasting effect on policy and the future training of both British and Sudanese officials. And where it was absent, it is possible to track different attitudes towards the work. Daniell's first Sudan post took him to a district vacated a year earlier by Wilfred Thesiger, who had been exempted from the training regimen for reasons that will be described in the next chapter. Arguably as a result of that omission, he was never able to sluff off the imperial romance and only served briefly, and unsatisfactorily, in the SPS before embarking on his long career as an anachronistic explorer and author.

4

The adventurer and the administrator

When Gawain Bell walked into Griffiths McAllister, of Warwick Street, Piccadilly, in 1931, he felt like an imposter. Mssrs Griffiths and McAllister had supplied the men of Empire for generations. Bell, a new, probationary officer in the SPS, had to walk through the narrow entranceway past a long line of crates on which were 'stenciled names and destinations well calculated to impress and indeed overawe: … "*Captain J.W.F. Horton-Gardiner, Accra,*" "*Mr. B.J. Bryanston, CMG, The Residency, Zanzibar.*"'[1] Bell had come to purchase all of the 'kit' he was told he needed for his first tour of duty. Moving up the stairs towards the main showroom, he was forced to pass under the gaze of 'many distinguished' men in framed photographs, 'some in uniform, and all [with] large and virile moustaches. Their eyes were steady, their mouths firm'. It was a familiar and universally agreed-upon catalogue of attributes that, while he made fun of it when recalling it years later, the young Bell most certainly failed to measure up to.[2] 'It was abundantly clear that without exception these paragons possessed in the fullest possible measure the qualities essential to a successful colonial administrator: resolution, fair dealing, integrity and supreme self-confidence.'[3] Bell was unsure he would prove to have any of these.

Mr Bryanston's status as a paragon of imperial manhood was at least supported by the CMG after his name. But what had Captain Horton-Gardiner done to awe the young Bell? Simply, he had his name and address stencilled on crates in Griffiths McAllister's. By the time the 23-year-old Bell went to buy his camp bed and mosquito netting, he had been immersed for decades in a fantasy of Empire and of Colonial Service that limited and guided Bell's sense of who these men were, with little need for any facts to fill in the details of their biographies. As has been discussed previously, Berny Sèbe argues that the role of these heroes was to 'personify the arguments of duty, responsibility and justice' and perform a 'highly mythologized meeting between conquerors and conquered'.[4] In other words, the role Bell was about to assume was, in part, a fantasy.[5] Men like Bell, who were just starting their careers in colonial administrations, felt that they had already been to the Sudan, or India, or Jamaica. Mr Bryanston and Captain Horton-Gardiner were known to Bell because they were both familiar and mythic in his young, well-read mind. What he wanted was to be included in a community that he thought he had already experienced through literature read in childhood and later.[6]

In the outfitters' emporium that day, Bell says that the assistant greeted him with a 'slightly patronizing' tone, but he was comforted by the thought that 'in a week or so the corridor would be filled with crates marked "*Mr G. W. Bell, Khartoum via Port*

Sudan'". Two years later, when he returned for his first leave, he went to Mssrs Griffiths McAllister again and recollected with satisfaction, 'I was no longer a cadet. I knew what I wanted. I had had fever and lost a stone in weight. My new status was clear. I was addressed constantly as "Sir". Although it was not yet eleven o-clock in the morning I was offered a whisky and soda.' The assistant serving as symbolic gatekeeper measured men against the metropole's understanding of imperial manhood. On his second visit, appropriate markers were identified, and Bell's status confirmed. He was now a man. Who but a man should or could drink whiskey and soda at eleven in the morning? He exhibited certain attitudinal markers: 'I knew what I wanted.' And visual ones: signs of fever and, we can assume, a deep tan. In other words, Bell ends the episode by implying that he now embodied the successful colonial administrator he had seen in the portraits two years earlier, although he never grew a moustache.[7]

This chapter will bring together the various threads explored in the first section of this book by looking at the mid-Condominium careers of two officers – one who attended the Colonial Administration Course and one who did not: the already introduced Gawain Bell went through the extensive year-long training course. Wilfred Thesiger, who later went on to make a name for himself as an explorer, photographer and memoirist, did not. Entering the service only four years after Bell, Wilfred Thesiger's motivations, understanding and preparations for the SPS were radically different. Thesiger embraced the hero narratives that Bell held at an ironic distance. Their initial impressions and interactions with the administrative apparatus once they arrived in the Sudan indicate that training, or the absence of it, influenced their ability to reconcile the ideal of imperial masculinity with the demands of post–First World War imperial administration and find their place as agents of evolving colonial policies.

When both men indicate in their correspondence and memoirs that they arrived in the Sudan already steeped in the popular memory of the soldier-hero, they are quite typical for their age and class. Graham Dawson points out that 'in the fascination that stories about fighting men beyond the frontier hold for boys far removed from those particular dangers, we find a clear example of the metaphorical use of narrative forms to organize imagined subjectivities'.[8] But unlike their metropolitan peers, these particular 'far removed' boys became men in the service of the Sudan; the subjectivities in which they are so heavily invested no longer live purely in the realm of the symbolic.

In understanding the relationship between psychic development, masculinity and imperial heroes, Graham Dawson still proves most useful. For young boys, 'the adventure hero as cultural form is drawn into the internal world of phantasy to operate as an imago'. But it isn't a one-size-fits-all situation. A multiplicity of cultural interventions and consumptions hold sway, says Dawson, and 'make possible different kinds of investment in the "same" heroic figure'.[9] In Dawson's original statement this 'same' is in quotes, acknowledging the amorphous nature of any archetype. The Gordon saga was not straightforward. Depending on who was describing him, Gordon was either a paragon of British Christian imperial virtue and the embodiment of the soldier hero, or he was a more-than-slightly-mad alcoholic with tendencies towards evangelical mysticism and a Messiah complex. The Sudan, in turn, was a territory of enslaved and desperate people who were admired for rising up against the despotic regime of the Khedive and/or for remaining loyal to Gordon instead of joining the Mahdi. Or it was a desolate and brutal nether region, devoid of any culture or society. For decades, articulating where one stood on the character of Gordon was to declare a position on the uses of imperial military power and the acceptable reach of the British Empire. More than a man, Gordon was an imperial Rorschach test.

Gordon and the Sudan entered Thesiger and Bell's minds at an age when the questions were much simpler: Could I be that brave? Am I my own man? Only later were the other dilemmas posed as they read and understood the debates at hand. Gordon claimed that 'the only reason which, to me, justifies [a colonial administrator] taking service is – that he wishes to benefit his fellow creatures' and that to do so successfully he 'should, for the time, entirely abandon his relations with his native land [and] put himself into the place of a native'.[10] Thesiger and Bell illustrate how differently Gordon's words could be personified. For Thesiger, the emphasis was on 'putting himself into the place of the native'. This meant reifying and valorizing what he believed an authentic Sudanese way of life to be. For Bell, being a colonial administrator was first and foremost a form of 'service', whereby he could 'benefit his fellow creatures' to a greater degree than if he had followed the path of his metropolitan counterparts. Along with the observations about training made by Rowe, Daniell, Wraith and others, Thesiger and Bell provide sufficient evidence to suggest that the training courses responded to and affected the administrative culture of the Sudan and, by extension, other colonial territories.

Wilfred Thesiger – Imperial adventurer

Wilfred Thesiger wrote popular travelogues in the 1950s and later about territories in Africa and Arabia that had managed to remain outside the reach of direct imperial rule or international development aid. In his time, he was quite famous. But in 1935, long before he wrote about these journeys in *Arabian Sands* or *The Marsh Arabs*, Thesiger joined the SPS. After five years spent in the western and southern regions of the country, he was seconded to the Sudan Defense Force to fight the Italians in Abyssinia and, in 1944, left the Sudan Service entirely. He was never a good fit, although in 1935 he, the Sudan Agent, and the Selections Board all thought he would be.

His family background was far more like John Philips's than what has been established as the typical profile for the SPS. Thesiger's great-grandfather was Lord Chelmsford, the Chancellor of the Exchequer, his grandfather served in the Crimea and then went to India in time for the Mutiny. His uncle was the Viceroy of India from 1916 to 1921, and father was in the Diplomatic Service, with postings ranging from St. Petersburg just after the failed revolution of 1905 to the Congo just after the release of the Casement Report. In 1909, Thesiger *père* began a ten-year post as head of the Legation in Addis Ababa, where Wilfred was born, in 1910. Soon after the family returned to England in 1919, his father died suddenly. Other members of the family took up the cost of his education and, after a stint at a prep school, Thesiger attended Eton and then Oxford.[11]

Despite the fact that he had only lived in Abyssinia as a small child, it loomed large in Thesiger's imagination. The Sudan was an attractive destination because of the intersection between the imperial saga of Abyssinia and the campaigns of the Mahdi army, and the simple fact of geographical proximity.[12] This interest was reinforced when family connections led him to be a junior staff member of the British delegation to Hailie Selassi's coronation in 1930 and he came to know the governor general of the Sudan, Sir John Maffey, and the civil secretary, Harold MacMichael, who were also in attendance.[13] This trip set him on two paths: he determined to explore a remote region of Abyssinia, the Danakil, once he finished his degree. And in his last year at Oxford he applied to join the SPS. His preparation for both of these ambitions consisted of reading Samuel Baker's and Winston Churchill's books on the Sudan and joining the Oxford Explorer's Club (OEC), of which he became secretary.

These were the peak years for the OEC. It was founded in 1927 by Max Nicholson (who went on to found the World Wildlife Fund), Colin Trapnell (who became a botanist and the preeminent surveyor of plant life in the British African colonies), Charles Elton (who later created the Bureau of Animal Population at Oxford and was a founder of the Nature Conservancy Council) and others. Between 1928 and 1933, its members undertook official Oxford University expeditions to Greenland, British Guiana, Lapland, the Hudson Strait, Borneo, the Arctic and the New Hebrides. When Thesiger arrived at Oxford in 1932, he was immediately interested in the group because he was already planning his expedition to Abyssinia.

John Buchan, the novelist, Member of Parliament and popular historian, was the OEC's president by this time. A recent inductee into the Order of the Companions of Honour for his service as a propagandist during the war, he had also accumulated a long list of other sinecures that labelled him a serious public figure dedicated to the Empire and to learning.[14] Thesiger had written to him asking his advice about planning an expedition because, as he put it, he was a 'passionate John Buchanite', whose style he tried to emulate. This letter earned him membership in the club and invitations to tea.[15] Thesiger's eventual expedition through the Danakil region of Abyssinia was not given the official Oxford imprimatur, perhaps because he undertook it as an individual journey, a la Richard Burton, rather than in the spirit of scientific exploration.

In the same year that Thesiger interviewed to join the SPS, Buchan published his account of the saga of General Gordon and the Sudan, *Gordon at Khartoum*. In 1934, he sets the scene with the following passage:

> The Soudan . . . had no unity and no history, nothing to bind it together except the long silver thread of the Nile. In 1883 to the Western world it was still largely unknown, though Speke and Baker, Gordon and Stanley had interested Europe in its southern fringes . . . Suddenly the fates set the play. From Darfur to the Red Sea, from Assouan to the Great Lakes, it became a single stage, lit by the fires of death, and as the months passed the drama drew to its climax in the few square miles of land where Khartoum stood at the junction of the two Niles. The ancient river of Egypt, which had witnessed in its lower course the making of so much history, now saw in its southern wilds a tragedy evolve itself with half the world as breathless spectators.[16]

Buchan's *Gordon at Khartoum* certainly had more in common with the romantic imperial tales of the Victorian and Edwardian eras than with the acerbic colonial commentaries of Joyce Cary's contemporary novels or Perham's comprehensive bibliographies. While its melodramatic style had not yet gone out of favour, no one would have looked to it for a serious assessment of the actual events that took place from 1883 to 1885. It was read, not for the basic information it provided but, rather, for the pleasure to be had from reading a familiar and much-loved author's take on a familiar and much-loved saga. Buchan's intent was to elicit emotion by recounting an exciting historical narrative; nevertheless, as with Slatin's memoir, the literary category for *Gordon at Khartoum* was still non-fiction.

Buchan certainly complimented Thesiger's own anachronistic leanings. In his memoir, Thesiger wrote that his desire to join the Sudan Government was based on the proximity of the Sudan to Abyssinia. He continued to be fascinated by the country he was born in and the feudal culture of the imperial court surrounding Haile Selassi.[17] He also listed as reasons for joining the richness of the big-game hunting in the south of the Sudan and the fact that while at Eton, he first came upon Winston Churchill's account of Kitchener's campaign to reconquer the Sudan, after which he read 'every book [he] could find about the rise and fall of the Dervish Empire'.[18] The characterization of the Sudanese followers of the Mahdi as 'dervishes' was prevalent in Slatin's era, certainly. But in the 1930s, when the Gezira Scheme was fully developed, Gordon Memorial College was providing administrative training to Sudanese students, and the Sudanese Student Association was gaining influence, Buchan's need to refer to the 'Soudan,' and Thesiger's interest in 'dervishes,' erased decades of history.[19] His account of his time in the SPS, even though written years later, unproblematically reproduces the vague disregard he had at the time for the politically constituted citizens of developing nation states.[20]

During his last year at Oxford, Thesiger spoke to the Sudan Agent in London about joining the SPS once he got back from his Abyssinia expedition to trace the course of the Awash River.[21] It is, perhaps, a glimpse into the changing ethos of the Sudan Government during this period that the Sudan Agent, who had served in the Sudan during the earlier military-oriented era before the war but who now represented the Sudan Government's interests in London, thought that a year exploring the Danakil region and then the brief Arabic language course at SOAS was a reasonable replacement for the year of colonial training.

For Thesiger, at least in his recollection years later, the original impulse to join was first and foremost about Africa as an experience he had already had or one that others had that he hoped to re-enact.[22] As he made his first journey into the Sudan, he wrote, 'So vivid had been the accounts I had read of the Sudan campaign that I felt that I had seen it all before.'[23] The Sudan was already a memory for Thesiger before he had even arrived – of imperial adventure and personal struggle against which he could measure himself and, hopefully, not be found lacking. His personal connections meant that he could imagine the Empire as a grand, personal testing ground.[24] He set his mind to exploring the source of the Awash because another explorer told him that the North and South Poles were 'all that had been left,' and he didn't like the cold.[25] A master of self-fashioning in his later writings, he similarly seems at the time to have seen a career in the Sudan as giving him access to vast expanses of land, and their anonymous inhabitants, as an arena in which he could enact and embody a particular selfhood increasingly anachronistic in the interwar period.

As a point of comparison, Jackson, who was discussed earlier as one of the earliest university recruits, was given his choice of postings in 1908 in recognition of that first year of service in a Khartoum office and chose the Fung Province in part because he too hoped to see some big-game hunting. But in his subsequent memoir, Jackson uses his animal stories as framing mechanisms for stories about interactions with Sudanese. By contrast, Thesiger's descriptions of hunting are as detailed as his descriptions of his job are brief, suggesting that, unlike Jackson, he saw his position as an administrator as a way to facilitate his hunting and exploration, rather than the other way around.[26]

When Thesiger returned from Abyssinia and finally came before the Admissions Board for his interview he was asked why he wanted to join the Sudan Service by a man he later recalled being named Hall, who must have been E. G. Sarsfield-Hall, the governor of Khartoum Province. Fresh from his adventures and feted by the Royal Geographical Society, Thesiger deemed the man and his question 'self-important' and almost answered, 'Because I want to shoot a lion.' He was 'sure the other members of the board would have approved of his answer, but [Hall] certainly wouldn't'.[27] Separate from his misperception of exactly who in that room was full of self-importance, Thesiger's misperceptions about the life and the responsibilities of a colonial administrator are indicative of the inter-war process of transition within colonial administrations.

Sarsfield-Hall, who joined the SPS in 1909, had, in fact, been stationed for four years in the same territory that Thesiger would be given as his first posting: Kutum, Darfur, but twenty years earlier. Sarsfield-Hall wrote numerous ethnographic and geographic articles and sketches during his time there, one of which was published in *Geographical Journal* in 1922. During the First World War, Sarsfield-Hall had been seconded from the SPS to the Egyptian Expeditionary Force and served in Palestine, as an Intelligence officer, much as Thesiger was seconded to its Second World War equivalent, the Sudan Defense Force. After his war service Sarsfield-Hall went on to serve as the governor of two different provinces, including Khartoum, before retiring the year after interviewing Thesiger. Thesiger's service in the SDF, on the other hand, was his last assignment before leaving the Sudan altogether.[28]

Thesiger didn't actually attend very much of his training course because, in the mode of his heroes, Burton, Speke, et al, he was preparing lectures for the Royal Geographical Society and writing articles for the *Times*. Enough senior officers in the SPS (from the pre–First World War generation) felt that his Abyssinian journey could stand in for much of his training that he was exempted from the requirement. His one comment on his limited training in Britain was that he 'always regretted missing the opportunity to learn classical Arabic'.[29] But he seems to regret this lack as a deficiency in his persona rather than a hindrance to fulfilling his role as a good administrator. He struggled with the Darfur Arabic of his first posting but mentions no effort to remedy the situation. After six months in the country, Thesiger writes home, 'I plod on with my Arabic and am at last beginning to feel that I have mastered the alphabet.'[30] He seems untroubled by his impending exams, however, taking time out from work and study to find bookcases to hold his 'complete sets of Conrad and Kipling, Blackwood's *Tales from the Outposts*, Gibbon's *Decline and Fall of the Roman Empire* ... Lawrence's *Revolt in the Desert*, Doughty's *Arabia Deserta*, Churchill's *River War*, and a number of other[s]'.[31] John Guille Millais's 1924 account of a safari, written with his son, *Far away up the Nile*, and the artist-naturalist Abel Chapman's 1921 travelogue, *The Savage Sudan*, fascinated him.[32] But the people and their society did not. As a result, a year after his arrival in the Sudan, he admits his 'Arab Examination was brief and to the point, consisting as it did on my part of [handing in] blank pages with my name at the top'.[33]

By comparison, when asked about friendships between Britons and Sudanese, K. D. D. Henderson, a contemporary, regretted that friendship was more difficult with Sudanese because 'one hadn't got the language'. He was frustrated that 'you could talk about herd tax or the various points of camels ... [but] when you were dining with a man who wanted to discuss Christian theology ... you found you were lamentably lacking in words'.[34] Henderson set the bar high for both language proficiency and friendship, betraying an interest in the people rather than the flora and fauna.

The lack of importance Thesiger put on training in irrigation, agriculture, sanitation or law was evident in how he described his approach to getting settled in once he arrived in Darfur. Chris Vaughan has analysed the complex intersection of British authority, Indirect Rule and the legacies of the Sultanate in Darfur. The 'incoherence' of British rule in the region was, perhaps, a reason why Thesiger was able to hold onto such a profound misapprehension of colonial administrating for so long.[35] As Vaughan points out, Thesiger wasn't alone in being ignorant of the unique characteristics of Darfur on arrival.[36] But, as a new and green officer in his first days on the job, he exhibited a resistance to any sort of corrective. Instead, he describes avoiding the officials who were discussing dry administrative matters and considers himself lucky that Charles Dupuis, the retiring governor of Darfur, was making his final rounds of the territory and was happy to reminisce about his hunting experiences. Dupuis, like Sarsfield-Hall, functioned as a projection of Thesiger's internal fantasy of the colonial administrator, which drew far more from the Gordon myth than from the bibliographies of Margery Perham and the lectures of Evans-Pritchard or even from Lord Lugard. Yet what Thesiger failed to understand is that Dupuis was extremely astute and eloquent about the mechanisms of effective and successful colonial administrative techniques.

Using Dupuis and others as foils for his own self-fashioning in his memoir, he characterizes the foundation of his rapport with Dupuis as connected to game hunting and an appreciation for the authentic Sudan. Ironically, Thesiger failed to grasp the particularism of Darfur, which he observed through a Manichaean, Buchanesque lens. He also admires Dupuis's wife, expressing relief that she knew not to intrude into the homosocial environment he was looking for, while neglecting to mention that the two families were neighbours back in England and that Mrs Dupuis and Thesiger's cousin, Sybil, planned and executed their own motor expedition across Africa from west to east in 1935.[37]

Thesiger had a clear expectation of what Dupuis's replacement, Guy Moore, would be like before he met him. Moore's success as a colonial administrator, and the respect he was able to command from Sudanese and British alike, led Thesiger to expect 'a tall, spare, weather-beaten man of few words,' reminiscent of the colonial heroes that Bell referenced, tongue-in-cheek, in Griffith McAllister's. It was a shock to Thesiger when Moore turned out to be 'short, tubby, talkative, with a red face [and] ... fluent Arabic'.[38] Thesiger's expectations of Sarsfield-Hall, Charles Dupuis and Guy Moore; the responsibilities of administration in Darfur; and the 'traditions' of the Sudanese were never challenged or shaped by the training course. Rather, the imperial romance was allowed to rest, unalloyed, in Thesiger's imagination.

Thesiger's lack of practical or professional training could have resulted in innovative and forward-thinking strategies unimpeded by institutional wisdom. When he rejects his predecessors' practices, however, he makes anachronistic rather than innovative choices. Despite lacking any experience of camel travel or of what his administrative treks around the territory would consist of, he asserted his preferences 'to travel light, fast and far rather than plod at the head of a caravan laden with tents, chairs, tables and the other customary impedimenta' and replaces pack camels with riding camels.[39] A key episode in the Gordon narrative occurred during his years working for the Khedive in the 1870s and involved riding out – alone – to confront the most renowned slave trader of the southwestern Sudan. Gordon believed that his *mano a mano* approach would flatter his adversary and give him additional status. Zubayr Pasha retreated and British-Egyptian oversight of the region was assured. Later, this event was seen as proof of Gordon's character by some and of his instability by others. Thesiger was apparently of the first opinion. The lone Englishman among the Arabs, or at odds with the elements, was the subject of many of those heavy books he had lugged all the way from London to Darfur. He had been able to bring the 'customary impedimenta' of metropolitan imperial fantasy to sit on his Darfur bookshelves because Sudanese labour built railways and roads connected to outlying stations by porters and, indeed, pack camels.

Thesiger imagined he inhabited a pre-Condominium world. In keeping with Buchan's empty 'Soudan', even in 1937, Thesiger was either blind to the people who were there, was uninterested in communicating with them or undertook elaborate plans to avoid them. Compared to the town and the office to which he was assigned, he described the campfires that he sat around with Darfur porters and soldiers as 'havens'. He was untroubled by the fact that he couldn't actually communicate fully with any of them.[40] In his memoir, Thesiger relays conversations with Darfur nomads without mention of translation except during official business, such as court cases. This creates the impression that outside the structures of the colonial administration some kind of magical process occurs by which he and the natives can communicate when, in fact, his *suffragi* (manservant) acted as interpreter.[41]

His attention (and imagination) was so focused on an ideal that sat outside the realities of the Anglo-Egyptian Condominium of 1937, that he was blind to the ramifications of his behaviour. When a fellow officer mentioned reports that the Italians had invaded Bir Natrum, Thesiger said he was just there and hadn't seen any. It had to be explained to him that *he* must be who they thought were the Italians. He failed to understand why London was alerted, alarms sounded and an international incident threatened because he didn't inform anyone that he was travelling along the border of fascist-controlled Libya.[42]

The *Guardian* obituary kindly described Thesiger's less-than-enthusiastic or effective colonial development efforts as a 'mystical regard for tradition'.[43] When overseeing a trial of Sudanese who had been coming down from the hills to raid livestock, he wrote to his mother, 'They were a fine-looking group and they had my sympathy. I should of course be a Mahdist if I was a Sudanese.'[44] Thesiger understood his environment as dichotomous – native/primitive/authentic vs European/civilized/inauthentic. He was unable to make space in his imperial romance for the complex history of Darfur's tribal resistance to both Turkish and Mahdiyya rule because those were contestations of power that did not take place under the British gaze.[45] Vaughan describes the reality on the ground as 'characterized by fluidity, competition and pluralism, rather than a clearly defined, fixed or impersonal hierarchy'.[46] For Thesiger, resistance to British authority was the Sudanese's primary and most appealing attribute. The varied relationships to power within Darfur society defied Thesiger's formulations.[47]

The *Guardian* obituary writer's use of the term 'mystical' was most likely intended at least in part as an indictment, echoing Lytton Strachey's characterization of Gordon decades earlier. By the post–First World War era, when Strachey and others discuss Gordon's religious fervour, it is not characterized as an admirable quality in the way Victorians would have seen it. Strachey's *Eminent Victorians* was written at a moment of attitudinal change. Mysticism and evangelical Christianity never really regained currency as admirable qualities in colonial administrators after the war. 'In the depths of Gordon's soul there were intertwining contradictions,' and, as Strachey saw it, these 'intricate recesses where egoism and renunciation melted into one another' lulled Gordon into a false sense of his own power over the 'swaying multitudes'.[48] So while Thesiger's 'sympathies were [also] with the indigenes,' it is clear that he could only actually understand the peoples of Darfur to a very limited extent, given his poor language skills and inability to recognize their lived experience in the 1930s, not the 1880s.[49]

After he returned from his first leave to England, Thesiger was surprised that his poor showing on the language exam resulted in his reassignment to the non-Arabic-speaking South, although that region – close as it was to Abyssinia – had originally been his focus. While expressing his surprise, in describing his new post to his mother he recalls his originally expressed priorities: 'I never … anticipated I would be helping … to administer these proud tribesmen in a virtually unknown area of the Southern Sudan teeming with wildlife.'[50] By the end of the year, however, the abundance of wildlife and close proximity to Abyssinia were not sufficient to make up for his responsibilities to its people. 'I know I am never going to settle to this life, and I have given it a fair trial trying to be unprejudiced. But I find myself tired of these naked, uninteresting, uncompanionable savages … [At least] at Kutum [Darfur] one was on the fringe of the Moslem world.'[51]

The government could no longer ignore his half-hearted efforts. When Thesiger returned from leave in 1939, he was seconded to the Sudan Defense Force. The prestige attached to his name could only carry him so far. The wartime secondment was a perfect way to shift Thesiger out of the administration. By 1942, the SDF had managed to thwart Italian efforts to invade the Sudan from Abyssinia, at which point Thesiger took up a new posting in Syria, fighting with Druze forces in a rear campaign against the

Vichy French, and was eventually transferred into the Special Air Service, the British wartime special forces unit. His career as a colonial administrator was over. Entering the SPS had been part of a larger strategy of self-fashioning, aligning his career choice and other aspects of his biography with the imperial imago he had internalized as a boy and carried with him into adulthood. Never attending the training year and learning the language, Thesiger was unable to connect with the contemporary realities of the Sudan and, instead, sought a life that looked and felt like the life he imagined.

Gawain Bell – Colonial administrator

Gawain Bell's motivations were, perhaps, based in a drive for self-fashioning but of a very different kind. His background was fairly typical for SPS recruits. Not the son of a doctor or a parson, his family was still sturdily middle class. Their only income was his father's salary. Bell spent his early childhood in South Africa where his father was posted as an agent for the New Zealand Shipping Company. Once his parents returned to England and his father became a stockbroker (which was not the high-flying career of today – more like that of a mid-level banker), Bell attended a minor prep school. Later, he gained entrance to Winchester because his uncle had taught there before becoming one of the school's heroes by dying in the Great War. Not even a typical 'legacy' student, he was related to the faculty, not alumni. But his parents were only able to take advantage of this little bit of nepotism because he was their sole child – the fees and expenses, first for Winchester and then Oxford, were almost beyond their means. He was a strong student and a poor athlete except that he was an exceptionally good shot; he came out the other end with a Second-class Honours in history and a shooting Blue.[52]

Bell had rejected a professional career because he liked the outdoors and a military career because, as he put it, Winchester had instilled in him an obligation to public service.[53] But he was worried that his poor performance at games and his solidly middle-class background would impede his application to the SPS. Two men reassured him that he was suited to life in the Sudan. The first was his medieval history tutor, who was scholarly, soft-spoken and cultured, but who was also known to have served with distinction in the war.[54] The other, Martin Parr, was the brother of one of his teachers at Winchester and the secretary to Governor General John Maffey at the time Bell applied. Both of them encouraged him to join, making it clear that his impulses beyond an adventurous life would be valued and satisfied.

The younger Bell, whom he describes as quiet and well-meaning but uncertain, was helped towards a colonial career by these men. He overcame the fears of inadequacy he so vividly remembered from his initial trip to the outfitters. The mentoring was aided by an evolving popular masculine ideal. In the interwar period, less aggressive male archetypes began to appear in boys' literature.[55] Gordon's virtues of service and selflessness were reconfigured as *secular* Christian attributes – peaceability, cooperation and paternal concern for the less fortunate – but devoid of confessional fervour that might erupt into militarism. Bell's awareness of the gap between who he was and who he was supposed to be if he was to be a successful imperial man is apparent in his correspondence from this period. Anxiety, however, is increasingly replaced by humour and ironic detachment as he begins to play with the divergence between type and self. In his account of going to Griffiths McAllister before his first tour, we see both.

Unlike Thesiger, Bell did take the additional year of training at Oxford after being accepted into the service in 1930. He was one of five Sudan Service probationers among sixty or so others bound for Africa territories. All of Bell's observations and self-characterizations were vigorously anti-romantic during this period. When the organizers of the course decided to train recruits in first aid and expose them to surgeries to ensure that they could deal with the blood and gore they might encounter in the field, Bell is quite happy to admit that he was 'overcome with nausea as soon as the knives got to work and obliged to lie on the floor of the operating theater to recover'.[56]

At the end of his year, he passed all of his exams (one of the five recruits didn't) and was, at age twenty-two, posted to south-eastern Sudan. In very short order, Bell was sent out on 'trek'. As a fledgling assistant district commissioner (ADC), he kept a running letter-diary for his parents. It is filled with descriptions of laying down a road or complaints about an insufficient well as he traversed a vast territory, oversaw infrastructure projects, adjudicated minor disputes and got to know the Sudanese. As he returned to headquarters, after five weeks of similarly mundane fare, he closed the diary with:

> The 8th of February then should see the travel worn and dusty caravan riding into Kassala with the setting sun turning the dust to powdered gold, etc, etc. The bronzed Empire builder mounted on his milk white racing camel salutes the first sight of the Union Jack – more etcs![57]

The CMGs with the authoritative moustaches were now the object of fun.

By the time he returned to the Sudan after his first leave, Bell's persona was fully invested in what he characterized as the appropriately 'modern' approach to colonialism. He railed against having to host the occasional 'explorers', passing through his territory with money and a desire for adventure. At one point, he complains to his parents, '3 more horrible explorers arrive tonight – they too want to "discover" Lake Tsana and Addis Ababa and they want 100 Abyssinians mules [to do it]! Where am I to get them 100 Abyssinian mules from?!'[58]

In addition to his ironic approach to his training and dismissal of imperial romance, many of his letters to his parents are filled with earnest concern once he was in the field. Foremost was his fear that he wouldn't be fluent in Arabic sufficiently to pass the exam that would end his probationary period. Bell's recollection of the training year included the same subjects that Rowe remembered from his earlier version, but Bell stressed that 'by far the most important of all the subjects which we were taught during that year was the language of the country where we were destined to serve'.[59] In his later memoir, Bell also recalls that a visiting lecturer during his training at Oxford stressed to him, 'You will be of little use in your job until you have mastered the language of your area sufficiently well to be able, as you walk through the village market, to set the merchants and bystanders guffawing with merriment.'[60] Once Bell was in the Sudan, he wasn't just anxious to find a tutor and practise his Arabic whenever possible because he was afraid his career plans would be thwarted if he didn't pass his exams. All of the work in the office, except correspondence, and all of an officer's interactions with the Sudanese were conducted in Arabic. He did pass his exams, but he also continued to be passionate about the language and observed that perhaps because Arabic was so difficult, it 'knocked some of the conceit out of' the British officials, making them less arrogant and more effective.[61] For Bell, unlike Thesiger, fluency in the language was central to effective administration.[62]

Bell expressed his good fortune in finding useful mentors. Martin Parr was a family friend who looked out for Bell in his first years. Unusual for the SPS, Parr was a vocal evangelist (*a la* Gordon). Perhaps because of his evangelism, he was stationed in the south for the majority of his career. He had a close relationship with the Christian Missionary Service, which only had permission to operate in the Southern provinces, under conditions of separate governance for the south, set down years earlier.[63] Parr's focus was on Bell's development as a good man. But Robin Bailey became a professional mentor, far more interested in government theory and the nitty-gritty of administration. Having joined the SPS during the war, he first arrived steeped in the romance of the soldier hero, then chafed at the old military model in the early 1920s, before being in a leadership position to demand better training for probationers as agriculture, infrastructure, health and education became more important.[64] And yet he was also drawn by the romance of the place. He tried to pass on to Bell how reconciling those competing impulses could create an effective officer in the SPS.

First of all, his advice was practical: 'You should call on [the] Nazir,' he wrote just before Bell took his first trek through the Ghash Grazing Area, 'and discuss with him where he would like you to go and what he thinks you should look out for particularly'.[65] Baily focused on the need to create practical relationships with Sudanese elites in keeping with Lugard's philosophy. He also signalled to Bell that the Sudanese knew more than he did. 'You should ensure liaison between his "retainer" patrol and yours. You will make yourselves word perfect over the regulation governing the use of patrols in this area.... You should take with you Acland's *Treatise on Camels*, a work crammed with information.'[66] Reliable, effective governments were only possible if strong personal relationships were backed up by objective knowledge.

Nevertheless, Baily also tells Bell to think of his first trek as his *Thousand and One Nights* adventure. He then explicitly adds, almost as an afterthought, that it wouldn't actually be a bad idea to learn the *Thousand and One Nights* by heart so that he can retell them to his 'campfire circle or under the shade of sumac trees'.[67] This combination of the practicalities of Acland's administrative notes (included in his treatise on camels) and the romance of the *Arabian Nights* articulates the in-betweenness that many of these officials navigated during this transitional period in the Sudan administration and which Bell was comfortable navigating – between the myth of the desert and the demands of development, the ideal of British expertise and the policy of Native Administration.

Bell's later descriptions of being on trek were focused on the Sudanese, his fear of failure and the mundane demands of his job. 'At each village there would be talk of the harvest, of the need to open a motor track or construct a river crossing. Trucks were beginning to take the place of camels as an economical means of transportation … There would be demands for a new … well, a dispensary.'[68] He never saw himself, 'likely to play a part of any significance in the development of the Empire'.[69] His conceptualization of his role as an administrator was undeniably paternalistic. But it was also rather realistic. 'Keeping the peace, developing local government, encouraging the spread of education, fostering economic development' were what he saw as his responsibilities.[70]

Bell's second posting took him to Talodi, in the Western Sudan where the Nuba people dominated. As he saw it, the anthropology lectures and methods he had been exposed to while in the training year were key to his ability to work well with the Nuba. He was not alone among the young recruits who saw anthropology as 'forming part of the business of administration,' even if they 'were all amateurs' who likely 'drew wrong conclusions from … the observations [they] made'.[71] In this same period, he remarked that one of his assigned Tropical Administration course texts, *Criminal Laws of India*, helped him set out the reasoning behind his findings in cases.[72] Bell drew a direct connection between aspects of his training – language, anthropology, jurisprudence – and his success on the job.

When Bell was coming to the end of his posting with the Nuba in Talodi, Thesiger was just starting his years among the Nuer in the next closest post, 150 miles to the south in the Upper Nile Province. It was 1937. E. Evans-Pritchard, who the next year would lecture to Paul Daniell, had just published his book on cultural practices among the nearby Azande.[73] After substantial fieldwork in the region during Thesiger's tenure there, he would write his three books on the Nuer.[74] A later generation of colonial administrator would read them as part of their administration course. Thesiger and Bell would never meet. But 1937 was a busy period for ironic coincidence because Bell did play host to Margery Perham.[75] Perham stayed with him for a few days during a research trip she was conducting as an observer on the De La Warr Commission on colonial education in East Africa and Sudan.[76] Bell described her as a consummate expert: 'informed, perceptive, sympathetic and stimulating'.[77] Bell and Daniell were likely to have both read the eventual report. No longer a colonial administrator by that point, Thesiger most definitely would not.

Part Two

Authoring the British-Sudani identity

5

Writing a new home

In 1932, Gawain Bell had been in his first posting as assistant district commissioner (ADC) in Gedaref, Kassala Province, for just a few months. Other than himself and another ADC named Evans, who had been there a year longer than he had, Sudan Defense Force officers constituted the rest of the British contingent in Gedaref. He and Evans were in the officers' mess, enjoying a drink and a chat before dinner one evening when the postbag arrived and, as he described the scene to his parents, 'What had been a cheerful and talkative company became for ½ an hour a completely silent gathering – everything [...] bridge, dinner and the gramophone had to wait until the post was read.'[1]

Across the geographical and occupational spectrum of the government, British administrators and their families expended huge amounts of time and emotional energy writing letters over the six decades of the Condominium. During the course of a twenty-five-year career, the typical official, who wrote each week to his parents, would have written them one thousand letters. Many, like Gawain Bell, wrote one or both of their parents far more often – sometimes twice or even three times a week. Officials and their wives also wrote to each other when separated; they wrote to each other's parents, to siblings, to friends and to their own children at school. Writing letters took time and effort, and so who wrote what, in what form and to whom were serious decisions.[2] Writers employed discursive strategies to cultivate, populate and maintain an epistolary Britain/Sudan space that was part of an ongoing preparation for their return.

Before the British-Sudani returned to Great Britain physically, their correspondence returned them there discursively again and again. Every week, sometimes more often, the British-Sudani arrived in Exeter, Aberdeen and Carlisle, through the mail slot. The mail was delivered twice daily. Ideally, their metropolitan partners wrote letters drawing them back to Britain while also travelling into the discursive space of the Sudan by asking questions, talking about an apropos book recently read or political events related to the region or the country. It was no exaggeration when Bell assured his parents that 'letters wait for nothing in the Sudan'.[3] With each exchange, both sides reaffirmed that British-Sudanis would be appreciated by and re-incorporated into their British community upon their return.[4]

Substantial research has been conducted on the epistolary strategies and forms for emigrant groups, ranging from the eighteenth through the twentieth centuries. With varying degrees of diligence, children and grandchildren in the adopted country, and parents and grandparents in the old, tried to maintain, over time, an epistolary version of familial relationships.[5] For the emigrant, the focus was the personal relationship that existed before the distance was put between them, wherever he or she was. Eric Richards points out in the case of Australian immigrant letters, there was a surprising lack of contextual content. Their letters de-emphasized the fact that they were in a new environment and commented little on their strange new world, in order to elide the distance. Nevertheless, it wasn't possible to deny the circumstances that made the letters necessary in the first place. Most immigrants' education level and socio-economic status made letter writing an extraordinary activity.[6] Their epistolary relationships only existed because of the distance between the correspondents, and the activity reinforced that distance.[7]

The epistolary relationship had very different underlying assumptions for the immigrant and the temporary colonial expatriate. British-Sudanis, for the most part, returned to the home country. Through their letters, the British-Sudani may have felt that by passing on news and gossip from 'home', their friends and families helped to keep them in Britain.[8] Their epistolary practices suggest, however, that their extensive correspondence was not an effort to remain but, rather, a form of returning that occurred, and recurred, long before their actual return took place.[9]

The first journey out to the Sudan and the first few months of acclimation constituted the first experiential milestone experienced away from 'home'. Then marriage (most British-Sudani married) symbolically marked the passage from youth to adulthood and, with the establishment of the marriage house, from visitor to resident.[10] These events, and the quotidian details of life in the Sudan, were commonly described in a cheery, neutral voice, suggesting these milestones and daily regimen were similar to life in Britain. By writing against the emotional impact of the content, they reduced the distance between their experiences and those of their audience and, in the process, mingled particular versions of Britain and the Sudan. Each became 'home', and each became a place that needed describing.[11] Their epistolic partnerships conflated two territories and two cultures. This began a pattern of strategic behaviour carried on throughout their lives, intended to insure that British-Sudanis would first be able to return to the 'home' culture and then seamlessly reincorporate themselves into it.[12]

This imagined space where Britain and the Sudan are equally knowable and familiar isn't really a British/Sudan hybrid because they aren't blended into one. More useful is a term borrowed from Homi Bhabha: a third space, which was neither Britain nor the Sudan, but in which both could be nearer to each other and be oneself in both places.[13] In this third space, where actual and experiential distance is shortened, the epistolary partners test the limits of knowing and understanding *despite* the incommensurability of their life experiences. The challenges of understanding – sometimes succeeding, sometimes failing – are seen as surmountable obstacles to communication and connection.[14]

These men (and later, women) first described efforts to acclimate to the Sudan. They then described their duties, living situations, budgets and surroundings. Nevertheless, it was extremely challenging for new arrivals to begin crafting a consistent narrative because they themselves lacked a clear understanding of their circumstances. We can see letter writers slowly working out for themselves the meaning of what it is that they're seeing and, through the process of writing, creating a narrative that is comprehensible to themselves as well as to their correspondents.

Sometimes, British-Sudanis failed to convince their British counterparts to participate and so the third space was never constructed. They exchanged pleasantries and managed the logistics of leaves and children's school holidays, but the distance between the two letter writers grew wider. British-Sudanis *were* leading extraordinary lives. There was a limit to what those back home understood and what British-Sudanis were willing, or able, to explain. Men and women who went to the Sudan had to live and write within a paradox: they wanted to experience a different kind of life but didn't want that difference to make them unsuitable to return.

Letter-writing technologies and their meanings

Even in the earliest period of the Condominium, prior to and including the First World War, its geographical proximity to Britain meant mail service could be quick – a letter from Khartoum could reach London in ten days.[15] But outside the capital, limitations and disruptions to corresponding caused by weather, road conditions, river height or the reach of the railway reinforced British memory of Gordon's isolation. In 1916–17, Lt. Col. S. T. Austin travelled up the Nile to Wau, the most far-flung outpost in the south-west, and was eventually stationed with the 14th Sudanese Regiment (and their families) beyond Wau, spending his time combating the slave trade and small pox. He remembered 'a post once a month ... letters being brought by native runner from Wau, which took 12–14 days according to the time of year ... It usually took 6 months for a reply to a letter to England'.[16] The *Sudan Almanac* warned staff in Austin's time that 'boats run ... when Sobat River is high enough', and 'Wau is only open to parcel service when the Jur River is open (approximately 1st June – 31st July).'[17]

The journey taken by Austin's correspondence was also a reliable measurement of British control of the Sudan. In 1916, he was the military arm of a barely present civilian administration. He was expected to represent the Sudan government, despite the fact that he was as distant from the centre of the nascent Sudan state as could be in terms of oversight and was performing tasks that were only half-heartedly supported from Khartoum. Active administration in the south-west certainly did not extend beyond Wau, and even there was tenuous at best. The forces of nature in the southern Sudan had yet to succumb to 'modernization', even at the behest of the British Empire and even in 1916.[18] Before a letter was opened, how long someone had to wait for it could either confirm or undermine British imaginings of life in the Sudan.[19]

In 1932, Gedaref, where Bell was stationed in Kassala Province, received mail once a week. In the 1910s, the mail was carried from Khartoum by donkey on a five-day journey in each direction, but by 1932, Gedaref was on the Kassala rail line.[20] The post schedule between Khartoum and London was three times a week. If the mail left Khartoum on Sunday it arrived in London ten days later on a Wednesday.[21] In reverse, someone in Gedaref commonly had to wait three or four weeks to receive a letter from

England. An improvement on Austin's experience, but still slow. In the later years of the Condominium, the comparative speed and reach of the postal service due to airmail may have created the opposite illusion, of geographic proximity. Weekly flights, connecting at Cairo, began in 1933 and reduced the Khartoum to London leg of the journey by eight days.[22] By 1941, there were twice-weekly flights,[23] and by 1953, daily flights to London were the usual mode of mail transport rather than a special expense.[24] Nevertheless, even once the transportation and communication infrastructure was at its most extensive, the mail still arrived in Kassala Province once a week, just as it had for ADC Bell twenty years earlier.[25]

In the first half of the twentieth century the letter, airmail letter, postcard, telegraph, note and package were all common forms of communication and people specifically chose one over another in different circumstances and content could be signalled based simply on which technology was being employed.[26] Once regular airmail service had been established in the 1930s, all-in-one, onion paper AIR MAIL letters became the norm. Persis Aglen, whose husband Peter was the DC in El Fasher, Darfur, was an expert at filling every possible bit of open space, writing sideways and around the edges, so that it was almost impossible to pick out the mailing address from the text around it. El Fasher would have been a distant outpost before airmail. In 1946, Aglen's sister, Grizel Warner, could be sure to get a letter in London six days after it was sent. But the barber's pole-edged airmail envelopes still highlighted the distance between Aglen and Warner, even as their banter and the air route shortened the miles that separated them.[27]

Austin employed a different writing strategy to mask that distance by writing much longer letters, in the form of a diary, that were only sent occasionally. 'I intend writing a little each day while I am travelling [*sic*]; a kind of diary of what happens.'[28] Before airmail service, letters written every few days or once a week would all be sent in the same mailbag, perhaps once a month, and arrive altogether. The decision to communicate through letter-diaries helped to disguise how remote the official's location was. Nevertheless, the letter-diary itself was almost always going to accidentally echo Gordon and his journals.

The content of Austin's letters *is* all about progress. He draws maps of his routes that create the illusion of control and predictability. He provides (rather boring) accounts of the movements of the 14th Sudanese and their activities – much like Douglas's and Bell's domestic descriptions. Austin was likely sanitizing his descriptions of ongoing 'pacification' campaigns undertaken in this region, which were often brutal and unsuccessful. In his descriptions, modern methods were being introduced to backwards populations. He seems genuinely proud of the inoculation campaigns against small pox.[29] Even the coded language that he uses to describe efforts to deal with the slave trade, while under strict instructions to leave practices of slavery untouched, still follows a narrative of progress.[30] But the pace of his exchange with family back home is a constant measure of how far away he is. The content might focus on the arrival of modernity to the southern Sudan, but the pace of the mail and the journal style remind the reader of Gordon and the 'Darkest Africa' of an earlier era.

In 1939, John Winder, a DC writing from the more remote regions of Upper Nile Province, apologizes to his fiancée for taking so long to respond to her letters, explaining, 'I have located the mail at last, though it has still to reach me. It had been running all round the country in a merchant's lorry and missed me once or twice.'[31] His job required trekking across vast territory so that even airmail couldn't find him quickly. For John Winder, the letter was even an animate object, 'running all round the country', actively seeking to connect the two writers.

The 'Bog Barons' of the south – those isolated and self-isolating holdovers from Kitchener and Windgate's era – die out just as airmail service arrives.[32] But airmail did not necessarily tie the south more to Khartoum. J. I. Parry, a missionary for many years in the south and connected to the Sudan Government Medical Service there, was separated for years from his family during the Second World War. After a lengthy mail delay, he discovered that 'all our mails, airmails as well, are held up at Lagos in West Africa because the planes are doing rather more important things'.[33] Parry learned that the chain of communication went through Lagos to London, rather than through Khartoum. For officials in outlying districts, southern or elsewhere, the distance from superiors in Khartoum might have well seemed pretty much the same as the distance from family in Derbyshire or Aberdeen. Winder, for example, worked and lived isolated from other Britons. He wrote to his wife in extreme detail about his work and counted on her to provide input. When the mail *did* find him, when he was at his administrative base in Pibor, Upper Nile Province, he might receive a response from her about some aspect of his work as promptly, or even more so, than from a ministry office in Khartoum.

Bridget Acland remembers being with her husband Peter in Geneina, in Darfur, when Imperial Airways began regular air service across Africa in 1935. 'It made a very big difference getting our airmail letters from England in such a short time,' she writes. But it also meant that 'Peter felt almost too close to Sudan Government HQ!'[34] Acland had been in distant outposts with her husband since they were married in 1927 and they enjoyed the physical isolation, in part because, as she points out, her husband could keep his distance from the politics and oversight of Khartoum. But their limited ability to communicate with England was a hardship.

Homemaking

British-Sudanis began writing home before they even arrived in the Sudan. They describe the trials and tribulations of getting passage on a ship from Liverpool, Edinburgh, Plymouth or Newcastle, or of finding one's way by train and ferry to Paris, to catch a train to Marseilles and boat passage to Africa from there.[35] Staff were given an allowance for their travel to and from the Sudan. It wasn't particularly generous; new probationers would have travelled third class to Egypt and then second class to Khartoum.[36] Even after years in the service, two weeks' travel to Khartoum invited a lot of letter writing; the journey was meticulously documented with an almost ritualistic regularity, as if it helped the British-Sudani to re-acclimate. They wrote gossipy letters recounting who was on the boat, what the amenities were like and anything of tourist interest.[37] Jock Miller, who first arrived in 1920 and would eventually rise to be finance secretary, describes his first journey to his parents. 'The boat is really very nice – bar the crowd – and we the Sudany quartet are lounging together,' in a way that allows him to claim membership in a community before he had even reported for duty.[38] Some ships, such as the P&O line ships, berthed people from the same service together, sharing the same second-class saloon, so the trip became a time to catch up with old friends, help new probationers and wives, and get a perspective on events and departments throughout the Sudan.[39] Officials and their wives entered the cultural territory of the British Sudan territory before they entered the actual geographic space.

In their early correspondence, sharing their initial impressions with their families was a low-risk way for probationers to begin their own Sudan narrative. Men like Bell could already be experts on the Sudan in the pages they wrote home. And by providing such rich descriptions of their new lives, they demand that their families take a virtual journey with them. As Elizabeth MacArthur explains, banal, domestic details have greater importance in the initial stages of a correspondence, 'as a means of marking the separation of their textual relationship from the outside world or other correspondences and as a means of stabilizing the exchange'.[40] The logical place to begin was with the domestic situation.

Scholarship has explored how homosocial culture was often romanticized in the imperial setting. Discussion continues as to the real and the rhetorical impact that the arrival of European women had on the nature of administrators' behaviour and policies.[41] Although Governor General Reginald Wingate's own wife travelled and lived with him in Cairo and Khartoum during his tenure from 1900–1916, there were official and unofficial bars to wives in more distant postings until well into the 1920s. And officers were not allowed to marry before completing two years of service.

All of this would suggest domestic arrangements would not figure prominently in correspondence until after these men get married. Nevertheless, these men were very keen to talk about their homes, furnishings, budgets, servants and efforts at hosting social events. Whether in the formally structured communities of Khartoum (the capital), Atbara (the railway hub) and Port Sudan (the main port), or in more distant reaches, new arrivals and seasoned veterans spend huge amounts of narrative energy on descriptions of their domestic situation, from the earliest day of the Wingate era, all the way to independence.

In Britain, a young man setting up house for himself would have given his parents a tour of his new digs. From the Sudan, one of the earliest efforts to bridge the distance was a virtual tour that would take the place of a parental visit. When Bell moves into his first house in Gedaref, he sends his parents both a floor plan and a sketch he has done, and while he admits, 'It is not a beautiful house, as no doubt you will have guessed,' he also proclaims, ' I think I am almost "house proud"!'[42] He apologizes and enthuses in equal measure. 'At present I haven't many comforts except the bath which is the best in Gedaref. I possess a desk and a chair and a native bed – left by my predecessor – a settee – very good with cushions £1 (very antique) … tables and a vast kind of book-case – quite the size of the one in the study where I keep my clothes.' By referencing a specific piece of furniture in his family home (the bookcase) and describing it in the present tense ('where I keep my clothes') he signals that their home is still his and he plans to return to it, even as he builds a new one in the Sudan.[43] Over the next few letters he keeps them up to date on his furniture purchases and the items he has ordered to be made. The carpenter gets a name – Ahmed Balal – and the furniture order grows. Balal eventually produces 'a dining room table – a sideboard – a book-case – a place for hanging suits and shelves in [the] kitchen' and the home furnishing enterprise gets a price tag – £5.[44]

Within a few weeks Bell declares, 'I am beginning to experience "the Everyman's house is his castle" feeling.'[45] Of course, his 'castle' is a little bit different than the bachelor flats of his contemporaries in Britain. For him, there is a cook and a *suffragi* (butler/housekeeper) but there is also no running water, no electricity, and at night, it's the British-Sudani practice to sleep on the roof under mosquito netting to escape the heat. There is a strategy in his writing of including the similarities and excising the differences. Does Bell provide the details and assurances to comfort the parents who are unable to have first-hand experience of their son's rite of passage? Or is he, himself, not able to imagine having these experiences without his parents' involvement? Both motivations are quite possibly coexisting in his and others' detailed, descriptions as an early attempt to furnish the third space – beginning, logically enough, with the literal furnishings.

Bell's enthusiasm for domestic details is not unusual among the newly arrived even though probationary officers are setting up house at the same time as they are taking up their duties, meeting other Britons, interacting with the Sudanese for the first time, and experiencing the climate and landscape. There is a strong focus on the domestic in many recent arrivals' correspondence despite these other subjects competing for their attention and for space in their letters. Like Bell, DC Allen Arthur, who was transferred from the Indian Service after independence, focuses on the details of setting up house but in his case, he is describing to his Anglo-Indian parents the differences between his domestic arrangements in the Sudan and India, rather than England. The shortcomings are not papered over nor are similarities to *English* home life accentuated. It seems that in their case, Arthur and his parents are creating a space of shared exile, rather than belonging. 'The house is certainly small, a drawing room and dining room and one bedroom with a large bathroom with long bath, hand basin and shower, kitchen, stove and a room on the verandah where I store all my boxes.'[46] This 'small' house is being compared to his Indian accommodations, and his parents are probably feeling the same way about their new home in England, where life might be feeling a bit cramped and grey after India, and the complaints that Allen makes tie his experiences to theirs.

He doesn't want to be too critical of the Sudan government; after all, he made the decision to join it and, even in 1947, thinks that he will be serving in the Sudan for a long time to come. Furthermore, he's engaged and this house will be the one that his new bride will call home. So he concedes, '[The house] is well built and will do us very well to start with but,' he can't help but add, 'it is absurd that the DC has no official house. As I am a new arrival and must mind my ps and qs I can not kick up a fuss'. Here, in his first posting in Omdurman, as in other places, officials rent their houses but from a list of available, sanctioned candidates. 'The garden is also small, but is being improved.'[47] His lack of control over housing and the fact that he must curb his desire to complain is occurring at the same time that his parents would be dealing with continued rationing in England, a similarly small garden, perhaps, as well as the decisions of a Labour government that they might find just as absurd as he finds things in the Sudan. Unfortunately, we can't know whether his tone was encouraged by a similar one in his parents' letters. But they were multi-generational Anglo-Indian up to this point. So the epistolary space that they are collaborating on is most certainly one in which Britain and the Sudan are both degrees of *foreign* rather than familiar.

Ian Douglas was a new arrival in the Audit Department, one of the practical branches of the government, in 1925, when he wrote describing his home and locating it within the Khartoum cityscape so that his sister could picture the scene. Douglas, feeling sorry for himself because he's stuck at home, nursing a bad cold, has the time to describe the scene to 'Duck' and, through discursive choices, draw her nearer to him. 'I'm sitting in the sun in our "garden" at the moment. This consists of a small brick tiled yard about 3ft above the level of the road. There are four small trees which greatly enhance the appearance of the place.' Written in the present tense, she sees with him what he describes. 'The road is a highway to + from [*sic*] the market but there is no wheeled traffic just donkeys with paniers + camels. There are, of course, an enormous number of donkeys here.'[48] Douglas's regular interjection of 'of course' invites her to become as nonchalant as he is about what have only very recently become everyday sights to him. 'The camel of course is a more expensive animal … A string of seven with loads of wood went by about a couple of minutes ago. The chief things one sees going by are onions, tomatoes, beans … lemons + sacks of durra (sort of maize).'[49] The street scene he is describing is a study in the everyday. Nursing a cold in his garden while watching the farmers' bringing their goods to the local market could be happening in Kent, except that his tableau includes camels. Along with the studied nonchalance, there are also hints of anxiety and homesickness, as everything is strange enough to warrant being recorded and shared with 'Duck'.

Many of these men and women felt compelled to provide visual aids to their family and friends in order to bring them into the territory they inhabit. When, in 1916, Lt. Col. Austin spent two years in military operations in the south-western Bahr al-Gezel Province, he sent his family maps of his routes, making it appear as if it was a manageable – and managed – territory.[50] In that early era, the southern boundary of the Sudan was contested, and the source of certain rivers still unknown. But Austin's map assures his family that he can be located, within British space. Similarly, Bell's sketch of the outside of his home in Gedaref, as seen from the road, allows his parents to approach his front door, at least in a virtual world, like regular visitors. And then the floor plan he provides also lets them come inside and walk around the space.[51] ADC John Kenrick, who spent his early years in the south, devised complicated diagrams of his territory and drawings of its inhabitants.[52] He doesn't have faith in the descriptive power of his prose. The postcard was also a popular choice of the reticent writer or the inadequate artist. The Karakashian Bros., merchants in Khartoum, did an extremely brisk business in postcards, very few of which seem to have actually been used as postcards. Many of the photo album collections in the Sudan Archive include postcards never written on or stamped or mailed. Presumably they were sent home with letters to give family and friends a better understanding of the people, landscape and architecture when the senders didn't think they could capture a better image themselves.[53] Nothing could replace the personal, however. As Elizabeth Buettner notes in her examination of long-distance family communications among Anglo-Indians, 'Photographs served not only as images that might underscore unfamiliarity but also as tangible, fetishized, material substitutes for those who were absent.'[54]

Many daily activities were also mapped out, in a way. As well as drawing a picture of home, or the street, or the Sudanese, the need to provide in excruciating detail the rundown of a 'typical day' is a recurring trope of new arrivals, the newly affianced or the newly transferred. Bell needs to tell his parents, 'I wake at 6 and am brought tea and biscuits – I ride from 6:30–7:30,' by which he means an inspection tour around the town, in uniform.

> At 8 I breakfast – fruit porridge and eggs generally. 9–2 is spent in the office and then lunch – cold soup – cutlets and vegetables perhaps … Then I read and sometimes but not often I sleep – at 4:30 I ride again (in mufti this time and often in shorts) or if it's a polo day, polo begins at 4:15. By 6 it is nearly dark and I have my tea in the garden followed by a pipe – then a bath … and usually I work at my Arabic until dinner at 8. I turn in as a rule about 9:30.[55]

Just like Douglas with his onions and beans, Bell finds the compulsive detailing necessary precisely because of the distance between him and his parents. He must negate the differences between his version of everyday life and theirs so that he can create a space within the correspondence where particular versions of Britain and the Sudan cohabitate, and the participants can coexist in each other's lives. It is possible that these extremely pedantic passages could simply be the writing of very boring correspondents, except that elsewhere most show an obvious flare. So, in these instances, their quotidian plodding on the page is a choice rather than an example of bad writing.

Friends and family

Typically, as men and women got older, married and had children of their own, the pace of their correspondence slackened. On the other hand, particularly for women, being married meant that they often had to write letters to in-laws as well. One parent was often designated as the primary epistolic partner in a continuation of the metropolitan family dynamics predating their time in the Sudan. Comments about how friends are doing pop up fairly regularly, signalling that at least some Anglo-Sudanis were able to keep up relationships with their contemporaries back home, as well, and that family helped maintain relationships with metropolitan friends on British-Sudanis' behalf.

Many address their letters to 'The Folks', or to both parents, or ask that their letters be passed around. This suggests that the writer in the Sudan was envisioning a community of people in Britain who accepted the invitation to occupy the shared space that was hopefully being created. Persis Anglen tells her sister that she 'wrote to Mummie an account of our Jebel Marra trip'. This is a dramatic volcanic mountain range that looms up to the west of El Fasher, in Darfur, where Persis and her husband, Peter, are stationed. But she goes on to explain that 'in case you would like to see it I have asked her to send it to you as I will not have time to write about it to you separately'.[56] Turning communication into a collective enterprise is a time-and-effort saving device. When Austin explained that he is going to write 'a kind of diary of what happens,' it is expressly because he wants it to 'be shown to anyone in the family as it's rather a big thing to write anything like fully to several people'.[57] But it also helps to create a standard narrative and to reinforce the collective nature of the family dynamic. If Aglen or Austin wrote separate accounts to everyone, it would atomize the group into a series of one-on-one relationships.

It is not remarkable that, over the years, parents would become familiar with the cast of characters. Bell is deft at creating a correlative to his peers' experiences in England, which his parents can appreciate. He facetiously reminds his parents in one letter, 'I spoke when I last wrote of the social whirl in Gedaref... 3 dinner parties and 2 native tea parties in less than a week left one feeling one was living in Mayfair Society'.[58] Providing updates to his contemporaries' life choices, Bell also keeps his parents connected to people they no longer see, now that he is gone. Comparing himself to such a friend from home, who was about to set out for '5 years in China... and [who] seemed quite cheerful about it', he also likely wishes to remind them that they will see him far sooner.[59]

Bell makes sure to update his perceptions of his Sudan government colleagues to his parents. He's generally fairly generous. And as with most young men, he's eager to find mentors. Bell is lucky enough to have a few, including Martin Parr, who become so familiar to the Bell family that he writes confidential letters updating them on their son's welfare.[60] And, of course, Robin Baily. When Baily is transferred and his replacement, in a rather confusing turn of events, is another Evans, Bell takes to calling his fellow ADC, 'Evans minor', and his DC, 'Evans major' for his parents' benefit, because he wants to be able to gossip with ease and clarity. In his first assessment of the couple, Bell writes home that Evans minor 'is... inclined... I feel to hurry and fuss... but he is very pleasant and anxious that we should all live happily together. He has a wife – they've been married a year – I think she feels she's rather a dazzler and very dangerous – I don't think I agree! Still as I said they are very friendly and kind'.[61] Unfortunately, that is the limit of Bell's kind words about her.

The friends and co-workers who populated people's lives become such regular characters that readers back in Britain are soon intimately familiar with them, their personalities and their back stories, joined in a virtual community that reinforced the possibility of a Britain/Sudan space in which distance and difference were erased. As the years go on, the British counterpart comes to be an expert.[62] Engineer Brian Storrar, who served in the Sudan Railways for more than two decades, oversaw the construction of the entire transportation system. He was a dedicated letter-diarist and photographer. A member of one of the practical branches rather than the SPS, his writings illustrate many habits and dynamics that were common across the entire British-Sudani community. If one were to read his record of these years, the cast of characters would be entirely British, in speaking roles, with a vast pool of extras made up entirely from the Sudanese population. Storrar was not inclined to political or diplomatic analysis, so what he recorded and provided for those back in Scotland were the day-to-day activities of an officer fulfilling practical requirements dictated from above.

Although he lived along what would become the main transportation route of Khartoum-Atbara-Port Sudan, and during most of his career had a house in either Atbara or Port Sudan, Storrar wrote in the letter-diary style that men in far-flung posts adopted and, like others, assumed that his letters, and the photos that accompanied them, would be passed around and read by people sharing varying degrees of intimacy with him.[63] At least in the early years, Storrar actually lived out of a railway car, sidetracked at whatever point on the line his engineers and labourers were working. But later, once he became a senior engineer in the civil service, he didn't leave the cities and the cast of characters around him became quite stable. Letter-diaries now included events such as the very first *thé dansée* held in Atbara, which Storrar also dutifully photographed.[64]

As opposed to Political Service, other service posts were seldom lonely because the practical administration was concentrated in the transportation and communications hubs and officers didn't get transferred at the rate of the SPS. So Storrar spent years surrounded by the same officials and their families. He watched children grow up, attended parties and threw some himself. Hugely house-proud, when he finally got to settle down, he sent many pictures back home to 'The Folks'. And the detailed accounts of all of these things slowly accrued so that he eventually stopped explaining who anyone was in his correspondence, unless they were new.

He, like Bell, seemed to have the same compulsion to share everything, even the details of preparing for and travelling on his leave, which meant that he would probably arrive in Scotland at the same time as his letter. But the only companions on the journey he gives any introduction to are those from outside his Sudan circle, therefore, outside his family's virtual circle.[65] The casual way that Storrar assumes his readers' knowledge, and writes his letter-diary as a diary that those at home can feel they are completely partaking of, is worth quoting at length.

> On Thursday, lunched at the Fyers with Claxton. Cochrane and he have just returned from their trip to Cairo, and the former has brought a little two-seater motor car back with him, and Claxton ran me over to the Sports Club after lunch in it, where I played squash with Knollys, Fisher and Waterfield.
>
> On Friday, I had lunch with the Drapers, and spent the afternoon there, and Junter coming in in the evening, we played bridge.
>
> Spent Saturday after-noon at the club, (Ladies' Day), and went to the Fyers farewell dinner at the hotel. There was a huge crowd there far more than one would think could be raised in Port Sudan. There were 34 all told, and I shall give a list of them so as to keep a record of it. Mr. and Mrs. Fyers, Major and Mrs. Wilson, Mr. and Mrs. Matthew, Mr. and Mrs. Wilkinson, Mr. and Mrs. Draper, Mr. and Mrs. Bates, four Manchester officers, Mackay, Knollys, Joyce, Havercroft, Hunter, Beilby, Claxton, Smith, Fisher, Bennett, Waterfield, Cochrane, Robinson, Laxton, Boxall, Cheesman, Osborne and myself. We had a very jolly evening dancing and playing bridge.[66]

Conclusion

Eric Richards points out that in the nineteenth-century Australian case, 'Migrants normally focused on their immediate circumstances. They were hardly likely to discourse on Malthusian pressures or income differentials at large in the world economy' and in some way the same can be said of the British-Sudani.[67] Their interests and their outlook were parochial, bounded, for most, by the borders of Great Britain and the Sudan. Nevertheless, unlike the typical migrants whose correspondence Richards and others have examined, the British-Sudani were highly educated and, as we will see in the next chapter, extremely interested in creating a cosmopolitan epistolary space for themselves and their British counterparts to occupy and adept at deploying discursive strategies to aid that project.

6

Writing to return home

While British-Sudanis offered detailed accounts of life in the Sudan, every choice of what to include and what to leave out turned the writer into an editor, but not necessarily an intentional dissembler. As David Gerber has aptly expressed in reference to the personal narratives of British emigrants to America, one must have sympathy for the absent individual's struggle 'between faithfulness and narrative truth, on the one hand, and absolute honesty and forthrightness, on the other hand'.[1] British-Sudanis and their epistolary partners back in Britain deployed strategies to cultivate a virtual space in which Britain and the Sudan are comprehensible and even familiar to both participants and in which a sense of proximity depends upon the selective arranging, exaggerating and eliding of certain details. As Macarthur points out, 'Letter writers do not merely reproduce the sentiments they feel and the events they observe; they transform them, whether consciously or unconsciously, into written texts whose organization, style, vocabulary, and point of view generate particular meanings.'[2] Given the general skill level of the writers, we should question whether these are unintentional or subconscious discursive strategies. 'Letter writers inevitably construct personae for themselves as they write, and if they are involved in a regular exchange they construct personae for the correspondent and plots for the story of the relationship as well.'[3] Therefore, the epistolary project was the creation of a mise en scène that these personae could inhabit, a middle territory, neither British nor Sudanese, where neither of them was 'away' or 'home'.[4]

A successful epistolic collaboration involved the appropriation of a particular role by each person. Elizabeth Macarthur talks about the existence of 'models' of behaviour or identity, which participants in long-term correspondence take on and act out. 'They become co-authors of a narrative in which they, or rather epistolary constructions of themselves, also play the leading roles.'[5] These models help to create a stable epistemological world in which both sides understand their obligations, not only to each other but to the correspondence as a creation.[6] Each side took on the role of the involved loved one, and a key responsibility of that role was to discursively reduce the distance between the two countries.

The dedicated 'British' writers showed an unflagging interest in the life that their sons, daughters, friends were leading in the Sudan. This signalled their enthusiasm and support and their acknowledgement that the Sudan life was 'extraordinary'. Meanwhile, British-Sudani' letters continued to demand the details of the life that they left behind. This, in turn, reinforced the value that they placed on those who remained in Britain and the 'ordinary' life there.[7] In this way, they maintained a domestic narrative that included them and that could easily be taken up by them later, because the writers in the Sudan wanted to reserve their right to return by continuing to participate, however vicariously, in their old life or the life that they would have led. In Britain, this ongoing epistolary return brought with it an accruing knowledge about the Sudan that became a kind of experience in itself.

The exchange had a rhythm and a presence in people's lives in the same way that a regular Sunday dinner engagement at one's parents' house or a regular lunch with friends might.[8] But unlike in those social encounters, the vicarious experiencers of the Sudan were, first and foremost, women. Mothers were more likely to keep up the parental end of family correspondence.[9] Sisters, girlfriends and, when separated, wives wrote more often than brothers and male friends. Women were also more likely to pass their son or brother's letters around to their female friends and relatives. So there developed a small but not insignificant female metropolitan population that actively participated in the dissemination of information and the creation of a space in which the British-Sudani were always present.[10]

Sharing culture

British-Sudanis typically arrived in the Sudan when they were in their twenties. Had they stayed in Britain, this would have been the decade when they were most likely to be avid consumers of entertainment; the latest movies, music, theatre and books would not have gone unnoticed, unattended or undiscussed. Even if it means being told about events that they can't possibly attend, many British-Sudani encourage their people back in the metropole to continue describing them. Cultural touchstones are used as markers of proximity. Ian Douglas, soon after arriving to work in the Audit Department, thanks his sister, Duck, for her 'description of St. Joan, which [he] found exceedingly interesting'. She had been to see George Bernard Shaw's groundbreaking play, in which Joan, who had just been made a saint by the Catholic Church in 1920, is instead a fully human, flawed and wilful young woman. Douglas admits, 'I'm quite heartbroken that I won't be able to see it myself.'[11] But he in no way discourages her from continuing to fill him in on the latest diversions available to her back in London. Young British-Sudanis wanted to remain immersed in metropolitan culture as much as possible for as long as possible.

Arriving six years after Douglas, Gawain Bell asked his parents to get him subscriptions to the weekly *Times*, which was a staple of the British-Sudani community, at least where it could arrive in a timely fashion. But he also wanted *The Listener*, which was the guide and companion to all BBC domestic programming, none of which he had access to until the World Service started the following year.[12] The majority of the British in the Sudan – who were not living in isolated posts – were not starved for word from back home or denied certain trappings of British middle-class life, such as the paper.

Daniell highlights the exotic nature of Khartoum's outdoor cinema.

> Never before have I seen such a strange and yet comfortable motion picture house as tonight here in Khartoum. Open to the sky, the moon and the stars shone down on our box where we sat in wicker chairs with our feet up on the bar in front and whiskey sodas at our elbows, chewing peanuts and watching the film *Elephant Boy*. An experience in itself worth the 3000–4000 miles.[13]

But Daniell was also signalling that he wasn't so far away that he couldn't participate in current cultural experiences – *Elephant Boy* had only been released in Britain the previous year. Bell recounted a similar visit to the Khartoum cinema on his way through town a few years earlier, in 1932, when the theatre burned down. 'On our arrival', he writes, 'a few thin wisps of smoke rising from the embers told us that a fire has destroyed it all'. For Bell, this story of visiting the cinema is about difference, rather than similarity. 'The people seem to take these things very calmly. "It was the will of Allah." But rather inconsiderate of him I thought as the film was to feature the great Greta Garbo.'[14]

Despite being unable to listen to them, his subscription to *The Listener* enabled Bell to write to his parents just a few weeks later about radio talks that Harold Nicholson had been giving about the state of modern literature, transcripts of which had been reproduced in the magazine. Bell *fils* is able to reference metropolitan events, like Nicholson's talks, to engage with his father. 'I think [Nicholson's talks] … are rather good', Bell tells his father. 'He says we are approaching a turning point in English literature – the modern writers are the last of a series of reactionary waves … in the near future [there will be] a reaction back to an earlier style and reaction against "All this stupid modern sex nonsense."'[15] The quote at the end is Bell's ventriloquism of his father's opinion. Bell's conversations with his father are classic generational and cultural debates. But Bell is also relaying metropolitan information that originated there. He is in the Sudan but participating in British culture simultaneously.

Robin Baily, who would later become Bell's senior officer and mentor, annihilated time and distance by taking on the roles of both his father and mother when penning imagined conversations. He signals that he doesn't need to be in the room with them physically to know what they would say after reading his letter. In 1919, he wrote to let them know that his leave was delayed because of political unrest and violence related to the question of Egyptian independence. Baily takes on both voices, writing,

> 'Oh, but I say!' 'Dem the boy!' … 'It's all the fault of our stinking politicians!'
> 'Sh! Father dear, "nasty", if you like, but not "stinking".'
> 'I don't believe the boy wants to come home. He likes his black wives and porcupines better than his poor old parents.'[16]

He imagines his closeness to them, overhearing their conversation, while at the same time, he imagines their complete misapprehensions about his imperial life with 'black wives and porcupines' and, as a result, gets at the anxiety underlying so much of their epistolary project: that their life experiences have rendered them incompatible with metropolitan society. Baily, of course, is also writing this at the beginning of the transitional period from military to civilian, and personal to bureaucratic, style within the Sudan government. Even though the administration was modernizing and university-educated men implementing economic development programmes were replacing military men suppressing the slave trade, correspondence partners in the metropole were getting little or no counter-narrative to the one created by Henty or Kipling twenty years earlier. So Baily is using his father's voice to vent his frustrations about leave, but also the gap between metropolitan misapprehensions about his life in the Sudan.

The metropolitan writers were predominantly women. They were equal participants with the British-Sudani, incorporating information, opinion and gossip from their lives. This third space, that these epistolary exchanges positioned discursively somewhere between Britain and the Sudan, was a hybrid space whose symbolic construction was both extra-domestic and yet feminized.[17] In a way, these women went out to the imperial setting as well as making room for it back home.[18] Additionally, in the case of wives and husbands separated from each other, the feminized discursive space was the intimate space of marriage. Separated by the war, J. W. E. (Jock) Miller, financial comptroller, wrote lengthy and extremely explicit letters to his wife in England in which he imagined them together, explicitly as a result of letter-writing.

> You are constantly in my thoughts and I am always stopping to think what you would think. What you would wish me to do. And so I feel that really we are not so far away and that love makes a bridge of thought – a kind of mental telephone … How I hope that it may be so with you too, love: that these letters may make you feel the love and longing that is constantly going out from me.[19]

The intended or expected audience might have influenced the content of the letters coming out of the Sudan, and so it must be remembered that this female network may have influenced what version of the Sudan was exported to Britain in this fashion. However, family dynamics and specific personalities seem to be more influential.[20] Robin Baily, in the SPS from 1909 to 1933, often wrote separate letters to his father and his mother about the same event; however, there is very little difference in their content and even less difference in their tone.[21] A family culture that inculcated a greater sense of adventure or was more outward looking, even in subtle ways, might have influenced those who chose a life in the service of Empire and resulted in less of a difference in the content of the correspondence based upon the sex of the recipient.

In DC Allan Arthur's correspondence, we can see how the frequency of the letter-writing creates the illusion that the participants are in close proximity. Allan Arthur wrote to his fiancée every second day until their marriage in 1949 when she came out to the Sudan. She wrote to him daily. His mother wrote twice a week and his father once, and he responded to them collectively, usually once a week. This volume of letter-writing was not at all unusual, and it meant that the correspondence took on more of the attributes of a conversation than a correspondence.

Persis Anglen and her sister, Grizel Warner, engaged in an amazingly dense and distance-erasing correspondence aided, as mentioned earlier, by the all-in-one airmail letter and extremely neat and tiny penmanship. But they had no need to resort to the discursive strategy of taking on all sides of the relationship. The two women bridge the gap in part with the aid of shared cultural interests, like Bell and Douglas do with their family correspondents. Anglen reminds her sister, after Warner describes a trip to visit some churches, that they had previously visited one of them together. She then goes on to connect this very English pastime, driving in the country to look at picturesque churches, with her community in the Sudan.

> Jimmy Burridge who is ADC to the Governor in headquarters is very interested in Romanesque Architecture and has lent me an enormous tome on the Romanesque Architecture of the Order of Cluny by a woman called Joan Evans. I wonder if you know of her? It is a tremendously documented work and I know too little in the first place to get full value from it but it has magnificent photographs.[22]

In a couple of sentences, Anglen has travelled back to England, then back to the Sudan. In the process she has pointed out that even separated by thousands of miles, she and her sister have actually been occupied by the same cultural interest at roughly the same time.

The third space created in the sisters' correspondence is one where they can also exercise the expertise that they have accrued but that they haven't got credentials for, because officially they are simply their husbands' consorts. In one exchange, Aglen responds to the news that Warner is reading *Arabia and the Isles*, a best-seller that Warner is primarily drawn to because her husband is working in the Middle East Bureau at the Foreign Office, and her sister is living in the Sudan. The author, Harold Ingrams, was a noted diplomat, but the book is mainly about his travels with his wife, Doreen, in an isolated region of the Aden Protectorate in the 1930s. Doreen Ingram had quite famously spent the last two years of the war establishing hospitals and famine relief centres. Aglen tells her sister that she enjoyed the book as well but then goes on to offer a bit of local gossip. 'Those who know him say he is not a very pleasant person and that his wife is the really able one of the pair.' She goes on to disclose, 'Evidently H.I. thinks a good deal of himself.'[23] In hindsight, her sources seem to have been reliable. Doreen Ingram's own *Survey of Social and Economic Conditions in the Aden Protectorate*, published in 1949, was a best-seller and was followed by a lengthy resume of related accomplishments.

In many letters, there is an almost ritualistic rhythm to the give and take of expressing interest and responding to expressions of interest, acknowledging each other's areas of expertise and deflecting suggestions of one's own. These sisters are extremely expert at the smooth transition from one mode to the other, so that their letters truly take on the cadence of a conversation. When Sir Robert Howe became governor general in 1947, Warner asked Aglen what she thought of the man, thereby, obviously, valuing her sister's insider knowledge. Aglen took the conversational baton, but then created an opportunity for it to continue. 'I don't know that we know what to think yet – and Khartoum reactions have not really percolated down here yet. Unfortunately, the only person in this Province who knew him in Abyssinia is not very encouraging about him and there is a slight feeling that he may be somewhat damp.' She trusts her sister really wants to know and postpones telling her until she can speak authoritatively. And then *she* asks, 'Is he married?' The ball is back in her sister's court.[24]

Of course, the contents of the correspondence were totally dependent on the personalities of the writers. In Allan Arthur's case, the conversational correspondence with his parents was fuelled in part by newspaper clippings that his mother sent with her letters and that he commented on at the beginning of his. Most often, they were clippings regarding political events in India, although they were also sometimes about Africa.[25] During his years in India, Arthur's mother continued to cultivate that shared experience after he relocated to the Sudan.[26] 'The article on Rajistan was particularly interesting', he replies to one offering, acknowledging her efforts.[27] He then discursively suggests that she shares his predicament as an ex-India official who isn't properly appreciated by immediately commenting that the current student protests in Khartoum should be taken more seriously by the government, 'It all seems pretty obvious to me but has escaped the notice of the Governor and higher authorities.'[28]

Increasingly, his mother included clippings about Africa, offering him proof of her interest and her expanding awareness of anything Sudanese. Within the correspondence, it becomes unclear who is the source and who the recipient of imperial information. She offers clippings, he then responds with questions and comments about events in Britain. At the beginning of the shooting season in Scotland, he writes, 'It is fitting that I should write to you on the occasion of the Glorious Twelfth. I hope that the weather has been kind and that you have had a lovely day on the Moors and that you got a good bag.'[29] In other instances he speaks with great anticipation about Ascot, Derby and Wimbledon as if he were going to attend these events as well, despite not having lived in Britain since university.[30]

Bell similarly relishes the fact that one of their family friends who is also in the SPS is home during the shooting competitions at Bisley. This brings the Sudan to Britain, and his family and his service contacts are all connected, as he tells his mother that his SPS friend 'is sending me the *Daily Telegraph* for the whole of Bisley fortnight as it always has by far the best shooting news'.[31] The spatial relationship of these topics and events is elided and, in the process, so is the distance between them and the events that they and their families are discussing.

The desire to erase the boundaries between the Sudan life and the British life leads to surprising and sudden juxtapositions that would appear completely inappropriate in another setting – non sequiturs that almost send the prose into nonsense. Just before heading home on leave, Baily, then acting governor of Khartoum, wrote a detailed account to his parents of the thwarted efforts (as he saw it) of the Egyptian government to influence negotiations with the new Labour government in Britain by sending agents to lobby two of the MPs involved. He concludes his letter,

> These two persons speedily developed disgust not only for these specimens but also for all Egyptians, with the satisfactory result that the particular section [the left wing of the Labour Party] which seemed most prone to sympathise with the Egyptian, is now rapidly becoming his bitterest foe.
>
> Though I have missed most of the cricket I shall be right in the middle of the blackberries and mushrooms, which is more important.[32]

Arthur similarly deployed abrupt subject shifts with the effect of erasing personal and professional, British and Sudanese life. In one letter he shifts from discussing his wedding plans to riots in Kampala to a picnic he went on to the weakness of the military position in the Middle East all in a single paragraph.[33] In a letter to his mother in November 1949, he thanks her for having taken care of processing the photographs of his recent wedding. He then says he hopes that a family friend's health is on the mend. Then, suddenly he suggests that 'Daud Abdul Latif, the Town clerk, Khartoum, at present on a course in England, would appreciate an invitation to a meal' and gives his contact information.[34] This is done without any change in tone or language to indicate that this would be in any way an unusual event.

In the collaborative, hybrid space created by the correspondence and in which its participants enacted their relationships to one another, racial identification took on a different meaning. In this instance, the casualness of the suggestion cannot reduce its potency or the startling position occupied by the Sudanese in this symbolic space. It was not unusual, however, for British-Sudanis to make an occasional demand to test the strength of the epistolary third space. Often, attitudes towards the Sudanese or the changing power structures in the Sudan as independence grew closer (as is the case here) were used as a marker of continued compatibility.[35]

Failed attempts at community

In terms of output and effectiveness, Persis Aglen and her sister, and Gawain Bell and his parents, sit at one end of a continuum that finds unfortunate letter-writers like T. A. Leach at the other. Leach, who was governor of Halfa when he retired from the SPS in 1927, described the keenly disappointing experience of an unsuccessful correspondence:

> It was annoying … when one received a letter reading something like: 'Dear John – Your Aunt Jemima is coming to Egypt on New Year's Day and she would like you to greet her and assist her through Customs.' The recipient might well be 10 days camel ride from the nearest civilization and 21 days by camel from the nearest railway, after which it would take 36 hours to get to Khartoum, which was four days' train ride from Cairo![36]

Leach's frustration is partly due to an obvious lack of any imaginative effort on the part of a metropolitan family member, who hadn't even bothered to look at a map. But he would not have felt quite so frustrated, perhaps, if he himself had not been extending himself to those at home and trying to maintain a connection.

Their repeated efforts give some idea of their desire to find a way; and sometimes they were more successful than they themselves were aware. When interviewed years later, Lesley Lewis had a very clear recollection of feeling that her mother had no interest in the details of her life in the Sudan and that, therefore, she never wrote about them.[37] In reality, however, Lewis's frequent and substantial letters were filled with descriptions of her day-to-day life, her husband's work and her own work during the war. She felt comfortable enough in their epistolic relationship to engage her mother about her father-in-law's wife, who was extremely difficult and frivolous, without respect for the importance or the difficulty of her husband's work in disease control. Upon the eruption of the latest family crisis instigated by David's stepmother, she wrote her mother, 'It makes me absolutely mad to have David worried like that on the eve of an undertaking more difficult than most people at home can ever imagine.'[38]

She was insistent that those at home share in their experiences and yet, at the same time, she was adamant that her life with David was outside metropolitan comprehension and had the memory, years later, that her mother hadn't really been fully engaged. Her mother was drawn into the third space, despite Lesley's later recollections, but her step-mother-in-law was not. Letters were exchanged, but the space was never created. As a result, Lesley expressed a version of what were very likely to be David's anxieties – if his parents couldn't share his life with him, then he would return to them a stranger.[39]

Inevitably, as Lesley Lewis's seemingly contradictory demand points out, there was a paradox. It appears self-defeating, but as scholarship has explored, many letter-writers experience a sudden impulse to accentuate the distance between correspondents, rather than attempting to erase it. Knowledge is, after all, power. And the desire to draw attention to how foreign life in the Sudan was is understandable within the normal assertion of ego that exists in any relationship.[40] Bell admits to his wife, in a 1941 letter,

> I saw Douglas Newbold [the Civil Secretary] this afternoon who had spent 6 weeks flying leave in London and Sussex. It was lovely to [hear] about bluebells and the woods which he says he's never seen so beautiful. He gave a lecture to the Supper Club just on England. The odd thing was that we felt we were listening to a lecture on some strange country… all about what people were eating and how they were dressing and what the undergraduates were like. It reminded me of the lectures we used to get at school about far away half imagined countries which one longed to visit some day.[41]

Occasionally, writers like to accentuate the distance, adding a certain tragic or at least nostalgic ingredient to the exchange. Over the years, these little bursts of incommensurability signal they accept a fundamental shift in the orientation of their relationship.[42] While on the one hand the accepted wisdom may be that mail is always used as a tool to keep in touch and shrink the distances between people, this doesn't happen through the letter-writing as an act in itself. It depends on the discursive strategy chosen by the writer.[43]

Being boring

The desire to establish and maintain a connection with Britain was in conflict with the desire to highlight the exceptional lives that British-Sudanis were leading. Despite Bell's dramatic account of the arrival of the mail to the isolated men 'in the mess' hungry for word from home, when he returned to Khartoum after his first stint in Gedaref, he commented to his parents that Khartoum 'was so drearily middle-class – it's all almost unbelievably like Surbiton with its little tennis courts and garages'.[44] Men and women repeatedly emphasized how far removed Khartoum life was from life in the provinces, how disconnected its British residents were from the 'real' Sudan. There was a pronounced tendency towards reverse snobbery that helped them deal with the hardships of life in the provinces.[45]

Bell's jokey comparison to Surbiton works on three levels and is emblematic of the discursive strategy that many officials seemed to employ. On the one hand, his offhand comment actually reinforces the exoticism of Khartoum because it is so obviously not like Surbiton at all. It also emphasizes how rough the outlying posts really were in relation to Khartoum. And it is also an example of the not-so-subtle observations that young officials begin to include, once they feel more confident about their surroundings, to indicate to those in Britain that they are acquiring experience and expertise and are no longer the uncertain young men they were when they left home.

When another ADC, E. A. Balfour, characterizes his first posting, which was in Khartoum, as 'the horrors of tropical suburbia', this is in part because of his disappointment to find the Sudan so far away from the imperial fantasy he had been anticipating.[46] He was a contemporary of Bell's, arriving just one year later. He also had childhood memories of the Sudan because his father, Dr. Andrew Balfour, had been the director of the Wellcome Laboratories in the 1910s. Balfour *fils* had a memory of the earlier rougher version of Khartoum combined with his expectations encouraged by metropolitan literature. He struggled to navigate his 'return' to the Sudan on two levels. Unlike Bell, however, he was posted to Khartoum at a time when the British community's amenities were fully established, but the educated Sudanese population was not yet politically or culturally asserting itself. The sterility of that environment was *not* what he had expected to encounter.[47]

It is difficult to ascertain to what degree British-Sudanis cultivated a certain nonchalance about their experiences as opposed to just naturally having a fairly even-keeled approach to their lives. Many of them saw their actions as ordinary in an era when colonial culture was so widespread as to actually *be* ordinary. For Arthur and others who came from Colonial Service families, the patterns of service and leave were familiar. For others like Balfour, whose father had actually been in the Sudan before him, letters careened between not bothering to explain context at all and repeatedly specifying the changes from the previous generation.

What is extraordinary to many British-Sudanis is how quickly their lives feel ordinary. Bell writes,

> I must admit that had I been told that within 6 weeks of my arrival in the Sudan I should be sent into the bush for a week alone with orders to set 45 men to build a road I should have been slightly alarmed, but curiously enough everything has seemed very easy and in no way out of the ordinary.[48]

But this fact, in itself, becomes worthy of comment and is shared with those at home. And this strangeness becomes part of the shared experience with others in the Sudan. He goes on to assure his parents that he isn't alone in thinking this. His fellow ADC, 'Evans minor', feels the same way, he assures them. 'He too was struck by the fact that although everything is so strange and different one takes it all for granted and nothing surprises one in the least.'[49] This allows the British-Sudani to describe a life that puts them squarely outside the norm of the British middle class while simultaneously denying that this life would have any transformative power over them. When Bell assures his parents 'I don't believe anything that happened here would surprise me', he is admitting that he lives an extraordinary life by British standards.[50] But he is also saying that, in its way, his life is as routine as theirs.

To some extent, personality determined one's attitude to adventure, and little else was needed to cultivate it. When asked years later what she thought it was in her personality that made her accept a marriage proposal that would mean a life in the middle of a desert, Annaliesa Dee, the wife of DC Brian Dee, responded, 'What woman wouldn't?' and was quite unwilling to entertain the thought that most of her female contemporaries in 1946 would not.[51] The fact that she was an Austrian national, trapped in Britain by Hitler's Anschluss while a visiting student, and that she had already had a career as a teacher and a social worker prior to meeting her husband, may speak to her more adventurous nature. But she didn't think so.

Lesley Lewis worked as librarian at the Agricultural Research Institute in Wad Medani in the mid-1940s while her husband was an entomologist there. 'When my husband and I were in Africa', she later remembered,

> our experiences always seemed perfectly ordinary and humdrum because so many of our colleagues were doing much the same things ... It is only after living in England for a year or so that one begins to feel that some of the things we did just as a matter of routine might really be thought quite exciting by ordinary standards, and that quite long travel books have been based on very little more.[52]

Lesley Lewis's ability to gage what should be considered ordinary was perhaps a little bit impaired to begin with. She was one of the first four graduates of the Cortauld Institute in 1932, and she later went on to write a number of books on art history, as well as a very popular and astute account of the fading culture of the English country estate using her own family as the central subject of study. During her eleven years in the Sudan, after she decided to leave the librarian post so that she could accompany her husband on his field trips to various inhospitable and obscure territories, she decided to study law through correspondence and was called to the Bar in 1956. Later in life, she also managed to find time to be the vice-president of the Society of Antiquaries and the Royal Archaeological Society, among other things.[53]

Nonchalance could also, of course, be a by-product of seniority. Storrar describes one of his many stopovers in Cairo in a way that emphasizes its ordinariness to him.

> I had the usual bustle round Cairo in the morning, going to the War office, the bank, and doing a lot of shopping. In the afternoon, Loake [new to the Sudan Government] and I drove out to the Pyramids, and did the orthodox round on donkeys ... Strolled round to the Turf Club for a little afterwards returning to Shepherds and playing billiards – I was here introduced to Prince Mahmoud Something or other, uncle of the Khedive.[54]

All of these events Storrar describes with studied boredom were probably described with wonderment by Loake in his first letter home.

Being bored themselves was very different from boring their readers. If their metropolitan counterparts were indeed as bored as often as the British-Sudani feigned concern about it, the entire enterprise would have been in serious trouble. But as a rhetorical assertion of all the participants' commitment to sharing the British-Sudan epistolary space, the pre-emptive apology for 'boring' the reader, or 'being tedious,' or telling people things that they 'probably already know,' was used to good effect. These phrases pop up over and over again, usually when the British-Sudani writer is about to dedicate a long letter to the discussion of Sudanese affairs. The reader in Britain is supposed to be interested, but there's always a worry that the writer's preoccupations have exceeded metropolitan interest. Recipients were the stand-ins for all of British society. Persis Anglen, never hesitant to share, writes, 'Our days fly by full of occupations but few of them seem worthy of reporting.'[55]But she goes on then, after begging her sister's indulgence in this way.

John Winder is, perhaps, the exemplar of insistent discursive practices. Winder and his fiancée had the misfortune of getting engaged just before the war broke out and civilian transportation was banned. Nevertheless, their intellectual intimacy is extraordinary. Is Winder testing his fiancée when he writes early in their forced separation, 'At the risk of boreing [*sic*] you I am going to look in to one of the local problems, as it will help me to understand it better myself if I try to expound it to you'?[56] Will she be a suitable wife for a colonial administrator? Will his preoccupations make him unsuitable to return to Great Britain? Here, before she had even arrived in the country for the first time, he begins to put his activities within the wider context of the Condominium's retreat from the policies of Indirect Rule. He explains that when the government first arrived, they gave authority to a group of 'magicians' who had usurped power from older tribal functionaries. 'For one reason or another, these men had had to be broken and today they are all either dead or in prison. Efforts were at first made to work through them but they failed entirely in most areas, and in the one area where this policy still exists up to a point I do not think it is working well.'[57]Apparently, his critique of Indirect Rule was not deemed too esoteric by his fiancée.

She invites him to share his day-to-day work: 'I am writing all this "shop" partly because you have said you would like to have it and also because it is the stuff which fills my mind while I write… Shortly I expect I shall be writing about the problems of Chieftainship… about the troubles of finding good chief policemen.'[58] As time goes on, his letters resemble correspondence between colleagues. 'I have spent a good deal of time today in writing out a letter about the Zeraf Cut Scheme, which I told you was coming forward. I do not think I shall send the letter as I think it needs rewriting. I will… send you a copy.'[59] In the case of the Winders, they were able to create a hybrid British-Sudan space and later, when she was back in England taking care of their small child, recreating that level of intimacy in an epistolary partnership was more easily done.

While much of the information that the people back home get sent is about the gossip of British-Sudani society, the nuts and bolts of governance and descriptions of the Sudanese cultures are regularly covered, if not in the same detail as the Winders. In this way, the British epistolary partner benefits – in a way the young recruit did not – from an alternative narrative of imperial administration that extended beyond Henty, Kipling and Co. When preparing for a long stint on trek, Bell involves his parents, explaining, 'Here is a map of the Butana and I have marked in the boundaries of the General Grazing Area to show you where I shall be for the majority of the time that I am out.'[60] His letters are filled with an enthusiasm for his work and a sincere desire to construct word pictures for his parents back home. The content of the letters was, of course, a particular performance of his activities in the country, but they included extremely detailed accounts of cultural and political happenings, as well as complex legal cases, epidemiological concerns, instructions for the construction of roads and lessons in the complexities of Islam.[61]

In writing to his mother, A. W. Polden, a veterinary inspector who arrived in 1949 and left in 1955, had little gossip to pass on. His job did not put him in Khartoum very often. But he did include a huge amount of casual information about the Sudanese and about Islam. His interest in the details of people's lives was obviously a learned trait, as his mother asked direct questions that he was often trying to answer, such as her curiosity about Arab cleanliness. He replies, 'The Arab seldom bathes for the simple reason that there is not sufficient water, 'though he is bound by his religion to cleanse the orifices of the body before his prayers; but if he could get plenty of water he would bathe constantly … as cleanliness is one of the big virtues according to the Prophet's teaching.'[62] Polden's mother, while inquisitive and intelligent, holds a world view that is informed by the racial stereotypes promulgated in other sources. But her son acts as a conduit that successfully bypasses the filter of the metropole and gives her access to more complex information that also strengthens their mother-son relationship.

A similarly detailed picture of the complex considerations that a good administrator was required to take on board can be seen in Jock Miller's description of his encounter with tribal Sudanese while on trek. Still an extremely remote area in 1924, there had reportedly been only one previous visit by a British official to the Red Sea Hills village he was in and that was a surveyor in 1906. Part of his job while there was to collect taxes, but he had a dilemma. 'As this was the first time an Inspector has come their way, and as they gave me so genuine a welcome, I couldn't face up to leaving them with the impression that the Inspector is merely a glorified tax collector with the latter official's heartlessness.'[63] He goes on to explain that he lengthened his stay and spent time talking with the village leaders and drinking tea before setting off. These kinds of trivial dilemmas, recounted to those at home, provided a more nuanced picture of the colonial project than that traditionally put forward for mass consumption.

But they weren't always descriptions that put the British efforts in the best light. In a much earlier era, Reginald Davies didn't hesitate to expose his family to the unofficial details of his work as a magistrate in Kordofan in 1912. He writes about a case where two people are both claiming to own the same slave. 'Of course, officially there is no such thing as slavery in the Sudan, so please don't show this letter … – in correspondence we call them "Sudanese Cases" and speak of "servants".'[64] The compulsive clipping sending of Arthur's mother, the detailed questions and answers of Polden's mother and Bell's parents, the ease with which Davies brushes aside the 'official' version of events and the teamwork of the Winders show how the exchange of information shortens the distances within the Briton/British-Sudani space. The necessary forward motion of the relationship must bring the participants closer together (or farther apart – if we remember Leach's silly aunt and Lesley Lewis's step-mother-in-law), but they cannot remain static. The epistemological geography does not continue to match the physical geography in which the correspondents find themselves located.

In later years, the obligations, duties and movements of officials eventually become appropriated in a 'royal we' by many wives, as the anxieties about reintegrating into British society become more pronounced.[65] Wives slide back and forth, discursively, between being of the Sudan government and outside of it. Lesley Lewis writes to her mother near independence, saying, 'There is great goodwill on the part of the Sudanese, which I am afraid may be somewhat [reduced] when they discover we have all given notice! However, they must have known it as we have made no secret of it.'[66] She hadn't worked in the government since her first two years in the country, almost a decade earlier, and yet it is the collective we that is giving notice. Winder betrays his ongoing desire for the boundaries to be extremely porous between Britain and the Sudan when he inserts lines into his letters to his wife, such as 'You know the Egyptian Irrigation have most of the say about the Nile water.' They read as segues in the conversation but also as little discursive tics that are meant to reassure him.[67] His wife had been with him in the Sudan for years and became so immersed in the country that she knows the most arcane details of irrigation policy, he's saying, but she was still able to return to a middle-class suburban life in Britain with little difficulty. Perhaps, then, so can he.

Conclusion

In the correspondence circuit of the British-Sudani and their family and friends in Britain, a particular geography was established unique to them. It helped both sides to occupy a space outside their actual location, making neither completely absent nor present in Britain or the Sudan. Furthermore, it helped them to initiate their return by paving the way – reserving a space for them to return home to – and allowing for their return to be a continuation of a narrative that they, their family and their friends were continuously creating. In the correspondence between the British-Sudani and their family and friends in Britain, positionality and strategy must be kept in mind. Not a direct representation of the events, their correspondence bolsters authority on both sides, as well as reassuring their continued connection, despite their profoundly different life experiences. The choices of content, tone, associations and juxtapositions in the organization of the letters suggest what the British-Sudani wanted their relationship to Britain to be.

Initially, the participants in the correspondence circuit are discovering the Sudan together. As time goes on, however, the British-Sudani can't help but accumulate knowledge their metropolitan counterparts will never have. Lived experiences are full of fragmented narratives and ambiguities that resist the discipline of the epistolary form. Everyone's Britain-Sudan space is conceived, populated and maintained in different ways, obviously without any conscious articulation that the project is even underway. But there is evidence that communities created in this space do appear to reassure everyone involved that the British-Sudani will be able to return to the 'home' culture and seamlessly reincorporate themselves into it. Nevertheless, the imposition of another version of events, promulgated by the British government or by the press, or the insistent intervention of the Sudanese themselves, could and did undermine all of their efforts. The Sudanese have appeared very little in the epistolary exchange so far. When events, driven by Sudanese actions, insistently push their way into the narrative space of the British-Sudani, it exposes the ephemeral nature of colonial control. After all, if officials can't control the narrative, then how can control even be defined?

7

The 1924 Mutiny – Narrative and alienation

Sir Lee Stack was the third governor general of the Anglo-Egyptian Sudan and sirdar of the Egyptian Army when, in the early afternoon of 19 November 1924, he was being driven through the always crowded streets of Cairo. With him were his driver, March, and his aide-de-camp. Given the time of day, the streets of Cairo were full of traffic and, inevitably, the car was forced to a crawl. At that moment, shots were fired from a cluster of Egyptian men standing on the sidewalk. All three in the car were shot, but March still managed to drive on to the Residency. Stack was quickly taken to the Anglo-American Hospital and operated on. He seemed to rally, but by the next afternoon the situation was grave and later that night, he died.[1]

Stack wasn't a particularly remarkable man. In fact, compared to other European men whose names were connected to Egypt and the Sudan, he was downright drab. His patient and perhaps even plodding nature might have been the key reason why he succeeded Sir Reginald Wingate as governor general and sirdar – Wingate could be confident that Stack wouldn't overshadow him. His strength and benefit to the Sudan lay in his readiness to concern himself far more with the actual issues of effective administration than had either of his predecessors. And yet his end was astoundingly consistent with the already developed narrative of Egypt and the Sudan as understood by the majority of Britons – full of tragedy that is, somehow, Egypt's fault.

Stack's assassination precipitated a series of events that included an ultimatum presented to the new government of Egypt, a media firestorm back in Britain, a mutiny in Khartoum and the brutal deaths of Sudanese soldiers whose only fault was loyalty to the wrong authority. Egypt was forced to remove its forces and its administrative staff and, despite the name continuing, the Anglo-Egyptian Condominium of the Sudan ceased to have an active Egyptian component. For some Sudanese nationalists, it has been called an aborted revolution. Martin Daly suggests that, more than anything else, it resembled a coup d'etat by the British.[2] Because its significance so outstripped the size of the actual series of events, the Egyptian Mutiny, as it came to be collectively referred to by British-Sudanis, was a flashpoint for heightened anxieties over their potential alienation – from the Sudan, to which their personal and corporate identity was joined, and from Great Britain, a version of whose identity they were ostensibly representing. This was recognized in the moment, but also compulsively revisited long after.[3]

British-Sudanis used the Mutiny to encapsulate the changes in the Sudan during the 1920s towards a corporate culture of efficient and calculated bureaucratization:

civilization through civil service.[4] At the time of the Mutiny, the Sudan government was waging a culture war, of sorts, within its own ranks, as it sought to recast itself while not abandoning the foundational fantasies of boyhood. 'The administrator who ruled by reports and decrees', as Hannah Arendt points out, 'grew out of a tradition of military discipline in the midst of ruthless and lawless men'. Administrators sought to wed the new with the old by holding on to 'the honest, earnest boyhood ideals of a modern knight in shining armor sent to protect helpless and primitive people'.[5] The British-Sudani, through their correspondence, were simultaneously interpreting the events both to illustrate the validity of their personal attitude regarding one or the other approach and to defend themselves as a corporate unit against the imagined coverage by the British press.

This cultural split within the British-Sudani community could be seen as the Condominium-specific manifestation of the post–First World War backlash against the old men who had led Europe into war and the early articulations of the resolutely professional class that only came into the ascendancy in Britain after the Second World War. As the tensions between these factions of the British public played out in Britain, the Mutiny in 1924 is the central event in the Sudan in this shift from one culture to another. Ironically, it is also the last time that the Sudan figures in any prominent way in the British imperial imaginary before the invasion of Abyssinia by Mussolini.

We can find the legacies of both Wingate and Kitchener in the events of 1924. Kitchener loomed very large as a celebrity soldier. This was aided by the fact that he died suddenly, in the line of duty, which insulated his persona from the postwar critique of military leaders. A broadly read and reproduced poem articulated his fixed position in the public imaginary as the vanquishing hero of the Gordon saga, even in 1916:

In woe's black watch, bereaved, earth weeps;
But the glad sea his body keeps,
And calls, triumphant, to the land
In tones none may misunderstand …

Though for your fame he chose to fight,
I am the measure of his might.
Ah, never now in vaulted gloom
Shall sleep the hero of Khartum [*sic*] …

To glorify this son of mars
And keep the memory of his wars.
To children on the beach at play
I'll shout the name of K. of K.[6]

The older administrative culture in the Sudan continued to value Kitchener and his type if for no other reason than the continuation of a direct administrative line of succession from Kitchener to Wingate and his appointees from the Egyptian Army. Nevertheless, with each passing year, the growing cohort of university-educated administrators brought their own expectations of colonial government with them. New recruits were signalled that university education was now valued above the military, the scientific and developmental activities of the government were going to replace 'peacekeeping' and Sudanese autonomy was to be valued and protected from Egyptian ambitions. Once the Egyptian Army was removed, an independent Sudanese force was created and, although there was an extremely low ceiling put on the ambitions of educated Sudanese, at the same time, the increased employment of Sudanese to replace some of the departed Egyptians created expectations among the small group of educated Sudanese and the impetus for expanding educational facilities. In 1924, the small Gordon Memorial College in Khartoum expanded its curriculum to include engineering, teachers' training, clerical work, accounting and science vocational courses.[7]

Benedict Anderson has characterized any effective 'national culture' narrative as homogenous and serial, providing the unifying influence of a shared time.[8] The coverage and treatment of the Mutiny show a disintegrating time where the discursive space created by the British-Sudani/British correspondence circuit became a territory capable of hosting multiple debates on identity and interpretation, but also straining under the narrative disruption that highlights the distance that participants' discursive strategies usually disguised. Lawrence Grossberg discusses how people attach themselves or are attached to 'a complexly structured set of practices and events, a milieu'. This milieu can span temporal and spatial boundaries because the 'milieu' is the intersection of time-space.[9] The British-Sudani and their metropolitan counterparts diligently created a stable symbolic structure through their correspondence where individual articulations were imagined to be part of a communal one. As James How describes epistolary spaces, they are 'continually there' and are 'common spaces other people are also always using' where 'their letters are jostling and bumping up against multitudes of other letters sent by a variety of different and unfamiliar people'.[10] The multitudinous voices engaged in the creation and transmission of a British-Sudani space defied management or manipulation – a messiness that was critical to its perceived authenticity but which made meaning unstable. Both on the page and in lived experience, 'there is no identity that is not both *mise-en-scène* and narrative'.[11] At moments of crisis, like the Mutiny, distances between participants became apparent and meanings attributed to events proliferated.

In the fall of 1924, how each government was going to justify and continue its imperial programme, and what the day-to-day running of the country would look like, was an ongoing debate in *both* Britain and the Sudan. At the moment of the Mutiny, the British-Sudani were imagining the metropolitan British as an older generation, associated with a pre-First World War, pre-League of Nations attitude towards empire. Simultaneously, the younger members of the British-Sudani community were expressing their impatience with the Kitchener and Wingate culture that might have both caused the conditions that prompted the Mutiny and dictated the heavy-handed response to it. In their correspondence, British-Sudanis who welcomed the increased civilian culture of the administration were simultaneously arguing against an outmoded imperial culture they imagined was still promulgated back in Britain and the more conservative elements of their own (Sudan) government.

The background to the 1924 Mutiny[12]

In 1919, there was a nationalist revolution in Egypt. It was put down, but it prompted the commissioning of a report by Viscount Milner on Egyptian constitutional development. Continued unrest, the untenable nature of continued direct British involvement in Egyptian governance, particularly in the postwar climate of the newly established League of Nations, led British High Commissioner to Egypt, Lord Allenby, to demand and get from Britain a declaration of Egyptian independence in 1922. In return, Britain retained control of the Suez Canal Company, and the question of the Sudan was left to be discussed at a future date. Control of the Nile headwaters provided the British with an element of control over Egypt. It was feared that the nationalist movement in Egypt would spread to the Sudan, however; the Egyptian population in the Sudan government and in the Army were seen as the primary sources of Sudan nationalist sentiment when it was first articulated in 1923. Prior to that, disturbances in northern Sudan were usually begun by religious or tribal leaders, and those in the south were most often the result of border disputes or British attempts to limit the slave trade. The White Flag League was new. It was a secular, Sudanese independence organization that advocated joining Egypt. Its pro-Egyptian stance was probably a strategic ploy to gain the support of the newly independent Egypt for the League's agenda; nevertheless, the League's efforts had the detrimental effect of uniting against it both religious leaders (led by the Mahdi's son, Sayyid 'Abd al-Rahman), who feared the growing popularity of a secular political organization, and tribal notables (led by Sheik Ali al-Mirghani), who were benefiting from the extension of Indirect Rule policies that accompanied the increasingly civilian administration and who feared the growing urban *effendi*-class.[13]

In January of 1924, Egypt's first parliamentary elections returned the Wafd Party under Sa'd Zaghlul as Prime Minister. After a summer of demonstrations in Khartoum and Atbara by students and young educated Sudanese, Zaghlul travelled in September to London to negotiate the future of the Sudan with Britain's first Labour prime minister, Ramsey MacDonald. For the first time, Sudan government representatives played a direct and major role in negotiations and, according to George Schuster, the financial secretary, who accompanied Stack to the meetings, officials were optimistic that the talks would result in Egypt having less, not more, involvement in the Sudan's affairs.[14] He conveyed this to Robin Baily, then deputy governor of Khartoum, the same man who would later be Bell's mentor in Kassala. The younger Baily passed on Schuster's confidence to his mother, in July, when he wrote,

> We have every trust in the Labour Government that they will end all this very soon. In fact, we hope for more from a Labour Government than from a Liberal or Conservative Government. Because Liberals and Conservatives allow their judgement to be warped by questions of diplomacy to a greater extent than the present people. I think there is an element in Labour more truly Imperial than anybody.[15]

The British-Sudani possessed a narrow political lens in their self-appointed role as the 'caretakers' of the country. The 'questions of diplomacy' that Labour eschewed were, in essence, the connection between British national interest and the actions of the Sudan government. Officers maintained the premise of independence until it had become a central tenet of their corporate identity. The details of the political wrangling that were going on at the highest levels of the Foreign Office, and within the Secretariat in Egypt, were not known to the majority of the British-Sudani or their epistolary counterparts. They seldom had to account for the British government's position on Egyptian and Sudanese politics in their correspondence.

Individuals like Baily, who was privy to details of the political machinations in London and Cairo, were suddenly called upon to reconcile the tension between multiple agendas that were public for the first time. Baily, in correspondence with Schuster as negotiations went on, maintained a disdain for 'questions of diplomacy' in correspondence with his mother. While officers had no problem reconciling the difference between official policy and the reality on the ground (as Reginald Davies did with the question of slavery), the identity of the Sudan government was built upon the idea of independence, that it was *not* a colony. This required that the place of the Sudan in British foreign policy ('questions of diplomacy') be elided as much as possible, resulting in what Baily later identified as 'the parochialism of the Sudan Political Service'.[16]

Tensions increased in Egypt just as the new MacDonald government collapsed in the fall of 1924. On 9 October, Parliament was dissolved following the defeat of Labour on the question of prosecuting the editor of the *Workers' Weekly* for inciting soldiers to mutiny rather than break up strikes. The British public barely noted the failure of the talks with Zaghlul as an election was held on 29 October bringing back a Conservative government. Sir Lee Stack's assassination in Cairo on 19 November competed with metropolitan press coverage of skyrocketing food prices, analysis of why the Liberals fared so poorly in the election and a dramatic mine collapse followed, eight days later, by a rescue in Wales.[17] It made the headlines in the British papers, but the framework of the stories was the meaning of the assassination for troubled Anglo-Egyptian relations. Always described as the sirdar of the Egyptian Army, rather than the governor general of the Sudan, the *Times* felt it necessary to remind its readers of Lee Stack's dual role. 'Nor should it be forgotten that in the summer [the Egyptian government] deliberately encouraged, in Parliament and subsequently, an agitation in regard to the Sudan with which the attack … is undoubtedly connected.'[18] Thus a pivotal event in the history of the British in the Sudan as far as British-Sudanis were concerned was relegated to side-show status in British public perception.

Sudan government leadership had been waiting since 1922 for an excuse to demand the removal of the Egyptian forces from the Sudan and, in the process, to reduce Egyptian influence on Khartoum's educated Sudanese population. 'Plan E', a complete evacuation plan, was ready.[19] Seizing the opportunity, Lord Allenby issued an ultimatum to the Egyptian prime minister, without clearing it with the new Conservative PM, Stanley Baldwin.[20] 'Striking Spectacle in Cairo' read the *Times*' headline, with a separate article describing Allenby's elaborate military escort as he delivered the ultimatum to the Palace.[21] The tone of the ultimatum was as strident as Allenby's mode of delivery, prompting criticism over the following weeks in some metropolitan press and a call for the League of Nations to step in.[22] Allenby's demands included an apology, reparations, an expansion of the amount of land the Sudan Cotton Syndicate could irrigate using the Nile and the evacuation of all Egyptian troops from the Sudan. In Britain, it was the irrigation water that became the main point of contention; the evacuation was seldom even mentioned.

The Conservatives were accused of using the assassination to circumvent the right of sovereignty of the newly independent Egypt.[23] Baldwin took the criticism over the ultimatum, even though he wasn't consulted on its content.[24] In Britain, the next chapter of the affair was a discussion of the differences between Conservative and Labour approaches to foreign affairs, rather than a discussion of Egypt, let alone a discussion over the fate of the Sudan. In the *Manchester Guardian*, letters to the editor deplored Conservative action and point out the 'gulf between Liberal and Labour thought on the one hand and Conservative thought on the other'.[25] Colonial events were commandeered to serve as a vehicle for the domestic political debate.

As a result, the mutiny of the 3rd Battalion of the Egyptian Army stationed in Khartoum North on 24 November, and Sudanese detachments stationed in Khartoum on 27 November, never acquired any footing in the larger story of the Egyptian crisis. On the evening of the 23rd, H. Huddleston, the acting sirdar, received the order for the evacuation. As it progressed on the morning of the 24th, an Egyptian regiment stationed in Khartoum North, across the Nile, refused to entrain because they would not recognize the legitimacy of the order, saying that they would only entrain if told to do so by the Egyptian king, to whom they owed ultimate allegiance. A sign of the Sudan government's lack of understanding about the sensitivity of the Egyptians to their position can be seen in Huddleston's 'Military Report on the Mutiny' in which he states that the soldiers' refusal prompted him to send a telegram 'for the King of Egypt to be *required* to give the necessary orders'.[26]

The rest of the Egyptian troops stationed in and around Khartoum were evacuated without incident, but in the tense atmosphere that developed between the 25th and late at night on the 27th – when an Egyptian official finally arrived from Cairo with the king's orders – rumours spread; and on the afternoon of the 27th a Sudanese unit stationed to the south of Khartoum began moving through the streets in an attempt to join up with the Egyptian forces, having decided that they too must recognize the Egyptian king as their commander.[27] After being fired on by the British when they refused demands to lay down their weapons, most men in the Sudanese unit took refuge in the Military Hospital, where six people were killed.[28] Although the night passed quietly, by morning there had been no resolution. Still refusing to take orders from the British, the remaining Sudanese soldiers who had not made their escape during the night were bombarded with heavy artillery until they were all killed and the hospital in which they had taken refuge was a pile of rubble.

British reaction to the Mutiny

During this crisis, British-Sudanis anticipated a difference between events in the Sudan and metropolitan press coverage of them. In Britain, the Sudan was always an adjunct to Egypt, whereas in the British-Sudani community, relations with Egypt were always influenced by its history in the Sudan.[29] British-Sudanis assumed that the events in the

Sudan were seen as important enough to warrant overblown reportage that they then needed to refute from their position of privilege. Instead, British papers, and those who wrote letters to their editors, were concerned with the unilateral appropriation of water supply from the Nile. The concerns differed within the political spectrum, with the left concerned with what was seen as a flagrant attempt by the British government (confused by the fact that the ultimatum was delivered between Parliaments) to further its exploitation of what was now a sovereign nation, Egypt, and the right concerned that Britain's international standing would be undermined by unilateral action so soon after the formation of the League of Nations.[30] On 28 November, the day of the second mutiny, Ramsey MacDonald (now in opposition) gave a speech in which he made it clear that he was not consulted on the ultimatum and where he grouped together all of the nations with whom Britain had disputes: France, Germany, the USSR and Egypt, in a broad indictment of British high-handedness.[31]

Florid accounts of colonial violence from Britain's imperial past had often been generated by events in the Sudan. Now, the press coverage of imperial events was decidedly ambivalent. In the interwar era of the League of Nations, a new narrative was evolving that could justify the continuation of the Empire under different terms.[32] Just a year earlier, delegates to the Empire Conference met in London. The Conference prompted few public events or articulations of imperial pride in the press at the time. Even the *Illustrated London News* was hard-pressed to fill its photo spread on the event, showing a posed picture of the delegates, and others of a naval display put on in their honour.[33] The *Manchester Guardian* profiled 'The Dominions and We' as well as including an editorial asking 'Does the Empire Count?'[34] The picture of delegates, reminiscent of delegation photos from the recent Versailles Conference, highlighted the business aspect of Britain's Commonwealth and Empire. The verdict of the *Manchester Guardian* was, in fact, that the Empire did count, but mainly for reasons of trade and security. Just a week after the Mutiny was quelled, amid the calls for responsible negotiation between Egypt and Britain, there was also coverage, including pictures, of Mohandas Gandhi ending a hunger strike in the name of Indian self-rule.[35] As Britain was increasingly confronted by the legacy of myth-building militarism, the image of civil service imperialism was becoming more common.

The corporate identity and priorities of the Sudan government were evolving and its leadership wanted the metropolitan population to know it. Models of the new, deep, Port Sudan were put on display at the Wembley imperial exhibition in 1924 and officers were required to be on hand at the exhibition to 'sell' the modernizing projects of the Empire to a metropolitan audience.[36] The planned city exemplified the modern imperial impulse to impose order through the administrative rather than military control of space.[37] This is a moment, therefore, that the two forms of imperial control, never completely divorced from one another, were in equilibrium, the question of which would become dominant not yet answered.

The Britain-Sudan third space contained the epistolary expressions of this struggle. As both Gerber and MacArthur have argued, it is virtually inevitable for long-term correspondence to develop into a quasi-fictional form. Letters encourage narratives in which protagonists and villains become consistent, and broad-brush strokes aid the narrative flow and reinforce the 'roles' correspondents adopt.[38] The stable subject position of the colonial actor, in relation to both the metropolitan population and the colonized one, was (re)produced in tandem with, or in opposition to, the subject positions fashioned in people's letters. The Mutiny was a litmus test for officials' opinion on the growing civilian rather than military corporate identity of those serving in the government. A similar ambivalence to that being expressed in the metropolitan press was becoming increasingly apparent within the ranks of the British-Sudani – or, rather, specifically within the population that was not in ranks: the new dominant population of civilian administrators. At the moment of the Mutiny and in its aftermath, the personae of Egyptians, Sudanese and the British public were strategically deployed to further whichever narrative a letter-writer espoused.

Creating meaning from the Mutiny

In July of 1919, Baily wrote to his father about a brief Mahdist uprising in Singa, south of Khartoum, in which Egyptians took part, after having seen newspaper coverage of it. 'The papers give rather a misleading account of the Egyptian rebellion. Whoever started the rebellion soon lost control… But it is very unfair to curse *all* Egyptians.' Going on to recount the criticism of an Egyptian friend who pointed out that the administration's disregard for the political ramifications of army appointments was a major source of resentment, Baily wrote, 'When they talk like that, all we can do is to hang our heads or change the subject, or fervently hope that Lord Milner and Co. will change the whole administration.'[39] His characterization of 'they' and 'we' gave little clue to those back home that there was any variety in opinion and attitude within the colonial administrative community.

K. D. D. Henderson summed up the clash of generations and philosophies: 'Serious-minded young civilians did not always find flamboyant characters easy to work under.'[40] They were the source of much amusement and, at the same time, fear. Bramble Bey (J. J. Bramble, SPS), who was known until retirement in 1933 by the Egyptian Army nomenclature that was abandoned by the government after the 1924 Mutiny, typified this older generation. Bramble Bey insisted that his subordinates join him in full dress regalia for a daily parade on horseback through Omdurman, their district.[41] Bramble was famous throughout the service – as an example of an effective administrator for some and as an embarrassing relic for others.[42] Far from embracing modern ideas, Bramble rejected even the need to speak the language. 'Only two [Arabic] words you need for governing this country… severity tempered by justice.'[43] The methods of other, older officials were deemed equally out of touch. Describing the insistence on certain regulations by senior officials in the remote Darfur district as late as the 1930s, Balfour writes, 'All harmless in their way and no doubt intend[ing] to build up a local morale but beginning to be queried by a new and slightly iconoclastic type of DC who was arriving in those remote parts.'[44]

In return, the younger generation were suspected of being less than capable of fulfilling the role of ruler. In the immediate, post–First World War years, there was a concern that the war had decimated the ranks of those who would have gone in to

Colonial Service. Those who were left showed a 'lack of enterprise and a tendency to stay at home', it was feared.[45] Those who were recruited out of the universities could prompt the older officials to ask, as Sir Sidney Low, trained at Sandhurst, did, 'perhaps you can tell me what they *do* learn at Oxford and Cambridge that can be of the smallest use to anybody?'[46]

Charles Dupuis, whom Thesiger encountered years later, was then deputy governor, Darfur. In a letter to his sister, written immediately following the Mutiny, he answers her anticipated question about why the British are in the Sudan if the Sudanese are mutinying against them. He admits it's 'partly, I suppose [because of] the money we have sunk in the cotton scheme, and partly a sort of sentimental feeling towards the country, which is a legacy of the Gordon business'.[47] Dupuis thus captures the tension between the multifarious considerations of increasingly global, economic and political responsibilities and influences and the imperial myth that continues to shape the British Sudan's identity. Dupuis was more ambivalent about the military/civil dichotomy than others from the earlier generation who arrived more as a result of 'that Gordon business'. But none of these categories are easy to delineate. He was also opposed to the increased number of British women in the Sudan, while simultaneously maintaining a long-term correspondence with his sister that included detailed discussions of politics and policy.[48] This resembled a similar concern about the delicate constitution of university men, prompting a pre–First World War policy that only men like Bramble could be stationed in the south.[49]

Dupuis's hunger to explain – to himself and his sister – resulted in a *twenty-two* page letter laying out the events of the Mutiny, his opinion as to their causes and his suspicions about their effects.[50] He proceeds to work out the meaning of the Mutiny for himself by imagining metropolitan ignorance or disinterest and asserting his own expertise. 'I don't know how much of it you'll get in the papers, but I think if you can stand it, I'd better write you a sort of essay on the whole business'.[51] A combination of history lesson and editorial, the letter presumes a level of knowledge and a visual understanding of the layout of Khartoum. He ends by asking her to pass his letter on to his mother, who has had 'scraps', but not a 'treatise', and to two other unidentified females, Ag. and V., who will also benefit from a corrective of that 'Gordon business' he assumes metropolitan Britain is imagining the Mutiny to resemble.[52]

Writing to his sister 'Duck', Ian Douglas takes a different approach. 'I refuse to write about our little war because a) I found it v. boring b) everyone talks of nothing else c) You probably know more about it than I do d) this letter will probably be censored. The only objection to pursuing this line of action is that it leaves me nothing to write about!'[53] Reducing the space between them by suggesting that she, through the media at home, may actually know more than he, and yet simultaneously suggesting that his information is so privileged that it might be censored, indicates his assumption that coverage of these events was flawed. As a recent arrival, Douglas signals his disinterest in the older style of imperial adventure. Dupuis's 'essay' similarly rejects the role of adventurer. When he lays out the intricate relationship between Egypt, Britain and the Sudan (with the Sudan as fulcrum), he forecloses the possibility that any detailed analysis was available to his readers elsewhere.

In a later letter home, Douglas writes, 'I hear Ward Price, the great Daily Mail correspondent is arriving on tomorrow's train so doubtless you will shortly hear "The Truth (?) about the Sudan."' He imagines reactionary and incomplete coverage by an influential member of the Fourth Estate and extends his dissatisfaction to include the entire metropolitan population.[54] The possibility of multiple metropolitan subject positions in relation to the Mutiny, as symptoms of a broader articulation of a diverse culture formation, was generally ignored.[55] The Mutiny produced a diffusion of cultural symbols generating tension and disagreement in the British-Sudani community that also highlighted their misunderstanding about the level of British interest.

Robin Udal, head of the soon to be expanded Gordon College, wrote to his parents immediately after the event. He bemoaned the fact that, due to their trusting nature, the Egyptians were able to manipulate the Sudanese, who 'followed them like sheep'.[56] Following a similar theme, Geraldine Forster, whose husband, Arnold, worked in the Audit Department, wrote to Grace Balfour that the mutiny (specifically of the Sudanese troops) was 'pitiful' and 'futile' and that many of them retreated like 'naughty children'. Interestingly, however, she went on to say that 'since we have allowed Egyptian officers to be over them ... I think *we* are mostly to blame'.[57] Following her own logic through to its end point, the Sudan government could not escape the indictment of failed stewardship.

Herein lay a troubling tension for the British-Sudani. The mutiny of the Sudanese was an indictment of British rule. The older military generation focused on the behaviour of the Egyptians, which they considered to be expected. The Sudanese deaths as the result of the ruthless British bombardment were treated as unfortunate collateral damage. The younger civilian class was preoccupied with the Sudanese soldiers' mutiny, and their manipulation by the Egyptians, but as an indictment of the Condominium's military culture. The deaths of the Sudanese became central to their collective narrative of the events of those few days.

In officials' descriptions of the night of the 27th, not only the Egyptians and the Sudanese occupy symbolic roles in the greater debate; the behaviour and presence of British women are also deployed to bolster the arguments. Although the British women themselves had complex responses to these events and to the social structure in which they functioned, they tended to come down on the side of the younger civil administrators even when their own husbands were more senior.[58] Once the initial confrontation sent the Sudanese soldiers into the Military Hospital, and the government realized things would not be immediately resolved, all of the British women and children in Khartoum were told to gather at the Palace, the better to protect them, although, as one wife of an officer wrote, 'A more hopeless place to defend than the Palace never existed'.[59] Accounts by those men in charge, such as Baily, who as acting governor of Khartoum had been successful in convincing another battalion of Egyptians to entrain when the first mutiny had occurred, stressed concern about potential danger to the eighty-one women and sixteen children: 'Women cramp one's style in a show like this', he wrote to his father.[60] Robin Udal, headmaster of Gordon College, on the other hand, wrote that 'the women were simply wonderful'. Caring for the children and keeping them from becoming upset, he described the women, including his wife, Margaret, as 'cheery and laughing and chatting as if it was a picnic'.[61]

Meanwhile, as he describes it, he found himself – a schoolmaster – as the number four man in a machine gun team.[62] While it may have been a tense few hours, Clare Willis, whose husband was a senior officer in Intelligence, wrote to her mother that 'the whole thing of course was really very small but they would not let any of us leave' and that her greatest concern was for her husband.[63]

Those who desired a decrease in the military culture within the Sudan government injected their accounts with the appropriate editorializing on the behaviour of the soldiers, as did those on the other side of the debate. And this included women's accounts. Geraldine Forster took great pains to explain to Grace Balfour that the Sudanese soldiers refused to interfere with British civilians as they marched through the streets, hinting that the military response of Huddleston was inappropriate. When a British colonel 'remonstrated' with the soldiers, their Egyptian officer, she says, ordered the men to shoot. 'Three times the officer gave the order to shoot him as he stood talking and three times the sergeant said no.' The confusion over who was in charge, and who owed allegiance to whom, she argues, was the result of 'a childish policy but we pursued it'. Her seemingly progressive stand should not be misunderstood. She believed that the use of 'blacks' and Egyptians within the officer corps was also a source of the difficulties, but in terms of the decision-making apparatus within the administration 'the position calls for a big man and clever at the head of affairs'.[64] Clare Willis, however, simply judged the entire event 'pitiful and futile and such an unnecessary waste of life'.[65]

Dupuis, on the other hand, saw a direct connection between the political exigencies and the military ones. He suggests to his sister that if the grievances had been treated as political, then 'perhaps one might have got more of them to surrender' and despairs that even after the Mutiny, 'for some inscrutable reason the authorities have decided that the nominal "condominium" is to continue'.[66] He points out that the Sudan was never a popular posting for Egyptian soldiers anyway and that, therefore, the evacuation would be welcome to them: 'reprieve, not banishment – whatever the Foreign Office and the Secretariat had in mind'.[67] Although his tone is highly dismissive of the grievances put forward by the Egyptians and the Sudanese, he is not confident in the efficacy of the response, in essence suggesting that the military culture would be necessary until the political complications of the Condominium arrangement were dealt with.

Dupuis's characterization of the decision-making process emphasized expediency. In others' correspondence, the imperial literary tropes overdetermined the meaning attached to British actions. The acting sirdar, Huddleston, who had failed to convince the Sudanese soldiers to put down their guns and who then, the next day, resorted to the indiscriminate bombardment of the Military Hospital to end the Mutiny, was described by Udal as 'simply splendid'. And Udal's vilification of the 'Gippies' is reminiscent of Henty's characterization. And his conviction that 'what we want now in the Sudan is a real display of force and to let the natives know we are here to rule' is followed by a Kiplingesque assessment that the Sudanese 'fought like tigers, and put up a wonderful show'.[68] Udal is also repositioning the Sudanese as people of character, which is necessary in order to justify the elaboration of Indirect Rule and a civil rather than military administration in the country. On the cusp between the reactionary attitude of Huddleston and Bramble Bey, and the more 'modern' approach of Kenrick, Douglass and others, Udal's attitudinal shifts illustrate the pre-existing anxieties about British-Sudani corporate identity.

Conclusion

The only other potentially violent incident in connection to the evacuation was at Talodi, a small settlement in the Nuba Mountains about seventy miles south of Khartoum, where three British officials oversaw Sudanese subordinates and an entire battalion of Sudanese soldiers was stationed under Egyptian officers.[69] The battalion in Talodi refused to take orders from the British officials, following their fellow soldiers in Khartoum in recognizing only the King of Egypt as their commander. They broke into the arsenal and took all the guns. There was nothing that the British officers could do to protect themselves, as they were grossly outnumbered and help was at least three days away. Events failed to escalate further, however, and the soldiers returned to their barracks. The Sudanese officials, Egyptian officers and soldiers all subsequently returned to their duties before the British 'rescue' mission even arrived from Kordofan to enforce the evacuation. The extent and limitations of British authority were abundantly apparent as the British officers had no choice but to 'allow' them to return to work, because there was no one to stop them.[70]

The ironic position of these few British-Sudani in Talodi was completely lost on Ysabel Hunter, whose husband was stationed there during the uprising. In her letter to an unidentified 'Chimp', she describes the British in an adversarial relationship with both Egyptians and Sudanese. Deploying the present tense to great effect, she writes, 'How much of the situation here do you know I wonder. Things have reached the crisis now – and the worst we feared has taken place. [Husband] Neil rushed in 2 hours ago to say that the whole battalion has mutinied and run amok. He armed me – and the 3 servants … I hear occasional shots.'[71] The fact that she could sit down and write a letter to her friend speaks volumes about just how dangerous (or not) her circumstances were but, nevertheless, her broken style reinforces that she is an eye-witness to a 'live' event. She is framing her 'exploits' as a *Boys Own* adventure tale.[72] 'I can hear the band playing – & – there is another shot – and another … One has blind faith in even 3 – Englishmen – even up against such odds as these but at the best the situation is pretty desperate.'[73] Her letter-writing is an invocation of a 'type' that harkens back to an earlier time of colonial, and particularly African, adventure story that glorified the daring do of colonial actors and a military imperial culture.[74] This contradicted the newly expressed policy to reduce the military presence and promote civilization through rational administration.

Ysabel Hunter was not concerned with trying to establish and maintain a balance between her British identity and her Sudanese experience, nor with attempting to reconcile the events of the Mutiny with the corporate narrative of benevolent and welcome colonial administration. What others didn't understand was that that their casualness was not playing back home in counterpoint to a version of events in the press that resembled Hunter's. The hybrid British-Sudan space which they had co-created with their correspondents was not even remotely similar to the metropolitan press and the British government's approach to the Sudan. The typical press coverage wasn't a florid account of a 'native uprising', as they feared it would be. The more progressive British-Sudanis' attempts to counterbalance what they erroneously imagined going on in the British press instead reinforced their distance from Britain and their lack of understanding of evolving official and journalistic attitudes towards the empire.

The Mutiny encouraged British-Sudanis to express their concerns that corporate identity within the British-Sudani community was changing either too quickly or not quickly enough. For some, Egypt continued to be blamed for any and all difficulties with the smooth running of the Sudan and its progress to wards self-rule.[75] For the younger cohort of DCs, usually with a greater command of Arabic, Egypt occupied a different symbolic space, as did the Sudanese.[76] The metropolitan audience for these letters were drafted into a larger debate about the nature of colonial rule – the subtleties of which may well have been lost on them.

Part Three

Remembering the Sudan

8

Writing the return[1]

In 1948, the Legislative Assembly of the Sudan, made up of northern Sudanese leaders of the various political factions, proposed a resolution of Sudanese self-determination. Egypt subsequently exacerbated the situation in 1951 by abrogating the 1936 Anglo-Egyptian Treaty that reiterated the Co-Dominion nature of the Sudan. Hoping to distract from a political crisis that would eventually lead to a coup, the new King Fauk declared himself sovereign of Egypt *and the Sudan*. This made the status quo in the Sudan untenable as far as the British members of its government were concerned. They had no choice but to declare themselves in favour of Sudanese self-determination and self-government at the earliest possible date despite the fact that this sentiment flew in the face of Whitehall's position, which was – simply put – to sacrifice the Sudan if necessary to maintain relations with Egypt and control of the Suez Canal. Margery Perham, seeing this process beginning in 1946, weighed in with a letter to the *Times* that summed up the post–Second World War situation.

> While Britain and Egypt have been arguing about the interpretation of a still undisclosed agreement, the Sudanese have been kept in a state of feverish suspense about their fate. If Britain has signed away her share of sovereignty and given it solely to Egypt, how can it honestly be maintained that there will be no change in the administrative *status quo*? The heart of that *status quo* is the guidance of the Sudanese towards full self-government by British officials; this will not easily survive either the penetration of Egyptian influence or the loss of faith in the British by the Sudanese, both of which are likely to follow upon the concession which Britain is said to have made.[2]

The raison d'être of British authority in the Sudan is, with Perham's help, being refashioned as stewardship towards a fairly rapid transfer of power. 'Everything must be done', she exhorts, 'to re-create the conditions in which the Sudan Government as at present constituted, will be free to give, and the Sudanese willing to accept, the last 10 or 20 years' service that is needed to round off half a century of skilful and devoted administration that has brought the Northern Sudanese within sight of full self-government'.[3] In this estimate, Perham imagines the shortest time span of any of the officials in the Sudan at the time, really. And she's not far off – nine years instead of ten.

As with the Mutiny in 1924, and Gordon in 1884, Perham notes that the Sudan is coming into the British public's consciousness only as an adjunct to Britain's relationship with Egypt. 'It is the misfortune of the Sudan that, neither a colony nor a foreign country, but lying in the twilight of its embarrassing status, it has been kept almost deliberately out of the public eye.' The implication, for Perham and others, is that the British public have a clearer idea about Egypt and the advantages gained by close relations with it in 1946 than with the Sudan. And, much like in the early days of British-Egyptian-Sudanese interactions, public pressure was bound to influence foreign policy. 'No comparable pressure of opinion in this country has supported our ministers against the pressure from Egypt', she worries.[4] If ill-informed officials are swayed by Egyptian claims that the Sudan was historically in the sphere of Egypt, who else in Britain was in a position to argue otherwise? How were the British people supposed to think about the Sudan? Was it an independent nation and therefore free to make its own decisions? Obviously not. It also didn't have the status of colony that would result in its protection becoming a rallying cry for pro-Empire members, particularly at a time when the sting of Indian Independence was almost upon them.

Perham tried to thread a needle. But it was extremely difficult to argue that Sudanese self-determination was better served if the British continued to occupy the upper echelons of the Sudan government until those positions were voluntarily passed to Sudanese at some future date. 'Those who know and care about the country should appeal for support for the government in its intention to safeguard the work and perhaps the security of a fine service, both British and Sudanese, which has been put by the events of the past few weeks into a position of acute difficulty.'[5] Here there are shadows of Gordon – the inheritance is still there. The security of the Sudanese, at the hands of Egyptian malfeasance, is once again dependent on the selflessness of British administrators. And just in case some of the *Times* readership needs a clearer reminder, she goes on to urge: 'Let us remember that the Sudanese are a high-spirited and intelligent people – and also that they are not remarkable for patience or docility.'[6]

Perham likens the Sudan to another colonial territory, and it is interesting that she is quite blunt in her assessment. 'It may be said that Egypt has quite literally vital interest in the Sudan … but she is more likely to secure them if her neighbour joins her as a Scotland rather than an Ireland and if the delicate modern mechanism of Nile water control in the Sudan is not jarred by discontent or disorder.'[7] She cautions and instructs much in the style of Stead, making sure that *Times* readers understand '"the unity of the Nile valley" is a slogan that has little support in history, race, politics, or, as those who have traced its immense course can see, in geography'.[8]

In all of this, the British are trapped by their own fiction. The British government wants to keep up good relations with Egypt and is inclined to support their claim to the Sudan in exchange for keeping their control of the Canal. But the foreign minister, Bevin, was on record making a pledge 'that no change should be made in the status of the Sudan as a result of treaty revision until the Sudanese have been consulted through constitutional channels'.[9] As Perham points out, 'The British, who promised the Sudanese, as part of the same pledge, that 'they shall decide their political future for themselves', will not, it appears, override such a decision. If we do not, it will then appear that we have offered Egypt something which it was not ours to give.'[10]

In many ways, the rhetoric had come full circle. Language used in semi-official documents between British officials in the upper echelons of the Sudan government and the Foreign Office (FO) echoed the tortured position taken by Gladstone's government seventy years earlier. British self-identification as stewards of Sudanese self-determination was increasingly retroactive.[11] Once again, Britain's complex relationship with Egypt forced an explicit articulation of the British-Sudanese relationship – more particularly, the success or failure of British stewardship.[12] The Sudan government was forced to retire British officials and raise Sudanese to senior posts in the administration. The British-Sudani were immediately anxious about the potential for ill-prepared and under-educated Sudanese being put in positions above their capabilities. These fears were voiced within the correspondence circuit of Condominium and Foreign Office officials, but it could not be publicly articulated without bringing the entire mission of the previous fifty years into question. In his review for H. C. Jackson's 1955 analysis of the sources of contemporary events in the Sudan, *Behind the Modern Sudan*, another senior SPS ex-official, J. Angus Gillan, recognizes Jackson's anxiety about both the Sudanese and the legacy of the British-Sudani. In the guise of a review, Gillan doesn't put too fine a point on his and Jackson's concerns. 'The too hasty expulsion of the British is already regretted in many quarters', he assures his readers in *African Affairs*.[13]

The audience for Perham, Jackson, Gillan and others was neither the Egyptians nor the Sudanese. While they were concerned for the fate of the Sudan, their narrative efforts were once again turned towards the British public. The British-Sudani attempted to assert their authority as the experts on the ground throughout the process of Sudanization and divestiture, but they were rebuffed by the Foreign Office. The Foreign Office felt they understood the Sudan within a broader, geopolitical framework and the British-Sudani were convinced that Whitehall didn't understand the subtleties of Egyptian and Sudanese relations. And blame was being apportioned. Competing claims to expertise and authority at the end of Britain's relationship with the Sudan seems apropos. The ghosts of Evelyn Baring, Lord Granville, W. T. Stead and General Gordon were present in the arguments on both sides even as British-Sudanis were anticipating and navigating their journeys home.

If a few thousand out of nine million could not be found suitably educated and prepared to take on administrative tasks, then what had the British been doing all this time? If administrators were concerned (and rightly so) that governmental policies that had separated the southern Sudanese from the north for decades would now, after independence, result in Sudanese at war with each other, and if rapid Sudanization was necessary in order to stop the Sudanese from being wooed into a new, inequitable association with Egypt, then what had all of those personal relationships meant? The triumphalist narratives promulgated by academics and politicians at the end of Empire have been challenged in recent decades. But for soon to be, or recently made, ex-colonial officers, what Michael Collins identifies as the 'empire-nation dichotomy' was already causing unease.[14] They understood their fates (at least in the eyes of posterity) as intertwined with those they had ruled over. As Chris Jeppesen observes, in the era of decolonization, the government struggled to reconcile the long-standing imperial project with the new narrative that 'underdeveloped' peoples needed British mentorship in order for the new Commonwealth to reach its full developmental potential. This sat uneasily with those whose careers had been defined by a Whiggish narrative of triumphant progress. 'Service to humanity at large' became the new recruitment message. But various policy shifts could also be taken as criticisms of the earlier generations.[15] The process of leaving the country and explaining to themselves what that meant will be the subject of the following chapters. During Sudanization, the narrative, and therefore the self-authorship of the British-Sudani, was threatened by what were characterized as unruly natives *and* uninformed metropolitan authorities and opinion makers. When external actions by the Sudanese or by British policymakers challenged whether the administrators were truly the servants of the Sudan, the British-Sudani narrative was undermined.

The silent return

When the moment finally came, most British-Sudanis returned to Britain with very little fanfare. All British members of the Sudan government were barred from settling in the Sudan once they retired and so from the first, every British-Sudani knew that they would be leaving the Sudan at the end of their service. Because retirement was mandatory at fifty, most British-Sudani men expected to embark on a second career upon their return, not only those whose careers were cut short by the rapid process of Sudanization and independence in 1956. The certainty of departure encouraged the development of elaborate 'final leave' rituals within the British-Sudani community in the Sudan. But curiously, this was followed by the complete absence of any comparable rituals of return once back in Britain.

It was common for wives to return to Britain once their children reached school age. Some officials, depending on their rank and financial wherewithal, rented modest homes for their families. Other wives and mothers returned to their own parents' homes. Wives tended to return again to the Sudan once the children went to boarding school (the usual practice for SPS officials' children and common for others in the higher ranks of the technical branches). Officials in the SPS had longer leave than in other services and, as discussed in an earlier chapter, the distance to get back to the British Isles was far more manageable. Nevertheless, for as much as twenty-five or twenty-seven of men and women's most active and impressionable adult years, a home in the Sudan was the stable point of reference, rather than one in the metropole.

At the moment of their final return, the British-Sudani fall strangely silent. There is an absence of material in the archive that pertains to their efforts to re-establish themselves in Britain. The British-Sudani are described repeatedly as compulsive recorders and preservers of their experiences. Kirk-Greene's assessment that 'the SPS was proportionally a notably literate service when it came to writing its memoirs' understates the manic self-production effort that generated multiple records of the same event. As a result, the consistent silence surrounding the return of so many of them is notable.[16]

It is possible that there was no space provided within the metropolitan imperial imaginary for the return of the colonizer because there was no established narrative of the returning imperial hero. As discussed earlier, the imperial hero sacrificed for the cause – as Gordon epitomized.[17] The literature of adventure, travel, conquest and empire lacked potent images of the return. The narratives of imperial travel were always imagined on an outward trajectory, and many of the myths of Empire derived a large measure of their potency from the one-way nature of the journey. The one-way journey was simple, a return journey messier. Without a denouement, the narrative as a whole was weakened, denying a compelling aspect of the imperial fantasy for those back home.[18]

Another possible reason for their initial silence may have something to do with an inability to continue the narrative flow of their lives, made particularly difficult at the time of independence, because their personal and corporate narrative was dependent upon the premise that they were wanted, welcome and doing good work.[19] Sudanization, like the Mutiny, is a moment when administrators and their wives show a considerable anxiety at the prospect of others suddenly getting to write the narrative. Asserting a unified British-Sudani identity was harder when members of the same community read the history differently.

The Mutiny became a signifier of generational shift: the removal of the Egyptian forces also meant a reconfiguration of governmental structures. The Egyptian Army was eventually replaced by the Sudan Defence Force, but Sudan government officials weren't military officers anymore. And the relationship between the British and the Sudanese had to stand on its own terms, without the Egyptians to blame. Twenty-five years later, the process of forced retirements brought on by Sudanization meant that the first generation of post-Mutiny British administrators and their wives were returning to Britain to take up new and unfamiliar identities. The Sudanese were quite publicly rejecting the British-Sudanis' right to be authors of the Sudan any longer and asking them to leave. The British community's ability to think of the Sudan as home, in any sense, was severely undermined; we are never asked to leave home – if we are, then it wasn't home.

In this and subsequent chapters, memory and identity become contested terrain. Our sense of ourselves within a wider collective is premised upon an original memory, however illusive, that anchors all other memories.[20] Pierre Nora, in his broad and deep examination of the relationship between memory and identity, notes that 'the intimacy of a collective heritage' allows us to then create our own memories, independent of or even in conflict with the collective one.[21] The rejection of the collective imperial memory of the Condominium undermined the authority of the British-Sudani. But it also undermined their collective identity. And this rejection could only be denied by also denying the departure. Colonial rejection was incommensurate with the imperial narrative, but the only other form of successful return was unavailable for those who returned at the time of independence.

Elizabeth Buettner provides ample detail of the variations in the Anglo-Indian 'return' spanning a century of British rule. In that case, the only one to predate Sudan independence, multiple generations of returning Anglo-Indians established a road map, a way to navigate that transition. Only the last generation were required to participate in 'ongoing re-evaluations and debates about the imperial legacy', in which they were called upon to embody 'a specific juncture when the colonial era itself remains a living memory'.[22] British-Sudanis constituted a tiny number compared to Anglo-Indians, no generation of them ever had the expectation of staying in the colony where they worked, and the generations of officials who had been able to return simply due to retirement barely outnumbered those whose return was forced due to Sudanization and independence. Consequently, there was little sense that returnees were following a well-trodden path.

This raised the possibility that these men and women would not be able, in a psychological and emotional sense, to return at all. Did the British-Sudani deny or attempt to downplay their return because they were already nursing concerns that their time abroad had left their personalities irretrievably different from their British contemporaries? Many of them later acknowledge how much their world view had been altered by their time in the Sudan.[23] In the first moments of returning, before they had been tested and when the anxieties brought on by so many life changes were high, some may have feared that these changes were potentially insurmountable.[24]

Many British-Sudani attempted to facilitate their reintegration into British society by eliding the boundaries between colony and metropole for their metropolitan audience and denying their return altogether. If the return journey didn't exist, then neither did their absence and distance from Britain. This strategy was only possible and successful up to a point, however. Inconsistencies and contradictions, such as their compulsion for commemorating their time in the Sudan, their subsequent choices in second careers and resettlement locations, and elaborate rituals of departure that were enacted while still in the Sudan, speak to their anxieties about returning and the tension between who they were and the contemporary British national culture to which they ostensibly belonged.

Home and family in the Sudan

The returnees fell into two groups: those who returned at the end of a normal length of duty in the Sudan and those who were forced to leave the Sudan in the early 1950s, before their time was up, due to the processes of Sudanization – whereby all positions in government that could 'affect the freedom of the Sudanese at the time of Self-Determination' had to be held by Sudanese.[25] As the retirement age for Sudan officials was so young, however, both groups shared the experience of 'retiring' while still being young enough that they were expected to pursue a second career. For the second group this meant a career out of necessity; for the first group the need to work again depended on the level of pension received, as well as the expectation that a man in his late forties or early fifties was too young to be idle.

For some women, the Sudan had offered a chance to explore a much less structured and prescribed life. Particularly in the later years of the Condominium, there were many wives who worked, either officially or unofficially. The war, the staffing shortages it created and the fact that some women were trapped in the Sudan by the unexpected nature of the Blitzkrieg at the end of the Phony War, all created excuses for women to engage in work outside the home, whether they were paid for it or not.[26]

In an era when most men stayed with the same employer for their entire career and, by fifty, were reaping the benefits of steady advancement, the British-Sudani in middle age had to begin all over again. The positions that they took up were generally senior ones, certainly. For their peers who had stayed put, however, the social and economic benefits of professional continuity cannot be underestimated. A middle class, public school educated man who had remained in Britain for the same years of his life created a place for himself – perhaps becoming a pillar of the community. He participated in local organizations and made connections through work and his community activities that extended into a social and cultural life beyond. And wives had similar experiences. British-Sudani women did not enjoy the same continuity that came from years of social interaction in Britain.

During their early years in the Sudan, most officers lived with few comforts and amenities. This was partly because of the clichés of bachelorhood, but also due to the greater mobility required of most junior officers in the technical branches and the SPS. They spent months at a time away from their station headquarters: sent on regular treks around their district to oversee various infrastructure projects or, if in the SPS, to deal with criminal cases, local grievances and tax collection. This doesn't mean that the desire for a homier atmosphere was absent. Bell's description of the simple yet carefully chosen items for his first house in Gedaref illustrates the point. Brian Storrar went to great lengths to build a model of a horse's head in order to hang it on the wall and use it to display various equine artefacts that he collected.[27]

The materially Spartan lives of the young British-Sudani men, at least in their personal belongings, were compensated for by the incredibly rich learning environment in which they were living. The young ADC Bell wrote to his parents less than six months after his arrival,

> On the evening of the 8th I rode dusty and rather dirty after 17 days in the complete wilds, into Kassala. At 9 am on the 9th I was attending … in full uniform – at midday I was galloping on a white Arab horse to meet … troops … who were arriving by air, at 5 I was playing in the most complete suburban tennis party with the Kassala railway officials and at 8 I was dining with the Governor at Government House: a full day.[28]

Their lifestyle swung between a condition of austerity while on trek and 'tropical suburbia' when at district headquarters.

By the middle of the 1920s, the regulations regarding marriage had been relaxed and the attitude of higher officials to the presence of British women, not only in Khartoum but also in the outlying provinces, had eased.[29] Even in the earliest years, British women in exceptional positions were in residence. Grace Balfour joined her husband in Khartoum when he became director of the Wellcome Tropical Diseases Laboratory in 1903.[30] By 1913, Mabel Struvé was accompanying her husband to postings in White Nile and Upper Nile provinces, where the landscape consisted of 'unlimited acres of black, cracked cotton soil with ant heaps several feet high'.[31] And by 1924, there were five British women employed in the Sudan government in positions with the Education and Medical departments that required travel to outlying territories.[32] And Brian Storrar's diary entries as early as 1909 make it clear that the 'all-male preserve' was less than a reality in the larger centres.[33] But when the military structure in the government ranks ended in 1924, so did the gender bar.[34]

By the 1930s, criticism was usually directed at particular women who are seen as being ill-suited to life in the Sudan, rather than the sex in general. That an 'unsuitable' wife was worth commenting on suggests how rare it was seen to be. The usually generous Bell gives a scathing critique of the wife of his boss, DC Evans: 'There was really nothing to tell you about her – very stupid, rather conceited and pretty selfish were her worst points: that she was cheerful and not altogether hideous and that she made an excellent cake were her best!'[35] Most were quite understanding that the climate was a brutal test of anyone's health and morale. Brian Storrar makes no derogatory comment when he writes, 'Passing through Shendi, I saw Anthony Pelham who was there for the last time packing up his things preparatory to leaving our service – I think the fact of his wife not being able to stand the climate is the principal reason of his leaving.'[36] In later years, many of the memoirs of officials include a comment that the wives seemed to have been chosen as effectively as the officials themselves in terms of temperamental suitability to the life and the climate.[37]

Male condescension aside, it really was not particularly remarkable that the women who came were quite successful at establishing a marriage home in such unusual settings. Most men of the SPS had gone from their parents' homes to their rooms at college to their first postings in the Sudan.[38] By comparison, a number of these women had been living independent lives with careers before their arrival. One of the earliest British women in the Sudan, Grace Crowfoot, had trained as an archeologist and had been on an extensive dig in Italy before marrying John Crowfoot, the Director of Education for the Sudan, in 1909. Mabel Wolff, nurse and midwife, joined the government to begin a maternity training service in 1920 and then was quickly joined by her sister.[39] Mary Rowley had been a nurse in London during the war and had come out to the Sudan as a midwife, before later marrying Deputy Governor Geoffrey Hawkesworth.[40] In the post–Second World War era, there were a number of women who continued their careers in the Sudan after getting married to SPS officers, such as J. S. R. Duncan's wife, Sheila, who was a doctor, and R. Simpson's wife, Evelyn, who was a teacher.[41]

British-Sudani men and women were both influenced by the unusual rhythm of life for Sudan government officials – a home in the Sudan and yet also long leaves in rented accommodation or as guests in other people's houses in Britain. They became experts at negotiating the disparity between their Sudan lives and their British ones.[42] But women, in particular, were required, on an annual basis, to revert to the family persona of child or sibling, long after they had established an adult life for themselves elsewhere. And particularly in the early years, and then during the Second World War, the role as spouse or parent could be interrupted for long periods of separation.[43]

The first few years of marriage also played out in strange communities where husband and wife knew few people and depended largely on each other. For the women, life-long habits of budgeting, shopping and entertaining for a family were formed in the Sudan because this was the first place that they had a marriage home, even if it wasn't for every month of the year. The women mimicked what they watched their mothers do back home; and the men were similarly often engaged in what appears to be an unconscious recreation of the British suburban life of their parents, even without female intervention.[44] In the couple's 'story', they might later downplay the man's domestic capabilities in order to establish the wife's value and credentials as homemaker, in an environment where there was little scope for her to do much else.[45]

Sudanese servants who cleaned the house and prepared meals was a domestic arrangement that many couldn't afford when they returned, particularly in the different British economic environment of the 1940s and 1950s.[46] And the men were always expected to be on call.[47] There was no separation of work and home: no 5:19 train to Woking. And for both, the experiences of life on trek cultivated improvisational skills that, perhaps, equipped them for such a profound change in lifestyle once they returned to Britain. When interviewed years later, Mary Rowley stated repeatedly, 'As I always said, "I can make roots … I can live in a tent. I shall be very happy."' And she certainly attributed that ability to her time in the Sudan.[48] And her repetition of this statement when interviewed in the early 2000s would seem to indicate that, even after having lived within a few miles of the same village in Berkshire for decades, it was still a trait that Mary Rowley valued highly.

Rituals of departure

Strict baggage limits for new recruits and equally strict regulations for a new wife's possessions limited the goods that could be brought in to the Sudan; years later, expense and conditions limited what could be taken on the return.[49] Women arrived to set up their first home with the silver and linens and the other accoutrements usually given as wedding gifts to middle-class couples during this period.[50] When the couple returned to Britain many years later the inventory lists were strikingly similar. The trappings of a British life in the Sudan were about to become the only tools of continuity for women (and men) in their first new home in Britain. This didn't usually extend to furniture because one of the most ubiquitous pests in the Sudan is the white ant, which will eat any wood or natural fibre that it encounters. The most common Sudanese mementos were small items made in local silver, which was of poor quality and usually extremely thinly worked, often into ashtrays or salvers and spears or other decorative objects used by the Nuer, Dinka and others in the south.[51]

Before the British left the Sudan, they auctioned off most of the household goods that they had acquired while there. Edward Willis described the 'miserable business of sorting and packing', separating what could be useful for the next person from the things that had slowly been brought into the country over the years, most notably wedding presents.[52] When W. A. Porter left Tokar, Kassala Province, in 1951, he and his wife had to ship or sell belongings that had accumulated since he first arrived in 1927, including the wedding presents that his wife brought with her in 1930. The auction netted 787 pounds, and the goods they were shipping back to England were insured at a value of 400 pounds, 100 of which were the surviving wedding presents. Of the rest, the most valuable item was a mahogany cabinet (ten pounds) that had miraculously survived white ants.[53] After over twenty years of marriage, this household was about to begin again with only 400 pounds worth of furnishings.

The auction was as much a social event as anything else. Storrar writes about a weekend auction in much the same tone as he would write about a tea party.[54] If those remaining in the Sudan could help with a purchase, it was a way to lend support to the departing family and also a way to compliment the couple on their taste. The auction was an institution and a rite of passage; although never codified, its function and form were absolutely understood and passed down through the British-Sudani generations. Its ritualistic and symbolic aspects were underpinned by its functionality. Newcomers needed household goods, and there was no sense in shipping home something that someone else would have to go to the expense of shipping out for themselves. So, better not to pay the costs twice but to spread them out over the community. The fact that this helped to define the community, to welcome new members to it, while giving others a supportive farewell as they left it, turned practicality into ceremony.

Diana Arthur is pleased to inform her mother after their auction in 1954 that 'there was great demand for all our things'.[55] Although the Arthurs don't mention it, auctions became much more politically fraught later in the Condominium when the officials were selling their belongings to new up-and-coming Sudanese officials, rather than the newly arrived or newly married British ones. Jane Britton, for example, talks about the tense period of waiting on the morning of her parents' auction in El Obeid in 1953, when no one came to buy anything. The implication was that the Sudanese didn't even want any of H. D. D. Henderson's family's possessions to remain in their community, let alone him and his family, even after he spent twenty-six years in the SPS. Although eventually there started a trickle of buyers which then grew to a respectable number as the day wore on, from a daughter's point of view, after her father's years of service, 'that was hard for him, I think'.[56]

Community support was also reinforced by a series of farewell parties. Depending on where an official was stationed and who he was, there could be an endless number of official and semi-official ones and then as many private, purely social ones as a person's popularity determined.[57] The centrepiece was the large, official farewell banquet hosted by the officer's specific branch of government. These testimonial dinners sometimes included the wives of officials and sometimes included the Sudanese members of the department. This depended most often on where the official was stationed. The greater the number of people within the returnees' Sudan community, the more compartmentalized the various farewell events would be.[58] In their personal letters, many give detailed accounts, including seating plans carefully noting everybody in attendance.[59] The social or sports club also had a banquet, and if an official's work brought him in steady contact with the non-British, non-Sudanese community in the Three Towns (Khartoum, Khartoum North and Omdurman) or the other larger towns with a substantial Greek and Syrian merchant community, there might also be a farewell banquet thrown by them.

There was at least one Sudanese farewell tea party. These parties produced the most elaborate tributes for the retiring official. In diaries, letter and memoirs both during their careers and after, numerous officials remark on the politesse of the Sudanese and its centrality in the culture. As Henderson noted, 'The Arab in general is the most skilled flatterer in the world.'[60] Interestingly, at the time of departure and after, the British-Sudani consistently failed to recollect that observation about Sudanese cultural practices when evaluating the sincerity of tributes, testimonials and expressions of good will coming from Sudanese colleagues. After independence, Sudanese popular opinion retroactively became extremely important in the creation and preservation of a particular corporate identity. These written tributes were carefully preserved and quite prominently placed in their memoirs and scrapbooks.[61]

And finally, if someone was senior, popular, had been living in a single town for a very long time or all three, then there was an obligatory, community-wide farewell at the train station or dockside. Many memoirs end with this set piece: a bitter-sweet departure with a huge multi-ethnic cast of well-wishers at the docks, or the train station, or the airport. John Kenrick remembers all of it as a continuum.

> During 1954 and 1955, British officials and their wives flowed in a steady stream through Khartoum and out of the country. Auctions of furniture were held... almost weekly.... For days before our departure every meal was engaged in being entertained by our Sudanese friends in their homes. At the station at Khartoum there was a large crowd on the platform to see us off.[62]

There are numerous photos of these kinds of farewells, and the preservation of the apparently 'spontaneous' act of community farewell in dozens of photographs makes it clear that this ritual took on a significant meaning.

Final leave

Embarking on their 'final leave', after weeks of preparation, these men, women and children returned 'home'. Although they had been home on ninety-day leaves every year, for many of the men their arrival in Great Britain marked the start of living in the country for the first time as mature adults. And yet, although many of the officials' diaries continue uninterrupted and private papers include the recording of important, even embarrassing or unflattering events, there is no mention of a welcome home party.[63] If they took place, they are unremarked upon. But there doesn't seem to be any evidence of them taking place at all.[64] There are no other papers in Sir Donald Hawley's private collection that pertain to his return, after having reached the position of Chief Secretary of the Judiciary, in 1955. And yet he kept an entire file of mostly unfavourable news coverage of a 1976 event, when a report on immigration that Hawley had written for the government was misleadingly cited by Enoch Powell to support his extreme right-wing stand on immigration. This resulted in accusations of racism against Hawley and intense media scrutiny.[65] And yet, on the subject of his return, Hawley has preserved nothing. Neither can anyone interviewed by the author recollect any parties or family reunions, gifts or commemorative gestures to mark their actual return.[66]

It seems a safe assumption that in most cases British-Sudanis were missed while they were gone. Diana Arthur, the wife of DC Allan Arthur, felt it necessary to establish boundaries with her over-eager parents and in-laws before one of their leaves: 'We shall certainly be with each of you for at least a month. So please parents don't squabble over us.'[67] And yet, at the time of their permanent departure, she feels it necessary to remind her parents 'that the children and I have only got another 3 weeks in the

Sudan' and that she is 'rather thrilled with the idea that we may be house-hunting this summer, I should love to get settled in a house of our own'.[68] She jumps over three intervening months that happen to be those in which the actual departure and arrival will take place and highlights the marker of adulthood, 'a house of our own'. This may be another reason why that period was elided in the memoirs and letters of returnees.[69] Years later, in her accompanying notes for her letters, Lesley Lewis summed up the entire return period by saying, 'then back to London to flat-hunting, finishing off my Bar final, learning to cook and generally repatriating ourselves to an unfamiliar post-war London'.[70] Her 'repatriation' is acknowledged but tempered by the assertion that it is specifically 'post-war London' that was unfamiliar, even after ten years of coming to it on leave.

Second homes, second careers

In the months leading up to retirement, during which the auctions and parties were taking place in the Sudan, a number of practical concerns about life in Britain occupied the British-Sudanis. Wives were concerned with establishing a new home and arranging appropriate schooling for children, or, if the children were older and at boarding school, there was the issue of continuing them there or removing them to a local day school.[71] Women often searched for a new home, and even selected one, prior to their husbands' return.[72] Often the wives had to wait until their husbands had found a new job before they could begin establishing a new home, as relocation would be dependent on where the husband ended up working. At a time when many women were unused to handling a checkbook, circumstances demanded that British-Sudani women were dealing with estate agents and school heads; and the logistics of shipping, storage, unpacking and furnishing fell to them, as did the need to set up accounts with merchants and arrange for utilities.

When her husband took a position in Nigeria, two years after they had returned from the Sudan and bought a house in England, it fell to Mary Hawkesworth to sell it before going to join her husband in Africa with their small son.[73] Common activities like buying a new home became occasions where returnees couldn't hide their different circumstances from their metropolitan audience. On the contrary, particularly in the circumvention of normative gender roles, these transitions exposed the reality that these women and their husbands had shared and accumulated very different experiences than their peers.

Despite the certainty of relocation, there was no established way by which new homes were bought or furnished in Britain. The Sudan Agent never arranged a contract with a particular company for the storage of goods once a family returned to Britain, but before they were able to find a home. Returnees had to arrange that for themselves. Winnifred Johnson, whose husband worked for the Sudan Cotton Syndicate, wrote as her departure was nearing that a friend 'very kindly gave us a list of people to enquire of if we go to Pembroke in search of a house'.[74] Companies such as Thomas Cook offered a range of services for those home on leave, such as house and car rentals, but these were never advertised as also being necessary requirements for returnees. Nor were house *sales* included in the Thomas Cook gazettes.[75] Although people stayed with family or friends when they first returned, many returnees needed to be in London to look for work, even if their families were not located in or near London. Annaliesa Dee remembered, years later, that there was a particular place where she and her husband stayed in London right after they got back that was known in 'colonial' circles as a good place to stay and which catered to that group. But no other interviewee remembers it or any other, even when asked about it specifically, and there is no mention of it in any other correspondence.[76] All of these practical concerns were left un-addressed by the Sudan government and Sudan Agency. Most resettled in the south of England even if originally Scottish or from the north. Although weather may have been a consideration as it was for older colonial retirees from other services, the second career needs of British-Sudanis focused them in the south. Some expressed a sincere regret that they weren't able to return to the region of their birth.[77]

In the men's letters and diaries, they are preoccupied with creating a smooth transition for their families, but are fearful there is little to which they were ultimately suited after so many years in the Sudan.[78] This concern can be seen in many of the speeches made at farewell parties in the Sudan, where post-Sudan career choices were often lampooned – a sure sign of displaced anxiety. After more than twenty years in the service, Brian Storrar was regaled with a poem that ended with:

> But I have thought that for a change, we might look in the future
> And visualize the time when he may be a local butcher.
> Perhaps he'll go to Peter Jones and stand behind the counter
> And issue yards of silken lace for every bargain hunter.
>
> A maiden wanders to his stand 'three yards of lace' says she
> 'I beg your pardon Miss' he says, 'reinforced, type B or C.'
> 'Perhaps you'd like it on the skew, or else like 1 in 8.'
> But I can't think that this is right, he deserves a better fate.
>
> I think I know where he will go, but this is between you and I
> He's going to be his own gay laird, up in the Isle of Skye
> A thousand acres he will buy, with birds and other cattle
> And dressed in a kilt, he'll spend his days, listening to children's prattle.
>
> But why speculate on what he'll do, He's a man of many parts
> He may be Bishop of Glasgow yet, or else a breaker of hearts.
> But whatever he does, wherever he goes, whatever he has in mind.
> He takes with him the very good wish, of those he leaves behind.[79]

What Storrar did take on as a second career is unknown but it is apparent, from the poem, that a second career, in a second country, was not a source of unmitigated, pleasant anticipation.

Particularly for members of the SPS, their work had, for the best of them, turned them into great generalists: men who were able to turn their attention to a great variety of tasks and who were comfortable in administrative positions that didn't require a large amount of specific skill or knowledge but that demanded an ability to reconcile the personal, political and economic concerns of unwieldy administrative units.[80] The Colonial Administration Course and later refresher courses known as the Devonshire Courses had provided training in specific fields, but with the assumption that there would be technicians and engineers taking care of the in-depth work. They were returning to an increasingly professionalized and technical metropolitan work culture, particularly after the Second World War. The men in the Sudan who would be considered technical staff, and the military, did not fare any better. In fact, 'staff of the railways and of the Customs Department and those occupying military posts … were the most difficult to resettle'.[81] In the non-military instances, this is likely because men like Storrar became adept at the specific engineering or bureaucratic demands of the Sudan environment but these did not translate to the British context. Doctors, educators, engineers and scientists usually had an easier time because they were, in essence, continuing their careers in different settings. John Kenrick definitely felt he was using 'administrative and secretariat [*sic*] skills learned in the Sudan', in his second career, and joked that 'the internecine strife between Departments reminded [him] of tribal disputes'.[82] Interestingly, the social hierarchy in the Sudan placed the specialists lower in status than the political officers. Back in Britain, however, the financial success of the specialists often outstripped their SPS colleagues. This had an impact on the identity of these men in later life and showed itself in the leadership of post-imperial British-Sudani organizations.

An ad hoc job placement network consisting of old university friends, other British-Sudanis, family and friends meant that very few had to resort to public announcements. Many large companies, town councils and schools contacted Oxbridge when interested in hiring at the managerial level. Oxford University had a questionnaire that alumni could fill out when seeking employment so that, when contacted, the university could provide an appropriate list of potential applicants. Some of the British-Sudani used this mechanism.[83] And yet, by 1950, although there were 993 Britons posted in the Sudan, and hundreds had already retired before them, there seemed to be no established custom of arrival and settlement, even an informal one. Within two years, the mass exodus of British-Sudani would begin as a result of Sudanization, but thirty years of returnees had not yet codified a process of return in a service that was explicitly set up for early retirement and where, overwhelmingly, its officers sought out second careers.

By 1953, the Ministry of Labour and National Service had established three offices in the country (London, Manchester and Glasgow) that dealt with 'filing vacancies of an administrative, managerial, professional and senior executive type' as well as 'an advisory service, which is available to older people who are making a major change in their careers',[84] within which the government was prepared to create a special Sudan Services Section, in the same way as the India and Burma Services Section was set up years earlier. Lessons from that influx had taught the Ministry that the circumstances of the returning British-Sudani would not be like that of other 'older people who [were] making a major change in their careers'.[85] The Ministry asserts, in fact, that that experience 'of other special resettlement problems and of the general employment situation in the field with which the Appointments offices are concerned, point to the need for special steps to seek openings, more particularly in industry and commerce, for the Sudan Service officers as soon as the number becoming available in the general employment market reach any size'.[86]

With Sudanization accelerating the rate of returnees, the Sudan government, through the Sudan Agency and under the aegis of the Foreign Office, set up the Sudan Government Re-Employment Bureau. Geoffrey Hawkesworth retired as a provincial governor from the SPS in 1954 and was immediately asked to head the new Bureau. Thanks to his efforts, some of the one thousand or so men became managers and executives in the newly nationalized industries in Britain, such as coal and electricity, with a total of 263 taking positions in commerce or industry.[87] Forty took posts in government services of some kind. Although town government structures were seen as closed units, dedicated to internal advancement, the 'new towns' in the postwar era provided an opportunity to ex-administrators.[88] Basildon, Essex, and Bracknell, Berkshire, both employed ex-British-Sudanis.[89]

In many cases a man's new career would take him (and, perhaps, his family) out of Britain a second time. One hundred and sixty-two entered government posts or academic posts in colonial territories. Therefore, the career choice made at twenty-one resulted in an expatriate lifestyle that lasted far longer than envisioned at the time. Many had a very strong desire to return to Britain and settle down in a society that they had missed. But reasonable employment for middle-aged generalists was not in abundance. 'Most of the officials were between 26 and 60 years of age. The re-employment of those under 35 years presented no problem; but it was more difficult to resettle those who were between 35 and 45 and still more difficult for those over 45 unless they possessed some professional qualifications.'[90] Geoffrey Hawkesworth, after having helped hundreds of others to find work, had so much difficulty finding something for himself that he applied for the post of Chairman of the Civil Service Commission of the Federation of Nigeria. 'This means selling my house and family separation during part of the next five years – In fact all those things I so much wanted to avoid. But at my age there is apparently no other choice.'[91] Others, such as John Kenrick, chose to take lower paying or less prestigious positions in order to remain in England. In his case, the desire to stay in England meant he turned down the Foreign Office's offer to appoint him Resident in Kuwait.[92]

Geoffrey Hawkesworth was not alone in being hired by the Colonial Service to help in the transition period of other African colonies nearing independence, such as Nigeria.[93] James Robertson also went to Nigeria and oversaw the transition to independence in 1960, as did Gawain Bell. Bell then went on to yet a third territory, Aden. Other senior members were recognized as possessing unique knowledge of the difficulties of colonial transitions and so were valued for their experience rather than penalized for their age. Fortunately for many of these men, increased demand for Middle Eastern oil in this period meant that the giant oil companies, such as BP and Shell, valued the generalist skills of ex-political officers who could speak Arabic.[94] Others acted as advisors and spokespeople for Middle East governments and relocated, at least temporarily, to various Gulf States. Forty-three officials took positions in foreign states or international organizations.[95]

Of course, for others a career choice that gave them the chance to travel again was not necessarily a problem, especially for the younger members of the service who were expecting to spend decades away and had, in fact, had their expectations cut short.[96] They accepted jobs overseas with equanimity because they had wanted to lead an expatriate life. The Sudan government stopped offering pensionable employment in 1952 because of the implementation of Sudanization. But of the seventy-seven post-probationary officers in the SPS in the last ten years of recruitment (1942–52), thirty-five took overseas employment after the Sudan.[97]

Bringing the Sudan with them

Although the emphasis here has been on the majority of British-Sudanis, who always planned to return to Britain, and who then wanted a seamless reintegration into British society as quickly and unproblematically as possible, there are two other groups of returnees that must be discussed because they did not engage in these efforts. Although there were constant and substantial fissures in the façade of reintegration for most members of the British-Sudani population, there were some who seemed less interested in erecting such a façade to begin with.

First, there were returnees who maintained their difference and perpetuated their Sudan life by openly declaring their British-Sudani identity within Britain. In some cases, those who asserted their British-Sudani-ness in Britain were deaf to the discordancy it produced. This was the choice of G. J. Clark, a former member of the Railways and Steamers Dept., headquartered in Atbara, a town on the banks of the Nile north of Khartoum. Upon returning to England, Mr. Clark and his family retired to a house in a north London suburb, on the city's busy ring road. His new address was '"Atbara," 21, North Circular Road, Finchley, N3'.[98] Whatever else he did, Mr. Clark was not concerned about disguising or downplaying how different his life story had been from his peers. He made his home, itself, a marker of difference. While the word 'Atbara' was drained of most of its meaning for those other than he and his wife when he decided to put a name plate on his front gate, what it retained was its exoticism. To call a suburban house by the same name as an entire town would not be done within a Western cultural framework: a returning Englishman would be unlikely to name his house 'Amsterdam', for instance, no matter how many years he had lived there. By bringing the name 'Atbara' into North London, G. J. Clark doesn't need his neighbours to understand its full meaning in order to effectively present at least a distillation of his personal identity as British-Sudani.[99]

It is difficult to make general pronouncements or make too many suppositions about the significance of these kinds of declarations. Nevertheless, there did appear to be a certain class element involved. In the list of pensioners from 1956, seventeen of them gave their homes names that evoke their Sudanese experiences. All of these individuals, save one, were from the ranks of the junior divisions or practical branches within the Sudan Service, which generally drew its numbers from a lower socio-economic background than the SPS.

Many people willingly decided to settle permanently somewhere other than Britain, which is also, perhaps, an inadvertent assertion of continuing British-Sudani identity. Len Newell, who had been a photographer with the Public Relations Office in Khartoum, decided to settle in Australia after independence, rather than return to Britain. He speaks of his 'homesickness for the Sudan' and suggests 'at least we were building something there... whereas it's very difficult here (and I imagine in the UK, too) to feel that one is doing a socially useful job'. His subsequent, dispassionate assessment of the benefits and flaws of Britain and Australia points out the distance he has travelled from British society. He offers his reader comparative assessments of British and Australian society that are from the point of view of someone distant enough from both societies that is able to see their constituent parts: Music is favoured in Australia over theatre in Britain as the primary cultural outlet, he feels, and the Australian social philosophy is more 'egalitarian', whereas the British are 'more respectful of authority'. Newell doesn't exoticized either country; nor does he exhibit any patriotic affection for one or the other. His choice to settle in Australia seems to be the result of weighing two *equal* options, neither of which possessed much emotional pull for him. 'At any rate, we're content here, and have made up our minds to settle permanently' is how he describes his verdict.[100]

'Homesickness' here is a relative term, and (as was the case with most ex-pat populations) the British in the Sudan always referred to Britain as 'home', even those such as Allan Arthur, whose family had been in India for generations before independence, and Reuben Cairo Garrett, born in Egypt, whose father had been in the employ of the Egyptian royal family before joining the Sudan Civil Service (SCS).[101] But Newell's admission of feeling 'homesick' for the Sudan may be an expression of longing for somewhere where his 'foreignness' is no greater or less than that of any other *British* person, whereas in both Australia and, tellingly, Britain, that is no longer the case for him.[102]

Very few of the women in the Sudan government pursued second careers. In many cases, they had retired from the service because of marriage and child-rearing. And in others, they took up or continued independent work. Lesley Lewis and Mary Crowfoot both authored multiple books, on art and botany respectively. And Lesley Lewis also studied law and was called to the bar. The wives of men who struggled to find second careers sometimes looked for work to bridge the gap. While her husband, Richard, had difficulty finding an academic posting after leaving the Sudan, Juliana Hill sought a job as a librarian given her experience at Gordon Memorial College in Khartoum.[103] For most women, their fates were tied to and depended on the career decisions of their husbands.

There are too few women who had full-length careers in the Sudan government, and none with husbands, to assess whether they approached their return and professional development in a substantially different way than their male governmental counterparts. Ina Beasley, a Doctor of Education, joined the Sudan Education Service after leaving Burma, where she had been a college lecturer. Divorced and with a daughter at boarding school in England, she took the posting in the Sudan because, as she said, 'I had been overseas before and thought I should like the opportunities offered.'[104] So, in her case, the Sudan *was* the second career that continued an expatriate life. She was the head of Girls' Education in the Sudan, before returning to Britain in 1949, where she continued her career as an educator. Another woman who had a full career in the Sudan, Elaine Hills-Young, never married. She was the Matron of

Khartoum Hospital and then Principal of the Midwives' Training School, from 1927 until 1943. Subsequent to retiring, she became the Principal Matron with the British Red Cross Commission for Refugees and was one of the first to enter Belsen death camp in May 1945 to organize Red Cross teams to bring out the survivors.[105]

These two women, although atypical as colonial administrators, typify many in terms of their physical relationship to Great Britain and what that might mean in terms of emotional and psychological attachment. With a similar dispassion to Len Newell, Beasley sought out a second career outside of Britain because she liked 'the opportunities offered'. Hills-Young returned to Britain during the war, *because of the war*, and worked for the Red Cross there. When the opportunity presented itself, however, she took up a position that would mean her departure yet again. It is unclear whether professional ambition or innate restlessness were the cause; in any case, the habits of a sedentary life, and the comforts of residing within a single cultural framework, were not sufficient draws to keep her at 'home'.

For whatever reasons, by the year of Sudan Independence, 1956, of the 1100 Sudan government pensioners, one in ten had an address outside of Great Britain. For those men and women, most of whom did slowly return 'home' as their second careers came to an end, the issues dealt with by others were taken up by them as well. Did Geoffrey Hawkesworth's return from Nigeria prompt celebrations that hadn't occurred the previous time? Probably not. But no matter how discreetly he and hundreds of others may have wanted to reinsert themselves into a very British life, they had not shared the uninterrupted narrative of that life and culture. Furthermore, they had experienced narratives of their own. Years after settling in Stanford Dingley, a very small village in Berkshire, the Hawkesworths were visited by an old Sudanese colleague who was in Britain on business. He and his two nephews came to their house in the village for lunch. As the afternoon progressed, Mary Hawkesworth realized that it was one of the Muslim prayer times. She offered the men, who were wearing the customary long, white robes of the northern Sudanese, a room, washing materials and rugs to kneel on and left them alone. As Mary Hawkesworth (later Rowley) tells it:

> The funniest thing was I'd got workmen working outside the house at the time, and they were going 'round the windows, or on the guttering or something. They were so amazed, they saw all these fellows doing their praying; you know, kneeling and that sort of thing. They couldn't believe their eyes. [From that point on, the workmen] always said, you know, they never knew what was going to happen when they were coming to my house. But, you know ... – well, you don't forget the customs, you just change the circumstances.[106]

It's not hard to imagine that the story of the Arab men who visited the Hawkesworths in Stanford Dingley would have been repeated and that even if nothing interesting ever happened again at the Hawkesworths', they were marked as slightly exotic people. However much many British-Sudanis might have wished to deny their 'different-ness', that didn't mean it was possible, because customs, which are learned, and circumstances, which are changeable, don't remain in sync. What is the result of this 'different-ness'? Kirk-Greene asks rhetorically what the impact of returnees might be, but he assumes it will be a conservative one because 'in social and attitudinal [terms] … the manners and mores of imperial life were … usually twenty years behind the times at home'.[107] A blanket application of that assumption might be problematic. While a culture may be more conservative in some of its practices, it may be more progressive in others. Robert Stack argues that 'modes [of thought] are social in the sense that individuals producing them are influenced by society and the organizations or communities to which they belong'.[108] An expatriate life, however, results in the production of modes of thought influenced by various societies, organizations and communities. As a result, a mixture of modes is possible whereby different members of a group have different relationships to their community. 'With … the complexities of social life which engendered such modes, comes a high degree of uncertainty, detachment and skepticism about the significant relationships between social order and geographic area.'[109]

Ramifications of this abound. Ex-colonial officials were in positions of power as the rest of decolonization occurred and as immigrants from former British colonies began to arrive in larger numbers in Britain. In the political arena, within the British-Sudani community alone, there were at least fifteen ex-SPS officials who went into the Diplomatic Corps. Four men became MPs. Countless men joined the Colonial Service for its final years. A large number of men (and women) went into education, either as teachers or as administrators. Others, who had enjoyed their judicial responsibilities while in the SPS, went in to the law. In terms of cultural impact, men from the Sudan government worked for the British Council – Reginald Davies was Assistant Director-General – and others for the BBC. Large industries such as coal and steel, brewing and electronics saw a number of men in their executive levels.[110] John Kenrick eventually became the Head of Personnel for Phillips Industries, joined the national Industrial Relations Court and the Home Secretary's Advisory Committee on Probation and After-care and was part of the Army Welfare Inquiry Committee.[111] At a time when the number of non-whites arriving in Britain was increasing, challenging the relationship between 'social order and geographical area', Hawley's report to the government and Kenrick's resumé are excellent examples of the potential influence of their British-Sudani background on the economic, political and cultural practices of an increasingly multiracial and no longer culturally monolithic society.[112]

Chris Jeppesen has illustrated that a colonial career was increasingly unpopular in the 1950s and 1960s. It was criticized for its 'antediluvian' gentlemanly ethos, even as it opened its doors to a broader range of socio-economic backgrounds to find recruits. Simultaneously, however, there was an ever-growing emphasis on 'professional competence and technocratic expertise'.[113] As 'ability rather than conditioning' was emphasized, middle-aged former Sudan government officials could still, if willing, find second careers in colonial governments. But Jeppesen points out that it was organizations such as the VSO (Voluntary Service Overseas) that largely took up the slack providing opportunities for young people to engage in new modes of 'service to humanity' in the post-imperial age.[114] The idealism of the new forms of service, untainted by the politically and morally problematic motivations associated with the Empire, set up an unfortunate delineation between even very recently hired Sudan government officials who were now 'post-colonial' and those setting out to the very same territories, but now under the aegis of the VSO and other organizations.[115]

The post-Sudan 'detachment and skepticism' about any sense of belong to the British metropole was also transmitted generationally. A substantial number of children of British-Sudani became ex-patriates, either for periods of their lives or permanently, as well. In just one instance, Sir Donald Hawley's daughter, Caroline, after travelling and working in the Middle East and serving as an occasional reporter for British media outlets, became the chief correspondent for the BBC in Baghdad during the US invasion and its aftermath in 2003. Either as a result of having spent at least part of their formative years living outside Britain or because of the attitudinal influences of their parents, the effects of the returnees' social discontinuity went on.[116]

Conclusion

It is clear then that ex-officials' second career opportunities could be hampered by their Sudan experiences and could benefit by them; in either case, it was very difficult to maintain the fiction that they generally shared the same life history as their peers. Wives, and perhaps even children, were also affected by the lost years of social interaction and community connection. And yet, although their initial strategy may have been to reinstate their Britishness by denying their return, most maintained their self-identification as British-Sudani for the rest of their lives. Their strategies speak of a desire to be 'returned', once and for all – to be British – in an uncompromised and unconflicted way. But perhaps their return, and that of so many other colonial personnel and their families, contributed in subtle ways to the creation of post-colonial Britishness, as well.

9

A change of masters[1]

With the coming of independence, the value placed on administrative artistry was replaced by the value of an honourable transfer of power. Retirement was inevitable; the characterization of that retirement was still, in the final years of the Condominium and after, an important component in the British-Sudani community's self-image. Pensions and pension terms constitute the one continuing relationship between employee and employer long after the work itself is finished, and so the pension arrangements of British members of the Sudan government were weighted with meaning that went beyond the practical concerns of financial security in their old age. As with other colonies, it was expected that the new government of the newly independent ex-colony bear the burden of paying the pensions of their former colonial masters. As a result, there was a residual relationship between colonizer and colonized that would extend into the post-colonial era. The struggle for the British-Sudanis to define the terms of that relationship against the continuous resistance of the metropolitan government was also part of their attempt to establish and articulate their location in the story of British imperialism and the process of decolonization and in the new lives they were living within the confines of Britain's domestic culture.

Three separate concerns arose regarding British-Sudani pensions when it became apparent that independence was near. Those who had retired before 1950 received a supplement to help bring their fixed pensions in line with the post-1950 variable pensions that fluctuated to match the value of the pound at the time of retirement. The continued devaluation of sterling since the war and the accompanying rise in inflation were not properly matched by these supplements.[2] Additionally, all pensions were tied to the Egyptian pound, which had been the currency of the Condominium, and which, it was assumed, would be less stable after independence. Finally, pensions were never paid out of a fund set aside for such a purpose but out of the annual budget of the Sudan government, voted on and ratified each year.[3] While the British ran the Sudan, pensions would be a budget priority, but there were concerns that a new government would not feel the same. The British pensioners wanted a guarantee from Whitehall that in case the future Sudan government repudiated their pension responsibilities, the British government would take over their payment.[4] There were unofficial assurances, but Whitehall feared that 'to make a firm guarantee might be to invite default, both here and in other territories'.[5] Whitehall contended that there was, in pension terms, no 'change of master' in the Sudan because the government was always independent, whether run by British or Sudanese.[6]

Their campaign began in earnest in 1952, three years before independence. It was 1962 before the British government finally agreed to pay a supplement sufficient to broach the gap between the rates of the fixed pensions of those who retired before 1950 and the skyrocketing cost of living in the post–Second World War II.[7] It was 1971 before Whitehall agreed to take over responsibility for the payment of pensions to its former colonial personnel. In pursuit of their goals over twenty years of campaigning, it became necessary for British-Sudanis to abandon certain elements of their corporate identity that had vacillated between the coterminous subject positions of master and servant. The independence of the Sudan government contributed to the exceptionalism that was central to the narrative of the Anglo-Egyptian Condominium: masters of the government but servants to the Sudanese, not servants of the Colonial Office and masters of the Sudanese.

Anyone who has watched *Yes, Minister* understands the institutional level of delay and prevarication for which Whitehall is famous. Therefore, it isn't remarkable that the pensioners were put off for years with highly skilled methods of deflection. What is worth examining is the particular form and tone that was chosen by Whitehall, and occasionally by Westminster, to manage the British-Sudani. In the early stages of their campaign, the pensioners positioned themselves discursively as the ex-rulers of one government speaking on equal terms with the current rulers of another, a strategy that quite possibly hindered their ability to look out for their interests as British citizens. Over time, however, the British-Sudani narrative more emphatically positioned them as loyal servants of Great Britain and eventually they abandoned the first position in favour of the second. But at both stages, and assisting the shift from one to the other, the Sudanese were positioned and repositioned within the constantly changing psychic landscape of British-Sudanis. Meanwhile, long-established class and gender delineations within the British-Sudani community were selectively invoked to provide stability to their identity position in the face of those challenges.

Associational membership bridges public and private persona and gives individuals a collective identity that isn't familial.[8] In this chapter and in the next, we will be looking at the actions of British-Sudanis in specifically collective environments between public and private. British-Sudani representative associations created space in which individuals could display reputation and prestige in public and, in so doing, manipulate public opinion towards accepting their desired collective identity.[9] In the case of the Sudan Government British Pensioners' Association (SGBPA), participating in the group helped individuals reconcile their identities as both private citizens and public servants. Colonial administrators were by definition the embodiment of the national imperial project and the SGBPA provided the comfort of contextual continuity for individuals who had for so long been defined by their participation in a community.[10] Although there was a very practical reason for the formation of the SGBPA, recasting their social identity in a decolonizing Britain became a compulsory additional project that can be traced over the course of their twenty-year campaign for economic and political recognition as British pensioners.[11]

Labor and management in the Sudan

1952 was the last year that the SPS recruited anyone for a pensionable position. For a number of years beforehand, and exclusively from that point on, British officers were hired on contracts in accordance with Sudanization efforts.[12] There were a few Greeks, Syrians and Lebanese in the government, and some Egyptians had come into the service again after the 1936 Treaty. Sudanization had less effect on any of their positions because the senior posts that might influence the 'free and neutral atmosphere' needed for self-determination were mainly held by British officials.[13]

Whoever the employer had been or would be in the future, prior to the decision to accelerate the process of Sudanization and eventual independence, there was no organization set up in the Sudan or in Great Britain to act as a lobbying organ for the employees of the Sudan government, whether they be British or another nationality. When, in 1951, a commission was established to look in to an overhaul of terms of service for Sudan Civil Service members, including the SPS, there was no pension organization to present a brief to the commission regarding changes to the pension arrangements. Most colonies had established pension organizations by this time, and there was an umbrella group for the entire Colonial Office. Between 1945 and 1947, the terms of service were revised for most of the colonies but the Sudan didn't undertake to revise *any* terms of service until 1951.[14]

The Senior Civil Servants' Association of the Sudan (SCSAS) was formed in 1950 to represent the interests of current employees, but they were unable to represent the interests of those who had already retired. Their remit, at least initially, was to represent the ongoing interests and concerns of Sudan government personnel during the process of Sudanization and the transfer of power, first to a governing council, then to a Legislative Assembly. Its membership crossed racial boundaries and the class hierarchy of the Sudani community, although its active members were drawn more from the technical and civil service departments than from the SPS. Despite the assertion that 'there is no upper limit to membership', meaning that even the most senior members of government could join, the regulations regarding public criticism of the government by its own political staff required SPS to be 'dormant members'.[15]

The political agenda of the association was certainly progressive. Among other matters, it supported equal pay for women, a subject then under debate in the British Parliament. And because of the forceful pursuit of other demands, the editorial board of the SCSAS's journal felt it necessary to reassure those who had yet to join that 'the Association is NOT a Trade Union (though for lack of any other legislation in the country we have perforce had to be registered for the time being under a Trade Union Ordinance)'. There were no other categories under Sudan law for registering an employees' organization, which suggests just how anomalous the SCSAS was.[16]

In a corporate culture where effective criticism and monitoring of government by its own professional class was uncommon, the pension campaign was slow to get going even as the younger generation of official still serving in the Sudan was increasingly more likely to take a publicly critical tone. By becoming members but not actively participating in the executive of the SCSAS, the younger SPS officials were able to support the organization's goals without coming in direct conflict with their own culture within a culture.[17] For the more active members, expressing discontent *along with* Sudanese officials signalled an interesting, short-lived moment in which superficial class solidarity was fostered by the racially and culturally neutral language that accompanied the transition to Sudanese authority.

In 1952, the make-up and the name of the SCSAS were changed when the Sudanese members left to form their own association. The cause of this split was, in fact, the pension question. The SCSAS recommended that the government solve the problem by creating a separate pension fund out of which all government employee pensions would be funded as was the common practice. The British-Sudani were unable to understand the delicate political position of the Sudanese government employees who 'did not see any difficulty over the funding of expatriate pensions but they saw difficulties, particularly on political grounds, over the funding of their own'.[18] And so the group became the Expatriate Civil Servants' Association of the Sudan (ECSAS), its new name signalling the inclusion of junior British civil servants as it lost its Sudanese members. From this point on, ECSAS members focused on what form their departure would take, in both practical and symbolic terms.

Meanwhile, in Britain, ex-members of the Sudan government were increasingly concerned about the future of their pensions after independence. Rather than more junior members of the Sudan government challenging the decisions of those at the top, Michael Hillary, the former auditor-general of the Sudan government who first brought the fate of the pension scheme to the attention of other retired officials, contacted retired senior members of the three Secretariat departments (Civil, Legal and Financial) that had constituted the political administration of the Sudan. These included Angus Gillan, a former civil secretary, J. W. Cummins, an ex-assistant financial secretary and A. E. Elkington, once the director of customs.

The first meeting of the SGBPA took place in May 1952, at Sudan House in London, where it was decided by the sixty-two people in attendance that it was worthwhile to organize.[19] Once a membership roll was established and an executive elected, Hillary became the SGBPA's Honorary Secretary, and Gillan was voted Chairman.[20] Other members of the executive were drawn from the senior ranks of other branches of the government, such as the railways, and the medical and education services. Thus the executive was more representative of the British-Sudani community in the Sudan than the Palace in Khartoum had been, but they were still all older members. Most had come in to the service during the 1920s. By 1954, virtually every pensionable British member of the Sudan government, or their widow, was a member of the SGBPA, approximately 1,100 people. The Annual General Meeting was soon connected to an annual reunion dinner to which families were invited, and the SGBPA quickly became the central organ of British-Sudani corporate identity in Britain.[21]

Negotiating with equals

During its early years, members exhibited an abiding faith in the power and connections of senior executive, assuming that status in the hierarchy of the Sudan government was transferable, somehow, to the political culture in Britain. Each of the succeeding chairmen were ex-civil secretaries and deputy secretaries, and they eventually invited a former governor general, Lord Rugby (previously Sir Geoffrey Archer), to function as a special patron for the group.[22] The core executive was always senior SPS and SCS retirees. Even after ten years of lobbying Westminster and Whitehall with no result, there was very little criticism of the executives' tactics, and the make-up of the executive was very stable. Between the first elections in 1952 and 1968, Sir Shuldham Redfern, once assistant civil secretary in the Sudan, and later private secretary to the governor general of Canada, was elected no less than nine times.[23]

The executive did not hesitate to keep information from the general membership if they felt it was prudent to do so.[24] C. G. Davies, then Sudan Agent in London, was concerned that the formation of the SGBPA might be diplomatically awkward. While telling Gillan, in confidence, that certain negotiations were going on behind the scenes, he suggested that Gillan 'might make a vague statement [to the general membership] to allay alarm and stop any hotheads from making too much fuss over things'.[25] The SGBPA began to deploy similar language about the potential emotionality of the rank and file pensioners as had been deployed about the Sudanese. Class affiliation replaced race to bolster the paternalism of the executive's efforts. The British-Sudani self-sacrifice was now directed towards the membership at large.

Every British woman in the Sudan government had been in the Civil rather than Political Service, and so their marginal involvement in association activities also paralleled the gender hierarchy in the Sudan. There were a couple of attempts in the early stages of the association to alter this dynamic. When discussing the formulation of the association's charter, Gillan, whom Davies referred to as one of 'the more moderns',[26] put forward the suggestion that one position on the executive should be reserved for a female member, but this was opposed by Sir Harold MacMichael, who had been civil secretary a quarter century before Gillan.[27] It was not raised again. And Dr. Ina Beasley put forward the request that the rate of membership fees for women should be 4/5 that of men because that was the current legal ratio of female to male salary levels for the same position. She apologized that she could not attend the meeting to put forward the resolution herself, explaining 'my present post requires *five* fifths of my time'.[28] But when Hillary wrote in response and told her that her suggestion was not to be incorporated initially but that she was welcome to continue a campaign for it at the next Annual General Meeting, she declined to pursue the issue. Initially, at least, rank-and-file members of the SGBPA were far less likely to rock the boat than those of the SCSAS.

Despite this evidence of members falling back on a familiar hierarchy, the formation of the SGBPA had an unsettling effect on the corporate identity of the British-Sudanis. From the first suggestion that such a group was necessary, many members expressed discomfort with its implications. There was a tension between the obvious practical need for such an organization and how this need contradicted British-Sudani self-representation. The response of J. W. Cummins, who was in the Finance Branch from 1919, to Hillary's letter about the need for such an association was emblematic. He respected the assessment of those above him that there was a problem, but he personally believed that 'most pensioners have the fullest faith in the Sudan Government'.[29] It was difficult, initially, for the membership to reconcile the formation of a lobbying group with recognition that there was a real need for it. While what prompted the creation of the SGBPA was concern about the possibility of Sudanese repudiation of pensions, Gillan began the very first meeting by stating, 'Needless to say, the proposal to form a Pensioners' Association contains no imputation of bad faith on anybody's part.'[30] In the initial stages the possibility that Her Majesty's Government would hesitate to alleviate their concerns was unimaginable.

By the autumn of 1953, the SGBPA had held its first Annual General Meeting, the transitional Sudanese Legislative Assembly had opened its first session and the speed of Sudanization was increasing, in preparation for the 1 January, 1956, date for full independence. The Foreign Office hall had failed to capitalize on its chance to put an assurance of the future of pensions into the independence agreement of 1953 and members of the ECSAS were conflicted, being both members of the current government and petitioners before the Sudanese Executive Council, which would set the terms for the next government. Their concerns were briefly assuaged by the governor general's promise to include a safeguard in the final agreement. Paul Daniell, now the Honorary Secretary of the ECSAS, issued a statement to the membership quoting Sir Robert Howe, to that effect.[31]

Daniell concludes with a personal appeal: 'I am further asked by His Excellency, in conveying this message to members … who are concerned, to request them to bear in mind that the information should be treated as confidential.'[32] Governors general's close contact with the Foreign Office had, in the past, brought their loyalty to the Sudan and the welfare of the Sudanese into question. In particular, the most recent governors general had been taken from other services or from the Foreign Office itself rather than being drawn from British-Sudani ranks.[33] Now, however, with Howe's *personal* assurances and request, those still in the Sudan government were increasingly affiliating themselves with metropolitan government structures and distancing themselves from the Sudanese.

In a 'top secret' summary of the compensation situation, the ESCAS expressed to its members its continuing dissatisfaction with the terms as laid out by the Sudanese, but concluded that 'it would be undignified to ask Sudan Government officials to wrangle further with the Sudanese over compensation terms. It would be a sordid exit after so splendid an entrance'.[34] Even after the failure to include pension assurances in the agreement, the executive was co-opted by the Palace's invitation to share in the greater burdens of the transition. W. H. Luce, Adviser to the Governor-General on Constitutional and External Affairs, told J. S. Owen, Daniell's predecessor,

> that he would regard any pressure brought to bear on H.M.G. through members of the House, however discreet and influential these might be, as both unhelpful and unwise until he had exhausted the possibilities of normal negotiation with the Foreign Office.[35]

In 1953, the ESCAS had met with the Foreign Office themselves but were given little additional assurance beyond the 'undesirably vague' official statement by Anthony Eden, then foreign secretary, that their interests would be looked after;[36] and so their decision to cooperate with the governor general's office meant that they now saw the Sudanese leadership and Her Majesty's Government firmly positioned on the management side of the employee/employer divide, with the governor general and the ECSAS, oddly, as labour. And when J. S. Owen left the Sudan in late 1954, Howe wrote him a personal farewell in which he told Owen, 'I have watched your handling of the affairs of the [ECSAS] with admiration during the recent difficult period of negotiations. I am aware too of your consistent loyalty to me in the best tradition of the Political Service, and I thank you for it.'[37] In Howe's characterization of the SPS as loyal, the question remains unanswered as to whom Howe saw as responsible for the more critical language of the ECSAS over the previous few years. Throughout 1954 and 1955, memberships in the ESCAS were transferred to the SGBPA as officials retired and returned to Britain. An increasing impatience with the SGBPA's faith in the British government can be detected in the final correspondence of the ECSAS, leading up to independence, and no one in the leadership of the ECSAS were active on the executive of the SGBPA.

From partners to petitioners

The Palace was attempting to elicit the cooperation of the executive of the ESCAS with language that stressed the historic unity of the Sudan government in response to the actions of the Foreign Office; the executive of the SGBPA was the target of a similar technique back in Britain. The initial letters from the SGBPA to Whitehall prompted responses suggesting that the situation in the Middle East was so precarious that it would be unpatriotic for the British-Sudani to press the issue, for fear of alienating the incoming Sudanese government, playing into Egypt's hands, or embarrassing Her Majesty's Government.[38] This position from Whitehall fed the ambivalent self-constitution of the SGBPA executive as both partners of government and as servants of it. Hillary and Gillan continued to offer assurances to the membership of the SGBPA even as the executive of the ECSAS sent them increasingly pessimistic letters.

Then, after much expectation, the Conservative government under Churchill also failed to include a guarantee of pensions in the final handing over agreement. Midnight on 31 December, 1955, came and went without the imposition of any conditions on the new Sudan. Any leverage that the British government had was now lost, and the petitioners were told that these concerns needed to be raised with the new Sudan government.[39] Simultaneously, however, H.M. government had repeatedly implied that direct dealing with the Sudan government could undermine British interests in other negotiations.[40] The British government had always maintained that the Sudan government had been independent: There had been no 'change of master'. Their employer had been the Sudan government and still was. While they continued to offer unofficial assurances that they would take over the pensions if they were repudiated, the British government would not make an official admission to that effect. Some on the SGBPA executive began to argue that 'we can no longer keep our members in ignorance'.[41] For many, this was the first time that they entertained the idea of Whitehall and Westminster as either grossly incompetent or flagrantly uncaring. Willoughby pointed out that Whitehall 'aren't making progress because they have left themselves nothing to bargain with'.[42]

Some pensioners were slower than others to internalize these actions and apportion blame anywhere. Angus Gillan resigned as Chairman in 1957, and his replacement, Sir Duncan Cumming, seemed reluctant to let go of similar assumptions about how to approach the government. But a meeting in September of 1958 changed everything. Cummings and Hillary met with A. R. Ross, head of the Levant Department of the Foreign Office, where they were received 'in a rather uncompromising manner'. When Ross 'would only say that he would keep in mind the points made by the Chairman', he appeared to repudiate even the unofficial assurances that the SGBPA had been given.[43]

Cumming was reluctant at first to attribute Ross's attitude to the Foreign Office at large and immediately sent a personal letter to the secretary of state, Sir Selwyn Lloyd, proposing that they meet, unofficially, to discuss matters. He suggested that 'some pensioners believe that they have now no alternative but to start parliamentary and public agitation', but that, between the two of them, something 'might be done to settle the matter without prejudicing either the position of H.M.G. or the interests of the pensioners'.[44] Although by this time the calls for pubic agitation were coming from the executive as well as the membership, Cumming was asserting his power by implying that he could stave off the 'agitation' if he could produce some concession.

Lloyd's response mimicked Cumming's language of presumed equality (Cumming, a former deputy civil secretary, the second man in the Sudan government, and Selwyn-Lloyd, secretary of state).[45] The subsequent meeting produced a reiteration of the unofficial assurance that Her Majesty's Government would not abandon pensioners. Lloyd did not say anything, however, that altered the Foreign Office's official stance that they 'must categorically repudiate any suggestion … of any liability for payment of pensions of British ex-officials of the Sudan Civil Service'.[46] This language was incommensurate with the British-Sudani identity; the unofficial assurance stemming from the personal meeting was emphasized, and the official repudiation downplayed between Cumming and many on the SGBPA executive.[47]

For other pensioners, however, the disillusionment was immediately registered by a change in attitude towards the British government. Jack Willoughby, a member of the executive, urged a more forceful approach because 'the FO have fallen down on their undertaking … (by reason of lethargy, complacency or some ulterior motive of which we have no knowledge)' and 'the Embassy are now embarrassed because we … have caught them up and are treading on their heels'. He went on to suggest that 'if the FO care to read into our letter the possibility of 1,000 members sending copies of the correspondence to 630 MPs, so much the better!'[48] This allowed for the possibility that it was the individuals in the Foreign Office rather than the British government itself with which the SGBPA was at odds.

Others made the interesting suggestion that loyalty to their fellow pensioners took precedence over loyalty to the British government, even a Conservative one. Sir Shuldham Redfern, who had continued a distinguished career in the British Diplomatic Service after leaving the Sudan, and who had, therefore, invested quite substantially in the prestige of the British government, illustrates what this meant for him in a 1958 letter to the executive.[49] 'We should write a *personal* letter to MacMillan and tell him we *must* have a settlement within say 24 hours … If we do not then get satisfaction we should hand the whole correspondence to Gaitskill [the Labour leader] or to the Press [my emphasis].'[50] Redfern, while still using language that reinforced this idea of equals and of a closed community of governors, was also threatening to go public and go to the Opposition. To become public petitioners was a grave challenge to British-Sudani exceptionalism and a step that many – especially those who had been in power – found difficult to take. A public approach implied that they were no different than any other petitioners and that these ex-rulers no longer shared a common purpose with Westminster. Just as the 'dormant' SPS officials in the ECSAS were unable to criticize the government in the Sudan, the executive of the SGBPA had to abandon their SPS identity in order to give themselves permission to publicly criticize the Conservative government.

It became increasingly difficult to maintain the narrative of 'equals' when Whitehall and Westminster were failing to provide the space in which it could be articulated. The SGBPA's change in strategy acknowledged their acceptance of the government's authority and their status as private British citizens. The civil service secretaries in Whitehall had been able to disavow the pensioners' status by using their own argument against them; if pensioners of a foreign government were no concern of Whitehall, then the British-Sudani had to make their identity as Britons less ambiguous. Redfern articulated this turn, 'We have been far too ready to accept that they are in no way responsible … After all, it *was* the *Anglo*-Egyptian Sudan.'[51] Retroactively, they wrote out their equality, reinscribing it as dependence, removing the disrespected equals and leaving the poorly treated servants to write in new boundaries.

For the British officials who lived and worked through the years of transition, such as Owen and Daniell, the illusion of the Anglo-Egyptian Condominium as an independent government was gone. Those like Gillan, Hillary and Cumming didn't have the benefit of that experience. They took longer to realize that modern political considerations had replaced the culture of government as a series of gentlemen's agreements. And by the 1958 Annual General Meeting, even Gillan was willing to propose that the SGBPA go public, although it would be almost two more years before they launched a modern, public campaign.[52]

Disillusionment and re-definition

It is difficult to assess what effect, if any, the Suez Crisis had on the attitudes and strategies of the British-Sudani. There is, perhaps, a change in tone towards members of government and, also, a slow change in strategy used to push their case. Despite Baily's assertions years earlier regarding Labour imperial policies, the majority of British-Sudanis voted Tory.[53] The Conservative governments of the 1950s left little chance for the pensioners to explain away the disappointing attitude of government as having anything to do with Labour Party policy. Blame had been argued away by focusing on the civil servants in the Foreign Office, but many were reluctant to damn their civil service counterparts.[54] It could have potentially created a rift between the Political Service and Civil Service pensioners from the Sudan government. Finally, in 1959, however, executive member A. E. H. Elkington submitted that 'further negotiations with the Foreign Office are useless and, with an impending election, we are in a stronger position than we have been in the past or are likely to be in the future'.[55] Dissatisfaction had resulted in the abandonment of party loyalty. By May 1962, just before the SGBPA knew that the Pensioners (Increases) Bill would be passed – finally improving and ensuring the supplements but still not assuring pensions – Willoughby was so completely disillusioned he was able to write, 'I am sorry to feel like this but much as I loathe most of the Labour Party policies I really believe the Sudan pensioners would get a better deal at their hands.'[56]

Many pensioners were actually employed in second careers that were connected to Britain's continued imperial concerns and were confronting nationalist movements in other colonies. Furthermore, by the early 1960s, Ghana and numerous other West African colonies had all been granted independence. The failure of the British to safeguard British-Sudani interests could no longer be blamed on the peculiar exigencies of the Anglo-Egyptian Condominium. Among other unsettling events, Britain had failed to affect reprisals on the Soviet Union after its invasion of Hungary; a coup in Iraq brought the deaths of the pro-British King Faisel II, his heir and the prime minister; the Mau Mau rebellion continued in Kenya; and the Suez Crisis resulted in Britain's loss to the United States of influence in the former British mandate, Palestine.

J. Carmichael, a pensioner, wrote to Hillary in 1958 that 'HMG have failed in the past four years … during which time, the pensioners themselves have been precluded from fighting their own case … It could be added that because of HMG's policy in the Middle East in the past two or three years it is probable that the Sudan Government's attitude to its British pensioners is less favourable than it otherwise would have been'.[57] And so by the end of 1959, not only their firm belief in the exceptionalism of the British-Sudani experience but also their confidence in British political skills had been seriously challenged. Elkington, when arguing for a large-scale public campaign, wrote,

> The F.O. may reply that we are prejudicing their negotiations with the S.G. This argument does not deserve much attention because, on several occasions in the past, they have been in an impregnable position … but they have failed to press our case … The letter from Mr. Selwyn Lloyd … is marked 'Confidential.' But … in all the circumstances we cannot be tied by this marking.[58]

The British government's tactics, although successful for a while, had thoroughly alienated the executive, who in turn could defend their decision to no longer cooperate by citing the incompetence of the Foreign Office, rather than their own loss of status.

Failure as the best option

With their exceptionalism abandoned, the executive began to actively affiliate itself with the pensioners' organizations of other territories, including the umbrella group for all Overseas and Commonwealth Office pensioners, the Overseas Pensioners Association.[59] They also went to the press: 'Our members have loyally served the Crown', the British-Sudani wrote to the *Times*, along with the Malayan and West African pensioners.[60] Citing the 'callous attitude of the Conservative Government',

Willoughby was happy to bring the Sudan pensioners rhetorically closer to their other colonial colleagues as poorly treated faithful servants.[61]

The new role as servants of the Crown allowed for the SGBPA to also relinquish mastery of their own fate. As private British citizens petitioning the British government, Sir Duncan Cumming and others became more comfortable exercising a freedom they hadn't previously enjoyed. Their cause was increasing urgent. By 1960, the pension gap had widened to the point that some older pensioners were in real financial trouble. The Sudan government, while still honouring its commitment to pay pensions at the sterling rate at the time of independence, refused to consider the pensioners' request for a supplement to bring it in line with inflation, arguing that they could not be held responsible for the rise in the cost of living in another country. Four hundred and fifty pensioners were over sixty by this point. Of these, 118 were over seventy and twenty-five were over eighty. The executive focused their concern on the older pensioners for whom time was running out and also the poor. After a direct appeal to Prime Minister MacMillan brought no result in 1959, the damage done to elderly and poor pensioners was put squarely on to the shoulders of government.[62] As long as the government refused to respond, it was feared that 'many pensioners would be reduced to what they could obtain in the way of National Assistance'.[63]

This increased urgency forced the British-Sudanis to deal with another paradoxical element of their corporate identity. Increasingly, it became apparent that the best way to deal with both key pension issues – a substantial increase in supplements and the end to any uncertainty about the reliability of funds – was for the new Sudan government to fail. Their self-ascribed status as governors and their symbolic location as servants of Britain were accompanied, prior to the pension struggle, by a loyalty to the Sudan and the Sudanese that was complimentary, not contradictory. As discussed earlier, in the postwar years the exceptionalism of their corporate identity was part of a discursive project that retroactively characterized their actions in the Sudan as selfless: as the last, finest version of colonialism and locating them firmly in the service of the Sudanese. Anthony Disney, ex-director of the Department of Economics and Trade, later asserted that he 'always knew, from the first that [we] would eventually leave … It was the "object of the exercise"'.[64] If the British government had given the SGBPA repeated private assurances that they would take over payment if the Sudan government stopped, and the Sudan government was refusing to recognize that economic conditions in Britain made the pensions inadequate, then Sudanese repudiation of their pension responsibility would be a valid excuse for the pensioners to demand that unofficial assurances become public policy.

This enlightened imperialism had been challenged by the Sudanese nationalist movement and resulted in the chagrined admission that the Sudanese had shown 'a strong inherent tendency to prefer inefficient government by fellow-countrymen to good government by foreigners'.[65] In the earlier days of the pension battle, the narrative of the ungrateful natives was reinvigorated, and to some degree the eagerness of the Sudanese for independence was written in to the story of the British-Sudani as the justification for the pensioners' lack of faith in their former charges, thus easing at least some of their ambivalence as former rulers and current petitioners. When writing to a fellow British-Sudani about an article that was being written about the

Mutiny, Reginald Davies said, 'I'm not at all sure how the Republic of the Sudan would view ... publication of an account of events which, from one point of view, at least, might appear to be discreditable to a number of Sudanese. Reprisals on the pension front would be unfortunate!!'[66] Although the punctuation implies that he means it as a joke, Davies connects events during the Mutiny, almost forty years earlier, to the current Sudan government's dependability as a pension provider. Rewriting their relationship with the Sudanese helped to cement their eventual over-determination as servants of Great Britain, but they had to abandon their role as caretakers of the Sudan. The pension debate was conducted in Britain but with the Sudanese offering the fixed point in a symbolic order of progress against which British-Sudani (and British) civility could be measured. This fixed point was maintained only through the strategic writing and re-writing of the relationship between the British-Sudani and the Sudanese. The Sudanese became the foil against which the seemingly mutually exclusive categories of former rulers and current petitioners could be reconciled.

When the British-Sudani strategy shifted and they began to argue that they had acted on behalf of Great Britain, the imminent failure of the new Sudanese government became central to their argument. The pensioners still tried to fashion themselves as benevolent caretakers by suggesting taking over pension payments as 'Her Majesty's Government's contribution towards the progress of the Sudan from its present undeveloped state towards a state of self-sufficiency'.[67] In this way, a lack of faith in the Sudan's ability to continue paying the pensions, or to provide the supplements to bring pensions in line with the cost of living, was more because of its economic burdens and not because of an inherent flaw in the national character. Expressed sympathy for the Sudanese position increased in direct relation to SGBPA frustration with the British government response.[68] 'But', asked the executive, 'how can the unfortunate Sudanese, for instance, who have their work cut out to keep their own country viable, be held responsible for inflation in the UK'?[69]

Redfern acknowledged the tactical error of allowing the government to co-opt the SGBPA for so long, missing opportunities as a result. 'When the Government's electoral fortunes were evenly balanced [prior to the 1959 election that returned a larger majority for the Conservatives], we might have scared them a bit by threatening to make an electoral issue' of their pensions.[70] As it was only in late 1959 that the executive finally made the shift towards a more combative stance, the idea of 'scaring' or 'threatening' the government was still anathema to their corporate identity. But in the same letter Redfern, who was one of the first to challenge the intentions of the government, abandoned not only his faith in the British government but, interestingly, his own subject position as a benevolent colonial administrator when he claimed that 'it is always a waste of time appealing to the Government – or any Government whatever its political complexion – on the basis of abstract justice'.[71]

Change of masters

Rewriting their relationship with the Sudanese was accompanied by the reconstruction of 'appropriate' gender identification that had also been challenged. The fifteen-year struggle with Whitehall and Khartoum had ignominiously turned them into supplicants. This was slightly ameliorated for the executive by their subject position as the caretakers of the pensioners themselves. The higher ranked members of the executive, who, in many cases did not actually need the Sudan government pension to live comfortably, were still able to maintain their self-identification as paternalistic leaders, but the petitioning process had challenged the easy correlation between imperial servant and masculine authority.

We can get some insight into the ambivalence of the average pensioner's gendered subject position in the astounding shifts of self-representation in one letter to Sir Duncan Cumming, in 1962. An elderly pensioner criticizes Cumming's tactics by asking, 'Does our traditional gentlemanly reticence get us anywhere?' This criticism is immediately undercut with an assertion of masculine outrage. 'Ought we not to thump a table somewhere, and if so, whose table would it be most advantageous to thump?'[72] But the undeniably masculine 'thumping' is framed as a useless show of impotent force because there's no access to power or even a recognition of who has the power. When the pensioner volunteers more gentlemanly tactics: 'I think I could raise a campaign in the press … [or] "Questions in the House"',[73] he immediately undercuts his authority evoking old-aged frailty and suffragettes' tactics from a half-century earlier: 'I would even chain my bathchair to the railing of the FO or Treasury, and scream blue murder if that would help.' In the end, he reclaims his paternal authority by saying 'many of us are in very much worse case than I am [*sic*]' but 'from a social point of view I would prefer that you keep my personal woes to yourself'.[74] This pensioner challenges the efficacy of SGBPA leadership but also acknowledges his own emasculation before reclaiming his gentlemanly dignity through stoicism and charity.

In 1963, the second Pensions (Increases) Act went into effect.[75] The SGBPA finally won a promise that Great Britain would pay a substantial supplement in order to bring pension levels in line with the domestic civil service. The uncertainty about pension takeovers in case of Sudanese repudiation was not settled for another eight years. But the practical, day-to-day problem of inadequate pensions was solved. The executive seizes this moment of victory to reclaim masculine prestige within the British-Sudani community. Before the new bill took effect, Hillary suggested it would be a good idea to make a proposal to the general membership that pensioners should make a one-time gift of the first month of their supplements to distribute among the *neediest* of the *widow* pensioners.[76] Angus Gillan agrees but, in his response, betrays some of the assumptions under which the suggestion was made. 'I entirely agree with your proposal that all ex-officials should be asked to forego their first month's increase for the benefit of widows on less than £200. (Should similar female annuitants, if any, be included?)'[77] For Gillan, all of the 'ex-officials' expected to participate in this act of noblesse oblige were men, despite the fact that the 'female annuitants' he is thinking of helping are also ex-officials. His response also betrays his inability to imagine a British, male, former member of the Sudan government in a dependent situation, not only incapable of contributing to this scheme but in need of charity themselves.

There was an immediate rush of correspondence as other members hurried to associate themselves with this plan and iron out its details in time to send out a circular before the new supplements began in 1963. The first criticism was in the initial cap of £200. Desmond Mulholland, who had been in charge of Supply for the Sudan Railways, thought that a set amount might result in those with higher pensions but also higher expenses being ineligible for help.[78] Another member makes the point of dependency clear when he also disagrees with the set cap and states, 'The intended purpose of the Fund will be vitiated unless the grant be paid to specific cases where the "NEED" is real.'[79] Once it's established that men of the Sudan government will be able to fulfill this last paternalistic act, the suggestion is made that the funds shouldn't be limited to men because there 'must be some officials themselves on very small pensions and with family commitments probably as badly off as the widows'.[80] And yet at the same time the difficulty is raised that 'while it is hoped that every official who can afford it will ante-up his contribution, it is realised that there are some who just can't afford to do so and they need feel no shame in refusing'.[81] Through all of these debates, and a final vote by the entire executive, chaired this time by Sir James Robertson, another former civil secretary, it became a separate and permanent 'Pension Supplementation Fund'.[82]

As donations began to arrive, including one for five hundred pounds, Redfern voiced his concern about people's generosity because the argument for supplements in the first place was the impecunity of *all* the pensioners. He also thought that, given the large donations, there might be a problem of never being able to distribute all the funds because 'very few pensioners will apply for assistance. Those that would consider it undignified to apply for National Assistance will be even more reluctant to apply for a subsidy from their erstwhile Sudan colleagues'.[83] Whether he was right or not is unknown because the trustees kept their word that all information would be kept strictly confidential. In any case, the almost frenzied creation of what everyone imagined to be a fund to aid women is an astounding bit of displacement: marking the end of their supplication, the men of the executive immediately created a highly gendered emblem for the expression of their restored status. And in July of the following year, Ina Beasley had her wish granted, as the membership fees for women were reduced, although it is questionable whether the motivation for the reduction would have pleased her.[84]

The Pensions Act included the former officials of all ex-colonies. British-Sudani exceptionalism was now completely abandoned. For members of the executive, the first campaign had seriously challenged their self-identity. They had continued their roles as leaders (of other pensioners) but were long unable to fulfil their role as providers and protectors. It was 1970 before the British government agreed to take over the payment of pensions. There was still no acknowledgement by what was now a Labour government of any moral obligation to pay pensions to British subjects employed in the national interest. Judith Hart, minister of Overseas Development, stated that 'the Government have decided that as part of their policy of aid to development', the British government would assume 'responsibility for the cost for pensions to expatriate officers in respect of pre-independence government service'.[85] Proposed by a Labour government, the bill was passed by Heath's Conservatives in 1971. All colonial officials of all independent or soon to be independent former colonies were covered under the bill. Assuming this burden even from countries with no intention of abrogating their pension agreements was the result of having 'recently given careful consideration to representations made by several governments of developing countries'. The efforts of the SGBPA and other pension groups were described as 'views expressed by many sections of informed opinion in this country'.[86] The exigencies of foreign affairs and the desire of their former charges, rather than a directly articulated concern for the welfare of Her Majesty's servants, were credited with bringing about the desired result.

Conclusion

The official role of the SGBPA was to acquire pension supplement increases and an official guarantee that the British government would take over responsibility of pensions if the Sudan government repudiated their obligation. The success of the SGBPA as an association, however, cannot be gaged by their success at doing so. In the end, it is debatable whether the executive's efforts had more than a negligible impact on the government's decision to take over pensions in 1971. And it is only by abandoning their exceptionalist status and becoming one of many groups petitioning that they succeeded in getting pension supplements for their members. Nevertheless, in many other ways, the SGBPA was extremely successful. It was a medium for the slow evolution of an articulated corporate identity. With some tensions as to its conservative nature, the SGBPA nonetheless managed to provide a focus for social identification, not only for those on the executive, like Hillary or Willoughby, or more vocal members of the membership, such as Ina Beasley, but also for the hundreds of British-Sudani who met every year after the General Meeting for a Tea Party and the few survivors who still meet in Salisbury for the Annual General Meeting.[87] While the next chapter explores the choices that have been made over the years as to the proper way to remember and commemorate the British-Sudani experience, for the crucial first decade the SGBPA was actively engaged in negotiating the *current* identity of the British-Sudani, and the contradictions between an identity formed of experiences while in the Sudan, and the evolving British social identity to which they returned.

10

Epilogue: Remembering the Sudan

The final form of authorship undertaken by British-Sudanis was the establishment of an official memory, one which accommodated the disjunction between their personal identity narrative and the British metropolitan narrative while also preserving and celebrating the experiences that created that disjunction. Beginning in the years immediately preceding Sudan's independence, many have engaged in projects that revisited and reworked the myth of the Sudan and their memories of living and working there. Although some efforts were inward looking, such as the creation of reunion groups, in many cases, including the numerous British-Sudani monographs and memoirs, these efforts were directed towards an audience outside their own circle.[1]

Memory text is not inherently tied to a linear narrative. Describing the process of writing autobiography, *the* self-conscious memory text, Annette Kuhn describes our constant and compulsive ordering: 'Events in the memory text seem often to have been plucked at random from a paradigm of memories and wrought into a "telling" that is by its nature linear, syntagmatic.'[2] To write autobiography is to put the self forward as a historical actor. The British-Sudani negotiation of private and personal identity can be approached in a similar way, both despite and because of their awareness of themselves as subjects of history – colonial actors. In telling the story of the Condominium, the 'I' of the writer is in the service of not only the national and imperial narrative but also the personal narrative. The returned British-Sudanis used memory retroactively to establish a narrative for an individual as well as collective loss.[3] The British-Sudanis wanted to reconcile what was becoming the standard post-colonial narrative of colonial administration with the improvisational narrative they created through life. Where the memories of one contradicted the narrative of the other, they often retroactively realigned them in order to come logically to the same point in the present.[4]

The British-Sudani community shared a desire to maintain and celebrate the particularity of their British-Sudani-ness across occupations and generations. Their experiences continued to inform their identities, and their successful return to metropolitan life was facilitated by a celebration of the Sudan that continued in the archive.[5] Annette Kuhn has identified that one of the roles of memory formation is to reassure the individual that their experiences fit within 'the regular course of human destiny'.[6] As was evident in the pension struggle, the British-Sudani felt that their story was left outside the narrative of the nation's destiny and, in the process, their lives were being forgotten in the broader cultural shift in the era of decolonization towards widespread metropolitan discomfort with the history of the imperial project. Maurice

Halbwachs observed that 'memories give us the illusion of living in the midst of groups that do not imprison us'. Through specific efforts, British-Sudanis asserted an identity that countered the identity imposed upon them by contemporary British society. But also, the British-Sudani wanted to create an outward representation of their own internal hybridity. Commemoration was a response to their perceived loss – of a Sudan that at least on some level could be called home – and the reformation or revitalization of an ongoing site of identity production.

The cross-cultural Anglo-Sudanese Association (ASA), which was obviously directed towards their former charges, was also less obviously intended as a retort to two factions in the British public: those who held increasingly negative attitudes towards colonial immigrants in the late 1950s and early 1960s and those who held increasingly negative attitudes towards the agents of the British imperial project during the same period. The creation of the Sudan Archive at the University of Durham was prompted, like the SGBPA struggle, by the unique corporate identity of British-Sudanis. The British-Sudani feared the Condominium would not be represented in the Public Records Office nor the Imperial and Commonwealth Archives at Rhodes House, would always be subsumed under Foreign Office or Cabinet papers, and never included in any collection that purported to hold records of 'the Empire'.[7,8] Initially prompted by this fear of erasure, the Sudan Archive at Durham University became the most vibrant and elastic mode of self-expression that the British-Sudani community created.

The other and far more long-lasting way in which British-Sudanis asserted their identity is complex in its formulation and surprisingly elastic in its composition. The Sudan Archive at Durham University, like the SGBPA, crossed the class/department boundaries of the entire British-Sudani community. The archive was, and is, an extremely egalitarian construct, both in terms of its contributors and in terms of the categories of knowledge and experience that it serves to represent. The Sudan Archive at Durham University is both the archive of the Anglo-Egyptian Condominium and an on-going project of self-fashioning for British-Sudanis. It is universal in its inclusivity and so the limits to its content are self-defined and policed solely by the choice to donate or not. The historical document and the active participants in its creation are not clearly delineated within the Sudan Archive. And yet there is a surprising compulsion to record everything, including the less flattering details, of the life of the Condominium. Of course, the creation of the archive doubles as an assertion that they belong(ed) to a special collectivity and that they continue to occupy a place in history can be recognized today as a common pattern in identity politics.

The Anglo-Sudanese Association

In 1949, the Sudan Agent in London, R. C. Mayall, wrote to M. J. Wheatley, MP, another ex-SPS man, to thank him: 'You and the other members of this unofficial "committee" ... have ... been very helpful in entertaining Sudanese' young men in Britain to study.[9] The fear was that the visiting Sudanese might fall prey to student Communist groups if left to their own devices.[10] Returned British-Sudanis already made a point of maintaining contact and being available to visiting Sudanese, but Allan Arthur's request that his parents invite Daud Abdel Latif for dinner, or Mary Hawkesworth's hospitality to visiting Sudanese at her home in Berkshire, was not prompted by geopolitical concerns. And once independence was imminent, private motivations prompted efforts to create an official mechanism for establishing British-Sudanese relationships in Britain, rather than the Sudan.

'There have been many suggestions that the time is opportune for the formation of some kind of "Sudan Association"', asserted Tom Mynors, governor of Blue Nile province, in a 1955 letter to colleagues in the Sudan and Britain.[11] Mynors, also editor of the scholarly *Sudan Notes and Records*, was focused on encouraging educated Sudanese and Britons to contribute, including on topical issues related to the process of independence.[12] At Mynors's instigation, British officials left in the country met and proposed that 'an Association of British persons should be founded in the United Kingdom'.[13] In their description, the object of this association was already described in a way that rewrote the narrative. The aim of 'maintaining and promoting British-Sudani friendship and understanding' elided the asymmetrical colonial relationship.[14] And the additional desire that the association would facilitate 'the reunion of its members' suggested that Mynors's focus on intellectual interest in the Sudan was only one motivator.[15] Paternalistic aid would take a new form – helping Sudanese after arriving in Britain – while British-Sudanis could maintain a corporate association despite the end of the British administration in the Sudan.

Simultaneously, another group from among the last British in the Sudan government, including J. S. Owen of the ECSAS, sent out an appeal to every retiring official as they left, soliciting donations to 'The Sudanese Scholarship Fund'. They suggested that despite the 'frustrations and unpleasantness of the last few years', the British and Sudanese had shared a 'generally happy human relationship'.[16] Consequently, 'a number of officials might welcome the opportunity of making a gesture to the Sudanese – a gesture of friendliness and fellowship for the future – which would form a fitting tail-piece to our service in this country'.[17] Their hope was to raise £15,000 (requiring a £15 donation from every retiring official) in order to provide a £400 scholarship in perpetuity to a visiting Sudanese for a four months' stay. Donors would be informed of the itinerary of each visitor and encouraged to 'offer some sort of personal hospitality'.[18] In this way, the ex-officials could keep in touch with events in the Sudan, as well as expressing 'personal friendliness and goodwill on the part of the ex-officials – which is the main object of the present proposal'.[19]

What makes both of these proposals surprising is the enthusiasm they both express about encouraging the growing educated class of Sudanese who, as in other colonial settings, were the most vocal proponents of independence and, as a result, were consistently singled out by officials and ex-officials as the least sympathetic. The Graduates Congress, formed in 1938 from the graduates of Gordon College who were increasingly filling the lower ranks of the government bureaucracy, began the campaign for self-determination during the 1940s and, as the Sudanization policy was implemented more rapidly than anticipated, the Sudanese 'intelligentsia' were seen by many to be overstepping their capabilities.[20] In 1943, G. C. Scott, one of the lecturers at Gordon College, thought that the tensions between British officials and

Sudanese graduates was getting serious enough that he co-authored, with his colleague Ibrahim Ahmen, a guide to lessening misunderstandings between the two cultures.[21] 'The object of these notes', they explained, 'is to help British and educated Sudanese to like each other better by understanding each other better'.[22] He singled out the educated Sudanese 'simply because it is between them and the British that the greatest difficulties exist', because 'when the Sudanese become educated … [c]onsciousness of self, race and nationality inevitably increase, and … he cannot help being emotionally resentful that his country is led and guided by foreigners [*sic*]'.[23] Now, independent of one another, and yet both initiated at the moment when Britain relinquished power, ex- and soon to be ex-officials expressed a desire to maintain connections with the educated Sudanese, to encourage their further education, and to cultivate friendships beyond the boundaries of the office or the suk.

When the scholarship fund failed to raise one-tenth of the target sum, it was proposed that the funds should be given over to the proposed ASA, the formation of which had itself been thwarted for a couple of years after independence, initially due to the Suez Crisis and then out of respect for the impending elections in the Sudan.[24] Finally, in December 1957, a group of British-Sudanis met to discuss the creation of an association with the blessing of the re-elected Sudanese prime minister, Sayyed Abdulla Khalil. Included in this group were representatives from a number of the subgroups within the British-Sudani community. Canon Harper of Khartoum Cathedral attended, as did Owen and Hillary from the pensioners' organizations. Senior officials like Gillan and Cumming, as well as members of the Education service, were there. Tom Mynors had since taken a job overseas, but Donald Hawley, who had been in the Judiciary, had taken over the role of pushing the idea forward.[25]

At the first meeting, support from political and business leaders, government officials and members of the official opposition was noted. These unofficial and semi-official contacts and negotiations had been going on throughout the period of the Suez Crisis and yet, both Sudanese *and* British-Sudanis seemed unconcerned about pursuing an agenda that was, at least temporarily, contradictory to the official line of their respective governments.[26] As with the pension debate, ex-administrators were increasingly comfortable taking positions critical of the British government, even a Conservative one. While an employee of the Foreign Office, in the Levant Dept., Hawley recounted a meeting with the Sudanese ambassador to voice his own discontent with the choices of the British government. Hawley stated the Sudanese ambassador saw little conflict of interest as 'British prestige would be restored in the Sudan and other Arab countries because popular opinion in Britain was hostile to the action which had been taken by its Government'.[27] 'What was now necessary', he opined, 'was that H.M.G. should at once obey the commands of the United Nations and withdraw all her forces from the Port Said area as soon as possible'.[28] Hawley finally described the ambassador as saying, 'The U.N. … was now the focal point of the hopes and aspirations of all small countries' and 'was in large measure the child of the U.K. so H.M.G. would not therefore wish it to die'.[29] This piece of studied ventriloquism elided the power dynamics of the Condominium period and reinscribed their relationship as one of fellow travellers. 'Throughout the meeting the Ambassador was most cordial – Sir Angus and I already knew him well … '[30] Hawley assured his audience.

Only a couple of years earlier, Tom Mynors suggested the formation of a group whose main purposes were to be for the reunion of a portion of the British-Sudani community that shared certain interests and as an informal hospitality and mentoring network for Sudanese visiting Britain but whose other purpose was to memorialize the trouble – free relationship that supposedly existed before the tensions leading up to independence. Now the still-as-yet unrealized ASA was imagined as a forum for discussion and exchange for educated Sudanese, many of them now in government, and their former bosses. These groups were to be augmented by those of both nationalities who had serious scholarly or social interests in the development of the Sudan.

By the time the first meeting was held at the Overseas Club in late 1957 to discuss the possibility of forming an association, British-Sudanis were beginning to settle in to their roles as private citizens or servants of Her Majesty's Government, rather than the Sudan government. The cultural climate of the imperial metropole was shifting; opinion was polarizing, partly due to the debacle of Suez. From the point of view of many British-Sudanis, their national identity associations had been undermined. As with the pension dispute, and perhaps in part because of it, it became increasingly common for British-Sudanis to express a different set of priorities than the official government line. As private citizens, they had the luxury of cultivating friendships with Sudanese whose views might similarly not be represented by their own government or who were not themselves representative of official Sudan policies in regard to members of the former government.

At the inaugural meeting of the ASA, which finally met in November 1960, around two hundred and forty people attended. There is no mention of the ratio of Sudanese to British. Of the thirty-two people who were elected to the General Council, however, five were Sudanese. In addition, two British women were elected, one of whom, Miss Buchanan-Riddell, was also elected to the Executive Committee, along with three of the Sudanese.[31] Although many of the members were the same as the SGBPA, this inclusion of women on the executive marked a distinct difference in the corporate culture of the association – one that the originators had been careful to cultivate. As Mynors wrote to Hawley after gaining the support of the SGBPA executive, 'Their ideas were rather in the line of those of their generation rather than of those who left the Sudan recently.'[32] And by this time, the stated objects of the association were 'to provide opportunities whereby Sudanese, British and other nationals with interests in the Sudan may maintain old friendships and sustain these interests' and 'to offer assistance and hospitality to Sudanese visiting or resident in the United Kingdom.'[33]

Concern or dissatisfaction about the idea of another reunion group began quite early. Hawley, in consultation with Mynors from the beginning, received a letter soon after Mynors's original proposal from a colleague who admitted, 'I am not entirely happy about the object. As you know I am doubtful about stressing the reunion motif.'[34] And Mynors himself characterized the original effort as being motivated by 'selfish reasons', – wanting a way to maintain ties with 'old friends and acquaintances'.[35]

By 1960, 'maintaining old friendships' was reimagined across the races. Representatives of the association were appointed in a number of university towns in order to arrange events and assistance to visiting Sudanese. Cambridge, Durham, Kirkcaldy (Edinburgh), Oxford and St. Andrews all had their own chapter. Liaison with the Union of Sudanese Students in the UK was also begun. Nevertheless, despite their apparent enthusiasm, the largest problem with the expansion of the association's aim for social interaction between British and Sudanese was the substantial gap between the interests of young professional Sudanese visiting Britain to extend their education and what older, retired officials, with time on their hands to plan events, thought constituted entertainment. 'With a view to stimulating interest in the Association and encouraging Sudanese students to become members', ASA members arranged for Sir Angus Gillan to give a talk in which he 'described his experiences during the early period of his service', which began in 1909.[36] Apparently, it was thought that Sudanese in 1961 would enjoy being regaled with stories of the military administration under Sir Reginald Wingate, a participant in the Battle of Omdurman in 1898.

Similarly, 'for the purpose of bringing members together', there was a reception for Lord Rugby, formerly John Maffey. Maffey had become governor general upon the assassination of Lee Stack in 1924. As a pretense to reunion, 'the reception was well attended but', it was observed, 'the attendance of Sudanese was rather disappointing'.[37] Those British-Sudanis who had been in the Sudan in the later years of the Condominium seemed better able to imagine and organize events that pertained to the current interests of the Sudanese, such as party held for the visiting Vice-Chancellor of the University of Khartoum, Sayed Nasr el Hal Ali.[38] But by 1963, it was suggested by the current chair, A. W. M. Disney, who had worked in the Sudan for a private company after independence and been the Sudan correspondent for the *Manchester Guardian* that 'as the students showed little enthusiasm for lectures, it should be left to them to ask for any talks they wanted'.[39]

By the second annual general meeting, in 1962, initial enthusiasm had waned and the efforts to foster corporate involvement on both sides were no longer mentioned. For the thirty-seven in attendance, practical concerns dominated the agenda: there was an appeal to anyone who could help visiting Sudanese find places to live because of the 'difficulty experienced by many Sudanese students in the United Kingdom (especially in the London area) in finding suitable lodgings'.[40] But by the following year, the council was forced to report that there had been little in the way of helpful response from members who were able to offer or suggest accommodation that would welcome Sudanese lodgers.[41] Similarly, at the 1962 meeting, Sir Angus Gillan raised issue of difficulties experienced by Sudanese wives who had accompanied their husbands to Britain. The responsibility for any project to reach out to the wives was left for the two female members of the council. By the following year, Elaine Hills-Young was forced to report that no one had come forward to offer any suggestions or assistance to include Sudanese wives in social activities, at least at the national level.[42]

The politics and practicalities of interaction between Sudanese and British were beginning to mirror those experienced in the Condominium: the more formal, artificial events dictated by senior British officials were met with little enthusiasm by Sudanese. The minutiae of organizational procedure took up more of the council's time than anything else and meetings were preoccupied with procedural niceties such as members complaining 'they had not received copies of the Rules of the Association'.[43] Some began to express impatience. Douglas Udal, once head of Gordon College, 'criticized the [annual report] on the grounds that it showed very little activity by the

Association in the past year'.[44] While at the same meeting it was noted that 'a vote of thanks... to the Honourary Treasurer was carried with applause', Udal and others felt that there was little to applaud.[45]

The only successes of the ASA came from the smaller, regional chapters, particularly those located in university towns where the interactions between British and Sudanese were informal, personal and practical. Their descriptions were in stark contrast to the activities of the council and the executive. A. B. Theobald, who had been in the Education Service, wrote to the executive presenting a surprising picture of a large Sudanese population in Leicester and an active British-Sudanese social calendar there:

> There were 23 Sudanese students in Leicester in the academic year 1962–1963; including wives and children the Sudanese community numbered 33. A committee was organized with Dr. A.B. Theobald as President and Sayed Ali Lufti Abdulla as Vice-President. Meetings were held monthly... the following programmes were carried out: -
> November: – Film show
> December: – Lecture by Dr. Theobald on 'Ali Dinar' – last Sultan of Darfur.
> January: – Evening of Sudanese Music.
> February: – Films – 'Education in Kuwait' and the Sudanese film 'White Gold'.
> March: – Visit to the *Evening Mail* Newspaper
> April: Lecture on 'Education in Russia'.
> June: – Garden Party, honoured by the presence of the Lord Mayor of Leicester.[46]
> Attendance at these meetings was a steady 30–40, with over 50 at the garden party; and there was always a good sprinkling of English friends of the students. Dr. and Mrs. Theobald also gave ten parties in their house.

The variety of events, the prominence of Sudanese subject matter and the apparently unproblematic and casual interaction between British and Sudanese were what the founders of the association had in mind.

There was also far more regional success in dealing with the isolation of Sudanese wives who had accompanied their husbands. K. S. Ferguson, an ex-SPS official who retired in 1955, wrote from Birmingham about the six women married to visiting Sudanese, 'Wives remained remarkably cheerful during a wretched winter. They enjoyed their contacts with the Y.W.C.A Young Wives Club which organized special parties for them... The wives are most appreciative of chances to be entertained at home and to learn about cooking, dress-making, etc.'[47] Condescension aside, Ferguson describes real, practical efforts at outreach that would be culturally acceptable to the Sudanese, something for which the women (or men) on the ASA Council showed little ingenuity.

The ASA did not last through another year. Mynors, working for Shell Oil, and Hawley, in the Foreign Service, were sent overseas, as were others in the younger generation of ex-officials who might have been able to partner with former colleagues to encourage social interaction between the two nationalities. Far from there being greater tension between the ex-officials and the Sudanese who were active in the Sudan government leading up to independence, there seems to be a general understanding that it was during this period that relationships were forged that were less under the strain of inequitable power dynamics. Many of those running the regional chapters were of this generation and had a more particular and practical approach to their interactions with the Sudanese and to providing visitors with helpful support. Thomas Hodgkin aptly identified the tension between the sources of the relationship between Africans and colonizers and the retroactively desired relationship in the context of decolonization: 'Put crudely', the relationship is defined by former colonizers as the result of 'adjustments, compromises, surrenders … in [the] face of claims of "African nationalists"'.[48]

As a result, the ASA suffered from a confusion of purposes. It is apparent from their choices of activity that many older British-Sudanis assumed that the ASA would reproduce British-Sudanese relationships (friendship may be too strong a word) that mimicked those that they remembered from their days in the Sudan. The younger generation of officials benefited from closer interactions with the Sudanese which had allowed them to establish informal relationships that actually had the potential to become friendships; but many of them were now the personnel overseeing the final stages of British colonialism elsewhere, participating in the newer efforts at economic and political influence of huge multinational corporations such as Shell Oil or educating the next generation of British citizens alongside their formal colonial subjects.

The two generations of officials pursued two different visions of the British and Sudanese relationship drawn directly from their experiences with the Sudanese in the Sudan.[49] The process of Sudanization meant that, despite tensions, the British and Sudanese had had the opportunity to interact in ways that older British officials would have found completely alien. Jamal Muhammad Ahmed remembers arguing about independence with British officers in the later years and, in his opinion, the officials who were most resistant were those older officials 'who thought they would protect us'.[50] Generally, these were the same officers who, during the 1940s, were the focus of G. C. Scott's pamphlet on the British and the educated Sudanese. Yusuf Bedri, son of the education pioneer, Bibekr Bedri, cogently delineated the generational attitudes of British officials:

> One is the old generation, of whom very few are left, and who … have very pleasant reminiscences … The [other] category is the young generation, who have the feeling there was something wrong done by their forefathers, this colonial, imperial … profession, let us call it. It was in fact a profession. They feel the British committed serious wrongs against the peoples of the colonies … you find among them the intellectuals and the social reformers.[51]

There were, of course, many younger officials who were not as self-critical as Bedri implies. John Phillips, who served in the SPS from 1945 to 1955, and was later appointed Ambassador to Khartoum, was not unique in his ability to rewrite the entire Sudanese nationalist struggle when he 'recalled' years later that 'many of the manifestations of [Sudanese] nationalism … seemed to me at the time to be unnecessary, like breaking down an open door'.[52] Nevertheless, distinct generational differences within the British-Sudani community – such as those that were expressed at the time of the Mutiny –

became apparent once again in the short-lived efforts of the ASA. This time, however, the British-Sudanis who criticized the pre-Mutiny leadership now occupied the space of the conservative elder statesmen, and the culture of empire had experienced a sea change yet again.

Just as there was a shift in metropolitan attitudes to the imperial project in the interwar period that played itself out in the Sudan as well as in Britain, the efforts of the association were taking place at another moment of profound change, this time in Britain's attitude and exposure to immigrants from former and current colonies. When put in the context of a country that was only just beginning to conceive of the multiracial possibilities of a post-colonial Britain, even the efforts of the older generation of British-Sudanis would have seemed radical in many circles. As Paul Rich points out, the creation of organizations in Britain dedicated to the improvement of race relations only began during the 1950s. These groups were coming out of the British political left and certainly would never, at the time, have associated themselves with the activities of ex-colonial organizations such as the ASA. Ex-colonial personnel advocating for progressive race relations was not yet seen as such an anomalous undertaking, before the heightened racial rhetoric of the late 1960s arrived.[53]

Although most of the Sudanese who were targets of the ASA's ministrations were not permanent immigrants, the racial context in which their visits were taking place is telling. In 1951, according to the census, there were 74,500 'colored' people in Britain. By 1961, there were 336,600. In 1962, when the association was at its most active, the Commonwealth Immigration Act was passed. This act was intended to stem the tide of immigration from the colonies because of the perceived threat to the resources of Great Britain.[54] It was only at that point that the boundaries of Great Britain were categorically defined as excluding the colonies rather than encompassing them.

For some older ex-officials expressing concerns over the welfare of Sudanese visitors allowed them to re-enact their paternal concern, and the ASA was a vehicle for them to commemorate a Sudan that no longer existed. And not every member of the younger generation deserves to be the recipient of Bedri's generous assessment. However, the ASA was also a mechanism through which membership could express complex racial categorizations than their metropolitan counterparts were unfamiliar with in the new immigrant society of 1950s and 1960s Great Britain. Their efforts at commemorating what they wanted to have been their relationship to the Sudanese, and their attempts at creating a new one were not compatible with what was *expected* to be their race politics in the nascent era of anti-imperialism on the left and fortress Britain on the right.

Of course, once again the Sudanese were drafted into the service of British-Sudani self-representation; but nevertheless, although the commemoration *in Britain* of their past relationships *in the Sudan* is most easily read as nostalgia, it should also be understood as a form of activism. The ASA was formulated at around the same time that the disillusionment of the pensioners was becoming acute. As a result, the creation of an organization that had as its mission aiding Sudanese students and others while in Great Britain – particularly as those efforts originated in the midst of tensions between the two countries as a result of the Suez Crisis and at a time when the established 'leaders' of the British-Sudani community were becoming alienated from the British government – allowed them to maintain a version of the autonomous relationship that they wanted to remember having had with Sudanese in the Sudan. Gone was the distrust of educated Sudanese. But they had to contend with the fact that they were now only helping, no longer ruling.

The Sudan Archive

The last Annual Report of the Anglo-Sudanese Association, in 1963, included the following note from Durham University:

> The Sudan Archive ... continues to be enriched by gifts of books, reports and papers of all kinds, including photographs. To the Collections of Sir Reginald Wingate and Slatin Pasha we recently added the papers of the late Mr. H.C. Jackson, formerly of the Sudan Political Service as well as a number of smaller collections, no less valuable as a historical record and no less welcome ... [The curator] would be only too pleased if members touring in the North-East would come and see for themselves the work upon which the University of Durham has been engaged in preserving and making available the records of the Sudan.[55,56]

The formation of the Sudan Archive, as this passage suggests, was the most expansive mode of commemoration undertaken by the British-Sudani community. Its founders sought to create the authoritative record of the Condominium through the breadth of its holdings rather than through the status of its choice donors or the 'significance' of their contributions. By extending the archive's remit to include *any* papers of people who had been in the Sudan, not only pertaining to their time there, the archive asserts the centrality of their Sudan experience to their identity. The notion that 'smaller holdings' were 'no less valuable as a historical record', mentioned in the same sentence as the papers of Wingate, set the tone for the archive as the source for the social history of a community, rather than merely a repository for the records of Britain's political efforts in a former colony. The invitation for Sudanis to 'come and see for themselves' was a clear articulation that, in a very material way, the archive was imagined as a space in which British-Sudanis could continue to be a community.[57]

People have included all their papers; the fearless declarative statements of a young and callow official are confronted by the more nuanced analyses of his older self. Certain contributions are repeated, such as the multiple perspectives of the same event permanently captured in the private photos of eyewitnesses; public and private papers are included, the private persona offering a running commentary on the public and political one. Contributions from wives not only challenge the masculine myths of the colonial endeavour but serve as proxies for real-life gender dynamics as husbands' acknowledge their dependence on wives contributions, supplementing their own memory and records when writing monographs and memoirs. As John Bodnar argues, 'Public memory emerges from the intersection of official and vernacular cultural expressions.'[58] The archive of the Condominium was created, in part, to preserve an established narrative. It has also, however, created an exuberant excess of narrative.

But rather than challenging or destabilizing the British-Sudani identity, that excess aids the creation and articulation of a community identity because the self-imagined story of a community *must* exceed the narrative confines established for it in order to be satisfying and authentic.

Central to the formation of any satisfying narrative are the activities of 'choosing and excluding' that imply excess.[59] Revisiting the colonial sphere in an archive that is always under construction contributes to the continued psychic immediacy of the colonial encounter. This temporal parallel challenges the established separation between the 'modern' narrative of metropolitan culture and the 'disturbing alterity' or belatedness of the colonial setting.[60] The plenitude of meanings that British-Sudanis attach to their colonial experiences is an integral part of the archive, one that is articulated in the premise upon which it was built: that the British-Sudani narrative can only be formed through the exuberant accumulation of a proliferation of texts. That this was articulated, however unself-consciously, by its first curator in the initial years of its formation is an interesting prefiguration of contemporary historiographical and narratological attitudes.

As with so many British-Sudani enterprises in Britain, the establishment of the Sudan Archive at Durham University was announced at the Annual General Meeting of the SGBPA, on 10 July 1957. The impetus for its creation came from three men, two of whom were ex-SPS. K. D. D. Henderson was a former member who had gone on to write a number of books about the Sudan. R. L. Hill had taken the interesting career path of being a former official of the Railways and Steamers Dept. who was subsequently seconded to the University of Khartoum and, upon retirement in 1949, took up a post as lecturer in Modern Near Eastern History in the School of Oriental Studies at Durham. T. W. Thacker was at that time its director.[61] Henderson's various connections in the SPS and with other ex-officials who took a scholarly interest in the Sudan were invaluable for the original solicitation of materials. He was diplomatically described as 'a sponsor in good standing with potential donors'.[62] But Richard Hill was the driving force behind the archive. He penned the appeal above and acted as curator, marketer and librarian for its first nine years, until his retirement in 1966.[63]

T. W. Thacker was receptive to Hill's urgent suggestion that Durham should take on such a project because he was convinced, as Hill was, that here was a substantial risk that materials would be lost if they were not collected in a timely fashion.[64] In Khartoum, the official documents of the Condominium remain in the possession of the current government – or at least those that were not destroyed by the departing British or by poor preservation in the years since.[65] And the National Archives hold any Foreign Office papers pertaining to the Sudan, under 'Egypt'. There were efforts underway at other universities to collect and preserve the documents of former British territories but it was noted that, yet again, because the Sudan was never technically part of the British Empire it was not mentioned in any discussions about the formation of other colonial archives.

After the initial announcement at the SGBPA, an appeal was sent out to 'all British people known to have been connected with the Sudan during the Condominium period'.[66] Henderson's connections with the SPS laid the groundwork for a rich collection of materials for political and economic historians of Africa and of the British

Empire – the kind of documents that were what came to mind in 1957 when thinking about 'historical' archives. But Hill's history with the Railways Dept. meant that even from the beginning those who might think their own papers were of little historic value because they were members of the practical rather than political departments were more likely to donate as well. The very first donation, in fact, was from Brian Storrar, the prolific and engaging diarist who built the Sudan Railway.

What has been created in the archive is what Edward Said would call 'contrapuntal ensembles', whose historical authority comes from their egalitarian multiplicity rather than their professional distance.[67] It is necessary to distinguish between the act of commemoration inherent in the archive and the act of construction that is not in contradiction with that first impulse but, rather, supports it. Thomas Richards describes the collection of information in imperial archives in Foucauldian terms, as the articulation of power through the accumulation of knowledge. But this nineteenth-century impulse to order was always illusive, it was 'an empire built on a series of flimsy pretexts that were always becoming texts'.[68] Consequently, it should be unsurprising that, as Bonnie Smith points out, the changing definition of historical evidence meant that even former agents of the Empire 'were becoming the agents of destabilization, confounding traditional efforts at orderly histories'.[69] As with other archives, the Sudan Archive destabilizes through the democratization of voices and memory. 'Acknowledging that the universe was riddled with individual force, that *everyone* had a history, and that facts were perspectival' has increasingly turned the creation of an archive into a proactive rather than a retroactive project.[70]

Certain former officials of the government took a personal interest in the archive and, from its inception, curatorial choices were made with input from British-Sudanis. Practical and monetary support as well personal interaction, first exemplified by Richard Hill, has continued until today. In 1960, papers belonging to Reginald Wingate that had not been included in his original donation were auctioned off at the time of his death. Unable to afford the purchase themselves, donations from former officials funded their acquisition.[71] Additionally, in 1982, by which time the success of soliciting donations had so far outstripped the manpower available to catalogue and care for it, it was again at a British-Sudani function – the Durham Sudan Records Conference, which was attended by many of those who had been active in the ASA – that Sir Donald Hawley challenged his fellow British-Sudanis to establish a fund through which a permanent archivist was hired by Durham, dedicated solely to the Sudan Archive.[72] British-Sudanis took it upon themselves to establish and maintain curatorial and conservancy standards.[73]

The British-Sudani felt a personal attachment that went beyond a sense that the political or economic history of Britain's involvement in the Sudan as a colonial territory should be recorded. Many of the collections read as a conversation between the individual as he or she was at the time that they first experienced and wrote about an event, and then a later version, sometimes more tempered by the years, but often voicing a more critical counter-narrative to their earlier account. As E. A. Balfour writes when compiling his papers from years earlier, 'I noticed from my letters that the public school spirit was strong in me at that time and perhaps throughout the rest of my career. Everyone I have to serve with appears to be an "awfully good fellow" or "a splendid chap".[74] Sounding as if he is quite surprised to be confronted by an earlier self that is markedly different, he comments that 'looking back from this distance I cannot help seeing a little clay mixed with the pure gold in my idols' feet'.[75] The archive thus not only preserves the original texts but also offers donors a symbolic space in which they can interact with their earlier selves and each other.

Processing the legacies of Empire occurred not only within the correspondences or diaries that sometimes span decades but also between the more polite, cautious and respectful young men and women, like Balfour, and their older selves, less intimidated by authority, who comment in the margins. Lesley Lewis included explanatory notes at the beginning of each set of letters that she donated, in which she explained topical references, identified individuals and provided editorial commentary. Sometimes, the later additions interjected a note of humour that would perhaps, at the time, not have been appreciated, such as Lewis's comment about her husband's horse allowance that accompanied one letter: 'It did not cost much to keep horses and David got an allowance for one, £5 a month but increased if the price of grain went up. The wife allowance was £5 a month too but never went up, which seemed unfair because the price of my food must have gone up too.'[76]

The archive was started at a time when the end of the story was not yet known but was imagined. Prior to independence, officials' fear was that there would be no repository commemorating their success. As Andrew Smith points out, in the processes of decolonization, 'Common sense held within it an internal logic of colonialism and power, and this is reflected in the archival collections that sprang from it.'[77] The Sudan Archive was created in layers. The records donated by contributors chart the loosening of that logic of colonialism in their minds and memories. The critical revisiting of Condominium institutions took on momentum both with the distance of time and the added confidence of age. Attitudinal shifts on a national scale – economic and political policies formed initially in the context of a hypothetical decolonizing metropole and then a real one – are replicated on the personal level.[78]

Generational differences are a natural evolution – changing with experience and exposure to the complexities of the world. But they also challenge the long-standing narratives of Empire. Robin Baily might not have had the same sense of humour as Lesley Lewis but he offered similarly instructive marginalia which not only expanded on his earlier statements but also pointed out that the existence of these earlier statements challenged general British assumptions at the time of his donation about what he and others as historical actors had been thinking. His discussion of the pros and cons of a Labour government in relation to Britain's imperial ambitions, mentioned earlier, is an example of this marginalia.[79]

None of these people would have bothered to write these comments if they didn't think that anyone would see them. This is the other conversation taking place: between the donor and his or her potential audience, the archive reader. Contributors address this imagined audience in ways that suggest they had understood what was expected of them and what traditionally constituted appropriate contributions to an archive: in other words, how they saw their shift from living individuals to historical subjects. Balfour informs his reader that he hasn't 'edited the letters so there is quite a lot of private matter which will be of no matter of interest to the historian' and yet he is compelled to include it because trying to separate the historically worthy from the rest of his experiences in the letter would have 'mutilated them sufficiently to spoil the picture'.[80] When the Sudan Archive explicitly solicited material of any kind, public or private, contributors were quite aware that this would result in a different 'picture' than other archives, where the definitions of personal and official, private and public, were decided by the participants rather than an outside authority.

Memoir and membership

The contributors' preoccupation with the 'picture' is most noticeable and varied in the substantial collection of memoirs contained in the archive. Forbes describes the decision to welcome memoirs as being 'in response to spontaneous suggestions from individual correspondents'[81] that the archive began to collect them in addition to the semi-official papers, correspondences and diaries that were written during the Condominium. In most cases, the 'raw' material of documents, letters and diaries and the carefully constructed memoir exist in temporal counterpoint to each other. But in some cases, a memoir, written after the fact, is the only contribution a person can make because they kept no documentation generated at the time their British-Sudani identity was established.[82] Instructions were given that all memoirs were to be 'in their own style, based on fact as far as possible, about their work and/or Sudanese experience'.[83] That they be 'based on fact as far as possible' speaks to one of two approaches to memoir writing in the archive collection. The elevation of 'Sudanese experience' signalled the other.

Some contributors preface their work, as A.W. M. Disney does, by qualifying its contents. His contribution is actually a compilation of stories written between 1943 and 1958. Some were written during the Condominium, although not necessarily at the time of the events they recount; others are written from England after retirement.[84] He explains that there are sixteen stories, fourteen of which are his, and two that were recounted to him, in one case, 'by the District Commissioner concerned… when the events were fresh in his mind'.[85] He has made a note at the bottom of one that 'this was written in 1944 and therefore "dates" in places; but it has been left, almost entirely, as it was written'.[86] And, in fact, he has only made factual corrections and clarifications, leaving untouched any of those things that he thought might have dated the piece. But he felt it necessary to reassure his reader of the verifiable nature of the historic record. In all of these efforts, Disney has taken on the persona of both contributor and recorder and appears to put on himself the responsibility to present an objective and reliable record of events. He believes that in order to turn his personal experiences into a historic record properly he is required to distance himself from the events; he positions himself as an eyewitness rather than a participant.

Although under the guise of an apologia, other memoir contributors highlight the personal nature of their memoirs and, in so doing, claim that their authority lays in the fact that they experienced the things they wrote about. Owen, who retired as governor from Bahr el Ghazal in 1953, opens his 209-page memoir, *Sudan Days*, with a typical statement of intent:

> I am fully aware that what follows in this book is hopelessly anecdotal, diffuse and personal. That is a grave defect. This is no detached and systematic description of the Sudan, of its manner of government, its people or its geography… since no official could, during his service, hope to know the whole of the Sudan intimately… any such description as appears here can only be partial.[87]

The conflicting stance that he takes in these few sentences show the competing aims of many of the memoirs, as well as the assumptions that their authors have about the nature of the authority upon which the memoirs are expected to rest. Owen goes on, in the present tense, leading his reader into his personal experiences of the Sudan. 'The great bulk of existence is made up of small things', he explains, as he asserts the worthiness of his contribution by highlighting its typicality: 'Let us therefore… live together the ordinary day of an ordinary District Commissioner.'[88]

Memoirists like Owen, while acknowledging that they are not following the rules of detached analysis that are the hallmarks of 'authoritative' texts, still feel compelled to forefront their personal experience. Those memoirs that actually were published did tend at least to have the veneer of detachment, although they've been lampooned for their adherence to a predictable style.[89] Sir James Robertson's *Transition in Africa*, Sir Gawain Bell's *Shadows in the Sand* and K. D. D. Henderson's *Set under Authority* all give evidence of the deeply held belief that the recounting of experiences needed to be couched – as much as possible – in the dispassionate voice of the scholar in order to make any claim at authority. That Owen and others forewent the possibilities of publication in favour of a more immediate approach to their subject speaks to their compulsion to articulate their expertise through their experience.

In some instances, scholars solicited memoirs or, at least, answers to questionnaires. Francis Deng and Martin Daly requested responses to questionnaires for their book, *Bonds of Silk*, throughout the 1970s and early 1980s.[90] J. A. Mangan explored the educational background of the SPS, which involved soliciting memoirs or responses to questionnaires.[91] Anthony Kirk-Greene solicited information for his profile of the SPS, and two requests for memoirs were made in the 1980s and another in the 1990s by fellow British-Sudanis.[92] Henderson solicited memoirs from former SPS officials when researching and writing *Set under Authority*; Rosemary Kenrick gathered memoirs from wives of SPS officials for her volume, *Sudan Tales*, and Donald Hawley edited stories written by ex-officials and their wives for *The Sudan Canterbury Tales*. In all three cases, the authors established with the various participants that, unless specified, they would pass the memoirs on to the archive.[93] And in the other cases, many of the contributors chose to answer the questionnaires in memoir form and then included them in their own donations to the archive.

In a way quite different than the other corporate articulations of British-Sudani identity, the memoirs and the archive's encouragement and collection of them enabled each person to participate equally in the continuing creation of the Sudani community. The potential for such egalitarianism was not lost on some memoirists. While there were those who highlighted the personal nature of their recollections, other contributors utilized the traditional dispassionate tone to disguise the fact that they were finally saying things about this community that they might not have been able to say while in the Sudan.[94] J. C. N. Donald, an SPS official who was stationed in the south, is extremely critical of the southern policy of the administration. Describing the moment when the Anglo-Egyptian Agreement was signed in 1952, deciding the course of independence, he refutes the standard narrative that independence was a mutually agreed upon transfer of power. On the contrary, it 'was greeted with incomprehension and dismay among chiefs, local government leaders, and most educated southerners'.[95] While the constitutional processes were revisited as a point of pride by many in their narratives, Donald takes care to point out that southerners 'had not been represented in any of the discussions' and 'though there was rejoicing amongst the Northerners', the sense of victory was not shared.[96]

Tom Mynors also wanted to use his memoirs as an opportunity to resurrect criticisms that had been silenced years earlier. 'I have felt it right to be critical', he explains in his introduction, 'not only to combat any tendency to euphoria in reminiscence, but because I often was critical throughout my service – and criticism was not welcomed in a hierarchical administration'.[97] Edward MacIntosh worked his way into a critical voice. Deployed first as a soldier in Egypt during the Great War, he was in the SPS from 1921 to 1945, and his early reminiscences are steeped in Gordon, Kitchener and other *Boy's Own* heroes. His memoir, *Middle Eastern Miasma*, begins in the tone of Rider Haggard; his chapters have titles such as 'The Egyptian Riots of 1919 and Subsequent Adventures' and 'Southward to the "Bog" ... A Land of Magic, Witchcraft and Hunting'. But by the time he reaches Chapter 8, 'The Southern Sudan in Retrospect', his language becomes much more prosaic and his criticisms more vocal. The final chapters are written as both criticisms of contemporary British government policy and of the British administration of the Sudan government, as the title of Chapter 16, 'Foreign Opinion, The Suez Canal, and the U.N.O', would indicate.[98] The independent nature of memoir production allowed MacIntosh and others to break free of the long-held habits of corporate responsibility.

The archive in general, and its collection of memoirs in particular, allowed British-Sudanis to articulate an individual version of British-Sudani community membership. 'The presumptive boundaries of "the archive"', Antoinette Burton argues, 'and especially its "concrete" location inside the nation, have been crucial to the security of the nation-state since the onset of modern processes of archive rationalization'.[99] But when the archive is not state sponsored but, rather, created by the 'authors' of a state, the Anglo-Egyptian Condominium of the Sudan, the rationalization of the archive has taken a different turn. The document, in the archive, in the nation, is paralleled by the personal identity, inside the official identity, inside the national identity, of the British-Sudani. Each new contribution and articulation of independent memory challenges one source of meaning or another. So, as Burton observes, 'What counts, what doesn't, where it is housed, who possesses it, and who lays claim to it as a political resource – is not theory, but the very power of historical explanation itself.'[100]

The belated democracy that the archive bestows on what was a hierarchical community is particularly enabling for the inclusion of women's voices, as well as the inclusion, by men, of those details that were not supposed to be of historic importance or which there was cultural pressure to devalue. Rosemary Kenrick's volume *Sudan Tales* is, in essence, a compilation of memoirs by a number of wives of SPS officials.

The longer memoirs of most of these women are included in the archive and they are the richest source for the social history of the Sudan. The day-to-day practicalities of living and the interaction of Sudanese and British in non-official capacities, such as between shopkeepers, servants and housewives, are detailed to a greater degree than elsewhere.

Owen's statement that 'the great bulk of existence is made up of small things' depends upon the recording and recollection of these small things to be recalled later. Tom Mynors, in the introduction to *his* memoir, states that he has depended on his wife, Dagmar's, writings in order to complete his own work.[101] And these personal contributions have also been seized upon by a number of the men as opportunities to articulate their dependency on and need for the women in their lives during their times in the Sudan. The masculine culture of the administration, and the public school tradition, did not provide the space for these acknowledgements earlier. Again, Tom Mynors singles out the contribution his Swedish wife made to his world view. 'My involvement (through marriage) with another country gave me a different view of British institutions and traditions', he asserts. And H. C. Jackson, who arrived in 1907, ends his memoir with a specific tribute to British women in the Sudan and dedicates the volume 'to my wife who shared with me the rough and the smooth, the sunshine and the storm of many happy years in the Sudan'.[102] The archive, rather than preserving the administration as it stood, was seized upon by many as an opportunity to retroactively include many aspects that were previously silenced.

Ongoing authorship

The archive results from personal and private participation in a larger collective undertaking. In this way, it harkens back to the foundational event in the British-Sudan narrative. The British public were taught (or given permission) by W. T. Stead to participate in a broad debate about the nature of Britain's relationship with the Sudan. One legacy of that campaign was the Gordon myth, which celebrated and enabled a particular kind of imperial project. The legitimate 'authors' of the Sudan for at least two subsequent generations were the creators of novels, poems, paintings and journalistic coverage of an imperial romance that saturated the culture and held fast in the British imagination. Another legacy of that campaign, however, was the birth of the colonial administrator as the expert in the field. Many of the British-Sudani, first in their letters, then in their fight to have the British government redefine their status as servants of Great Britain, privileged their individual identity over official classifications and the individual colonial expert over the metropolitan one, gradually asserting slightly different corporate identity.

The establishment of the Anglo-Sudanese Association and the creation of the Archive occurred just as the metropolitan desire to create distance between British identity and the imperial project was growing. Pierre Nora describes the impulse as feeling 'called upon to accumulate ... any tangible sign of what was – as if this expanding dossier might someday be subpoenaed as evidence before who knows what tribunal of history'.[103] In the era of decolonization, there was substantial pressure to abandon any evidence of Britain's imperial past. There was no specific event that marked this change in public attitude, but as independence was granted to one former colony after another, it was no longer possible to unproblematically tie Britain's empire to Britain's national identity. That British-Sudanis and others embodied that project meant that its erasure from history was their erasure as well. So the potential loss was not only personal but existential.[104] Nostalgia can be a creative force. They were simultaneously located in the time of the colonial encounter and that of the metropolitan repudiation of that encounter. And this was their motivation.[105]

Coming full circle to be the subject of history as well as a private citizen, they endeavoured to forefront their experiences rather than subsume their own personal memory beneath the larger narrative of the colonial endeavour. Antoinette Burton's description of marginalized subjects' efforts at alternative archival activity can be borrowed to describe the motivations of many who contributed to the Sudan Archive. 'The intersection of their peripatetic lives with crises of imperial and nationalist history... led them to appreciate the partiality of official history... Inevitably, their mobility left its imprint on the archives they created.'[106] The authority of the archive typically comes from its impression as static and immovable, even when it is not. Its instability comes from what Svetlana Boym identifies as nostalgia's 'fundamental ambivalence... the repetition of the unrepeatable, materialization of the immaterial'.[107] Administrators and their wives authored, edited and revised their British-Sudani identity through the rewriting and reasserting of a shifting identity over decades.

And it continues. By the turn of the current century, approximately four to six visits were made to the archive each year by contributors, their children and grandchildren. Children and grandchildren describe the donations as a 'fitting memorial' to their parents' efforts, and Jane Hogan, the chief archivist, says that they always 'get a thrill out of seeing them in boxes on shelves', as well as the inclusion of their family's photos in the database.[108] But this aura of permanence belies the fact that although the archive was created to preserve the Anglo-Egyptian Condominium for posterity, it has become a site of individual expression as well as personal memorialization.

Modern memory is understood as a creative enterprise – a form of authorship. It is 'concerned not with collecting fragments and elegiac images of the past, but with acting and making judgments in the present'.[109] In the formation of the ASA and the Sudan Archive at the University of Durham, the British-Sudani responded to what they saw as a threat to their memory of themselves through the process of decolonization and the metropolitan renunciation of Britain's imperial history.

The British-Sudani community was first created in the literary world that predated any reader's personal relationship with the actual territory. It was then shaped in the shared literature of the probationers' training, in the epistolary exchange with friends and family, in the public fight for pension recognition and then, finally, in the archive. The archive is, in fact, where that community is now located. This is the case in both a literal sense – as the actual individuals die and their records are what remain – and symbolically – as the individual expressions of community identity have modified and enriched what was, before, 'pretexts that were always becoming texts' and nothing more. This archive is now a more egalitarian community. It is unified by the personal experiences of its donors, whatever their relationship with the Sudan. The Anglo-Egyptian Condominium of the Sudan is no longer geographically or temporally bounded. The men and women who were once imagined as the unproblematic embodiment of a national agenda in a territory synonymous with imperial sacrifice now comment on and amend that chapter of the imperial narrative. It is still a British version of the Sudan. The collection of papers generated at the time of the Condominium sit side by side with the later reordering and modification of that version. Through this conversation the authorship of the British-Sudani community continues.

Notes

Introduction

1 Francis M. Deng and M. W. Daly, *Bonds of Silk: The Human Factor in the British Administration of the Sudan* (East Lansing: Michigan State University Press, 1989), 13.
2 Ibid., 17.
3 Andrew Griffiths, *The New Journalism, the New Imperialism, and the Fiction of Empire, 1870–1900* (New York: Palgrave Macmillan, 2015), 3.
4 Ibid., 56.
5 Ibid., 57.
6 Ibid., 62.
7 Doris Sommer, *Foundational Fictions: The National Romances of Latin America* (Berkeley: University of California Press, 1991), 6.
8 Ibid.
9 Among others, Shauna Huffaker identifies the reinforcing reality of metropolitan fantasy and imperial events, in 'Representations of Ahmed Urabi: Hegemony, Imperialism, and the British Press, 1881–1882', *Victorian Periodicals Review* 45, no. 4 (Winter 2012): 375–405: 'British newspapers and magazines recognized that the story's key ingredients suited the sensibilities of their readers. Their reports included action and adventure, a central antagonist, colorful and exotic extras, and brave British servicemen in an ancient and majestic setting', 376.
10 Most notable in this category is the Manchester University Press series 'Studies in Imperialism', edited by John M. MacKenzie. He offers a helpful survey of the wealth of cultural texts through which British knowledge of and support for the Empire over the past two centuries has been articulated in 'Passion or Indifference: Popular Imperialism in Britain, Continuities and Discontinuities over Two Centuries', in *European Empires and the People: Popular Responses to Imperialism in France, Britain, the Netherlands, Belgium, Germany, and Italy*, ed. John M. MacKenzie (Manchester: Manchester University Press, 2011), 57–89.
11 Edward Said, *Orientalism* (New York: Vintage, 1979).
12 Patrick Brantlinger, *Rule of Darkness: British Literature and Imperialism, 1830–1914* (Ithaca: Cornell University Press, 1988).
13 Kelly Boyd, *Manliness and the Boys' Story Paper in Britain: A Cultural History, 1855–1940* (New York: Palgrave, 2003), 1.
14 Ibid., 47.
15 Ibid., 49.
16 Gail S. Clark, 'Imperial Stereotypes: G. A. Henty and the Boys' Own Empire', *Journal of Popular Culture* 18, no. 4 (2008): 43–51.
17 Boyd points out that the respectability of some of the boys' magazines, including one coedited by Henty, meant they were less popular with boys; *Manliness*, 45.
18 Ibid., 47.

19 George William Joy, *Death of Gordon*, 1892. The cultural potency of visual images of Gordon (and Kitchener) is detailed by Berny Sèbe in *Heroic Imperialists in Africa: The Promotion of British and French Colonial Heroes, 1870–1939* (Manchester: Manchester University Press, 2013), 99.

20 Geoffrey Cubitt, 'Introduction: Heroic Reputations and Exemplary Lives', in *Heroic Reputations and Exemplary Lives*, eds. Geoffrey Cubitt and Allen Warren (Manchester: Manchester University Press, 2000), 8.

21 Robert H. MacDonald, *The Language of Empire: Myths and Metaphors of Popular Imperialism, 1880–1918* (Manchester: Manchester University Press, 1994), 81.

22 Ibid.

23 Ibid.

24 John Tosh, *Manliness and Masculinities in Nineteenth-Century Britain: Essays on Gender, Family, and Empire* (Harlow, UK: Pearson Longman, 2005), 197.

25 Bell, letter to parents, 22 January 1932, SAD 697/5/27.

26 Most Anglo-Egyptian Condominium documents fall under the FO Egypt heading. Series FO 867, the only series dealing directly with the Condominium, was created after its end to contain documents inherited from previous incarnations of other ministries.

27 Christopher Prior, *Exporting Empire: Africa, Colonial Officials and the Construction of the British Imperial State, c. 1900–39* (Manchester: Manchester University Press, 2013), 115.

28 Martin Daly, *Empire on the Nile: The Anglo-Egyptian Sudan, 1898–1934* (Cambridge: Cambridge University Press, 1986), 87.

29 See H. C. Jackson, *Sudan Days and Ways* (London: Macmillan, 1954), on the earlier model. See H. A. MacMichael, *The Anglo-Egyptian Sudan* (London: Faber and Faber, 1934), on the middle era. See K. D. D. Henderson, *Set under Authority* (London: Castle Cary Press, 1987); and Gawain Bell, *Shadows on the Sands* (London: Palgrave, 1984), on this later period.

30 Ann Laura Stoler and Frederick Cooper, 'Between Metropole and Colony: Rethinking a Research Agenda', in *Tensions of Empire: Colonial Cultures in a Bourgeois World*, eds. Frederick Cooper and Ann Laura Stoler (Berkeley: University of California Press, 1997), 9.

31 Ibid.

32 Daly, *Empire on the Nile*, 219.

33 Homi K. Bhabha, 'Signs Taken for Wonders: Questions of Ambivalence and Authority under a Tree outside Delhi, May 1817', *Critical Inquiry* 12, no. 1, 'Race', Writing, and Difference' (Autumn 1985): 144–65.

34 For various treatments of letter-writing, see Janet Gurkin Altman, *Epistolarity: Approaches to a Form* (Columbus: Ohio State University Press, 1982); Rebecca Earle, ed., *Epistolary Selves: Letters and Letter Writers, 1600–1945* (Aldershot: Ashgate, 1999); Elizabeth Macarthur, *Extravagant Narratives: Closure and Dynamics in the Epistolary Form* (Princeton: Princeton University Press, 1990); Dena Goodman, *Becoming a Woman in the Age of Letters* (Ithaca: Cornell University Press, 2009); David A. Gerber, *Authors of Their Lives: The Personal Correspondence of British Immigrants to North America in the Nineteenth Century* (New York: NYU Press, 2008).

35 David Lambert and Alan Lester, 'Imperial Spaces, Imperial Subjects', in *Colonial Lives across the British Empire*, eds. David Lambert and Alan Lester (Cambridge: Cambridge University Press, 2006), 8.

36 Ibid., 9.
37 Paul Ricoeur, *Hermeneutics and the Human Sciences* (Cambridge: Cambridge University Press, 1981), 165.
38 Lawrence Grossberg, 'History, Imagination, and the Politics of Belonging: Between the Death and the Fear of History', in *Without Guarantees: In Honor of Stuart Hall*, eds. Grossberg et al. (London: Verso, 2000), 504.
39 Charlotte Lydia Riley, '"The Winds of Change Are Blowing Economically": The Labour Party and British Overseas Development, 1940s–1960s', in *Britain, France and the Decolonization of Africa: Future Imperfect?* eds. Andrew W. M. Smith and Chris Jeppesen (London: UCL Press, 2017), 57. Accessed 21 June 2018: DOI: 10.2307/j.ctt1mtz521.7
40 This was a gradual and uneven process whereby officials in the Sudan vacillated between concern for Sudanese autonomy in relation to Egypt but stalled efforts at self-determination in Khartoum. M. W. Daly, *Imperial Sudan: The Anglo-Egyptian Condominium, 1934–1956* (Cambridge: Cambridge University Press, 1991), 251.
41 Alan Burns, *Colonial Civil Servant* (London: George Allen & Unwin, 1949), 159.
42 Andrea L. Smith, 'Introduction: Europe's Invisible Migrants', in *Europe's Invisible Migrants*, eds. Andrea L. Smith (Amsterdam: Amsterdam University Press, 2003), 10–13.
43 Lambert and Lester, 'Imperial Spaces, Imperial Subjects', 15.
44 Elizabeth Buettner, *Empire Families: Britons and Late Imperial India* (Oxford: Oxford University Press, 2005), 151, 156, 175.
45 MFC 2/18.
46 Georg Simmel, *On Individuality and Social Form*, ed. Donald N. Levine (Chicago: University of Chicago Press, 1971), 144.
47 Ibid.
48 Emile Durkheim's description of 'anomic suicide' has influenced wider theorization on anomie resulting from the lack of limitations produced by a regulating relationship between individual and society. He explains the higher rate of economically related suicide among the well-off as compared with the poor thus: 'Those who have empty space above them are almost inevitably lost in it, if no force restrains them.' Durkheim, *Suicide* (New York: Simon and Schuster, 1997), 257.
49 Julia Kristeva, *Strangers to Ourselves*, trans. Leon S. Roudiez (New York: Columbia University Press, 1991), 181.
50 Ibid., 17.
51 Frederick Cooper discusses the unique problems posed by returning imperial populations, in 'Postcolonial Peoples: A Commentary', in *Europe's Invisible Migrants*, ed. Andrea Smith, 173.
52 Ibid.
53 Burns, *Colonial Civil Servant*, 159.
54 Barry Crosbie, *Irish Imperial Networks: Migration, Social Communication, and Exchange in Nineteenth-Century India* (Cambridge: Cambridge University Press, 2012); Ulrike Hillemann, *Asian Empire and British Knowledge: China and the Networks of British Imperial Expansion* (London: Palgrave Macmillan, 2009).
55 Peter Berger, Brigitte Berger, and Hansfried Kellner, *The Homeless Mind* (New York: Random House, 1973), 206. 'This external mobility has correlates on the level of consciousness. A world in which everything is in constant motion is a world in which certainties of any kind are hard to come by. Social mobility has its correlate in cognitive and normative mobility. What is truth in one context of the individual's social career becomes wrong in the next.'

56 Inderpal Grewal, *Home and Harem: Nation, Gender, Empire, and the Cultures of Travel* (Durham: Duke University Press, 1996), 85.
57 Caren Kaplan, *Questions of Travel: Postmodern Discourses of Displacement* (Durham: Duke University Press, 1996), 169; Grewal, *Home and Harem*, 85.
58 For a discussion of the impulse to create fixed templates of power and meaning in the imperial territory, see Timothy Mitchell, *Colonizing Egypt* (Cambridge: Cambridge University Press, 1991), 165.
59 Edward Said, *Culture and Imperialism* (New York: Vintage Books, 1993), 332.
60 Ibid.
61 Buettner discusses the self-identification of ex-India personnel through their choice to retire in particular communities, such as Cheltenham. This was less common in the British-Sudani community due to small numbers and second careers. *Empire Families*, 218.
62 John Darwin, 'British Decolonization since 1945: A Pattern or a Puzzle?' *Journal of Imperial and Commonwealth History* 12 (1984): 188.
63 Cooper, 'Postcolonial Peoples', 172.
64 Jürgen Habermas, *The Structural Transformation of the Public Sphere: An Inquiry into a Category of Bourgeois Society*, trans. Thomas Burger and Frederick Lawrence (Cambridge, MA: MIT and Polity Press, 1989), 3.
65 William B. Cohen offers an excellent analysis of this phenomenon in relation to returnees in 'Pied-Noir Memory, History, and the Algerian War', in *Europe's Invisible Migrants*, ed. Andrea L. Smith, 130.
66 Gayan Prakash, 'Introduction: After Colonialism', in *After Colonialism: Imperial Histories and Post-Colonial Displacements*, ed. Gayan Prakash (Princeton: Princeton University Press, 1995), 4.
67 Susannah Radstone, 'Working with Memory: An Introduction', in *Memory and Methodology*, ed. Susannah Radstone (Oxford: Berg, 2000), 12.
68 See Zig Layton-Henry, *The Politics of Immigration: Immigration, Race, and Race Relations in Post-War Britain* (Oxford: Blackwell, 1992).
69 Jay Winter, *Sites of Memory, Sites of Mourning: The Great War in European Cultural History* (Cambridge: Cambridge University Press, 1995), 48.
70 Annette Kuhn discusses inserting autobiography into official memory to enrich the dominant ideology by exposing its contingency. See 'A Journey through Memory', in *Memory and Methodology*, ed. Susannah Radstone, 180.
71 Bernard Porter and others have argued that there was little domestic impact from or engagement with the Empire; see *Absent-Minded Imperialists: Empire, Society, and Culture in Britain* (Oxford; New York: Oxford University Press, 2004). See a nicely succinct treatment of the debate, and rebuttal of Porter et al.'s position, by Bill Schwarz in *White Man's World: Memories of Empire*, Vol. 1 (Oxford: Oxford University Press, 2011), 13–18.

Prologue

1 Griffiths, *New Journalism*, 56.
2 *PMG*'s central role in creating the imperial myth of Gordon is examined by, among others, Cynthia F. Behrman and Michael Wolff, in 'The Creation of Social Myth; Journalism and the Empire [with Comments]', *Victorian Periodicals Newsletter* 4, no. 1 (1971): 9–16.

3 James Mussell, 'Characters of "Blood and Flame": Stead and the Tabloid Campaign', in *W. T. Stead – Newspaper Revolutionary*, eds. Roger Luckhurst, Laurel Brake, James Mussell and Ed King (London: British Library, 2012), 29.
4 Alan J. Lee, *The Origins of the Popular Press, 1855–1914* (London: Croom Helm, 1976), 122.
5 Rachel Matthews, *The History of the Provincial Press in England* (New York: Bloomsbury Academic, 2017), 91.
6 Ibid., 85.
7 Tony Nicholson, 'The Provincial Stead', in *Newspaper Revolutionary*, Luckhurst et al., eds., 29.
8 This is framed as the 'something must be done' approach by Tony Nicholson, in 'The Provincial Stead', in *Newspaper Revolutionary*, Luckhurst et al., eds., 39.
9 Ibid.
10 Michael de Nie, '"Speed the Mahdi!" The Irish Press and Empire during the Sudan Conflict of 1883', *Journal of British Studies* 51, no. 4 (October 2012): 888.
11 Mark Hampton, *Visions of the Press in Britain, 1850–1950* (Urbana: University of Illinois Press, 2004), 119.
12 Kate Campbell, 'W. E. Gladstone, W. T. Stead, Matthew Arnold, and a New Journalism: Cultural Politics in the 1880s', *Victorian Periodicals Review* 36, no. 1 (Spring 2003): 27.
13 Hampton, *Visions of the Press in Britain, 1850–1950,* 39.
14 Campbell, 'W. E. Gladstone, W. T. Stead, Matthew Arnold, and a New Journalism', 25.
15 John Morley, editor of the *Fortnightly Review* and later a Liberal Cabinet minister, as quoted by Paul Auchtertlonie in 'From the Eastern Question to the Death of General Gordon: Representations of the Middle East in the Victorian Periodical Press, 1876–1885', *British Journal of Middle Eastern Studies* 28, no. 1 (May 2001): 5–24, 8.
16 http://www.attackingthedevil.co.uk/steadworks/gov.php. Accessed 10 January 2012.
17 Mark Hampton marks this moment as the shift from an educational model to a representative model – the press becoming the Fourth Estate. This is compatible with the emergence of the reader/expert and the press as representative of the reader rather than educating him/her: *Visions, 106.*
18 J. O. Baylen, 'Politics and the "New Journalism": Lord Esher's Use of the *Pall Mall Gazette*', *Victorian Periodicals Review* 20, no. 4 (Winter 1987): 127.
19 *PMG*, 27 November 1883.
20 Ibid., 26 November 1883.
21 For purposes of continuity, Stead's spelling of Zubeyr has been used herein.
22 *PMG*, 26 November 1883.
23 Ibid.
24 *Times*, 4 December 1883.
25 *PMG*, 26 November 1883.
26 Hampton, *Visions*, 69.
27 *PMG*, 4 December 1883.
28 Ibid., 10 December 1883.
29 Ibid., 9 January 1884.
30 Ibid.
31 Ibid.
32 Stead had every 'Epitome of Opinion' section concerned with the Sudan question between his Gordon interview issue on 9 January 1884 and the announcement of Gordon's appointment on 18 January.

33 W. T. Stead, 'Government by Journalism', http://www.attackingthedevil.co.uk/steadworks/gov.php. Accessed 10 January 2012.
34 'From Our London Correspondent', *Manchester Times*, 12 January 1884.
35 Baylen, 'Politics', 128–29.
36 Ibid., 127.

Chapter 1

1 Harold McMichael, 'Introduction', in *Sudan Political Service, 1899–1956*, eds. Gawain Bell and D. Brian Dee (Oxford: Oxonian Press, n.d.), 1. Birthdates of early officials in the SPS range from 1866 to 1877, putting the age of young readers in 1884 between childhood and late youth.
2 Ibid., 40.
3 Griffiths, *New Journalism*, 84. 'The extent to which the public was invited to buy into the news narrative was striking and extended well beyond the later publication of adventure stories.' Griffiths traces this relationship between journalism and literature by focusing on the central role of Gordon in this new model. Multiple chapters are dedicated to Gordon, his vanquisher Kitchener, the editor who brought Gordon to prominence, Stead, and the decades-long model of interpolated fact and fiction.
4 Ibid., 46.
5 Multiple studies have marked this connection between literacy and more-aggressive imperial policy. There has been a reconsideration more recently, however, about the degree to which newspapermen pushed statesmen into more-aggressive diplomatic stances. Simon J. Potter, 'Jingoism, Public Opinion, and the New Imperialism', in *Media History* 20, no. 1 (2014): 34–50, argues that editors were as much used by, as used, politicians.
6 Alex Nalbach, '"The Software of Empire": Telegraphic News Agencies and Imperial Publicity, 1865–1914', in *Imperial Co-Histories: National Identities and the British and Colonial Press*, ed. Julie F. Codell (Madison, NJ: Fairleigh Dickinson University Press, 2003), 69.
7 Griffiths, *New Journalism*, 183; Potter, 'Jingoism', 43.
8 Sèbe, *Heroic Imperialists*, 66–73.
9 Berny Sèbe, 'French and British Colonial Heroes', in *Resurgent Adventures with Britannia: Personalities, Politics and Culture in Britain*, ed. Wm. Roger Louis (London and New York: I.B. Tauris, 2011), 58.
10 David Finkelstein examines the deployment of metropolitan periodical literature to represent the Empire to its imperial centre in 'Imperial Self-Representation: Construction of Empire in *Blackwood's* Magazine, 1880–1900', in *Imperial Co-Histories*, ed. Julie F. Codell, 100.
11 Among many examples, Dorothy O. Helly and Hellen Callaway describe the accrual of details culminating in a rich metropolitan narrative for South Africa in 'Constructing South Africa in the British Press, 1890–92: *The Pall Mall Gazette*, the *Daily Graphic*, and the *Times*', in *Imperial Co-Histories*, ed. Julie Codell, 125.
12 Max Jones, Berny Sébe, John Strachan, Bertrand Taithe and Peter Yeandle, 'Decolonising Imperial Heroes: Britain and France', *Journal of Imperial and Commonwealth History* 42, no. 5 (2014): 787–825, 790.
13 Novelists' negative characterizations of journalists can also be taken as evidence of their symbiotic relationship. They were a threat because they had the potential

to shape perceptions that novelists had previously had a monopoly over. Matthew Rubery, *The Novelty of Newspapers: Victorian Fiction after the Invention of the News* (Oxford: Oxford University Press, 2009), 84.

14 Haggard.

15 Edgar Wallace.

16 As Cora Kaplan argues in 'Imagining Empire: History, Fantasy and Literature', 'in the fantasmatic register in which literature operates an alternative history opens up, with a complicated narrative of its own, but one that is at the same time constitutive of the social real'. In *At Home with the Empire*.

17 Anonymous, *A School History of England* (Oxford: Clarendon Press, 1901), unnumbered publisher's note.

18 J. A. Mangan, ed., *Benefits Bestowed? Education and British Imperialism* (London: Routledge, 2012).

19 Mangan argued this as far back as 1975, in 'Play Up and Play the Game: Victorian and Edwardian Public School Vocabularies of Motive', *British Journal of Educational Studies* 33, no. 3 (October 1975): 324–35.

20 Richard Aldrich discusses this shift towards history as a tool to create metropolitan support (and staff) for the Empire in Edwardian Britain in 'Imperialism in the Study and Teaching of History' in Mangan, *Benefits Bestowed?* Mangan furthers this analysis in 'Images for Confident Control: Stereotypes in Imperial Discourse', in *Imperial Curriculum: Racial Images and Education in the British Colonial Experience*, ed. J. A. Mangan (London: Routledge, 2012), 11. 'The colonial curriculum was a means of establishing and perpetuating political inequalities.'

21 Anonymous, *School History*, 354.

22 Ibid.

23 Ibid.

24 Ibid., 355.

25 Trevor Royle provides a detailed assessment of Kitchener's various attractive and troublesome attributes that the public had to embrace, reject and ignore in their pursuit of a bona fide imperial hero in *The Kitchener Enigma* (London: Michael Joseph, 1985), 1–4.

26 Donald Leinster-Mackay, 'The Nineteenth-Century English Preparatory School: Cradle and Crèche of Empire?' in *Benefits Bestowed?*, ed. J. A. Mangan, 63.

27 'With the exception of Winston Churchill in 1940 no other British war leader has excited so much public enthusiasm.' Royle, *Kitchener Enigma*, 3.

28 J. A. Mangan, *The Games Ethic and Imperialism: The Diffusion of an Ideal* (New York: Viking Penguin, 1986), 47.

29 Kenneth O. Morgan, 'The Boer War and the Media, 1899–1902', *Twentieth-Century British History* 13, no. 1 (2002): 1–16.

30 Robert Baden-Powell, *Scouting for Boys: A Handbook for Instruction in Good Citizenship*, ed. Elleke Boehmer (Oxford: Oxford University Press, 2005), 242.

31 Boehmer in Baden-Powell, *Scouting*, editor's note, 380.

32 Rudyard Kipling, *Barrack Room Ballads* (London: Methuen, 1892); for the broader picture of best-selling high-, middle- and low-brow literature in the era, see Troy J. Bassett and Christina M. Walter, 'Booksellers and Bestsellers: British Book Sales as Documented by *The Bookman*, 1891–1906', *Book History* 4 (2001): 206–36. Edition print information, WorldCat.

33 Deng and Daly, *Bonds of Silk*, 224.

34 Rudyard Kipling, 'Fuzzy Wuzzy' in *Barrack Room Ballads*, 10–12.
35 Alison Blunt and Robyn Dowling, *Home* (New York: Routledge, 2006), 144. The assertion that there was a late-Victorian 'flight from domesticity' is debated. This term, coined by John Tosh in 'Imperial Masculinity and the Flight from Domesticity', in *Gender and Colonialism*, ed. Timothy Fowley (Galway: Galway University Press, 1994), is supported and extended into the Edwardian period by Michael Roper in 'Maternal Relations: Moral Manliness and Emotional Survival in Letters Home during the First World War'. The distances and dynamics of colonial administrative service, as imagined in popular literature and lived experience, also strongly suggest that this dynamic carried into the interwar period. See *Masculinities in Politics and War: Gendering Modern History*, eds. Stefan Dudink et al. (Manchester: Manchester University Press, 2004).
36 Boyd, *Manliness*, 124.
37 Bassett and Walter, 'Booksellers and Bestsellers', 216.
38 Francis Adams, from an 1893 review in *Fortnightly*, quoted in *A Kipling Primer*, ed. F. L. Knowles (Boston: Brown, 1899), 119.
39 Nancy Robertson, quoted in Rosemary Kenrick, ed., *Sudan Tales: Recollections of Some Sudan Political Service Wives, 1926–56* (Cambridge: Oleander Press, 2000), 12.
40 Henry W. Wells, 'Kipling's Barrack-Room Language', *American Speech* 18, no. 4 (December 1943): 273–78.
41 G. A. Henty, *A Chapter of Adventures; or, Through the Bombardment of Alexandria* (London: Blackie and Son, 1891).
42 Elizabeth van Heyningen, *The Concentration Camps of the Anglo-Boer War: A Social History* (Johannesburg: Jacana Media, 2013), 329. In note 85, pertaining to her discussion of casualties on pages 16–19, van Heyningen describes the difficulty of pinning down an accurate number. The number provided here was promulgated in the propaganda of the era, both anti-imperial writings by Britons such as E. H. Hobhouse and the Afrikaner propagandists of the immediate postwar era.
43 Henty, *Chapter*, 134.
44 Ibid.
45 Ibid., 135.
46 These issues still hadn't been resolved by the First World War. International law was modernized in the wake of the conflict. With Egypt as its own agent, Britain signalled its willingness to abandon the capitulations and redefine the structures and expectations of foreign investment but 'Independence in 1922' wasn't what they had in mind. See Philip Marshall Brown, 'The Egyptian Capitulations', *American Journal of International Law* 12, no. 4 (October 1918): 820–23.
47 Henty, *Chapter*, 121.
48 John Buchan, *Gordon at Khartoum* (London: Peter Davies, 1934),14.
49 Ibid.
50 Henty, *Chapter*, 134.
51 Ibid.
52 Ibid., 135.
53 Salisbury supported the attempt to hold the Sudan prior to 1884, the partition of Africa and the creation of Rhodesia. His government approved Kitchener's Nile Expedition and subsequently supported further deployment up the Nile, bringing about the Fashoda Incident. He also took Britain into the Second Boer War.
54 Henty, *Chapter*, 166–78.

55 Roger Owen details the efforts of Lord Cromer to reconcile his perceived reality on the ground in Egypt with that understood by Gladstone's fractious cabinet and the increasingly vociferous assertions of Gordon's expertise leading up to and following Gordon's mission to Khartoum. Roger Owen, *Lord Cromer: Victorian Imperialist, Edwardian Proconsul* (New York: Oxford University Press), 183–214.

56 G. A. Henty, *The Dash for Khartoum: A Tale of the Nile Expedition* (New York: Charles Scribner's Sons, 1891).

57 Mawuena Kossi Logan, *Narrating Africa: George Henty and the Fiction of Empire* (Psychology Press, 1999), 95.

58 Aldershot is a large military instillation in Surrey.

59 Henty, *Dash*, 118.

60 See, for example, http://www.heirloomaudio.com/; https://yourvibrantfamily.com/best-homeschool-history-curriculum/. Accessed 1 June 2017.

61 Rudolph Slatin Pasha, *Fire and Sword in the Sudan: A Personal Narrative of Fighting and Serving the Dervishes, 1879–1895* (London: Edward Arnold, 1896).

62 Father Joseph Ohrwalder, *Ten Years Captivity in the Mahdi's Camp: 1882–1892* (London: Low, 1892).

63 Connections to Sudan narratives are more pronounced in the Mediterranean section where the power dynamics are less unidirectional, and in the India section where the political utility of captivity narratives for the promotion of an imperial agenda in the metropole is quite similar. Linda Colley, *Captives: Britain, Empire, and the World, 1600–1850* (New York: Pantheon, 2002), 4–12.

64 Churchill was employed by the *Morning Post* throughout the campaign.

65 Ohrwalder was a German Catholic priest whose memoir *Ten Years' Captivity*, like Slatin's, was translated by Francis Reginald Wingate.

66 Henty, *With Kitchener in Soudan: A Story of Atbara and Omdurman* (New York: Charles Scribner's Sons, 1902), vi.

67 Robert MacDonald points out 'the adult fictional world begins … to reflect the boys' world', and the paradox of the 'man-boy' or 'boy-man', in *Language*, 209.

68 J. M. Rawa, discussing point of view in E. M. Forster's *Passage to India*, suggests the di-ease of imperial relationships was the catalyst for a growing awareness of subject positionality and its relationship to culture and community. *The Imperial Quest and Modern Memory from Conrad to Greene* (New York: Routledge, 2005), 71.

69 See Stephen Ross, *Conrad and Empire* (Columbia: University of Missouri Press, 2004), 31. Ross describes Conrad, and other novelists of this period, as combining and compressing 'the distinction between the realms of the psychic and the social, casting each in terms of the other to illuminate their interdependence and contiguity'.

70 A. E. W. Mason, *The Four Feathers* (New York: Macmillan, 1905), 73.

71 I. Zangwill, *Pall Mall Magazine* 42 (1908): 480.

72 Ibid.

73 Angela Woolacott, *Gender and Empire* (New York: Palgrave, 2006), 7.

74 Richard H. Brodhead, *Cultures of Letters*, 8. 'Writing always takes place within some completely concrete cultural situation, a situation that surrounds it with some particular landscape of institutional structures, affiliates it with some particular group from among the array of contemporary groupings, and installs it in some group-based world of understandings, practices, and values. A work of writing comes to its particular form of existence in interaction with the network of relations that surround it.'

75 On the representation of period-specific emotion (Edwardian manly emotion), see Mary Floyd Wilson, 'English Mettle', in *Reading the Early Modern Passions: Essays in the Cultural History of Emotion*, eds. Gail Kern Paster et al. (Philadelphia: University of Pennsylvania Press, 2004), 130–46.

76 Brantlinger, *Rule*, 11.

77 Miles Gloriosus, review of Frederick Austin's *A Source Book of Medieval History*, in *Public School Journal* 35 (1916): 305.

78 Angela Woolacott gives an interesting gendered reading of Kipling's story 'The Bridge-Builders', as well as of Joyce Cary's *Mister Johnson*. This later story in the Kipling oeuvre, written in 1919, takes place on a massive construction site. Kipling replaces soldiers with engineers and barracks with building sites. Cary's 1939 novel also centres on an engineering project. In this classic critique of empire, determination of the colonizer to get the job done by whatever means necessary requires the sacrifice of the colonized subordinate, as with adventuring explorers of an earlier era. Woolacott, *Gender and Empire*, 85.

Chapter 2

1 Sèbe, 'Colonial Heroes', 46.

2 Ibid.

3 Dane Kennedy, in 'Imperial Parasitism: British Explorers and African Empires', argues that the historical narrative that European powers and interests were the ultimate drivers of explorers and adventurers' efforts has been accepted as a real component of European imperial exceptionalism. In the process, erstwhile African rulers, enablers, partners and foes, have been relegated to roles of lesser importance. This also means that their British agents were seen as actors of Britain, rather than misfits of Empire. In *Echoes of Empire* (London: I.B. Tauris, 2015), 20.

4 C. J. Lowe, *The Reluctant Imperialists: British Foreign Policy, 1878–1902* (New York: Macmillan, 1969), 52–72. Lowe puts Egypt and the Sudan in the centre of the process by which Gladstone's government moves reluctantly towards the late-nineteenth-century interventionist and populist-driven imperial policies that Salisbury subsequently embraces.

5 MacDonald, *Language of Empire*, 82.

6 SPS and practical branch officers appear compelled to begin with a recapitulation of the Gordon narrative regardless of the era that is otherwise the subject of the memoirs and monographs. See *Days and Ways*, by H. C. Jackson, dated 1954, and *The Anglo-Egyptian Sudan from Within*, edited by J.A. de C. Hamilton, dated 1935 for evidence that this was not a phenomenon unique to the earlier period of the Condominium.

7 There is a tension between historians' need to use individuals as exemplars in order to tell broader stories and their desire to unearth the 'typical' and the quotidian. This is evident in even the most excellent historical treatments of colonial administrators. The recent volume, *Colonial Lives across the British Empire*, edited by David Lambert and Alan Lester has this problem, where some of the figures being discussed are so far from typical of the colonizers' experience that, while fascinating subject studies, they aren't as useful as examples of the vast majority of 'colonial careering'.

8 Woolacott, *Gender and Empire*, 60.

9 Barnett Singer, *Cultured Force: Makers and Defenders of the French Colonial Empire* (Madison: University of Wisconsin Press, 2004), typically ends his discussion of the

cultural component of French military decision-making at the point of indigenous capitulation even as he asserts that we need to look beyond the negative aspects of colonial military destruction.

10 Deng and Daly, *Bonds of Silk*, 19.
11 Ibid., 18.
12 MacDonald, *Language of Empire*, 81.
13 Tosh, *Manliness*, 197.
14 Andrew Griffiths argues quite the opposite that his moniker of Chinese Gordon stayed with him throughout his career and after his death. Griffiths, *New Journalism*, 60.
15 Berny Sèbe supports this point; the Khartoum chapter of the Gordon myth obliterated his earlier career except when used as a reference to what was often framed as a 'lifetime of service' to the Crown. *Heroic Imperialists*, 155.
16 Tosh, *Manliness*, 197.
17 Charles Gordon, *General Gordon's Last Journal. A Facsimile of the Last of the Six Volumes of Journals Dispatched by General Gordon before the Fall of Kartoum* (London: Kegan Paul Trench, 1885).
18 Charles Gordon, *The Journals of Major-Gen. C. G. Gordon, CB., at Khartoum. Printed from the original manuscript. Introduction and Notes by A. Egmont Hake* (London: Kegan Paul Trench, 1885).
19 Ibid., 278.
20 Griffiths, *New Journalism*, 60.
21 See Stephanie Laffer, *Gordon's Ghost: British Major-General Charles George Gordon and His Legacies, 1885–1960*. Dissertation (Talahasee: Florida State University, 2010); and Sèbe, *Heroic Imperialists*.
22 Gordon, *Journals*, x.
23 Ibid.
24 Deng and Daly, *Bonds of Silk*, 15.
25 Gordon, *Journals*, xiv.
26 Ibid., xxxvii (original emphasis).
27 Ibid., xxii.
28 Winston Churchill, *The River War: An Historical Account of the Reconquest of the Soudan* (London: Longmans Green and Co., 1900), 63.
29 Rt. Rev. Llewellyn Henry Gwynne, 'Makers of the Sudan', SAD 421/1/174.
30 Ibid.
31 Ibid.
32 *The Sudan Diocesan Review*, II, 5 (January 1950), 15.
33 Gordon, *Journals*, 57.
34 Hake's introduction to Gordon, *Journals*, xxxii.
35 Ibid., 353.
36 Gordon, *Journals*, 289.
37 See Nalbach, 'The Software of Empire', 69.
38 Gordon, *Journals*, 289.
39 Ibid.
40 Ibid.
41 Ibid., 292; emphasis in the original.
42 Daly, *Empire on the Nile*, 148–51.
43 Henderson, *Set under Authority*, 26.

44 Father Joseph Ohrwalder sets out the intent of the English version's publication in his Preface, hoping that 'those concerned come to a right and just decision . . . to restore to civilization this once happy and prosperous country'. In Slatin, *Fire and Sword in the Sudan*, 3.
45 Slatin, *Fire and Sword in the Sudan*, 239.
46 Robert O. Collins, 'Introduction' in *The British in the Sudan*, Collins and Deng, eds., 9.
47 Sèbe, 'Colonial Heroes', 52.
48 Ibid.
49 MacDonald, *Language of Empire*, 83.
50 Churchill, *The River War*.
51 Ernest Bennett, *The Downfall of the Dervishes: Being a Sketch of the Final Sudan Campaign of 1898* (London: Methuen, 1898).
52 Churchill cites both authors' work in his own. And at times, quite frankly, passages border on plagiarism.
53 Churchill, *River War*, 65.
54 Ibid.
55 Winston Churchill, 'Gordon: A Christian Hero's Sacrifice', *Overseas Daily Mail*, 4 February 1933, quoted in 'In the Beginning', by Michael S. Coray, in *The British in the Sudan, 1898–1956*, edited by Robert O. Collins and Francis M. Deng, London: Macmillan, 1984, 29.
56 Jackson, *Sudan Days and Ways*, 1–14.
57 Ibid., 15.
58 Ibid., 18.
59 Robert MacDonald and Berny Sèbe both identify Gordon's myth as singularly useful to these purposes. See MacDonald, 'Deeds of Glory' in *Language of Empire*, and 'Imperial Heroes in the Market', I and II in *Heroic Imperialists in Africa*. Importantly, the commercial and moral utility of Gordon should be seen as mutually reinforcing rather than mutually exclusive properties.
60 In order, A. W. M. Disney, K. D. D. Henderson, J. F. S. Phillips and T. R. H. Owen, all quoted in Deng and Daly, *Bonds of Silk*, 13–14.
61 Lytton Strachey, *Eminent Victorians* (New York: Oxford University Press, 2003), 176.
62 'List of Books of Interest – Recommended for Reading by Candidates Appointed to the Sudan Political Service', in Brian Carlisle's materials; SAD 725/6/55-57.
63 Alfred Milner, *England in Egypt* (London: Edward Arnold, 1893), 85.
64 Ibid., 86. It's interesting that Milner is, in 1893, already using the more modern spelling of 'Sudan'. There is a correlation between the perpetuation of romantic characterizations of 'the Soudan' into a later era (see Buchan, *Gordon at Khartoum*), and the new generation's push towards 'the Sudan's' development and modernity.
65 Gordon, *Journals*, 306.
66 Ibid.
67 Ibid.
68 Milner, *England in Egypt*, 47, 57, 219.
69 Roger Owen, *Lord Cromer: Victorian Imperialist, Edwardian Proconsul* (Oxford: Oxford University Press, 2004), 198.
70 Andrew Griffiths, 'Winston Churchill, the Morning Post, and the End of the Imperial Romance', *Victorian Periodicals Review* 46, no. 2 (Summer 2013): 167.
71 Evelyn Baring, Lord Cromer, in Sidney Low, *Egypt in Transition* (New York: Macmillan, 1914), xv.

72 The incessant quoting of Cromer's words cannot be overstated. It becomes a kind of tic that infects the entire publishing population of the British in the Sudan. Just a few include Bell, Henderson, MacMichael, Kenrick, etc. It is then repeated by historians of the SPS almost as faithfully.
73 Cromer, in Low, *Egypt in Transition*, xvi.
74 Ibid.
75 Ibid., xvii.
76 Ibid.
77 Ibid., xviii.
78 Strachey, *Eminent Victorians*, 76.
79 For a detailed account of the intersection of these three men, see Brian Thompson, *Imperial Vanities: The Adventures of the Baker Brothers and Gordon of Khartoum* (New York: HarperCollins, 2001).
80 Ibid., 219.
81 Samuel Baker, letter to the *Times* and interview with the *Pall Mall Gazette.*
82 Thompson, *Imperial Vanities*, 224.
83 Cromer, in Low, *Egypt in Translation*, xiv.
84 Ibid., xvi.
85 Charles Gordon, 'Foreigners in the Service of Oriental States' reproduced by Sudan Agent, undated, *c.* 1933, sent to Gawain Bell, SAD 700/7/34-36.
86 Sudan Agent correspondence, forms and lists sent to Brian Carlisle, SAD 725/6/24-50. The reproductions are *c.* 1952, but within the documents it is noted that they are reproductions from 1935 and earlier, still being used.
87 Hake's introduction to Gordon, *Journals*, xxvii.

Chapter 3

1 Fouracres, unpublished memoir; SAD 815/15/25.
2 Ibid.
3 Ibid.
4 Ibid.
5 Anthony Kirk-Greene, *Britain's Imperial Administrators: 1858–1966* (London: Palgrave Macmillan, 2000), 18.
6 Prior, *Exporting Empire*, 37.
7 Joseph Hodge, *The Triumph of the Expert: Agrarian Doctrines of Development and the Legacies of British Colonialism* (Athens: Ohio University Press, 2007), 4.
8 Ralph Furse, *Aucuparius: Recollections of a Recruiting Officer* (Oxford: Oxford University Press, 1962), 138–39.
9 P. J. Cain and A. G. Hopkins, *British Imperialism, 1688–2000* (New York: Longman, 2002), 587.
10 Margery Perham, 'Some Problems of Indirect Rule in Africa'; this was originally a lecture and discussion conducted at the Royal Society of Arts in March 1934. It is reproduced in *Colonial Sequence, 1930–1949* (London: Metheun and Co., 1967).
11 Margery Perham, 'The Politics of Emancipation', in *The Colonial Reckoning* (New York: Knopff and Co., 1962), 69.
12 'Agricultural Research and Administration in the Non-Self-Governing Dependencies', quoted in Furse, *Aucuparius*, 138–39.

13 Anthony Kirk-Greene, 'Forging a Relationship with the Colonial Administrative Service, 1921–1939', *The Journal of Imperial and Commonwealth History* 19, no. 3 (October 1991): 74.
14 Furse, *Aucuparius*, 151.
15 Furse later characterized himself as of the old guard. But at this moment, he was on the cutting edge. Prior, *Exporting Empire*, 22.
16 Hodge, *The Triumph of the Expert*, 146.
17 Christopher Prior's *Exporting Empire* thoroughly examines many details of recruitment, training and application for members of both the colonial services and the SPS during the time under examination in this chapter.
18 Deng and Daly, *Bonds of Silk*, 224.
19 Robert O. Collins, 'Introduction', in *The British in the Sudan, 1898–1956*, eds. Robert O. Collins and Francis M. Deng (Stanford, CA: Hoover Institution Press, 1984), 1.
20 For detailed descriptions of the educational background of SPS officials, see J. A. Mangan, 'The Education of an Elite Imperial Administration: Sudan Political Service and the British Public School System' unpublished manuscript, SAD Durham University; and for a survey of SPS biographies, see Anthony Kirk-Greene, 'The Sudan Political Service, 1899–1955', in *Britain's Imperial Administrators*.
21 Henderson quoted in Deng and Daly, *Bonds of Silk*, 15.
22 Mangan, *The Games Ethic and Imperialism*, 93.
23 Furse, *Aucuparius*, 11.
24 Ibid.
25 Ibid., 12.
26 J. F. S. Phillips, unpublished memoir, SAD 721/5/1-2.
27 Ibid.
28 Ibid.
29 Ibid.
30 Ibid.
31 Furse, *Aucuparius*, 223.
32 Charles Garrett, interview with the author, 2 February 2003.
33 J. P. Daniell, diary entry, 3 June 1937, SAD 777/13/4.
34 E. G. Rowe, interview with John Tawney, 24 September 1969. Rowe Papers, MSS Africa S. 1698, 3.
35 A. V. Arthur, quoted in Kirk-Greene, *Britain's Imperial Administrators*, 15.
36 J. P. Daniell, diary entry, 3 June 1937, SAD 777/13/8.
37 Kirk-Greene, *Britain's Imperial Administrators*, 11.
38 Mangan, *Benefits Bestowed*, 8.
39 Furse, *Aucuparius*, 152.
40 Ibid.
41 Ibid., 151.
42 Ibid.
43 Ibid.
44 MacMichael, 'Introduction', *Sudan Political Service*, 3.
45 Jackson, *Sudan Days and Ways*, 28.
46 Ibid., 26.
47 Ibid., 15.
48 Ibid., 29.
49 Ibid.

50 MacMichael, 'Introduction', *Sudan Political Service*, 1.
51 Kirk-Greene, *Britain's Imperial Administrators*, 20.
52 Ibid.
53 Robert O. Collins, 'The Sudan Political Service: A Portrait of the "Imperialists"', *African Affairs* 71, no. 284 (July 1972): 296.
54 Rowe, interviewed by Tawney, Rowe Papers, MSS Africa S. 1698, 3.
55 M. W. Daly, *The Sirdar: Sir Reginald Wingate and the British Empire in the Middle East* (Philadelphia: American Philosophical Society, 1997), 245.
56 In earlier years, he hosted royalty in the Palace of Khartoum so frequently that Cromer had to put an end to it because it was so disruptive. C. W. R. Long, *British Pro-Consuls in Egypt, 1914–1929: The Challenge of Nationalism* (London: Routledge Curzon, 2005), 35.
57 Daly, *Empire on the Nile*, 271.
58 Ibid.
59 Ibid.
60 Ibid., 272.
61 Ian M. Drummond, *British Economic Policy and the Empire, 1919–1939* (London: George Allen & Unwin, 1972), 20.
62 Ibid., 23.
63 Michael Havinden and David Meredith, *Colonialism and Development: Britain and Its Tropical Colonies, 1850–1960* (London: Routledge, 1993), 146.
64 Stephen Constantine, *The Making of British Colonial Development Policy, 1914–1940* (London: Frank Cass, 1984), 63.
65 L. C. A. Knowles, *The Economic Development of the British Overseas Empire* (London: G. Routledge and Sons, 1924); Allan McPhee, *The Economic Revolution in British West Africa* (London: G. Routledge and Sons, 1926); quote from Peter Duignan, review of *Economic Change in Precolonial Africa: Senegambia in the Era of the Slave Trade*, by Philip D. Curtin, in *The Journal of Economic History* 38, no. 2: 525–27.
66 Margery Perham, *Colonial Government: Annotated Reading List on British Colonial Government with Some General and Comparative Material upon Foreign Empire, Etc.* (London: Oxford University Press, 1950), x.
67 Daly, *Empire on the Nile*, 275.
68 Forster, letter to his wife, 15 March 1920, SAD 600/10, quoted in Daly, *Empire on the Nile*, 274.
69 C. E. Lyall, quoted in Daly, *Empire on the Nile*, 273.
70 Ibid.
71 'List of Books of Interest – Recommended for Reading by Candidates Appointed to the Sudan Political Service', in Brian Carlyle's papers, SAD 725/6/55-57.
72 Brian Carlisle, Condominium probationary material, SAD 725/6/55-57.
73 Cain and Hopkins, *British Imperialism*, 623.
74 'Books of Interest'; SAD 725/6/55-57.
75 For a detailed explication of the ramifications of repeated dependence on Sale by later translators and scholars, see Ron Geaves. 'Correcting English Versions of the Qur'an: The Throne (*'arsh*) and the Footstool (*Kursi*) Controversy in 1902', *Victorian Review* 37, no. 2 (2011): 31–35.
76 'Books of Interest'; SAD 725/6/55-57.
77 See for a discussion of the variety of attitudes and opinions on Indirect Rule, 'Managing Social and Political Change: Tradition, Modernity and Indirect Rule', in Prior, *Exporting Empire*, 147–65.

78 H. C. Jackson, *Osman Digna* (London: Methuen, 1926).
79 Ibid.
80 These texts include Stoddard's *The New World of Islam* (1921); Harklot's *Islam in India* (1921); Kennett's *Bedouin Justice* (1925); Baron Carra de Vaux's five-volume *Les Penseurs de l'Islam* (1921–26); and O'Leary's *Islam at the Cross Roads* (1923), described in the list as 'a brief survey of the present position and problems of the world of Islam'. SAD 725/6/55-57.
81 See, in particular, Heather Bell, *Frontier of Medicine in the Anglo-Egyptian Sudan, 1899–1940* (Oxford: Clarendon Press, 1999), 55–89.
82 H. E. Wraith, interviewed by Kirk-Greene, MSS Africa S. 1719, 7.
83 Rowe, interviewed by Tawney, Rowe Papers, MSS Africa S. 1698, 3.
84 Ibid., 7.
85 Ibid., 8, 10.
86 Wraith, interviewed by Kirk-Greene, 56, MSS Africa S. 1719.
87 C. G. Seligman, 'Some Aspects of the Hamitic Problem in the Anglo-Egyptian Sudan', *The Journal of the Royal Anthropological Institute of Great Britain and Ireland* 43 (July–December 1913): 593–705.
88 Paul Daniell describes his lectures on service but also on Islam and particular ethnic/tribal groups from both Evans-Pritchard and Margery Perham. Specifically singles out Evans-Pritchard as fascinating; diary, October 1937, SAD 777/13/10.
89 Margery Perham, 'Problems of Indirect Rule in Africa', addressed to the Royal Society of Arts, 24 March 1934, published in the Journal of the Society of Arts, May 1934; reproduced in, *Colonial Sequence 1930–1949: A Chronological Commentary upon British Colonial Policy, Especially in Africa* (London: Methuen, 1967).
90 Perham collected detailed bibliographies throughout the 1930s. See MSS Perham 272/1 and 272/3 for bibliographies on materials found in the Colonial Office Library and at Chatham House, respectively (the CO having moved from Chatham), and for correspondence seeking additional bibliographical information on German and French colonial theory, see MSS Perham 272/7.
91 Perham, 'Problems of Indirect Rule in Africa', 104.
92 Margery Perham, Introduction to 5th Edition of Lugard's *The Dual Mandate* (London: Archon, 1965), xlviii.
93 MSS Perham 272/1, 272/3 and 272/7.
94 For a detailed discussion of how Indirect Rule was, or wasn't, central to administrative training during this period, see Prior, *Exporting Empire*, 43–50.
95 Margery Perham, *Native Administration in Nigeria* (Oxford: Oxford University Press, 1937), 353.
96 Ibid., 352.
97 Thomas Spear, 'Neo-Traditionalism and the Limits of Invention in British Colonial Africa', *Journal of African History* 44, no. 1 (2003): 15. Another analysis of Indirect Rule that focuses on the widened gap between the forms of administrative knowledge and the imposition of power from the metropole is Peter Pels, 'The Pidginization of Luguru Politics: Administrative Ethnography and the Paradoxes of Indirect Rule', *American Ethnologist* 23, no. 4 (November 1996): 738–61.
98 Perham, *Native Administration in Nigeria*, 352.
99 Daniell, diary, October 1937; SAD 777/13/10.
100 Ibid., 11.
101 Ibid., 10.
102 See MSS Perham 244/4 for syllabi, exams and other materials related to various classes over the period.

103 Daniell, diary, October 1937; SAD 777/13/11.
104 MSS Perham 244/4.
105 Daniell, diary, October 1937; SAD 777/13/17.

Chapter 4

1 Bell, *Shadows*, 17.
2 Among others on the 'type' of colonial hero, see Graham Dawson, *Solider Heroes: British Adventure, Empire and the Imagining of Masculinities* (London: Routledge, 1994); Prior, *Exporting Empire*; Sèbe, *Heroic Imperialists*.
3 Bell, *Shadows*, 18.
4 Sèbe, *Heroic Imperialists*, 1.
5 Jacqueline Rose, *States of Fantasy* (New York: Oxford University Press, 1996), 5.
6 Metropolitan imaginings of imperial spaces were shaped by cultural input that wasn't intended for didactic purposes. For examples of the influence of leisure travel and advertising on the perception that metropolitans 'knew' colonial spaces, see Panivong Norindr, *Phantasmatic Indochina: French Colonial Ideology in Architecture, Film, and Literature* (Durham, NC: Duke University Press, 1996); for the influence of travel writing on metropolitan notions of imperial geography, see F. Driver's *Geography Militant: Cultures of Exploration and Empire* (Oxford: Blackwell, 2000).
7 Bell, *Shadows*, 18.
8 Dawson, *Soldier Heroes*, 254.
9 Ibid., 233.
10 Tosh, *Manliness*, 197.
11 Thesiger, *The Life of My Choice* (Glasgow: William Collins, 1987), 64.
12 Ibid., 89.
13 Ibid.
14 Among others, he had been a trustee of the National Library of Scotland and the president of the Scottish Historical Society.
15 Maitland, *Wilfred Thesiger: Life of the Great Explorer* (London: Harper Press, 2006), 89.
16 John Buchan, *Gordon at Khartoum* (London: Peter Davies Limited, 1934), 16.
17 Thesiger, *My Choice*, 89.
18 Ibid.
19 Ibid., 84.
20 Ibid., 102.
21 Ibid.
22 As Prior points out, particularly in other African colonies, a prior connection to the continent was what drove young men to enlist in the Colonial Service. So Thesiger was not unique in this. *Exporting Empire*, 17.
23 Ibid.
24 Alexander Maitland, *Wilfred Thesiger: A Life in Pictures* (London: HarperCollins Publishers, 2004), 18.
25 Thesiger, *My Choice*, 89.
26 For examples, see ibid., 203–13, 243.
27 Maitland, *The Life of the Great Explorer*, 123.
28 The similarities and differences in tone, preoccupations and ambitions, between Sarsfield-Hall and Thesiger, are interesting to note. For comparison, see

Sarsfield-Hall's correspondence with his mother and fiancée on attitudes towards postings in Darfur, desire to see service during the war and descriptions of treks. SAD 680/1/1-57.

29 Thesiger, *My Choice*, 89.

30 Thesiger, letter to brother, Roddy, 27 June 1935. Eton MS 433 02 02.

31 Thesiger, *My Choice*, 186.

32 Maitland, *The Life of the Great Explorer*, 129.

33 Thesiger, letter to mother, 29 January 1936. Eton MS 433 02 02. In his later memoir, his self-fashioning as a Arab expert over the subsequent years influences his memory. He asserts in *The Life of My Choice* that at the time when he was writing to his mother that he failed his exams, he had become fluent in Arabic; 251.

34 K. D. D. Henderson, quoted in Deng and Daly, *Bonds of Silk*, 42.

35 Chris Vaughan, *Darfur: Colonial Violence, Sultanic Legacies, and Local Politics, 1916–1956* (Rochester, NY: James Curry, 2015), 2.

36 Ibid., 16.

37 Thesiger, letter to brother, Roddy, 27 June 1935. Eton MS 433 02 02.

38 Maitland, *The Life of the Great Explorer*, 134.

39 Thesiger, *My Choice*, 187.

40 Thesiger, letter to his mother, 15 April 1934.

41 Ibid., 171.

42 Thesiger, *My Choice*, 218.

43 Michael Asher, 'Obituary: Sir Wilfred Thesiger', *The Guardian*, 27 August 2003.

44 Thesiger to his mother, 9 June 1935. Eton MS 433 02 02.

45 Kirsten Holst Pedersen describes the 'imperial benevolence' of Karen Blixen as bounded by assumptions about the need for it, and the European's ability to determine what form it should take. This is similarly, repeatedly present in Thesiger's superficially complimentary characterization of Muslim over animist Sudanese. 'Blixen's Africa: Wonderland of the Self', in *Burden or Benefit: Imperial Benevolence and Its Legacies*, eds. Helen Gilbert and Chris Tiffin (Bloomington, IN: Indiana University Press, 2008), 103–07.

46 Vaughan, *Darfur*, 54.

47 Ibid.

48 Lytton Strachey, *Eminent Victorians*, 181.

49 Michael Asher, 'Obituary: Sir Wilfred Thesiger'.

50 Quote from *The Danakil Diary*, quoted in Maitland, *The Life of the Great Explorer*, 162.

51 Letter to mother dated 18 May 1938. Eton MS 433 02 02

52 Bell, *Shadows*, 16.

53 Ibid., 17.

54 Ibid.,16.

55 Kelly Boyd, 'Knowing Your Place: The Tensions of Manliness in Boys' Story Papers, 1918–1939', in *Manful Assertions*, Roper and Tosh eds., 147.

56 Bell, *Shadows*, 16.

57 Bell, letter to parents, 22 January 1932, SAD 697/5/27.

58 Bell, letter to parents, 17 April 1932, SAD 697/6/28.

59 Bell, *Shadows*, 17.

60 Ibid.

61 Ibid., 50.

62 Ibid., 20.

63 Most of Parr's papers are about or with various Christian organizations in the Southern provinces. He continued to express concern for the fate of the southern

Sudan after independence, framed largely as concern for the Christian minority population. SAD 817/2-9.

64 Robin Baily was very critical of his own younger self in notes he included with the materials he donated to the Sudan Archive. 'Many read now as very jejune and school-boyish'. SAD 268/11/3

65 Letter from Baily to Bell, 1 June 1932, SAD 697/7/4.

66 Ibid.

67 Bell, letter to parents, 17 April 1932, SAD 697/6/28.

68 Bell, *Shadows*, 35.

69 Ibid., 20.

70 Ibid., 21.

71 Ibid., 35.

72 Ibid., 36.

73 E. Evans-Pritchard, *Witchcraft, Oracles, and Magic among the Azande* (Oxford: Oxford University Press, 1937).

74 Evans-Pritchard, *The Nuer: A Description of the Modes of Livelihood and Political Institutions of a Nilotic People* (Oxford: Clarendon Press, 1940); *Kinship and Marriage among the Nuer* (Oxford: Clarendon Press, 1951); *Nuer Religion* (Oxford: Clarendon Press, 1956).

75 Robert Boyce, 'The Significance of 1931 for British Imperial and International History', *Histoire@Politique* 11, no. 2 (2010): 1–8, https://www.cairn.info/revue-histoire-politique-2010-2-page-8.htm. Accessed 12 January 2016.

76 C. Brad Faught, *Into Africa: The Imperial Life of Margery Perham* (London: I.B. Tauris, 2012), 87.

77 Ibid.

Chapter 5

1 Bell, letter to parents, 8 April 1932; SAD 697/6/18.

2 David Gerber discusses strategies surrounding whom to write, what to write and how to frame the correspondence, in *Authors of Their Lives*, 93–94; as does Eric Richards, 'The Limits of the Australian Immigrant Letter', in *Letters across Borders: The Epistolary Practices of International Migrants*, eds. Bruce S. Elliott et al. (New York: Palgrave, 2006), 58.

3 Bell, letter to parents, 8 April 1932; SAD 697/6/18.

4 Immigrant correspondence is not always about wanting to go home. See, for example, letters of British migrants to the United States, in Charlotte Erickson, *Invisible Immigrants: The Adaptation of English and Scottish Immigrants in Nineteenth-Century America* (Coral Gables, FL: University of Miami Press, 1972), 154.

5 Gerber, *Authors of Their Lives*, 93.

6 Eric Richards addresses the issue of literacy in 'The Limits of the Australian Emigrant Letter', 57.

7 Ibid., 59.

8 Richard H. Brodhead, *Cultures of Letters*, 8. 'Writing always takes place within some completely concrete cultural situation, a situation that surrounds it with some particular landscape of institutional structures, affiliates it with some particular

group from among the array of contemporary groupings, and installs it in some group-based world of understandings, practices, and values.'

9 Janet Gurkin Altman discusses how the participants understanding of the potential conclusion was central to forming the epistolary narratives. For the British-Sudani, the correspondences were almost always premised on the understanding that the narrative would end because of reunion, not because of death or impossible separation. *Epistolarity: Approaches to a Form*, 150.

10 Stanley Cavell states in his 'Introduction' to *Home: A Place in the World* 'that owning or belonging to a place is the promise and power of leaving it, say of staking one's name'. Arien Mack, ed. (New York: NYU Press, 1993), 5.

11 Gwendolyn Wright describes the collective and personal nature of 'home' in similar hybrid terms: 'The ideal of home, while universal, exists simultaneously as a deep-rooted individual concept – at once fantasy, memory, and longing'; 'Prescribing the Model Home', in Mack, 214.

12 Gerber uses the term 'negotiation' to describe the evolution of an unspecified contract between epistolary partners, in *Authors of Their Lives*, 94.

13 The 'Third Space of Enunciation' is described in 'Signs Taken for Wonders', in *The Location of Culture* (New York: Routledge, 1994), 218. This is specifically in the context of the colonizer/colonized relationship, but the dynamics are recognizable in any relational assertions of cultural exclusivity and authority.

14 Altman, *Epistolarity*,150.

15 The estimated time for the journey is given in the earlier Almanacs. See *Sudan Almanac 1912* (London: His Majesty's Stationary Office, 1912).

16 Later recollection of Lt. Col. S. T. Austin, *c*. 1963, of events of 1916–17, SAD 863/4/11.

17 *Sudan Almanac, 1912.*

18 Ibid.

19 Altman, *Epistolarity*, 13.

20 The mode of post transport is detailed as well as the estimated time for the journey in the earlier Almanacs. For donkey journey of five days to Gedaref see, for example, *Sudan Almanac 1912*. For 1932 details, see ibid., 1932.

21 *Sudan Almanac*, 1912.

22 *Sudan Almanac*, 1933.

23 *Sudan Almanac*, 1941.

24 *Sudan Almanac*, 1953.

25 *Sudan Almanac*, 1953. Each of these almanacs offers the postal rates for various departure points and destinations, as well as a comprehensive schedule of postal deliveries.

26 For details of the development of letter-writing technologies and their relation to mail delivery, see M. J. Daunton, *The Royal Mail: The History of the Post Office since 1840* (New York: Athlone Press, 1985).

27 Altman, *Epistolarity*, 13: Letters can emphasize the distance *or* the bridge.

28 S. T. Austin, letter to parents, 27 July 1916, SAD 863/4/2.

29 For a discussion of the relationship between colonial power and medical policies, see Bell, *Frontiers of Medicine*, 14–15.

30 Daly discusses at length the problematic nature of slavery – as opposed to the slave trade – and particularly as it had to be finessed for public consumption back in Britain, in *Empire*, 239.

31 Winder, 22 February 1939. SAD 863/7/31.
32 Daly, *Empire*, 150.
33 J. I. Parry, letter to parents, 20 August 1942, SAD 541/13/18.
34 Bridget Acland, undated and unpublished memoir, SAD 777/15.
35 See 'Passage Section of the Sudan Agent Office' document in letter of acceptance to Sudan government recruits. Example in Carlisle papers, SAD 725/6/51.
36 'Sudan Civil Service: General information for Candidates' Carlisle papers, SAD 725/6/24.
37 Storrar, letters from onboard ship. Examples can be found in SAD 51/1/4 and 21/11/1.
38 J. W. E. Miller, letter to mother, 5 June 1920, SAD 966/5/1.
39 This was obviously a desired situation because it was specifically advertised. See, for example, *Burma and Ceylon Information for Travellers and Residents* (London: Thomas Cook & Sons, 1912).
40 Macarthur, *Extravagant Narratives*, 159.
41 For explorations of imperial masculinity, see Tosh, *Manliness*; Dawson, *Soldier Heroes*. The effects of European women on the colonial arena are also well explored. See Mary Procida, *Married to the Empire: Gender, Politics and Imperialism in India 1883–1947* (Manchester: Manchester University Press, 2002); Antoinette Burton, *Burdens of History: British Feminists, Indian Women, and Imperial Culture, 1865–1915* (Chapel Hill: University of North Carolina Press, 1994).
42 Bell, 29 September 1931, SAD 697/4/25.
43 Ibid.
44 Bell, letter to parents, 17 October 1931, SAD 697/4/35-36.
45 Ibid.
46 Arthur, letter 4 September 1949, SAD 726/4/55-6.
47 Ibid.
48 IW Douglas, letter to sister, 19 February 1925, SAD 707/9/28.
49 Ibid.
50 Later recollection of Lt. Col. S. T. Austin, *c.* 1963, of events of 1916–17, SAD 863/4/11.
51 Bell, letter to parents, 29 September 1931, SAD 697/4/25.
52 J. Kenrick, unpublished memoir, SAD 647/5.
53 Brian Storrar's collection in the Sudan Archive is an excellent example of this. He compiled photo albums that are full of his own pictures but that also contain, mixed in with his photos with no differentiation between them, postcards, as well. See, for example, SAD A93/1-289.
54 Buettner, *Empire Families*, 138.
55 E. A. Balfour, letter to mother, 3 October 1932, SAD 606/3/85.
56 Persis Aglen to sister, Grizel Warner, 15 June 1947, SAD 895/8.
57 S. T. Austin, letter to parents, 27 July 1916, SAD 863/4/2.
58 Bell, 26 November 1931, SAD 697/4/60.
59 Bell, letter to parents, 29 September 1931, SAD 697/4/25.
60 Martin Parr, letter to Bell's mother, 5 April 1932, SAD 697/6/39.
61 Bell, letter to parents, 26 November 1931, SAD 697/4/60.
62 Charles Bazerman, 'Letters and the Social Grounding of Differentiated Genres', in *Letter Writing as a Social Practice*, eds. David Barton and Nigel Hall (Philadelphia, NL: John Benjamins Publishing Company, 2000), 25; ProQuest ebrary Web. Accessed 15 January 2017.

63 For an example of Storrar's collectively addressed letter-diary style, see SAD 51/1/5.
64 Photographs of Walmsleys's *thé danseé*; SAD 54/1/84.
65 Storrar, 6–18 June 1912. 'On board were Mrs. Col. Radcliffe, Capt. Kelly of the Cavalry, Drummond and Beam of Gordon College, Young and Baily, Province Inspectors and Drower, Advocate Khartoum. Arrived Cairo 11 am Monday and left for Port said same evening, staying at "Savoy" Hotel and joining the Bibby boat "Warwickshire" on Tuesday morning with Drummond, Beam and Young. Reached London on Monday 24th June.' SAD 51/1/234.
66 Storrar, 25–28 February 1915, SAD 52/1/69.
67 Eric Richards, 'The Limits of the Australian Emigrant Letter', in *Letters across Borders*, 58.

Chapter 6

1 David A. Gerber, 'Epistolary Masquerades: Acts of Deceiving and Withholding in Immigrant Letters', in *Letters across Borders: The Epistolary Practices of International Migrants*, eds. Bruce S. Elliott, David A. Gerber and Suzanne M. Sinke (New York: Palgrave Macmillan, 2006), 142.
2 Macarthur, *Extravagant Narratives*, 118.
3 Ibid.
4 See Altman, *Epistolarity*, 150. She points out that correspondence is never undertaken 'out of a desire to merely express oneself without regard to the eventual reader', but rather are 'the result of a union of writer and reader'.
5 Macarthur, *Extravagant Narratives*, 135.
6 Gerber, *Authors of Their Lives*, 60.
7 Gerber, 'Epistolary Masquerades', in *Letters across Borders*, 151.
8 Macarthur, *Extravagant Narratives*, 134–35.
9 Hartley, 'Letters Are Everything These Days', in Earle, 185.
10 Every person whose letters are quoted in this chapter wrote to women. Unless specified, letters quoted are all addressed either to the mother or to both parents. Many did have separate correspondence with fathers as well, but the default correspondent within families was the mother.
11 IW Douglas, 19 February 1925. SAD 707/9.
12 Bell, 14 October 1931, SAD 697/4/33-34.
13 Daniell, letter to parents, 2 September 1938, SAD 777/13/27.
14 Bell, letter to parents, 26 September 1932, SAD 697/8/15.
15 Bell, letter to parents, 15 November 1931, SAD 697/4/55-7.
16 Baily, letter to father, 3 July 1919, SAD 533/1/39.
17 Bhabha, *Location of Culture*, 38–39. The disruption of the unquestioned and seamless national and imperial narrative occurs in multiple sights of discourse, one of which is this one. '… it is the "inter" – The cutting edge of translation and negotiation, the *in-between* space – that carries the burden of the meaning of culture. It makes it possible to begin envisaging national, anti-nationalist histories of "the people." And by exploring this Third Space, we may elude the politics of polarity and emerge as the others of ourselves'.
18 Carolyn Steedman uses women writing letters to challenge the stark delineation of the public and private sphere established by Jürgen Habermas in *The*

Structural Transformation of the Public Sphere. See Steedman's 'A Woman Writing a Letter' in Earle.

19 J. W. E. Miller, letter to wife, 29 August 1942, SAD 969/2/12.

20 A similar insistence on participation is talked about by Jenny Hartley, when she discusses the correspondence between mothers and sons and daughters who are at the front in the Second World War. She writes about the 'need to take the parent into the new terrain', in a way that might go against our preconceived notions of mothers being shielded from grim details in correspondence. '"Letters Are Everything These Days": Mothers and Letters in the Second World War', in *Epistolary Selves*, 190.

21 Examples of this are R. E. H. Baily, letter to mother, 10 December 1924, SAD 533/2/11; and letter to father, November 1924, SAD 533/2/8.

22 Persis Aglen to sister, Grizel Warner, 15 June 1947, SAD 895/8.

23 Ibid.

24 Ibid.

25 See, for example, letter, 3 May 1949, SAD 726/4/27-8; and 4 July 1949, SAD 726/4/38-9.

26 A. Arthur, letter to parents, 21 February 1949: In response to his mother's queries, he asserts that the British will be in the Sudan for another 20 years. 'The country is not nearly so far advanced as India was, and the process of Sudanisation in the Services will not reach 50% until 1964.' SAD 726/4/10.

27 Arthur, letter to mother, 19 April 1949, SAD 726/4/23-24.

28 Ibid.

29 Arthur, letter to parents, 12 August 1949. This letter is the first acknowledgement that he can't participate in an event back home. SAD 726/4/48-9.

30 In other instances (see SAD 726/4/36 for example), Arthur has an interesting discursive strategy of writing about events as if he is there.

31 Bell, letter to parents, 17 July 1932, SAD 697/7/25.

32 Baily, letter to parents, 25 July 1924, SAD 533/2/4.

33 Arthur, letter to parents, dated 27 April 1949, SAD 726/4/25-26.

34 Arthur, letter to parents, 18 November 1949, SAD 726/4/69-70.

35 Macarthur, *Extravagant Narratives*, 156: She argues that metaphor and metonymy are both required to string out the dynamic narrative. There must be occasional tests of unity and provocations of tension, in order to maintain discursive energy.

36 T. A. Leach, reported in clipping from unidentified *Bath* newspaper, dated *c*. 1930–33, speaking to the Bath Rotary Club after retirement, SAD 770/3/26.

37 Lesley Lewis interviewed by author, 4 February 2003.

38 Lewis, letter to her mother, 21 November 1949, SAD 338/6/49.

39 Gerber discusses the power of withholding in correspondence, particularly as a tool to shift the power dynamics between parents and children; see 'Epistolary Masquerades', in *Letters across Borders*, 151.

40 Jacques Rancière, 'Discovering New Worlds: Politics of Travel and Metaphors of Space', in *Travellers' Tales: Narratives of Home and Displacement*, edited by Jon Bird, Barry Curtis, Melinda Mash, Tim Putnam, George Robertson, Lisa Tickner (New York: Routledge, 1994), 31. Rancière argues that the traveller gains authority and power through the journey – the implication being that the positive additions to individual identity greatly outweigh the negatives of distance and separation.

41 Bell, letter to wife, December 1941, SAD 698/4/1-43.

42 An excellent example of this in another colonial setting can be found in Nicholas Thomas's analysis of the ne'er do well and failed colonial adventurer, Vernon Lee

Walker, in *Colonialism's Culture: Anthropology, Travel and Government* (Princeton: Princeton University Press, 1994), 143–69. In his letters, Walker had a compulsive need to remind his mother of how different he had become, how unsuited he was for life in Britain after his experiences and how closely he lived to the native standards in Fiji, where he was attempting (without success) to make his fortune.

43 Kristeva, *Strangers amongst Ourselves*, 7–9.
44 Bell, letter to parents, 26 September 1932, SAD 697/8/15.
45 In many areas, the lack of understanding in Khartoum gave officials latitude in their actions, in both the earlier era and later. See Daly, 'Administration in the Southern Sudan, 1920–33', in *Empire*. For examples of the later era, see Winder's detailed exchanges with his wife when he describes his difficulty in getting what he thinks is appropriate support for aspects of the Jonglei Irrigation Scheme, in 1949. SAD 541/13/18.
46 E. A. Balfour, cover note to collection of letters to mother, undated, SAD 606/3/1.
47 A good example of this is E. A. Balfour's letter to his mother on the anniversary of his father's death, 27 January 1933, SAD 606/3/137-40.
48 Bell, trek letter-diary, 1 November 1931, SAD 697/4/45-46.
49 Ibid.
50 Ibid.
51 Annaliesa Dee, interviewed by the author, 3 February 2003.
52 Lesley Lewis, undated commentary accompanying correspondence, SAD 338/13/11.
53 Lewis lived to be 100, dying in 2010. Her book about her upbringing is *The Private Life of a Country House* (1912–39); her most notable art history monograph is *Connoisseurs and Secret Agents in Eighteenth Century Rome.*
54 Storrar, letter diary, 16 November 1910, SAD 51/1/4.
55 Persis Anglen, letter to sister, 4 April 1947, SAD 895/8/52.
56 Winder, letter to fiancée, 19 February 1939, SAD 541/13/18.
57 Ibid.
58 Winder, letter to fiancée, 29 October 1938; SAD 541/13/10.
59 Ibid.
60 Bell, letter to parents, 17 July 1932, SAD 697/7/25.
61 For a good sampling of Bell's correspondence to his parents, and his descriptions of his work and the country, see SAD 697/7-8 and, for later years, SAD 698/1-4.
62 A. W. Polden, letter to mother, 20 March 1950, SAD 759/6/6.
63 Miller, trek diary letter to mother, 26 February 1923, SAD 968/9/5.
64 SR. Davies, letter to parents, 18 January 1912, SAD 882/8/3.
65 See Rosemary Kenrick, *Sudan Tales*, passim, for consistent remembrances framed as 'we' statements by wives of what were actions by husbands.
66 Lewis, 4 January 1955, SAD 338/12/1.
67 Winder, letter to his wife, date unclear, 1949, SAD 541/13/18.

Chapter 7

1 Details come from M. W. Daly, *British Administration and the Northern Sudan, 1917–1924: The Governor-Generalship of Sir Lee Stack in the Sudan* (Nederlands Historisch-Archaeologische Institut, Istanbul, 1980).
2 Daly, *Empire*, 309.

3 Although I can't be categorical, I would hazard to assert that every official who was in the Sudan government (or wife) at the time of the Mutiny and has written a memoir that is held in the Sudan Archive has felt it necessary to give some treatment of it.
4 Dawson, *Soldier Heroes*.
5 Hannah Arendt, *The Origins of Totalitarianism* (New York: Harcourt Brace Janovich, 1973), 186.
6 Lily Young Cohen, *In Memoriam Kitchener, June 7, 1916*, pamphlet reproduction as printed in the *New York Times*, 26 June 1916.
7 Public Relations Office, Civil Secretary's Department, Khartoum, *Sudan Almanac 1924* (Khartoum: Sudan Government and McCorquodale & Co., 1924).
8 Benedict Anderson, *Imagined Communities* (London: Verso, 1991), 7.
9 Lawrence Grossberg, 'History, Imagination and the Politics of Belonging', in *Without Guarantees: in Honor of Stuart Hall*, 154.
10 James How, *Epistolary Spaces: English Letter Writing from the Foundation of the Post Office to Richardson's Clarissa* (Aldershot: Ashgate Publishers, 2003), 4.
11 Burgin, *In/Different Spaces: Places and Memory in Visual Culture* (Berkeley: University of California Press, 1996), 193.
12 For a more detailed account of the causes and ramifications of the Mutiny, see Holt and Daly, *A History of the Sudan: From the Coming of Islam to the Present Day* (London: Longman, 2000), Ch. 4; and Daly, *Empire*, Ch. 7.
13 Daly, *Empire*, 295–96.
14 Sir George Schuster, financial secretary, letter to R. E. H. Baily, dated 3 July 1924, details the efforts that the Sudan Agent in London and other sympathetic MPs are undertaking to limit the influence of Zaghlul's envoys, SAD 533/2/2.
15 Baily, letter to mother, dated 25 July 1924. In the marginalia, he later added, 'My opinion about the Labour foreign policy under Ramsey MacDonald was shared by most Sudan officials at this critical time.' SAD 533/2/7. For further reading about Labour's imperial involvement, see Partha Sarathi Gupta, *Imperialism and the British Labour Movement, 1914–1964* (New York: Holmes and Meier Publishers, 1975).
16 Baily, cover note to letter and diary entries from 1924 to 1925, *c.* 1965, SAD 268/11/3.
17 As well as on other days, on the date of the mutiny in Khartoum, 28 October 1924, the editorial in the *Times* was about rising food costs. During the week of the assassination, beginning on 17 November 1924, the *Manchester Guardian* ran a series of articles detailing the Liberal Party's failures in the recent election and a discussion of what should be the new direction of the party. Particularly in illustrated magazines, such as the *Illustrated London News*, an event as photogenic as the pit collapse (the miners were rescued on 30 November, two days after the mutiny) was serious competition for the story in Khartoum for which there were no immediate pictures.
18 *Times* editorial, 20 November 1924.
19 P. D. Mulholland, chief of security, kept a copy of the 'SECRET evacuation plans for Egyptian Army', undated, but *c.* Spring 1924, which include instructions for railways, post and telegraph, Port Sudan camp commandant, chief embarkation staff officer, reception staff at Wadi Halfa and orders to officers commanding stations and districts outside Khartoum. SAD 479/7/6. Plans were for the evacuation by both rail and boat, up the Nile and through Suez, depending on where the soldiers were stationed and also in an attempt to keep groups separate. It also included a plan by which British troops were able to quickly take over the jobs of Egyptian civil servants who might

also leave. It was thought that as many Egyptians were unhappy to receive postings in the Sudan, they would be happy to leave.

20 Daly, *Empire*, 306.
21 *Times*, 29 November 1924.
22 Ibid.; sympathetic coverage of speech by MacDonald on 29 November, when he called for a League of Nations Mandate to end the dispute; *Manchester Guardian* editorial, 20 November, stated that 'British involvement [in Egypt] is vague, anomalous and impossible to justify . . . but good work has been done and there is more to do'.
23 *Manchester Guardian* editorial, 27 November 1924. Also, *Times* editorial, 29 November 1924.
24 Holt and Daly, *Sudan*, 134.
25 *Manchester Guardian*, letter to the editor, 28 November 1924.
26 'Official Report on the Evacuation'. SAD 479/7/46-52; emphasis added.
27 Daly points out that the respect, however grudging, for the Egyptian determination that the order come from the King of Egypt, to whom they took their oath of loyalty, and the disregard for the Sudanese who articulate a similar concern show the different footing the British saw themselves as having with both groups of soldiers. Daly, *Empire*, 310–11.
28 The official report on the evacuation gives no details on the Sudanese mutiny, SAD 479/7/46-52.
29 All papers pertaining to the Sudan in the National Archives reflect this reality, as they are contained within the 'Egypt' division of the 'Levant' and later 'Africa' department within the Foreign Office, rather than a separate designation.
30 *Manchester Guardian* editorial, 27 November 1924. Also, *Times* editorial, 29 November 1924.
31 The *Manchester Guardian* printed MacDonald's speech on 29 November 1924, and used it to continue advocating the involvement of the League of Nations.
32 For examples of government discussion of changing economic relationships with colonies and its impact on traditional power relations, see Cabinet Memorandum. 'Proposals for financial assistance to accelerate the development of Imperial Resources. Joint Memorandum by the Secretary of State for the Colonies and the President of the Board of Trade', 8 February 1923, CAB 24/158; Cabinet Memorandum, 'Ottawa Agreements Bill', 28 September 1932, CAB 24/232; for an overview of the gradual change in imperial relations in the interwar period, see I. M. Drummond, *Imperial Economic Policy: 1917–1930: Studies in Expansion and Protection* (London: Allen & Unwin, 1993).
33 *Illustrated London News*, 10 November 1923.
34 *Manchester Guardian*, 2 October 1923.
35 *London Illustrated News*, 6 December 1924.
36 Miller, letter to mother, 15 May 1924, SAD 968/11/1.
37 The most insightful treatment of this phenomenon/methodology is Timothy Mitchell's *Colonizing Egypt* (Cambridge: Cambridge University Press, 1988).
38 MacArthur, *Extravagant Narratives*, 134; Gerber, *Authors of Their Lives*, 60.
39 Baily, letter to his father, 3 July 1919, SAD 533/1/39-40.
40 Henderson, *Set under Authority*, 15.
41 E. A. Balfour, SAD 606/3/1.
42 E. A. Balfour includes a description of these 'old school' officials in 'The District Commissioner's Tale', in *The Sudan Canterbury Tales*, ed. Sir Donald Hawley

(Norwich, England: Michael Russell, 1999), 39. John Kenrick also mentions Bramble's rides, saying they made him feel 'ashamed', in 'Notes for the History of the Sudan Political Service', SAD 815/4/16.

43 Balfour, 'The District Commissioner's Tale', 42.

44 Ibid., 50.

45 Colonial Office memo on recruitment, undated, *c.* 1925, CO 323/981/1.

46 Sir Sidney Low, *Egypt in Transition*, as quoted by Michael S. Coray in 'In the Beginning', in *The British in the Sudan, 1998–1956*, 82–83.

47 C. G. Dupuis, letter to sister, 21 December 1924, SAD 780/1/4.

48 K. D. D. Henderson recalled, 'It was considered the old belief of men like Baily and Dupuis that [wives] distracted a man's attention from his work.' Deng and Daly, *Bonds of Silk*, 45.

49 In the military era, 'civilian DCs were not allowed to serve further south than Sennar'. Henderson, *Set under Authority*, 24.

50 C. G. Dupuis, letter to sister, 21 December 1924, SAD 780/1/4-17.

51 Ibid.

52 Ibid.

53 I. W. Douglas, letter to sister, 5 December 1924, SAD 707/9/12.

54 Douglas, letter to mother, 15 December 1924, SAD 707/9/15-16.

55 British newspaper cuttings regarding the Mutiny, SAD 770/3/2.

56 R. Udal, letter to parents, dated 30 November 1924, SAD 750/5/12.

57 Forster, SAD 209/11/31-38.

58 Clare Willis, letter to mother, 30 November 1924, SAD 209/11/38-39.

59 Geraldine Forster, letter to Grace Balfour, 17 December 1924, SAD 606/3/33.

60 Baily, letter to father, 30 November 1924, SAD 533/2/8.

61 R. N. Udal, letter to parents, 30 November 1924, SAD 750/5/10.

62 Ibid.

63 Willis, letter to mother, 30 November 1924, SAD 209/11/38-39.

64 Forster, SAD 606/3/33-34.

65 Willis, letter to mother, 30 November 1924, SAD 209/11/40.

66 Dupuis, SAD 780/1/4-17.

67 Ibid.

68 Udal, letter to parents, 30 November 1924, SAD 750/5/12.

69 This barely makes it in to the official accounting of the Mutiny. See Appendix III of the 'Military Report of the Evacuation'. SAD 479/7/52

70 This fact is dealt with euphemistically in Huddleston's official report, which he concludes by saying, 'Owing to the state of affairs it was necessary to allow the Egyptian and Sudanese officers to resume normal duties in the Battalion for the time being.' SAD 479/7/50.

71 Y. Hunter, letter dated 24–26 November 1924, SAD 745/4/4.

72 Martina Kopf, 'European and African Narrative Writing', in *Developing Africa: Concepts and Practices in Twentieth Century Colonialism*, eds. Joseph M. Hodge, Gerald Hödl, Martina Kopf (Manchester, UK: Manchester University Press, 2014), 344.

73 Ibid.

74 Kopf, 'European and African Narrative Writing', 344.

75 Udal, letter to parents, 30 November 1924, SAD 750/5/12.

76 Richard Hill, of the Railways Dept. and later lecturer of Near Eastern Studies at Durham University and the founder, per se, of the Sudan Archive, drew a direct line

between education level and the ability to speak Arabic, and the different relationship the military, the civil service and the political service had with the Sudanese. Quoted by Coray, in 'In the Beginning', in *The British in the Sudan*, 60.

Chapter 8

1 'Bringing it all Back Home: the Project of Return for the Anglo-Sudanese, 1940-1965,' in Patrick Manning, ed. *World History: Global and Local Interactions* (Princeton, NJ: Markus Weiner, 2005).
2 Margery Perham, letter to the *Times*, 10 December 1946, reproduced in *Colonial Sequence, 1930–1949*, 292–93.
3 Margery Perham, letter to the *Times*, 10 December 1946, in *Colonial Sequence*, 292–93.
4 Ibid.
5 Ibid.
6 Ibid.
7 Ibid.
8 Ibid.
9 Ibid.
10 Ibid.
11 Smith, *Europe's Invisible Migrants*, 15.
12 HMG was forced to reiterate the long-standing policy of the British government during this period. See, for example, FO 371190141, no. 284, minutes of a meeting to prepare for Egyptian abrogation of the Condominium Agreement, 10 October 1951. And the subsequent statement from HMG: 'They reaffirm the two fundamental principles of their policy in regard to the Sudan, namely that they will agree to no change in the status of the Sudan without consultation with the Sudanese, and that they will maintain the right of the Sudanese freely to choose their ultimate status.' Reproduced in *British Documents on the End of Empire: Series B, Vol. 5: Sudan, Part II, 1951–56*, ed. Douglas H. Johnson (London: The Stationary Office, 1998), 47–48.
13 J. A. Gillan, 'Review of H.C. Jackson, *Behind the Modern Sudan*', *African Affairs* 55, no. 219 (1 April 1956): 146–47, https://doi.org/10.1093/oxfordjournals.afraf.a094389. Accessed June 17, 2018.
14 Michael Collins, 'Nation, State and Agency: Evolving Historiographies of African Decolonization', in *Britain, France and the Decolonization of Africa: Future Imperfect?* (London: UCL Press, 2017), 41.
15 Chris Jeppesen, 'The Colonial Service during Decolonization', in *Britain, France and the Decolonization of Africa: Future Imperfect?*, edited by Andrew W.M. Smith and Chris Jeppesen, 140–42.
16 Kirk-Greene, *Britain's Imperial Administrators*,198.
17 Berny Sèbe, 'French and British Colonial Heroes, 58.
18 Dawson, 114. He points out that the idea of the 'hero' was a man of action. A retired solider did not register symbolically in the imperial imaginary.
19 Kirk-Greene, *Britain's Imperial Administrators*, 15. 'In the case of the SPS, of course, they were *de jure* the servants of the government ... never of His Majesty's Government.' He then acknowledges the difficulty of US scholars believing this culture existed. But, at least in the case of the British-Sudani, it was true to the point

of political myopia. Furthermore, the British-Sudani self-fashioned in reaction to the Egyptian Civil Service and the Indian Civil Service; see 64–71. They fought against a Sudan equivalent to the sahib and memsahib personae. And yet it should be noted that the percentage of government positions occupied by Sudanese was far below the rate of Indians in the ICS. By 1952, only 41 of 136 DC posts were held by Sudanese and all 39 governors and deputy governors were British; see 195.

20 Nicola King, *Memory, Narrative, Identity: Remembering the Self* (Edinburgh: Edinburgh University Press, 2000), 28.

21 Pierre Nora, 'Generations', in *Realms of Memory: Rethinking the French Past, Vol. 1: Conflicts and Divisions*, ed. Pierre Nora, English edition, ed. Lawrence D. Kitzman, trans. Arthur Goldhammer (New York: Columbia University Press, 1996), 2.

22 Buettner, *Empire Families*, 254.

23 See Chapter 1, 'Preconceptions and Early Contacts', in *Bonds of Silk*.

24 The denationalization of individuals, particularly those in diasporic communities, is addressed by many, including James Clifford who talks about 'diasporic paradigms', 246.

25 Annex III of Cmd 8904, 1953: the 'Agreement between the Government of the United Kingdom of Great Britain and Northern Ireland and the Egyptian Government concerning Self-Government and Self-Determination for the Sudan', dated Cairo, 12 February 1953. Article I is more explicit: 'In order to enable the Sudanese people to exercise Self-Determination in a free and neutral atmosphere, a transition period providing full self-government for the Sudanese shall begin.' Reproduced in *British Documents on the End of Empire*, 508–15.

26 Kenrick explores the relationship between the earlier military culture and the inconsistency of the policy versus the experiences of wives and other women in the service; *Sudan Tales*, 21–28.

27 Storrar, letter diary entry, 2–8 October 1920, regarding horse's head, SAD 54/1/159.

28 Bell, letter to parents, 12 February 1932, SAD 697/5/54.

29 As the original barrier to women's presence was never a hard and fast one, it is impossible to identify a fixed date when the policies changed. But anecdotal evidence makes it clear that by 1925, British women were allowed in all stations for at least part of the year.

30 E. A. Balfour, cover letter to correspondence, SAD 606/3/1.

31 M. E. Struvé, memoir, *c*. 1966, SAD 294/18/50.

32 *Sudan Almanac*, 1924.

33 There are daughters and sisters as well as wives in residence in the 1910s. For examples specific to Atbara, see SAD 52/1/368.

34 Prior to the evacuation of the Egyptian Army, civilian officials were given military titles. By the end of the 1920s, the administration had completely changed over to a civilian structure.

35 Bell, letter to parents, 1 April 1932, SAD 697/6/15.

36 Storrar, letter diary, 21 November 1920, SAD 51/1/10.

37 Deng and Daly, *Bonds of Silk*, 46–49.

38 There is the stereotype of the young woman going on a 'hunting expedition' for a husband during a trip for that purpose to a colony. In most cases, however, men met and married their wives in Britain, and most of these women were slightly older than usual 'marrying age', as were the men.

39 Obituary, *Palestine Exploration Quarterly*, 1957: 2 (July–December), 153–54.

40 Mary Rowley, interview with the author, 8 February 2003.
41 Kenrick, *Sudan Tales*, 146–50. It is interesting in Kenrick's book that, although it is an account of the experiences of SPS wives, the husbands' careers are detailed as a way to track the women's lives in the Sudan.
42 'Dagmar's Sudan Recollections (1938–1955)', by Dagmar Mynors, *c.* 1980, includes a passage about the strangeness of leading two lives, HAW 8/3/17.
43 Most British-Sudani kept their children with them until they were of school age. Most wives chose to be with their husbands rather than their children if a choice had to be made, although an unhappy marriage could be ameliorated by the wife's decision to be with the children. Charles Garrett speaks of this possibility in regard to his own parents in an interview with the author, 7 February 2003. During the Second World War, separation was a particularly difficult decision because whatever choice was made at the beginning of the war was the family reality for six years.
44 See Bell's, letter to parents, 14 October 1931, detailed account of efforts to create a home in his new house, SAD 697/4/33-34.
45 During 1949, the correspondence of Allan and Diana Arthur with their families gives an excellent description of Diana's efforts at adjusting to the Sudan and her desire to behave as a proper middle-class adult. For example, see SAD 726/4 and 707/16.
46 Mynors, memoir, HAW 8/3/17.
47 E. G. Sarsfield-Hall, *From Cork to Khartoum* (Keswick, Great Britain: the author, *c.* 1975), appendix, vii. 'It was a tradition that a DC was on duty at all times.'
48 Rowley, interview with the author, 8 February 2003.
49 Due to the destruction of documents held by the Sudan Agency, it is necessary to extrapolate from shipping and transportation agreements undertaken by the Colonial Office. In 1949, Brian Carlisle was given an allowance of £40 to take his belongings to the Sudan. For normal leave passage, which didn't involve substantial baggage, the allowances were smaller. See, for example, CO 323/1042/7: Circular No. 163, dated 8 May 1929: Regulations regarding assisted passages to the Untied Kingdom ... for Gibraltar. 'No allowance ... may exceed an amount equivalent to 50% of a 1st Class P & O return passage'; final leave usually granted a similar allowance to the initial outward passage.
50 Arthur, letter to parents, 3 May 1949, is having the furniture that came with the house replaced by furniture designed by his fiancée, at a cost of £200, SAD 726/4/27-8; Lewis, letter to sister, 3 November 1944. She writes that her husband was concerned that the servants that he had been employing were alright for a bachelor but that now that they were to have a proper married household, they might not be good enough. Her concern is to learn Arabic quickly so that she can have a proper relationship with them, SAD 338/1/5.
51 SAD is in possession of hundreds of these items, most similar in nature. Spears, arm bands and shields were commonly collected.
52 Edward Wallis, letter to Udal, 23 June 1950, SAD 781/3/2.
53 W. A. Porter, inventory of auction and baggage, 30 May 1951, SAD 700/14/23-32.
54 Storrar, letter diary, 18–31 January 1927, SAD 57/1/153.
55 D. Arthur, letter to mother, 14 April 1954, SAD 707/17/65.
56 Jane Britton, née Henderson, interviewed by author, 3 February 2003.
57 Storrar, various entries, describing a total of seven farewell parties, SAD 57/1/100-280.
58 For Storrar, for example, Atbara was a sizable town and so there were various different communities within it that held parties for him. There was not, however,

a differentiation, for example, among 'non-British staff' as he calls them, SAD 57/1/271.

59 Storrar, SAD 57/1/100-280.

60 Deng and Daly, *Bonds of Silk*, 'What I think … one is bound to remember is that the Sudanese are an extremely courteous people …', Bell, 27; 'The Arab in general is the most skilled flatterer in the world', H. D. D. Henderson, 29.

61 See, for example, testimonial by Bushara Abdulla for Bailey, 27 June 1932, SAD 533/1/35-7, and testimonial by Abdel Said Effendi Abdel Koddous for Storrar, 8–11 July 1927, SAD 57/1/272.

62 John Kenrick, 'Reminiscences around the Transfer of Power', in *The Condominium Remembered: Proceedings of the Durham Sudan Historical Records Conference, 1982; Vol. 1: The Making of the Sudanese State*, Working Paper, Deborah Lavin, ed. (Durham: University of Durham, Centre for Middle Eastern and Islamic Studies, 1991), 164.

63 D. Hawley, essay letters, *c.* 1953–25 March 1955, HAW 1/6/1-53.

64 It is difficult to prove a negative. However, the head archivist of SAD, Jane Hogan, was consulted regarding this claim and agrees. She has never encountered a description of any kind of homecoming celebration, whatsoever.

65 Hawley, assorted papers pertaining to immigration report, 1976–77, HAW 22/8/1-70.

66 Each interview subject was specifically asked this question.

67 D. Arthur, letter to parents, 9 March 1950, SAD 707/17/16-9.

68 Rowley, interview with the author, 8 February 2003.

69 Buettner discussed example of, and motivations for, silences about family separations, but silences about returning seem less common in the Anglo-Indian instance. See *Empire Families*, 139–45.

70 Lewis, note on final letter from the Sudan, dated 25 April 1955, SAD 338/12/15.

71 These were the concerns of Juliana Hill, wife of Richard Hill, who had worked for the Sudan railways and then taught at Gordon College. SAD 970/3 includes letters from early 1949 from J. Hill to various universities inquiring about positions for both her and her husband; see 970/3/6-10. Also correspondence with placement agencies for short-term work, see 970/3/35-37.

72 Marigold Best, daughter of Reginald Davies, Dir. of Economics and Trade, retired 1935, interviewed by the author, 3 February 2003; also Rowley.

73 Rowley, interview with author, 8 February 2003.

74 W. Johnson, diary, *c.* 1954; SAD 752/16/4.

75 There wasn't a specific Thomas Cook publication for the Sudan. Others for the Middle East, India and Malaya, however, show a general structure that was shared by all. Ship passage to and from the Sudan, for example, could be seen in the schedule for ships passing through the Suez Canal and down the Red Sea, stopping at Port Said, and then Port Sudan. The Sudan Agents papers are, for the most part, lost. So the detailed contracts between transport companies and colonial governments in other colonies at a comparable distance from Britain have been combined with the vaguer mention of such contracts on the part of the Sudan government in recruitment and employment contract literature to establish that similar contracts existed for the Sudan.

76 Dee, interview with author, 3 February 2003.

77 Rowley, interview with author, 8 February 2003.

78 See, for example, letter from D. M. H. Evans to G. Hawkesworth, head of the Re-Employment Bureau, *c.* 1956, SAD 712/10/1-2. Evans identified his generalist skill set as an impediment to employment.

79 Poem written by Thompson, a storekeeper, on the occasion of the retirement of Brian Storrar, Railways and Steamers Department, most likely given at the Atbara Sports Club dinner held in Storrar's honour on 7 July 1927, SAD 57/1/277.
80 A particularly interesting example can be found at Exeter College, Oxford. Four consecutive bursars of the college were ex-SPS officials. Kirke-Greene, 269–70.
81 Sudan Agency Memo, 'Sudan No. 3 (1956)', SAD 712/13/18.
82 J. Kenrick, unpublished memoir, SAD 815/4/21.
83 D. M. H. Evans completed the Oxford Questionnaire in early 1954. In response, the Educational Secretary at the Oxford Appointments Committee, A. R. Wooley, asked, 'Am I right in thinking that you are now in the same position as a number of other Oxford men from the Sudan who have been to see me?' For those who went to Oxford (and one would assume, the other old universities), it was understood, therefore, to be a normal step in re-establishing a life in Britain and a second career to turn to one's university for potential referral services, SAD 714/6/2.
84 Minute of the Ministry of Labour and National Service, 'Resettlement of Officers of the Sudan Government. Assistance that could be offered by the Ministry of Labour and National Service', 10 June 1953; LAB 8/1788.
85 Ibid.
86 Ibid.
87 Sudan Agency Memo, 'Sudan No. 3 (1956)', SAD 712/13/18:
88 Rowley, interview with author, 8 February 2003.
89 Gawain Bell and Brian Dee, eds., *Sudan Political Service, 1899–1956* (Oxford: Oxonian Press, n.d.), 58–59. D. M. H. Evans worked for Basildon; J. V. d'A. Rowley worked for Bracknell.
90 Sudan Agency Memo, 'Sudan No. 3 (1956)', SAD 712/13/18.
91 G. Hawkesworth, letter to D. M. H. Evans, *c.* 1956, SAD 712/10/1-2.
92 J. Kenrick, SAD 815/4/21.
93 Most notably Sir James Robertson, governor general of the Federation of Nigeria, and G. Hawkesworth, chairman of the Civil Service Commission of the Federation of Nigeria.
94 Brian Carlisle, interviewed by author, 5 February 2003.
95 This number was arrived at by reviewing the second career entries in Bell and Dee, eds., *Sudan Political Service.*
96 Between 1956 and 1972, Lesley Lewis and her husband, David, travelled extensively together and apart, following his work. L. Lewis has catalogued their correspondence during this period: SAD 338/14.
97 Gawain Bell and Brian Dee, eds., *Sudan Political Service*, 58–59.
98 'Sudan Government British Pensioners' Association: List of Members' (London: Sudan Government British Pensioners' Association, *c.* 1957).
99 'Place – the region, the city and the neighborhood – condenses a whole complex history of economic, social and political processes into a simple cultural image.' John Clarke, '"There's No Place Like …": Cultures of Difference', in *Geography Matters! A Reader*, eds. Doreen Massey and John Allen (Cambridge: Cambridge University Press, 1984), 54.
100 L. Newell, letter to D. Evans, 9 June 1957, SAD 712/11/3.
101 Garrett, interview with author, 2 February 2003.
102 For an interesting examination of the changing status of British immigration to Australia, but that offers interesting insight into the 'invisible' white migrants within the Commonwealth, see Stephen Constantine, 'British Emigration to the Empire

Commonwealth since 1880: From Overseas Settlement to Diaspora?' in *The Journal of Imperial and Commonwealth History* 31, no. 2 (2003), 16–35.

103 Librarian employment card of Juliana Hill included in material sent when seeking employment in England, SAD 424/10/3.

104 Ina Beasley, *Before the Winds Changed*, Oriental and African Studies Series (Oxford: Oxford University Press, 1992), 1.

105 Obituary for E. Hills-Young, saved by Helen Foley who also worked for the Red Cross in the Sudan during the Second World War, SAD 784/18/30.

106 Rowley, interview with author, 8 February 2003.

107 Kirk-Greene, *Britain's Imperial Administrators*, 289.

108 Robert Stack, 'The Societal Conception of Space', in *Geography Matters!* Massey and Allen, eds., 34.

109 Ibid.

110 Kirk-Greene, *Britain's Imperial Administrators*, 269–70.

111 J. Kenrick, memoir. Considering that there are so few other markers of the return set out by British-Sudani, it is interesting to note that in his twenty-page memoir Kenrick provides no section breaks or headings, except one. The last section is called 'Readjustment' and deals with his post-Sudan life, SAD 815/4/21.

112 Elizabeth Buettner, *Europe after Empire: Decolonization, Society, and Culture* (Cambridge: Cambridge University Press, 2016), 63.

113 Chris Jeppesen, 'The Colonial Service during Decolonization', 145.

114 Ibid., 148–53.

115 Ibid.

116 This is an anecdotal assessment, based on interviews, memoirs and other biographical material.

Chapter 9

1 '"Change of Masters": The Sudan Government British Pensioners' Association and the Negotiation of Postcolonial Identities,' in *The Journal of Colonialism and Colonial History*, Vol. 7 Issue 2 (Summer 2006).

2 M. Hillary to D. Cumming, 25 September 1958. 'The amount required to meet our request for a revision of the pensions of the 511 officials who retired before 1950 … is £E 94,089.' This was the SGBPA executive's assessment in 1958 of the cost, SAD G//S 1186, Box 2/3.

3 *The Journal of the Senior Civil Servants' Association of the Sudan*, no. 7 (August 1951): 2. 'The pensionable official has 4 percent or 5 percent of his monthly salary deducted at source towards pension and the amount deducted is placed in the general revenue. Pensions of retired officials are paid out of general revenue. There is no special Pension Fund.'

4 For a detailed account of the pensioners' demands, see *Sudan Pensions: They also serve who only stand and wait…?*, a pamphlet to members of Parliament, published by the SGBPA, distributed in March 1961, SAD G//S 1186, Box 2/3.

5 J. R. Shaw, 'Brief record of a meeting at which the Minister of State, The Right Hon. Selwyn Lloyd, C.B.E., Q.C., met representatives of the Expatriate Civil Servants Association on March 23rd, 1953', SAD G//S 1186, Box 1/6.

6 There is discussion of this in numerous documents. See, for example, 'Note of Interview with His Excellency the Governor-General on 27th May, 1952', in *The*

Journal, no. 10 (August 1952): 11. 'With regard to the Association's contention that self-government implied a "change of Master" and a breach of existing contracts of service, His Excellency stated that in the opinion of his legal advisors this was not so.'

7 *Sudan Pensions: They also serve ...?*, 1, SAD G//S 1186, Box 2/3.

8 Habermas, *The Structural Transformation of the Public Sphere*, 231–32.

9 Mark E. Warren, *Democracy and Association* (Princeton: Princeton University Press, 2001), 39.

10 Michael A. Hogg and Deborah J. Terry, 'Social Identity Theory and Organizations Processes', in *Social Identity Processes in Organizations Contexts*, eds. Hogg and Terry (Philadelphia: Psychology Press, 2001), 3: 'People have a repertoire of ... discrete category memberships that vary in relative overall importance ... Each category membership is represented in the individual member's mind as a social identity that both describes and prescribes one's attributes as a member of that group.'

11 For a discussion of popular metropolitan efforts to discuss, define, remember and forget Britain's imperial history, see, among many others, Andrew Thompson and Meaghan Kowalski, 'Social Life and Cultural Representation: Empire in the Public Imagination', 287–96; Krishan Kumar, 'Empire, Nation, and National Identity', 320–28; and Andrew Thompson, 'Afterward: The Imprint of the Empire', 330–45; in Andrew Thompson, ed., *Britain's Experience of Empire in the Twentieth Century*, Oxford History of the British Empire: Companion Series (Oxford: Oxford University Press, 2012). Also, Buettner, *Europe after Empire*, 440–49.

12 'Of the sixty-five ... recruited from 1945 onwards ... only twenty-six were given pensionable terms; the others were given contracts.' Harold MacMichael, 'Introduction', in *Sudan Political Service, 1899–1956*.

13 Annex III of Cmd 8904, 1953.

14 G. D. Lampen, letter to Michael Hillary, 14 February 1952, SAD G//S 1186, Box 1/4.

15 Letter to membership of the SCSAS, written by W. G. Piper, Honorary General Secretary, March 1950, SAD 830/6/11.

16 *The Journal*, no. 7, August 1951, 1.

17 The SCSAS attracted more junior members to begin with and those on contracts. And the entire executive of the organization was from the technical and civil braches of government. For a list of initial membership, see *The Journal*, no. 1, July 1950, 20–22. For a list of executive, see, for example, *The Journal*, no. 10, August 1952, 32.

18 *The Journal*, no. 7, August 1951, 2.

19 C. G. Davies, letter to James Robertson, 15 May 1952, SAD 523/3/2.

20 Initially J. A. Willoughby was elected Honorary Secretary but he took an overseas position and Hillary stepped in. Hillary then held the post for more than twenty years.

21 The SGBPA was the only post-Sudan service organization that had a universal membership. Other groups were limited to those who fit specific sub-categories within the Sudani community, such as the Sudan Defence Force Dinner Club or the Sudan Church Association.

22 The initial suggestion was made by Hillary in letter to the executive, 27 April 1960. In subsequent correspondence (same citation) he is asked and accepts, SAD G//S 1186, Box 2/4.

23 For a list of the executive election results between 1952 and 1968, see SAD G//S 1186, Box 3/2. The make-up of the executive was very stable over those sixteen years, with some members elected as many as nine times.

24 D. C. Cumming, letter to Lloyd, F.O., dated August 1957.

25 C. G. Davies, letter to James Robertson, 15 May 1952, SAD 523/3/2.

26 Ibid.
27 'Minutes of 1st meeting of the SGBPA, October 10, 195[2]', chaired by Gillan, SAD G//S 1241, Box 1/2.
28 Beasley, letter to M. Hillary, 23 September 1952, SAD G//S 1186, Box 1/5.
29 J. W. Cummins, letter to Hillary, 13 February 1952, SAD G//S 1186, Box 1/4.
30 A. Gillan, speech before the first meeting of pensioners, 16 May 1952, SAD G//S 1186, Box 1/4.
31 J. P. S. Daniell to Province Representatives of ECSAS, 29 December 1954, SAD G//S 1165, Box 1/7. Quote from Howe: 'Her Majesty's Government in the United Kingdom accordingly make known their intention, when the Sudan determines its future status, to ensure observance of this safeguard by securing its embodiment in a formal agreement to be entered into between H.M. Government and the Government of the Sudan.'
32 J. P. S. Daniell to Province Representatives of ECSAS, 29 December 1954, SAD G//S 1165, Box 1/7.
33 Robert Howe was governor general from 1947 to 1955. He was from the Foreign Office and had been appointed to oversee the process of Sudanization and independence. In discussing an earlier struggle between the Palace and Whitehall, Douglas H. Johnson states in his Introduction to *British Documents on the End of Empire: Series B, Vol. 5: Sudan, Part I, 1942–1950* (London: The Stationary Office, 1999), 'The confrontation which now developed … was the product, in part, of the Sudan administration's long-standing distrust of the Foreign Office, compounded by the isolation from contact with the wider empire which attachment to the Foreign Office had fostered', lvii.
34 SAD G//S 1186, Box 1/6: author unknown, most likely Owen or Daniell, 1954, SAD G//S 1186, Box 1/6.
35 Owen, letter to W. H. Luce, 16 July 1954, SAD G//S 1165, Box 1/7.
36 'Brief Record of Meeting …', J. R. Shaw, 23 March 1953, SAD 1186, Box 1/6.
37 R. Howe, letter to Owen, 14 December 1954, SAD G//S 1165, Box 1/8.
38 There was a long series of letters between officials in the Foreign Office and Gillan. For a summary, see 'Brief Record of Negotiations with Foreign Office', 1953–58, SAD G//S 1186, Box 2/3.
39 See, for example, D. Cumming to Sayed Ibrahim, minister of Finance and Economics, 13 September 1958, SAD G//S 1186, Box 2/3.
40 'Brief Record of Meeting …', J. R. Shaw, 23 March 1953, SAD G//S 1186, Box 1/6.
41 At the same time that the official assurances of the governor general and the Foreign Office were being passed on to members, there was correspondence between the executives of the two associations that betrayed a more cynical attitude, most notably on the part of the ECSAS. See SAD G//S 1186, Box 1/6: letter from Owen to Hillary, 17 June 1953.
42 Willoughby to Hillary, 31 July 1957, SAD G//S 1186, Box 2/3.
43 Hillary, notes on meeting with A. R. Ross, 31 October 1958, SAD G//S 1186, Box 2/3.
44 Cumming to Lloyd, 27 October 1958, SAD G//S 1186, Box 2/3.
45 Lloyd to Cumming, 6 November 1958, SAD G//S 1186, Box 2/3.
46 Hillary, 31 October 1958, SAD G//S 1186, Box 2/3.
47 Willoughby to unknown pensioner, 10 February 1963. In this letter he details his frustrations about the paternalism of the Executive and his belief that the general membership should not have been protected from the details of the campaign over the years and that, given the lack of success that the executive had for so long,

new difficulties should not be kept from them either. He argues that the general membership should be allowed to make fully informed decisions based on complete disclosure. SAD G//S 1186, Box 2/3.

48 Willoughby to Hillary, 31 July 1957, SAD G//S 1186, Box 2/3.

49 Redfern had been the private secretary to the governor general of Canada and the director of the Commonwealth Dept. of the British Council, among other things. Bell and Dee, *Sudan Political Service*.

50 Redfern to Hillary, 1 September 1958, SAD G//S 1186, Box 2/3.

51 Ibid.

52 This was instigated by A. E. H. Elkington in a 'Paper submitted ... for consideration at the Fiftieth meeting of the Committee', *c.* 1960. SAD G//S 1186, Box 2/4.

53 This claim is based mainly on received knowledge but also on a survey of the newspapers read by British-Sudanis while in the Sudan (Weekly *Times* being the most common) and those interviewed for this project (mainly the *Times* and the *Daily Telegraph*).

54 Willoughby to Sir Hugh Lucas-Tooth, MP, 14 May 1962, SAD G//S 1186, Box 2/6.

55 Elkington, note to committee members, *c.* February 1959, SAD G//S 1186, Box 2/4.

56 Willoughby to Lucas-Tooth, 14 May 1962, SAD G//S 1186, Box 2/6.

57 Carmichael to Hillary, 9 October 1958, SAD G//S 1186, Box 2/6.

58 Elkington to the SGBPA Committee, 6 February 1959, SAD G//S 1186, Box 2/4.

59 By 1959, the executive was actively compiling statistics that compared their situation with that of former colonies. For an example, see 'Note for the Committee', 25 June 1959, in which the executive sets out arguments and facts prepared in advance of the Annual General Meeting, SAD G//S 1186, Box 2/4. By 1961, the OSPA and the SGBPA were submitting joint letters to Members of Parliament. SAD G//S 1186, Box 2/3. See also the legal assessment of the SGBPA case by Mr. Justice Bennett, Q.C., 24 May 1961, in which his assessment is compiled in part by comparison with other colonial situations, SAD G//S 1186, Box 2/3.

60 Letter to the editor of the *Times*, 9 February 1959, signed by the chairmen and presidents of the Malayan, Sudan and West African Pensioners' Associations, SAD G//S 1186, Box 2/3.

61 Willoughby, 14 May 1962, SAD 1186, Box 2/6.

62 'Memorial: Sudan Government British Pensioners' Association', undated, April 1959, SAD G//S 1186, Box 2/4.

63 Anonymous, 'Case for HMG taking over Sudan Government Pensions in the same way as pensions of retired members of the Indian Civil Service were taken over', *c.* 1959, SAD G//S 1186, Box 2/4.

64 Deng and Daly, *Bonds of Silk*, 71.

65 Anthony Eden, letter to R. Howe, 20 February 1953, FO 3711102746, no 269. Reproduced in *British Documents on the End of Empire, Part II*, Douglas H. Johnson, ed., 214.

66 Letter from R. Davies to 'Robin', 1 September 1963, SAD 533/2/17.

67 Anon., 'Case for HMG ...', SAD G//S 1186, Box 2/4.

68 Willoughby, 14 May 1962, SAD G//S 1186, Box 2/6.

69 Ibid.

70 Redfern to Hillary, 27 September 1959, SAD 1186, Box 2/4.

71 Ibid.

72 Letter to Sir Duncan Cumming from 'Elliot', *c.* 1959, SAD G//S 1186, Box 2/3.

73 Ibid.

74 Ibid.
75 For the specific implications of the act in regard to Sudan pensioners, see SAD G//S 1186, Box 3/3. 'Pensions (Increases) Act, 1962: Note on Regulations', SAD G//S 1186, Box 3/3.
76 Hillary's suggestion is mentioned in Gillan's written response, 20 November 1962, suggestion that Hillary brought it up at an executive meeting in early November of the same year, SAD G//S 1186, Box 3/3.
77 SAD G//S 1186, Box 3/3.
78 P. D. Mulholland to Hillary, 29 November 1962, SAD G//S 1186, Box 3/3.
79 F. S. Halide to Hillary, 3 December 1962, SAD G//S 1186, Box 3/3.
80 Gillan to Hillary, 12 December 1962, SAD G//S 1186, Box 3/3.
81 Ibid.
82 Form letter to all members of the SGBPA from Gillan, as chairman of Trustees of the Fund, SAD 696/4/24.
83 Letter from Redfern to Hillary, 6 May 1963, SAD G//S 1186, Box 3/3.
84 Letter to members from Hillary, July 1964. Men's annual subscription rates set at £20 and women's at £10, SAD 696 4/27.
85 'Statement by the Minister of Overseas Development', 11 March 1970, G//S 1186, Box 3/2.
86 Ibid.
87 For an example of numbers for the Tea Party, see SAD G//S 1186, Box 2/3: at the Tea Party on 4 July 1958, there were 245 in attendance.

Chapter 10

1 It is too much of a diversion to go into detail about the efforts to get Westminster Abbey to include a commemorative plaque to British service in the Sudan. Suffice it to say that there was a substantial split within the community, even within those who would be considered leaders of the British-Sudani community. Some even went so far as to write letters specifically stating that they wanted nothing to do with such an effort.
2 Kuhn, 'A Journey through Memory', in *Memory and Methodology*, 190.
3 Anderson, *Imagined Communities*, 187–206.
4 Mark Freeman, 'Telling Stories: Memory and Narrative', in *Memory: Histories, Theories, Debates*, eds. Susannah Radstone and Bill Schwarz (New York: Fordham University Press, 2010), 267.
5 It is interesting to note that in the years between when this portion of this study was originally written and the version that is included here, the author has found it necessary to replace present tense verbs with past tense ones. The act of creation was still underway then and so 'British-Sudanis revisit and rework their memories' has become 'British-Sudanis revisited and reworked their memories'.
6 Annette Kuhn, 'A Journey through Memory', in *Memory and Methodology*, ed. Suzannah Radstone (London: Berg Publishers, 2004), 189.
7 Maurice Halbwachs, 'The Reconstruction of the Past', in *On Collective Memory*, ed. and trans. Lewis A. Coser (Chicago: University of Chicago Press, 1992), 50.
8 Various archives used in this book were originally accessions of Rhodes House, then taken into the broader Bodleian Library Special Collections Archives. The entire

collection of FO documents pertaining to the Sudan at the National Archives are under the Egyptian Office heading.

9 Letter from R. C. Mayall to M. J. Wheatley, 18 July 1949, SAD 703/1/27.

10 J. W. Robertson to Wheatley, 16 April 1949, SAD 703/1/14. Robertson, then civil secretary, was concerned that 'the reason why the Communists were making headway in British universities and technical colleges was the open hospitality which they extended to coloured students, whereas other British – Conservative, Liberal and Labour alike – stood aloof… The students from Oxford were particularly emphatic that the white students in Colleges not only refrained from offering them hospitality but from making friends with them'.

11 Form letter from T. H. B. Mynors to prospective members, *c.* 1955, SAD 725/9/67.

12 T. H. B. Mynors, introduction to unpublished memoir, March 1982, SAD 777/8/1. He writes that when he tried to broaden the scope of the journal, he received more support from 'departmental officials' (meaning non-SPS) and remembers being 'officially warned to avoid controversy'.

13 Form letter from T. H. B. Mynors to prospective members, *c.* 1955, SAD 725/9/67.

14 Ibid.

15 Ibid.

16 W. O'B. Lindsay, H. A. W. Morrice, J. S. Owen, J. V. Rintoul, R. C. Wakefield and A. E. T. Walkley, form letter, *c.* 1955, SAD 712/10/5.

17 Ibid.

18 Ibid.

19 Ibid.

20 See Chapter 4, 'Nationalism and Independence', in Deng and Daly, *Bonds of Silk*. For example, John Winder, a provincial governor at the time of independence, argues 'the Sudanese then seemed unable or unwilling to believe that the British did not at heart wish or intend to control the Sudan as long as possible in their own interests, and they were reluctant to accept that the tendency of the British not to move faster in a declared policy of de-control was dictated by the impracticalities of the situation (for example, lack of education and social cohesion) rather than by latent imperialism', 75.

21 G. C. Scott and Ibrahim Ahmed, draft of 'The British and the Educated Sudanese', *c.* November 1949, SAD 517/8/11-19.

22 Ibid.

23 Ibid.

24 Form letter to subscribers from J. S. Owen, *c.* 1957, SAD 712/10/9.

25 Draft Minutes of meeting held on 19 December 1957 'to consider the foundation of an Anglo-Sudanese Association', HAW 6/6/17.

26 Ibid.

27 Donald Hawley, circular on Anglo-Sudanese Association, 30 November 1956, HAW 6/6/15.

28 Ibid.

29 Ibid.

30 Ibid.

31 'Report of the Council', *c.* May 1961, SAD G//S 971.

32 Mynors to Hawley, 27 November 1955, HAW 6/6/13.

33 'Rules of the Anglo-Sudanese Association', n.d., SAD G//S 971.

34 Author unknown, letter to Hawley, 12 February 1952, HAW 6/6/8.

35 Mynors to Hawley, 12 February 1955, HAW 6/6/7.

36 'Minutes of the First Annual General Meeting', 22 June 1961, SAD G//S 971.
37 Ibid.
38 Ibid.
39 'Minutes of the Third Annual General Meeting', 9 July 1963, SAD 691/4/21.
40 'Minutes of the Second Annual General Meeting', 29 August 1962, SAD G//S 971.
41 'Minutes of the Third Annual . . .', SAD 696/4/23.
42 Ibid.
43 'Minutes of Second Annual . . .', SAD G//S 971.
44 Ibid.
45 Ibid.
46 Appendix to 'Minutes of Third Annual General Meeting': Extracts from reports from regional representatives, SAD 696/4/23.
47 Ibid.
48 Thomas Hodgkin, *Nationalism in Colonial Africa* (London: Frederick Muller, 1956), 10.
49 A. Arthur, letter to parents, 4 November 1949, SAD 726/4/65-6.
50 Jamal Muhammad Ahmed, quoted in Deng and Daly, *Bonds of Silk*, 143.
51 Yusuf Bedri, quoted in Deng and Daly, *Bonds of Silk*, 153.
52 John Phillips, quoted in Deng and Daly, *Bonds of Silk*, 75.
53 Paul B. Rich, 'End of Empire and the Rise of Race Relations', in *Race and Empire in British Politics* (Cambridge: Cambridge University Press, 1986), 169–200.
54 James Walvin, *Passage to Britain: Immigration in British History and Politics* (Harmondsworth, England: Penguin Books, 1984), 109–11.
55 In Paul Gilroy's exploration of the official efforts of the Greater London Council to address racism in Britain, we can see little place for the cross-cultural efforts of mostly Conservative-identifying ex-colonial officials and the 1970s attempts to respond to radical right-wing articulations of racism by Labour governments. See 'Two Sides of Racism', in '*There Ain't No Black in the Union Jack': The Cultural Politics of Race and Nation* (Chicago: University of Chicago Press, 1987), 149 in particular.
56 Appendix to 'Minutes of Third Annual General Meeting', SAD 696/4/23.
57 Durba Ghosh discusses the imposed discipline of archival standards and expectations in 'National Narratives and the Politics of Miscegenation: Britain and India', in *Archive Stories*, ed. Antoinette Burton (Durham, NC: Duke University Press, 2005), 39–40.
58 John Bodnar, 'Public Memory in an American City: Commemoration in Cleveland', in *Commemorations: The Politics of National Identity*, ed. John R. Gillis (Princeton: Princeton University Press, 1994), 75.
59 Ricoeur, *Hermeneutics and the Human Sciences*, 130.
60 Bhabha, '"Race," Time, and the Revision of Modernity', *Oxford Literary Review* 13, nos. 1–2 (1991): 193–219. When talking about the imposition of colonial temporality and experience on to the European conceptualization of Modernity 'it suggests that what is read as the futurity of the modern, its ineluctable progress, its cultural hierarchies, may be an "excess," a disturbing alterity, a process of the marginalization of the symbols of modernity', 204.
61 Lesley Forbes, 'The Sudan Archive of the University of Durham', in *Middle East Studies and Libraries: A Felicitation Volume for Professor J.D. Pearson*, ed. B.C. Bloomfield (London: Mansell, 1980), 49.
62 E. S. B. Cory and Lesley Forbes, 'Resource for Sudanese Studies: The Sudan Archive of the University of Durham', *African Research and Documentation* 31 (1983): 1.
63 Ibid.

64 Forbes, 'The Sudan Archive of the University of Durham', 49.
65 Ibid.: 'There are many district records still in the old provincial headquarters, substantial numbers in the southern region now being in a deplorable state of preservations', 57.
66 Ibid., 50.
67 Edward Said, 'Secular Interpretation, the Geographical Element, and the Methodology of Imperialism', in *After Colonialism: Imperial Histories and Post-Colonial Displacements*, ed. Gayan Prakash (Princeton: Princeton University Press, 1995), 29.
68 Thomas Richards, *The Imperial Archive: Knowledge and the Fantasy of Empire* (London: Verso, 1993), 4.
69 Bonnie G. Smith, *The Gender of History: Men, Women, and Historical Practice* (Cambridge: Harvard University Press, 2000), 225.
70 Ibid., 235.
71 Forbes, 'The Sudan Archive of the University of Durham', 53.
72 Hogan, interview with the author, 5 July 2004.
73 Ibid.
74 Balfour, cover letter to correspondence collection, 19 February 1978, SAD 606/3/2.
75 Ibid.
76 Lewis, note accompanying letter of 18 July 1949, SAD G//S 1129/3.
77 Andrew W. M. Smith, 'Futures, Contingencies and the End of the French Empire', in *Britain, France and the Decolonization of Africa: Future Imperfect*, edited by Andrew W.M. Smith and Chris Jeppesen (London: UCL Press, 2015), 89.
78 Ibid.
79 Baily, marginalia included with letter to mother, dated 25 July 1924, SAD 533/2/7.
80 Balfour, cover dated 19 February 1978, SAD 606/3/1.
81 Forbes, 'The Sudan Archive of the University of Durham', 57.
82 E. H. MacIntosh's memoir is an example of this. SAD 895/2-4.
83 Forbes, 'The Sudan Archive of the University of Durham', 50.
84 A. W. M. Disney, 'All in the Day's Work in the Sudan, 1926–1957', unpublished memoir. Cover letter dated 1975, SAD 716/1.
85 Disney, unpublished memoir, SAD 716/7/7.
86 Ibid., SAD 716/7/61.
87 T. R. H. Owen, *Sudan Days*, unpublished memoir, written 1960/61, SAD 769/10/3.
88 Ibid., SAD 769/10/11.
89 Ashley Jackson offers generic categories that she argues are predictably represented in most administrators' memoirs, in 'Review: *Governing Empire: Colonial Memoirs and the History of HM Overseas Civil Service*', *African Affairs* 103, no. 412 (July 2004), 479–82. Published by: Oxford University Press on behalf of the Royal African Society.
90 Deng and Daly, *Bonds of Silk*, 8.
91 Mangan, *The Education of an Elite Imperial Administration*.
92 Kirk-Greene, *The Sudan Political Service: A Preliminary Profile* (Oxford: Oxford University Press, 1982), passim.
93 Jane Hogan, interview with the author, 5 July 2004.
94 John Gillis states, 'Commemorative activity is by definition social and political, for it involves the coordination of individual and group memories.' Donors' explicit awareness of this is found in these apologia and marginalia. 'Introduction', in *Commemorations*, 5.

95 J. C. N. Donald, n.d., after 1970, SAD 761/8/37.
96 Ibid.
97 Mynors, unpublished memoir, March 1982, SAD 777/8/1.
98 SAD 895/4.
99 Antoinette Burton, *Dwelling in the Archive: Women Writing House, Home and History in Late Colonial India* (New York: Oxford University Press, 2003), 138.
100 Ibid.
101 Mynors, SAD 777/8/1.
102 Jackson, *Sudan Days and Ways*. For contribution of British women, see 247–48.
103 Pierre Nora, 'Between Memory and History', in *Realms of Memory*, 9.
104 Frederick Cooper, in 'Postcolonial Peoples: A Commentary', in *Europe's Invisible Migrants*, ed. Andrea L. Smith, discusses the unique problems posed by returning imperial populations: 'Thus to the extent that the assertions of particularity and claims to recognition ... are patterns of identity politics, it was a politics that resonated badly with its time and social context. These were not recognition claims like any other: they were assertions of a past that risked getting in the way of a future', 173.
105 Matt Matsuda, *The Memory of the Modern* (New York: Oxford University Press, 1996), 46.
106 Burton, *Dwelling in the Archive*, 142.
107 Svetlana Boym, *The Future of Nostalgia* (New York: Basics Books, 2001), xvii.
108 Jane Hogan, interview with the author, 5 July 2004.
109 Matsuda, *The Memory of the Modern*, 206.

Bibliography

Archives

Cabinet (CAB); Colonial Office (CO); Foreign Office (FO); Labour Office (LAB). National Archives, UK.

Donald Hawley Archive. Durham University (HAW).

E.G. Rowe Papers. Weston Library. Oxford University (MSS Africa).

Margery Perham Papers. Weston Library. Oxford University (MSS Perham).

Sir Ronald Furse Papers. Weston Library. Oxford University (MSS Furse).

Sir Wilfred Thesiger Papers. Eton College.

Sudan Archive. Durham University (SAD).

Thomas Cook Archives. Thomas Cook Company. Peterborough, UK.

William Gladstone Papers. British Library.

Interviews by the author

Annaliesa Dee

Brian Carlisle

Charles Garrett

Jane Britton

Jane Hogan

Lesley Lewis

Marigold Best

Mary Rowley

Newspapers and periodicals

Illustrated London News

The Journal of the Senior Civil Servants' Association of the Sudan

Manchester Guardian

Manchester Times

Pall Mall Gazette

The Sudan Diocesan Review

Times of London

Westminster Gazette

Printed material

Adair, Gilbert. *Myths & Memories*. London: Fontana, 1986.

Aldrich, Richard. 'Imperialism in the Study and Teaching of History' in Mangan, *Benefits Bestowed? Education and British Imperialism*. Edited by J. A. Mangan. Manchester: Manchester University Press, 1988.

Altman, Janet Gurkin. *Epistolarity: Approaches to a Form*. Columbus: Ohio State University Press, 1982.

Anderson, Benedict. *Imagined Communities: Reflections on the Origin and Spread of Nationalism*. London: Verso, 1991.

Anonymous. *A School History of England*. Oxford: Clarendon Press, 1901.

Anonymous. 'Obituary for Mabel Wolff'. *Palestine Exploration Quarterly* (1957): 2 (July–December): 153–54.

Arendt, Hannah. *The Origins of Totalitarianism*. New York: Harcourt Brace Janovich, 1973.

Auchtertlonie, Paul. 'From the Eastern Question to the Death of General Gordon: Representations of the Middle East in the Victorian Periodical Press, 1876–1885'. *British Journal of Middle Eastern Studies* 28, no. 1 (May 2001): 5–24.

Baden-Powell, Robert. *Scouting for Boys: A Handbook for Instruction in Good Citizenship*. Ed. Elleke Boehmer. Oxford: Oxford University Press, 2005.

Bassett, Troy J. and Christina M. Walter. 'Booksellers and Bestsellers: British Book Sales as Documented by *The Bookman*, 1891–1906'. *Book History* 4 (2001): 205–36.

Baumgarten, Murray and H. M. Daleski, eds. *Homes and Homelessness in the Victorian Imagination*. New York: AMS Press, 1998.

Baylen, J. O. 'Politics and the "New Journalism": Lord Esher's Use of the *Pall Mall Gazette*'. *Victorian Periodicals Review* 20, no. 4 (Winter 1987): 126–41.

Beasley, Ina. *Before the Winds Changed*. Oriental and African Studies Series. Oxford: Oxford University Press, 1992.

Behrman, Cynthia F. and Michael Wolff. 'The Creation of Social Myth; Journalism and the Empire: [with Comments]'. *Victorian Periodicals Newsletter* 4, no. 1 (1971): 9–16.

Bell, Gawain. *Shadows on the Sand: The Memoirs of Sir Gawain Bell*. London: C. Hurst and Company, 1983.

Bell, Gawain. *An Imperial Twilight*. London: Lester Crook Academic Publishing, 1989.

Bell, Gawain and Brian Dee, eds. *Sudan Political Service, 1899–1956*. Oxford: Oxonian Press, n.d.

Bell, Heather. *Frontier of Medicine in the Anglo-Egyptian Sudan, 1899–1940*. Oxford: Clarendon Press, 1999.

Bennett, Ernest. *The Downfall of the Dervishes: Being a Sketch of the Final Sudan Campaign of 1898*. London: Methuen, 1898.

Berger, Peter, Brigitte Berger, and Hansfried Kellner. *The Homeless Mind*. New York: Random House, 1973.

Bhabha, Homi K. 'Signs Taken for Wonders: Questions of Ambivalence and Authority under a Tree outside Delhi, May 1817'. *Critical Inquiry* 12, no. 1. 'Race, Writing, and Difference' (Autumn 1985): 144–65.

Bhabha, Homi K. 'Race, Time, and the Revision of Modernity'. *Oxford Literary Review* 13, nos. 1–2 (1991): 193–219.

Bhabha, Homi K. *The Location of Culture*. New York: Routledge, 1994.

Bodnar, John. 'Public Memory in an American City: Commemoration in Cleveland'. In *Commemorations: The Politics of National Identity*. Edited by John R. Gillis. Princeton: Princeton University Press, 1994, 74–89.

Boyce, Robert. 'The Significance of 1931 for British Imperial and International History'. *Histoire@Politique* 11, no. 2 (2010): 1–8. https://www.cairn.info/revue-histoire-politique-2010-2-page-8.htm. Accessed July 12, 2018.

Boyd, Kelly. *Manliness and the Boys' Story Paper in Britain: A Cultural History, 1855–1940.* New York: Palgrave, 2003.

Boym, Svetlana. *The Future of Nostalgia*. New York: Basics Books, 2001.

Brah, Avtar and Annie E. Coombes, eds. *Hybridity and Its Discontents: Politics, Science, Culture*. New York: Routledge, 2000.

Brantlinger, Patrick. *Rule of Darkness: British Literature and Imperialism, 1830–1914.* Ithaca: Cornell University Press, 1988.

Brodhead, Richard H. *Cultures of Letters: Scenes of Reading and Writing in Nineteenth Century America*. Chicago: University of Chicago Press, 1993.

Brown, Philip Marshall. 'The Egyptian Capitulations'. *American Journal of International Law* 12, no. 4 (October 1918): 820–23.

Buchan, John. *Gordon at Khartoum*. London: Peter Davies, 1934.

Buettner, Elizabeth. *Empire Families: Britons and Late Imperial India*. Oxford: Oxford University Press, 2004.

Buettner, Elizabeth. *Europe after Empire: Decolonization, Society, and Culture*. Cambridge: Cambridge University Press, 2016.

Burgin, Victor. *In/Different Spaces: Place and Memory in Visual Culture*. Berkeley: University of California Press, 1996.

Burns, Alan. *Colonial Civil Servant*. London: George Allen & Unwin, 1949.

Burton, Antoinette. *Burdens of History: British Feminists, Indian Women, and Imperial Culture, 1865–1915*. Chapel Hill: University of North Carolina Press, 1994.

Burton, Antoinette, ed. *Archive Stories: Facts, Fictions, and the Writing of History*. Durham, NC: Duke University Press, 2005.

Cain, P. J. and A. G. Hopkins. *British Imperialism: Crisis and Deconstruction 1914–1990*. London: Longman Group, 1993.

Cain, P. J. and A. G. Hopkins. *British Imperialism, 1688–2000*. New York: Longman Group, 2002.

Campbell, Kate. 'W. E. Gladstone, W. T. Stead, Matthew Arnold, and a New Journalism: Cultural Politics in the 1880s'. *Victorian Periodicals Review* 36, no. 1 (Spring 2003): 20–40.

Chatterjee, Partha. *The Nation and Its Fragments: Colonial and Post-Colonial Histories*. Princeton: Princeton University Press, 1993.

Churchill, Winston. *The River War: An Historical Account of the Reconquest of the Soudan*. London: Longmans Green and Co., 1900.

Clark, Gail S. 'Imperial Stereotypes: G. A. Henty and the Boys' Own Empire'. *Journal of Popular Culture* 18, no. 4 (2008): 43–51.

Clarke, John. '"There's No Place Like ...": Cultures of Difference'. In *Geography Matters! A Reader*. Edited by Doreen Massey and John Allen. Cambridge: Cambridge University Press, 1984, 54–67.

Clifford, James. 'On Orientalism'. In *The Predicament of Culture: Twentieth-Century Ethnography, Literature, Art*. Cambridge, MA: Harvard University Press, 1988, 255–276.

Clifford, James. *Routes: Travel and Translation in the Late Twentieth Century*. Cambridge, MA: Harvard University Press, 1997.

Codell, Julie F., ed. *Imperial Co-Histories: National Identities and the British and Colonial Press*. Madison, NJ: Fairleigh Dickinson University Press, 2003.

Cohen, William B. 'Peid-Noir Memory, History, and the Algerian War'. In *Europe's Invisible Migrants*. Edited by Andrea L. Smith. Amsterdam: University of Amsterdam Press, 2003, 129–145.

Cohn, Bernard. *Colonialism and Its Forms of Knowledge: The British in India*. Princeton: Princeton University Press, 1996.

Colley, Linda. *Captives: Britain, Empire, and the World, 1600–1850*. New York: Pantheon, 2002.

Constantine, Stephen. *The Making of British Colonial Development Policy, 1914–1940*. London: Frank Cass, 1984.

Constantine, Stephen. *Emigrants and Empire: British Settlement in the Dominions between the Wars*. Manchester: Manchester University Press, 1990.

Collins, Robert O. 'The Sudan Political Service: A Portrait of the "Imperialists"'. *African Affairs* 71, no. 284 (July 1972): 293–303.

Collins, Robert O. and Francis M. Deng, eds. *The British in the Sudan, 1898–1956: The Sweetness and the Sorrow*. London: Palgrave Macmillan, 1984.

Constantine, Stephen. 'British Emigration to the Empire Commonwealth since 1880: From Overseas Settlement to Diaspora?' *The Journal of Imperial and Commonwealth History* 31, no. 2 (2003): 16–35.

Cooper, Frederick. 'Postcolonial Peoples: A Commentary'. In *Europe's Invisible Migrants*. Edited by Andrea L. Smith. Amsterdam: Amsterdam University Press, 2003, 169–183.

Cooper, Frederick and Ann Laura Stoler. *Tensions of Empire: Colonial Cultures in a Bourgeois World*. Berkeley: University of California Press, 1997.

Coray, Michael. 'In the Beginning'. In *The British in the Sudan, 1898–1956*. Edited by O. Collins Robert and Francis M. Deng. London: Macmillan, 1984, 28–64.

Cory, E. S. B. and Lesley Forbes. 'Resource for Sudanese Studies: The Sudan Archive of the University of Durham'. *African Research and Documentation* 31 (1983): 1.

Crosbie, Barry. *Irish Imperial Networks: Migration, Social Communication, and Exchange in Nineteenth-Century India*. Cambridge: Cambridge University Press, 2012.

Cubitt, Geoffrey. 'Introduction: Heroic Reputations and Exemplary Lives'. In *Heroic Reputations and Exemplary Lives*. Edited by Geoffrey Cubitt and Allen Warren. Manchester: Manchester University Press, 2000, 1–27.

Cubitt, Geoffrey and Allen Warren, eds. *Heroic Reputations and Exemplary Lives*. Manchester: Manchester University Press, 2000.

Daly, M. W. *Empire on the Nile: The Anglo-Egyptian Sudan, 1898–1934*. Cambridge: Cambridge University Press, 1986.

Daly, M. W. *Imperial Sudan: The Anglo-Egyptian Condominium, 1934–1956*. Cambridge: Cambridge University Press, 1991.

Daly, M. W. *The Sirdar: Sir Reginald Wingate and the British Empire in the Middle East*. Philadelphia: American Philosophical Society, 1997.

Darwin, John. 'British Decolonization since 1945: A Pattern or a Puzzle?' *Journal of Imperial and Commonwealth History* 12 (1984): 187–209.

Dawson, Graham. *Soldier Heroes: British Adventure, Empire and the Imagining of Masculinities*. London: Routledge, 1994.

De Nie, Michael. '"Speed the Mahdi!" The Irish Press and Empire during the Sudan Conflict of 1883'. *Journal of British Studies* 51, no. 4 (October 2012): 883–909.

Deng, Francis M. and M. W. Daly. *Bonds of Silk: The Human Factor in the British Administration of the Sudan*. East Lansing: Michigan State University Press, 1989.

Derrida, Jacques. *Writing and Difference*. Translated by Alan Bass. London: Routledge and Kegan Paul, 1978.

Driver, Felix. *Geography Militant: Cultures of Exploration and Empire*. Oxford: Blackwell, 2000.

Drummond, Ian M. *British Economic Policy and the Empire, 1919–1939*. London: George Allen & Unwin, Ltd., 1972.
Dudink, Stefan, Karen Hadgeman, and John Tosh, eds. *Masculinities in Politics and War: Gendering Modern History*. Manchester: Manchester University Press, 2004.
Duignan, Peter. Review of *Economic Change in Precolonial Africa: Senegambia in the Era of the Slave Trade*, by Philip D. Curtin. In *The Journal of Economic History* 38, no. 2: 525–27.
Durkheim, Emile. *Suicide*. New York: Simon and Schuster, 1997.
Earle, Rebecca. 'Introduction: Letters, Writers and the Historian'. In *Epistolary Selves: Letters and Letter Writers, 1600–1945*. Edited by Rebecca Earle. Aldershot: Ashgate Publishers, 1999, 1–13.
Evans-Pritchard, E. *Witchcraft, Oracles, and Magic among the Azande*. Oxford: Oxford University Press, 1937.
Evans-Pritchard, E. *The Nuer: A Description of the Modes of Livelihood and Political Institutions of a Nilotic People*. Oxford: Clarendon Press, 1940.
Evans-Pritchard, E. *Kinship and Marriage among the Nuer*. Oxford: Clarendon Press, 1951.
Evans-Pritchard, E. *Nuer Religion*. Oxford: Clarendon Press, 1956.
Faught, C. Brad. *Into Africa: The Imperial Life of Margery Perham*. London: I.B. Tauris, 2011.
Finkelstein, David. 'Imperial Self-Representation: Construction of Empire in *Blackwood's* Magazine, 1880–1900'. In *Imperial Co-Histories: National Identities and the British and Colonial Press*. Edited by Julie F. Codell. Madison, NJ: Fairleigh Dickinson University Press, 2003, 95–108.
Forbes, Lesley. 'The Sudan Archive of the University of Durham'. In *Middle East Studies and Libraries: A Felicitation Volume for Professor J.D. Pearson*. Edited by B. C. Bloomfield. London: Mansell, 1980, 49–57.
Freeman, Mark. 'Telling Stories: Memory and Narrative'. In *Memory: Histories, Theories, Debates*. Edited by Susannah Radstone and Bill Schwarz. New York: Fordham University Press, 2010, 263–280.
Furse, Ralph. *Aucuparius: Recollections of a Recruiting Officer*. Oxford: Oxford University Press, 1962.
Geaves, Ron. 'Correcting English Versions of the Qur'an: The Throne (*'arsh*) and the Footstool (*Kursi*) Controversy in 1902'. *Victorian Review* 37, no. 2 (2011): 31–35.
George, Rosemary. 'Homes in the Empire, Empires in the Home', *Cultural Critique* (Winter 1993–94): 95–127.
Gerber, David A. *Authors of Their Lives: The Personal Correspondence of British Immigrants to North America in the Nineteenth Century*. New York: NYU Press, 2008.
Ghosh, Durba. 'National Narratives and the Politics of Miscegenation: Britain and India'. In *Archive Stories: Facts, Fictions, and the Writing of History*. Edited by Antoinette Burton. Durham, NC: Duke University Press, 2005, 27–44.
Gilbert, Helen and Chris Tiffin, eds. *Burden or Benefit: Imperial Benevolence and Its Legacies*. Bloomington, IN: Indiana University Press, 2008.
Gillan, J. A., 'Review of H.C. Jackson, *Behind the Modern Sudan*'. *African Affairs* 55, no. 219 (April 1956): 146–47. https://doi.org/10.1093/oxfordjournals.afraf.a094389. Accessed June 17, 2018.
Gillis, John R., ed. *Commemorations: The Politics of National Identity*. Princeton: Princeton University Press, 1994.
Gilroy, Paul. *'There Ain't No Black in the Union Jack': The Cultural Politics of Race and Nation*. Chicago: University of Chicago Press, 1987.

Goodman, Dena. *Becoming a Woman in the Age of Letters*. Ithaca: Cornell University Press, 2009.

Gordon, Charles. *General Gordon's Last Journal. A Facsimile of the Last of the Six Volumes of Journals Dispatched by General Gordon before the Fall of Khartoum*. London: Kegan Paul Trench, 1885.

Gordon, Charles. *The Journals of Major-Gen. C. G. Gordon, CB., at Khartoum. Printed from the original manuscript. Introduction and Notes by A. Egmont Hake*. London: Kegan Paul Trench, 1885.

Grainger, J. H. *Patriotisms: Britain 1900–1939*. London: Routledge, 1986.

Grewal, Inderpal. *Home and Harem: Nation, Gender, Empire, and the Cultures of Travel*. Durham: Duke University Press, 1996.

Griffiths, Andrew. 'Winston Churchill, the Morning Post, and the End of the Imperial Romance'. *Victorian Periodicals Review* 46, no. 2 (Summer 2013): 163–83.

Griffiths, Andrew. *The New Journalism, the New Imperialism and the Fiction of Empire, 1870–1900*. London: Palgrave Macmillan, 2015.

Grossberg, Lawrence. 'History, Imagination, and the Politics of Belonging: Between the Death and the Fear of History'. In *Without Guarantees: In Honor of Stuart Hall*. Edited by Lawrence Grossberg, Angela McRobbie, and Paul Gilroy. London: Verso, 2000, 148–164.

Grossberg, Lawrence, Angela McRobbie, and Paul Gilroy, eds. *Without Guarantees: In Honor of Stuart Hall*. Edited by Lawrence Grossberg, Angela McRobbie, and Paul Gilroy. London: Verso, 2000.

Gwynne, The Rt. Rev. Llewellyn Henry. 'Makers of the Sudan'. unpublished MS. Sudan Archive.

Habermas, Jürgen. *The Structural Transformation of the Public Sphere: An Inquiry into a Category of Bourgeois Society*. Translated by Thomas Burger and Frederick Lawrence. Cambridge, MA: MIT and Polity Press, 1989.

Halbwachs, Maurice. *On Collective Memory*. Edited and translated by Lewis A. Coser. Chicago: University of Chicago Press, 1992.

Hall, Catherine and Sonya O. Rose, eds. *At Home with the Empire: Metropolitan Culture and the Imperial World*. Cambridge: Cambridge University Press, 2006.

Hamilton, J. A. de C., ed. *The Anglo-Egyptian Sudan from Within*. London: Faber and Faber, 1935.

Hampton, Mark. *Visions of the Press in Britain, 1850–1950*. Urbana: University of Illinois Press, 2004.

Harper, Marjorie, ed. *Emigrant Homecomings: The Return Movement of Emigrants, 1600–2000*. Manchester: Manchester University Press, 2005.

Hartley, Jenny. '"Letters Are Everything These Days": Mothers and Letters in the Second World War'. In *Epistolary Selves: Letters and Letter Writers, 1600–1945*. Edited by Rebecca Earle. Aldershot: Ashgate Pub., 1999, 183–195.

Havinden, Michael and David Meredith. *Colonialism and Development: Britain and Its Tropical Colonies, 1850–1960*. London: Routledge, 1993.

Hawley, Donald, ed. *The Sudan Canterbury Tales*. Norwich, England: Michael Russell, 1999.

Helly, Dorothy O. and Hellen Callaway. 'Constructing South Africa in the British Press, 1890–92: *The Pall Mall Gazette*, the *Daily Graphic*, and the *Times*'. In *Imperial Co-Histories: National Identities and the British and Colonial Press*. Edited by Julie F. Codell. Madison, NJ: Fairleigh Dickinson University Press, 2003, 125–144.

Henty, G. A. *A Chapter of Adventures; or, Through the Bombardment of Alexandria*. London: Blackie and Son, 1891.

Henty, G. A. *The Dash for Khartoum: A tale of the Nile Expedition*. New York: Charles Scribner's Sons, 1891.

Henty, G. A. *With Kitchener in Soudan: A Story of Atbara and Omdurman*. New York: Charles Scribner's Sons, 1902.

Heussler, Robert. *Yesterday's Rulers: The Making of the British Colonial Service*. Syracuse, NY: Syracuse University Press, 1963.

Hillemann, Ulrike. *Asian Empire and British Knowledge: China and the Networks of British Imperial Expansion*. London: Palgrave Macmillan, 2009.

Hodge, Joseph. *The Triumph of the Expert: Agrarian Doctrines of Development and the Legacies of British Colonialism*. Athens: Ohio University Press, 2007.

Hodge, Joseph M., Gerald Hödl, and Martina Kopf, eds. *Developing Africa: Concepts and Practices in Twentieth Century Colonialism*. Manchester, UK: Manchester University Press, 2014.

Hogg, Michael A. and Deborah J. Terry. 'Social Identity Theory and Organizations Processes'. In *Social Identity Processes in Organizations Contexts*. Edited by Hogg and Terry. Philadelphia: Psychology Press, 2001, 1–12.

How, James. *Epistolary Spaces: English Letter Writing from the Foundation of the Post Office to Richardson's Clarissa*. Aldershot: Ashgate Publishers, 2003.

Howe, Stephen. *Anticolonialism in British Politics: The Left and the End of Empire, 1918–1964*. Oxford: Clarendon Press, 1993.

Huffaker, Shauna. 'Representations of Ahmed Urabi: Hegemony, Imperialism, and the British Press, 1881–1882'. *Victorian Periodicals Review* 45, no. 4 (Winter 2012): 375–405.

Jackson, Ashley. 'Review: *Governing Empire: Colonial Memoirs and the History of HM Overseas Civil Service*'. *African Affairs* 103, no. 412 (July 2004): 471–91.

Jackson, H. C. *Osman Digna*. London: Methuen, 1926.

Jackson, H. C. *Sudan Days and Ways*. London: McMillan and Co, 1954.

Jameson, Fredric. 'Modernism and Imperialism'. In *Nationalism, Colonialism and Literature*. Minneapolis: University of Minnesota Press, 1990, 43–68.

Johnson, Douglas H. *British Documents on the End of Empire, Series B, Vol. 5: Sudan. Vol. II, 1951–1956*. London: HMSO, 1998.

Johnson, Douglas H., ed. *British Documents on the End of Empire: Series B, Vol. 5: Sudan, Part I, 1942–1950*. London: HMSO, 1999.

Jones, Max. 'What Should Historians Do with Heroes? Reflections on Nineteenth- and Twentieth-Century Britain'. *History Compass* 5, no. 2 (March 2007): 439–54.

Jones, Max, Berny Sébe, John Strachan, Bertrand Taithe, and Peter Yeandle. 'Decolonising Imperial Heroes: Britain and France'. *Journal of Imperial and Commonwealth History* 42, no. 5 (2014): 787–825.

Joy, George William. *Death of Gordon*, 1892.

Kaplan, Cora. 'Imagining Empire: History, Fantasy and Literature'. In *At Home with the Empire: Metropolitan Culture and the Imperial World*. Edited by Catherine Hall and Sonya O. Rose. Cambridge: Cambridge University Press, 2006, 191–211.

Kaplan, Caren. *Questions of Travel: Postmodern Discourses of Displacement*. Durham: Duke University Press, 1996.

Kennedy, Dane. 'Imperial Parasitism: British Explorers and African Empires'. In *Echoes of Empire: Memory, Identity, and Colonial Legacies*. Edited by Kalypso Nicolaïdis, Berny Sèbe, and Gabrielle Maas. London: I.B. Tauris, 2015, 17–28.

Kenrick, Rosemary, ed. *Sudan Tale: Recollections of Some Sudan Political Service Wives, 1926–56*. Cambridge: Oleander Press, 2000.

King, Nicola. *Memory, Narrative, Identity: Remembering the Self.* Edinburgh: Edinburgh University Press, 2000.

King, Russell. 'Generalizations from the History of Return Migration'. In *Return Migration: Journey of Hope or Despair?* Edited by Bimal Ghosh. Geneva: International Organization for Migration and the United Nations, 2000, 7–55.

Kirk-Greene, Anthony. 'Forging a Relationship with the Colonial Administrative Service, 1921–1939'. *The Journal of Imperial and Commonwealth History* 19, no. 3 (October 1991): 62–82.

Kirk-Greene, Anthony. *Britain's Imperial Administrators: 1858–1966.* London: Palgrave Macmillan, 2000.

Kipling, Rudyard. *Barrack Room Ballads.* London: Methuen, 1892.

Knapman, C. *White Women in Fiji, 1835–1930: The Ruin of Empire?* Sydney: Allen & Unwin, 1986.

Knowles, F. L., ed. *A Kipling Primer.* Boston: Brown, 1899.

Kopf, Martina. 'Developing Africa in the colonial imagination: European and African narrative writing of the interwar period'. In *Developing Africa: Concepts and Practices in Twentieth Century Colonialism.* Edited by Joseph M. Hodge, Gerald Hödl, and Martina Kopf. Manchester, UK: Manchester University Press, 2014, 341–366.

Kristeva, Julia. *Strangers to Ourselves.* Translated by Leon S. Roudiez. New York: Columbia University Press, 1991.

Kuhn, Annette. 'A Journey through Memory'. In *Memory and Methodology.* Edited by Susannah Radstone. Oxford: Berg, 2000, 187–206.

Kuklick, Henrika. *The Imperial Bureaucrat: The Colonial Administrative Service in the Gold* Coast, *1920–39.* Stanford, CA: Stanford University Press, 1979.

Laffer, Stephanie. *General Charles George Gordon and His Legacies, 1885–1960.* Dissertation. Tallahassee, FL: Florida State University, 2010.

Lambert, David and Alan Lester. *Colonial Lives across the British Empire: Imperial Careering in the Long Nineteenth Century.* Cambridge: Cambridge University Press, 2006.

Layton-Henry, Zig. *The Politics of Immigration: Immigration, Race, and Race Relations in Post-War Britain.* Oxford: Blackwell, 1992.

Leinster-Mackay, Donald. 'The Nineteenth-Century English Preparatory School: Cradle and Crèche of Empire?' In *Benefits Bestowed? Education and British Imperialism.* Edited by J. A. Mangan. Manchester: Manchester University Press, 1988.

Lewis, Reina. *Gendering Orientalism: Race, Femininity, and Representation.* Routledge: London, 1996.

Logan, Mawuena Kossi. *Narrating Africa: George Henty and the Fiction of Empire.* New York: Routledge, 2011.

Long, C. W. R. *British Pro-Consuls in Egypt, 1914–1929: The Challenge of Nationalism.* London: Routledge Curzon, 2005.

Loomba, Ania. *Colonialism/Postcolonialism.* London: Routledge, 1998.

Low, Sidney. *Egypt in Transition.* New York: Macmillan, 1914.

Lowe, C. J. *The Reluctant Imperialists: British Foreign Policy, 1878–1902.* New York: Macmillan, 1969.

Luckhurst, Roger, Laurel Brake, James Mussell, and Ed King, eds. *W. T. Stead – Newspaper Revolutionary.* London: British Library, 2012.

Lugard, Frederick. *The Dual Mandate.* London: Archon, 1965.

Macarthur, Elizabeth. *Extravagant Narratives: Closure and Dynamics in the Epistolary Form.* Princeton: Princeton University Press, 1990.

MacDonald, Robert H. *The Language of Empire: Myths and Metaphors of Popular Imperialism, 1880–1918*. Manchester: Manchester University Press, 1994.
MacKenzie, John M. *Propaganda and Empire: The Manipulation of British Public Opinion, 1880–1960*. Manchester: Manchester University Press, 1984.
MacKenzie, John M., ed. *Imperialism and Popular Culture*. Manchester: Manchester University Press, 1986.
MacKenzie, John M. 'Heroic Myths of Empire'. In *Popular Imperialism and the Military, 1850–1950*. Edited by John M. MacKenzie. Manchester: Manchester University Press, 1992, 109–138.
MacKenzie, John M. 'Passion or Indifference: Popular Imperialism in Britain, Continuities and Discontinuities over Two Centuries'. In *European Empires and the People: Popular Responses to Imperialism in France, Britain, the Netherlands, Belgium, Germany, and Italy*. Edited by John M. MacKenzie. Manchester: Manchester University Press, 2011, 57–89.
Maitland, Alexander. *Wilfred Thesiger: A Life in Pictures*. London: HarperCollins Publishers, 2004.
Maitland, Alexander. *Wilfred Thesiger: Life of the Great Explorer*. London: Harper Press, 2006.
Mangan, J. A. 'Play Up and Play the Game: Victorian and Edwardian Public School Vocabularies of Motive'. *British Journal of Educational Studies* 33, no. 3 (October 1975): 324–35.
Mangan, J. A. 'The Education of an Elite Imperial Administration: The Sudan Political Service and the British Public School System'. *The International Journal of African Historical Studies* 15, no. 4 (1982): 671–699.
Mangan, J. A. *The Games Ethic and Imperialism: The Diffusion of an Ideal*. New York: Viking Penguin, 1986.
Mangan, J. A. *'Benefits Bestowed?' Education and British Imperialism*. Manchester: Manchester University Press, 1988.
Mangan, J. A., ed. *The Imperial Curriculum: Racial Images and Education in the British Colonial Experience*. New York: Routledge, 2014.
Mangan, J. A. and James Walvin, eds. *Manliness and Morality: Middle-Class Masculinity in Britain and America, 1800–1940*. Manchester: Manchester University Press, 1987.
Mason, A. E. W. *The Four Feathers*. New York: Macmillan, 1905.
Massey, Doreen and John Allen, eds. *Geography Matters! A Reader*. Cambridge: Cambridge University Press, 1984.
Matthews, Rachel. *The History of the Provincial Press in England*. New York: Bloomsbury Academic, 2017.
McMichael, Harold. 'Introduction'. In *Sudan Political Service, 1899–1956*. Edited by Gawain Bell and Brian Dee. Oxford: Oxonian Press, n.d, 1–8.
McPhee, Alan. *The Economic Revolution in British West Africa*. London: G. Routledge and Sons, 1926.
Miles, Gloriosus. Review of Frederick Austin, 'A Source Book of Medieval History', *Public School Journal* 35 (1916): 305.
Mills, Sara. *Discourses of Differences: An Analysis of Women's Travel Writing and Colonialism*. London: Routledge, 1991.
Milner, Alfred. *England in Egypt*. London: Edward Arnold, 1893.
Mitchell, Timothy. *Colonising Egypt*. Berkeley: University of California Press, 1991.
Mohammed, Khaleel. 'Assessing English Translations of the Qur'an', *Middle East Quarterly* 12, no. 2 (Spring 2005): 58–71.

Morgan, Kenneth O. 'The Boer War and the Media, 1899–1902'. *Twentieth-Century British History* 13, no. 1 (2002): 1–16.

Mussell, James. 'Characters of "Blood and Flame": Stead and the Tabloid Campaign'. In *W. T. Stead – Newspaper Revolutionary*. Edited by Luckhurst et al. London: British Library, 2012.

Nalbach, Alex. '"The Software of Empire": Telegraphic News Agencies and Imperial Publicity, 1865–1914'. In *Imperial Co-Histories: National Identities and the British and Colonial Press*. Edited by Julie F. Codell. Madison, NJ: Fairleigh Dickinson University Press, 2003, 68–94.

Nandy, Ashis. *The Intimate Enemy: Loss and Recovery of Self under Colonialism*. Delhi: Oxford University Press, 1983.

Nicholson, Tony. 'The Provincial Stead'. In *W. T. Stead – Newspaper Revolutionary*. Edited by Luckhurst et al. London: British Library, 2012.

Nicolaïdis, Kalypso, Berny Sèbe, and Gabrielle Maas, eds. *Echoes of Empire: Memory, Identity and Colonial Legacies*. London: I.B. Tauris, 2015.

Nicolson, I. F. and Colin A. Hughes. 'A Provenance of Pro-Consuls: British Colonial Governors, 1900–1960'. *Journal of Imperial and Commonwealth History* 4 (1974–75): 77–106.

Nora, Pierre. 'Between Memory and History'. In *Realms of Memory: Rethinking the French Past, Vol. 1: Conflicts and Divisions*. Edited by Pierre Nora. English language edition edited by Lawrence D. Kitzman and translated by Arthur Goldhammer. New York: Columbia University Press, 1996, 1–20.

Nora, Pierre. 'Generation'. In *Realms of Memory: Rethinking the French Past, Vol. 1: Conflicts and Divisions*. Edited by Pierre Nora. English language edition edited by Lawrence D. Kitzman and translated by Arthur Goldhammer. New York: Columbia University Press, 1996, 499–513.

Norindr, Panivong. *Phantasmatic Indochina: French Colonial Ideology in Architecture, Film, and Literature*. Durham, NC: Duke University Press, 1996.

Ohrwalder, Father Joseph. *Ten Years Captivity in the Mahdi's Camp: 1882–1892*. London: Low, 1892.

Oliver, Caroline. *Western Women in Colonial Africa*. Westport, Conn: Greenwood Press, 1982.

Owen, Roger. *Lord Cromer: Victorian Imperialist, Edwardian Proconsul*. Oxford: Oxford University Press, 2004.

Partha, Sarathi. *Imperialism and the British Labour Movement 1914–1964*. London: Macmillan, 1975.

Pels, Peter. 'The Pidginization of Luguru Politics: Administrative Ethnography and the Paradoxes of Indirect Rule'. *American Ethnologist* 23, no. 4 (November 1996): 738–61.

Perham, Margery. *Native Administration in Nigeria*. Oxford: Oxford University Press, 1937.

Perham, Margery. 'Introduction'. *Colonial Government: Annotated Reading List on British Colonial Government*. London: Oxford University Press for Nuffield College, 1950.

Perham, Margery. 'Introduction'. In *The Dual Mandate*. Edited by Frederick Lugard. London: Archon, 1965, 1–7.

Perham, Margery. 'Problems of Indirect Rule in Africa'. In *Colonial Sequence 1930–1949: A Chronological Commentary upon British Colonial Policy, Especially in Africa*. London: Methuen, 1967, 91–118.

Perl, Jeffrey M. *The Tradition of Return. The Implicit History of Modern Literature*. Princeton: Princeton University Press, 1984.

Porter, Bernard. *Absent-Minded Imperialists: Empire, Society, and Culture in Britain*. Oxford: New York: Oxford University Press, 2004.

Potter, Simon J. 'Jingoism, Public Opinion, and the New Imperialism'. *Media History* 20, no. 1 (2014): 34–50.

Prakash, Gayan. 'Introduction: After Colonialism'. In *After Colonialism: Imperial Histories and Post-Colonial Displacements*. Edited by Gayan Prakash. Princeton: Princeton University Press, 1994, 3–17.

Pratt, Mary Louise. *Imperial Eyes: Travel Writing and Transculturation*. London: Routledge, 1992.

Prior, Christopher. *Exporting Empire: Africa, Colonial Officials and the Construction of the British Imperial State, c. 1900–39*. Manchester: Manchester University Press, 2013.

Radstone, Susannah. 'Working with Memory: An Introduction'. In *Memory and Methodology*. Edited by Susannah Radstone. Oxford: Berg, 2000, 1–22.

Radstone, Susannah and Bill Schwarz, eds. *Memory: Histories, Theories, Debates*. New York: Fordham University Press, 2010.

Rapport, Nigel and Andrew Dawson. 'Home and Movement: A Polemic'. In *Migrants of Identity: Perceptions of Home in a World of Movement*. Edited by Nigel Rapport and Andrew Dawson. Oxford: Berg, 1998, 9–15.

Rawa, J. M. *The Imperial Quest and Modern Memory from Conrad to Greene*. New York: Routledge, 2005.

Richards, Thomas. *The Imperial Archive: Knowledge and the Fantasy of Empire*. London: Verso, 1993.

Ricoeur, Paul. *Hermeneutics and the Human Sciences*. Cambridge: Cambridge University Press, 1981.

Riley, Charlotte Lydia. '"The Winds of Change Are Blowing Economically": The Labour Party and British Overseas Development, 1940s–1960s'. In *Britain, France and the Decolonization of Africa: Future Imperfect?* Edited by Andrew W. M. Smith and Chris Jeppesen. London: UCL Press, 2017, 43–61. JSTOR. Accessed 21 June 2018: DOI: 10.2307/j.ctt1mtz521.7

Roper, Michael. 'Maternal Relations: Moral Manliness and Emotional Survival in Letters Home during the First World War'. In *Masculinities in Politics and War: Gendering Modern History*. Edited by Stefan Dudink, Karen Hagemann, and John Tosh. Manchester: Manchester University Press, 2004, 295–315.

Roper, Michael and John Tosh, eds. *Manful Assertions: Masculinities in Britain since 1800*. New York: Routledge, 1991.

Ross, Stephen. *Conrad and Empire*. Columbia, MO: University of Missouri Press, 2004.

Royle, Trevor. *The Kitchener Enigma*. London: Michael Joseph, 1985.

Said, Edward W. *Orientalism*. New York: Vintage Books, 1979.

Said, Edward W. *Culture and Imperialism*. New York: Vintage Books, 1993.

Said, Edward W. 'Secular Interpretation, the Geographical Element, and the Methodology of Imperialism'. In *After Colonialism: Imperial Histories and Post-Colonial Displacements*. Edited by Gayan Prakash. Princeton: Princeton University Press, 1995, 21–39.

Samuel, Raphael, ed. *Patriotism: The Making and Unmaking of British National Identity, 1–3*. London: Routledge, 1989.

Samuel, Raphael and Paul Thompson, eds. *The Myths We Live By*. London: Routledge, 1990.

Schwarz, Bill. *White Man's World: Memories of Empire*, Vol. 1. Oxford: Oxford University Press, 2011.

Sèbe, Berny. *Heroic Imperialists in Africa: The Promotion of British and French Colonial Heroes, 1870–1939*. Manchester: Manchester University Press, 2013.

Seligman, C. G. 'Some Aspects of the Hamitic Problem in the Anglo-Egyptian Sudan'. *The Journal of the Royal Anthropological Institute of Great Britain and Ireland* 43 (July–December 1913): 593–705.

Simmel, Georg. *On Individuality and Social Forms*. Edited by Donald N. Levine. Chicago: The University of Chicago Press, 1971.

Singer, Barnett. *Cultured Force: Makers and Defenders of the French Colonial Empire*. Madison: University of Wisconsin Press, 2004.

Slatin, Rudolph. *Fire and Sword in the Sudan*. London: E. Arnold, 1896.

Smith, Andrea L., ed. *Europe's Invisible Migrants*. Amsterdam: Amsterdam University Press, 2003.

Smith, Andrew W. M. and Chris Jeppesen, eds. *Britain, France and the Decolonization of Africa: Future Imperfect?* London: UCL Press, 2017. JSTOR. Accessed 21 June 2018: DOI: 10.2307/j.ctt1mtz521.7

Smith, Bonnie G. *The Gender of History: Men, Women, and Historical Practice*. Cambridge: Harvard University Press, 2000.

Sommer, Doris. *Foundational Fictions: The National Romances of Latin America*. Berkeley: University of California Press, 1991.

Spear, Thomas. 'Neo-Traditionalism and the Limits of Invention in British Colonial Africa'. *Journal of African History* 44, no. 1 (2003): 3–27.

Stack, Robert. 'The Societal Conception of Space'. In *Geography Matters! A Reader*. Edited by Doreen Massey and John Allen. Cambridge: Cambridge University Press, 1984.

Stead, W. T. 'Government by Journalism'. http://www.attackingthedevil.co.uk/steadworks/gov.php. Accessed January 10, 2012.

Steedman, Carolyn. 'A Woman Writing a Letter'. In *Epistolary Selves: Letters and Letter Writers, 1600–1945*. Edited by Rebecca Earle. Aldershot: Ashgate Pub., 1999, 35–46.

Stewart, Susan. *On Longing: Narrative of the Miniature, the Gigantic, the Souvenir, the Collection*. Durham, NC: Duke University Press, 2007.

Stoler, Ann Laura. 'In Cold Blood: Hierarchies of Credibility and the Politics of Colonial Narratives'. *Representations* 37 (Winter 1992): 151–89.

Stoler, Ann Laura and Frederick Cooper. 'Between Metropole and Colony: Rethinking a Research Agenda'. In *Tensions of Empire: Colonial Cultures in a Bourgeois World*. Edited by Frederick Cooper and Ann Laura Stoler. Berkeley: University of California Press, 1997, 1–57.

Strachey, Lytton. *Eminent Victorians*. New York: Oxford University Press, 2003.

Strobel, Margaret. *European Women and the Second British Empire*. Bloomington: Indiana University Press, 1991.

Thomas, Nicholas. *Colonialism's Culture: Anthropology, Travel and Government*. Princeton: Princeton University Press, 1994.

Thompson, Andrew, ed. *Britain's Experience of Empire in the Twentieth Century*. Oxford History of the British Empire: Companion Series. Oxford: Oxford University Press, 2012.

Thompson, Brian. *Imperial Vanities: The Adventures of the Baker Brothers and Gordon of Khartoum*. New York: HarperCollins, 2001.

Thurston, Anne. *Records of the Cabinet, Foreign Office, Treasury and Other Records*. London: The Stationary Office, 1998.

Tosh, John. 'Imperial Masculinity and the Flight from Domesticity'. In *Gender and Colonialism*. Edited by Timothy Fowley. Galway: Galway University Press, 1994, 72–85.

Tosh, John. *Manliness and Masculinities in Nineteenth-Century Britain: Essays on Gender, Family, and Empire*. Harlow, UK: Pearson Longman, 2005.

van Heyningen, Elizabeth. *The Concentration Camps of the Anglo-Boer War: A Social History*. Johannesburg: Jacana Media, 2013.

Vaughan, Chris. *Darfur: Colonial Violence, Sultanic Legacies, and Local Politics, 1916–1956*. Rochester, NY: James Curry, 2015.

Walvin, James. *Passage to Britain: Immigration in British History and Politics*. Harmondsworth, England: Penguin Books, 1984.

Warren, Mark E. *Democracy and Association*. Princeton: Princeton University Press, 2001.

Webster, Wendy. *Imagining Home: Gender, 'Race' and National Identity, 1945–64*. London: UCL Press, 1998.

Wells, Henry W. 'Kipling's Barrack-Room Language'. *American Speech* 18, no. 4 (December 1943): 273–78.

Wilson, Mary Floyd. 'English Mettle'. In *Reading the Early Modern Passions: Essays in the Cultural History of Emotion*. Edited by Gail Kern Paster, Katherine Rowe, and Mary Floyd-Wilson. Philadelphia: University of Pennsylvania Press, 2004, 130–146.

Winter, Jay. *Sites of Memory, Sites of Mourning: The Great War in European Cultural History*. Cambridge: Cambridge University Press, 1995.

Woolacott, Angela. *Gender and Empire*. New York: Palgrave, 2006.

Young, Robert J. C. *White Mythologies: Writing History and the West*. New York: Routledge, 1990.

Young, Robert J. C. *Colonial Desire: Hybridity in Theory, Culture and Race*. New York: Routledge, 2000.

Zangwill, Israel. *Pall Mall Magazine* 42, 1908.

Index

www.ingramcontent.com/pod-product-compliance
Lightning Source LLC
Chambersburg PA
CBHW070520100726
47907CB00004B/921